MW00776636

Akhenaten

The AUC History of Ancient Egypt

Edited by Aidan Dodson and Salima Ikram

Volume One

Akhenaten

A HISTORIAN'S VIEW

Ronald T. Ridley

The American University in Cairo Press
Cairo New York

First published in 2019 by
The American University in Cairo Press
113 Sharia Kasr el Aini, Cairo, Egypt
200 Park Avenue, Suite 1700, New York, NY 10166
www.aucpress.com

Dar el Kutub No. 26251/15
ISBN 978 977 416 793 5

Dar el Kutub Cataloging-in-Publication Data

Ridley, Ronald T.
        Akhenaten: A Historian's View / Ronald T. Ridley.—Cairo: The American University
    in Cairo Press, 2019.
        p.   cm.
        ISBN: 978 977 416 793 5
        1. Egypt—Antiquities
        932

1 2 3 4 5   23 22 21 20 19

Designed by Jon W. Stoy
Printed in the United States of America

To the Memory of

Norman de Garis Davies (1865–1941), indefatigable recorder,

Cyril Aldred (1914–1991), inspiring biographer,

William Murnane (1945–2000), great Amarnan scholar, and

John Albert Wilson (1899–1976), my first inspiration in Egyptology

Most of what is written about the momentous events in the history of the Amarna Period in our secondary sources is speculation.

—*Geoffrey Martin, The Hidden Tombs of Memphis*

Contents

Preface

This is, I believe, the first book about Akhenaten written not by an archaeologist, a philologist, or an art historian, but by a historian. What that means should become clear as the text progresses.

I have tried to document each statement with evidence. That can come from an amazing array of sources: epigraphic, archaeological, artistic, or literary. I confess that finding them has often caused me great pains; for example, others can refer simply to 'a block from Hermopolis' (there are thousands and thousands of them), or an object in the Louvre or in the Metropolitan (the same). They are identified here as exactly as possible.

Each chapter is subdivided with subheadings. In this way, I have tried to avoid a common feature of writing on Akhenaten: nothing is treated comprehensively in one place, but each topic is scattered throughout the text with multiple references. With my system, one should find a substantial discussion of any topic in one place, with adequate signposting.

Illustrations are vital evidence. They will be found at the most important point where they are discussed, not in erratic order or bunched together at various points.

As a historian, I am not competent to deal with art history. There is no chapter as such on Amarnan art. And there is no chapter on the infamous problem of a coregency between Akhenaten and his father. After oceans of ink being spilled, that has most recently been nonchalantly consigned to the 'outdated matters/no longer of interest' box.

There are two matters I should signal. First, I had hoped to present the essential primary sources drawn from both text and art directly in my own text, as historians like to do, but they are hidden in the endnotes. Second, I have given full names in the first reference to each person in each chapter, but used only surnames for subsequent references in that chapter. On another matter of names, I have generally called Akhenaten and Tutankhamun by those names, rather than switching to and from 'Amenhotep IV' and 'Tutankhaten,' although I have, on occasion, highlighted a particular occurrence of a name where it is necessary for the purposes of the narrative.

My sincerest gratitude must be expressed to the original publishers of the wonderful illustrations without which such a subject would be incomprehensible, and who have so generously allowed them to be reproduced here.

There are three women without whom this book would never have been published: my best editor, my wife Therese; Ingrid Barker, who impeccably transformed typescript into a digital version; and Salima Ikram, the essence of kindness.

Abbreviations

Ashmolean	Ashmolean Museum, Oxford
Berlin	Ägyptisches Museum, Berlin
BM	British Museum, London
Brooklyn	Brooklyn Museum, New York
Cairo	Egyptian Museum, Cairo
EA	*Amarna Letter* number
Fitzwilliam	Fitzwilliam Museum, Cambridge
KV	Valley of the Kings tomb number
MFA	Museum of Fine Arts, Boston
MMA	Metropolitan Museum of Art, New York
Ny Carlsberg	Ny Carlsberg Glyptotek, Copenhagen
Petrie	Petrie Museum, University College London
San Diego	San Diego Museum of Man, San Diego
TA	Tell el-Amarna tomb number
TT	Theban tomb number
WV	Western Valley of the Kings tomb number

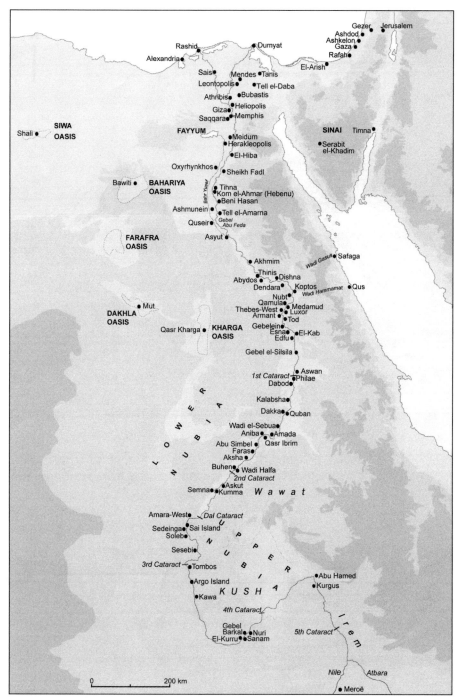

Map. 1. The Nile Valley.

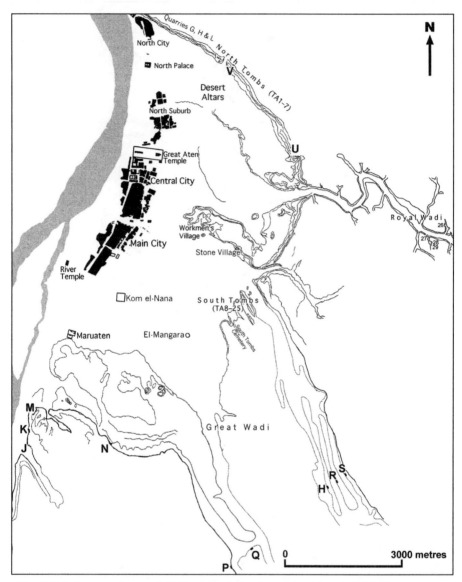

Map. 2. Tell el-Amarna. The capital letters denote the boundary stelae of Akhet-Aten..

Map. 3. The Near East during the fourteenth century BC.

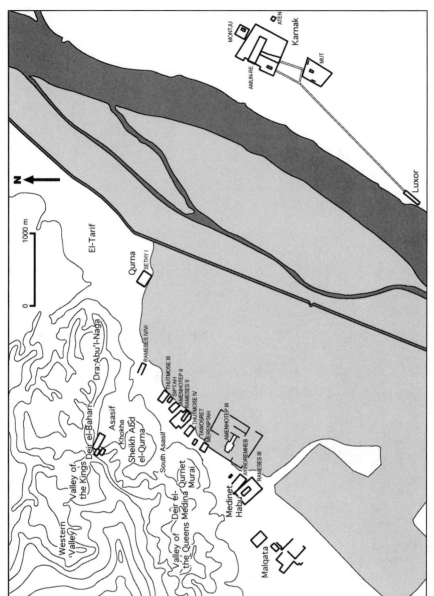

Map. 4. Thebes.

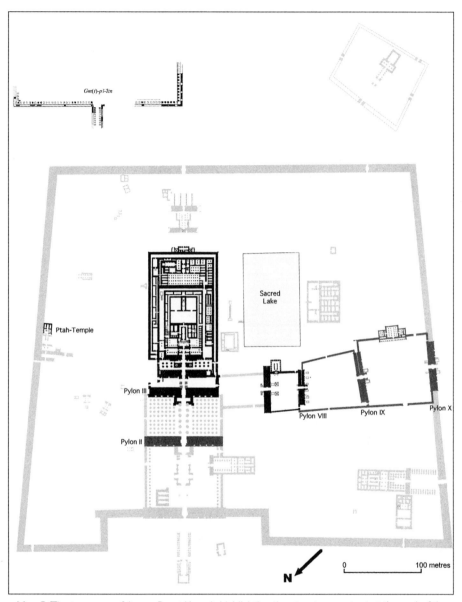

Gm(t)-pȝ-Itn

Ptah-Temple

Sacred
Lake

Pylon III

Pylon II

Pylon VIII

Pylon IX

Pylon X

0   100 metres

N

Map. 5. The temenos of Amun-Re at Karnak, highlighting the structures extant at the end of the Eighteenth Dynasty.

1 Akhenaten: Fashion, Fantasy, and Fact

FOR ABOUT ONE and a half centuries now, anyone interested in Egypt has been aware of a king either fascinating or alarming, depending on reactions. These extreme responses have arisen primarily because of his appearance—at least in some of his portraits—and his position in the religious history not only of Egypt, but also of the East. Modern reactions were prefigured by those of his contemporaries, including those who tried to obliterate him from history, but his brief reign has given its name to what is now the best-known period in Egyptian history.

We begin with three generalizations, put forth by several authors:

Few sovereigns have been so pitifully mistreated by posterity as Amenhotep IV; it seems that modern historians have been bent on worsening the curses with which the Theban priests have burdened his memory. Most wish to see in him only a lofty fanatic, others charge him with madness, others again state that he was a simple eunuch.[1]

Of all the personalities of Egyptian antiquity, Akhenaten and Nefertiti are undoubtedly the most famous. The royal couple of Amarna exercise such a fascination that they are now part of Western cultural mythology. Seemingly so close to us, they represent the image of the ideal couple, touching in their adversity,

1

struggling against the established strength of a traditionalist society, and attempting to establish a religion of love in a selfish world. The companion of a mystical king with fragile health, the queen moves us by her fidelity and her constant presence next to her frail husband. And then, Nefertiti is so beautiful. This vision is real, but it is a reality of the contemporary world that is always ready to find in the past the reflection of its hopes and ideals.[2]

Akhenaten is precisely one of those figures that tempt writers to go to extremes.[3]

Changing interpretations

Richard Lepsius (1810–84) must be acknowledged as the scholar who first, in 1851, understood the main lines of the history of Akhenaten, but he revealed no judgment.[4]

Flinders Petrie (1853–1942), first excavator at Amarna, was highly impressed by the man and his cult: "Akkhenaten stands out as perhaps the most original thinker that ever lived in Egypt, and one of the greatest idealists of the world."[5] "If this were a new religion, invented to satisfy our modern scientific conceptions, we could not find a flaw in the correctness of this view of the energy of the solar system."[6]

Alexandre Moret (1868–1938), a student of Gaston Maspero (1846–1916) and historian of Egyptian society, religion, and law, painted a broad picture: "If the reign of Akhenaten counts for little in the history of Egypt, it counts infinitely in the history of humanity."[7]

One of the most influential commentators was James Henry Breasted (1865–1935), founder of American Egyptology. Akhenaten was "the first individual in history," "the world's first revolutionist," and the earliest idealist.

Consciously and deliberately, by intellectual process he gained his position, and then placed himself squarely in the face of tradition and swept it aside. He appeals to no myths, to no ancient and widely accepted versions of the domination of the gods, to no customs sanctified by centuries—he appeals only to the present and visible evidences of his god's dominion, evidences open to all.[8]

Norman de Garis Davies (1865–1941), indefatigable copyist and publisher of tomb inscriptions, said that Akhenaten "scarcely had the dignity of a heretic. His theology was ignored after his death, not refuted. . . . it was in undermining the unity of Egypt, the magnificence of her temple service, and her imperial prestige, that he most offended."[9]

The German excavator of Amarna Ludwig Borchardt (1863–1938) saw the Amarna period as "a violent, bad exaggeration of good, old religious ideas, which throttled the possibility of their further development."[10] His great rival Heinrich Schäfer (1868–1957), who paradoxically despised Amarnan art, saw the age as the "Egyptian people's imperishable claim to fame."[11] The Ramessides may have called him "that criminal of Akhet-Aten," but one does not, he admonished, judge Socrates or Jesus by their judges.

For those who disapprove of Akhenaten, either his policies or his character, fantasy knows no bounds. According to Henry Hall (1873–1930) of the British Museum, he died "possibly insane."[12] The Reverend James Baikie (1866–1931) judged that Akhenaten "seems to have been the world's first pacifist" and that "Egypt duly produced her great man, a man who in some respects is the greatest she ever produced." In 1923, that would have rung a bell with many. For Baikie, he was "an idealist dreamer," "undoubtedly a fanatic, but he was by no means a fool."[13] Baikie also had to caution Wallis Budge (1857–1934), Keeper of Egyptian and Assyrian Antiquities at the British Museum, who insinuated that Akhenaten may have been guilty of wholesale murders,[14] though he admitted that there was no evidence to prove such a thing: "It would be difficult to imagine a worse conclusive example of prejudice usurping the place of unbiassed judgement."[15]

Étienne Drioton (1889–1961), the last French director of the Egyptian Antiquities Service, and Jacques Vandier (1904–73) of the Louvre declared Akhenaten to be "a dreamer, incapable of concentrating his mind on the practical necessities of government."[16] Jaroslav Černý (1898–1970), professor of Egyptology at the University of Oxford, similarly declared Akhenaten to be a dreamer and fanatic.[17]

Sir Alan Gardiner (1879–1963), the greatest English Egyptian philologist of his generation, wrote of Akhenaten's "fanatical determination": he was "self-willed but highly courageous," and Gardiner judged that it was "in the moral courage with which the reformer strove to sweep away the vast accumulation of mythological rubbish from the past that

Fig. 1. Cyril Aldred (1914–1991).

his true greatness lay; a negative greatness, no doubt, but one that has been unjustly denied him."[18]

The remarkable study, for many the foundation of the modern understanding of Akhenaten, by Cyril Aldred (1914–91, fig. 1) of the Royal Scottish Museum denied any revolution in Akhenaten's politics or social character, but judged that his monotheism "disorganised the machinery of government" and brought his innovations to an "inglorious end."[19]

A totally different view of Akhenaten was offered by the Russian Egyptologist Yuri Perepelkin (1903–82). His *Secret of the Golden Coffin* appeared in English translation in 1978, but the original Russian edition was published in 1968, a highly significant year in Soviet history. The king was "least of all a complacent dreamer. . . . He was a strong-willed formidable ruler, who ruthlessly eliminated those who defied his will." One can hear in that description the tanks rolling into Prague, but Perepelkin was also relying on a text from the tomb of Tutu,[20] which he translated as referring to scaffolds, swords, and fire. And he was impressed by the quarrying corvée[21]—as if this was previously unknown in Egyptian history. For him, Akhenaten was "the most despotic of the pharaohs."[22]

Frederick Giles described Akhenaten as an insane king who was allowed to rule by himself for only two and a half years [sic].[23] For Erich Hornung, Akhenaten was not a visionary but a "methodical rationalist" whose changes in logic "for a few years anticipated Western modes of thought."[24]

Most recently, a new obsession has taken hold. According to the Canadian archaeologist Donald Redford, Akhenaten was "hideous to behold" and enforced "a rigid, coercive, rarefied monotheism." Although he was not a good administrator, it is admitted that he was a great poet and made an important contribution in art. Overall, however, he was a voluptuary and a totalitarian. Much attention is paid by Redford to Horemheb's "Edict of Reform,"[25] and lurking over all is some amateur psychology: Akhenaten was ignored by his father, but was certainly close to his mother—and then the Aten became his father.[26]

Fellow Canadian Ronald Leprohon also attempted to use the Edict of Reform, which dates from the beginning of Horemheb's reign, to detail the inefficiency and corruption of Akhenaten's time.[27] This ignores the fact that some thirteen years and the reigns of two pharaohs (Tutankhamun and Ay) had intervened. It is more instructive that the army was complicit in much of this inefficiency and corruption—and Horemheb had been a leading general all this time.

Herman Schlögl imagined that spies and informers must have denounced those who held fast to the ancestral gods—but then admitted that we have no precise information about such matters. One important text has often been used to paint a dark picture of the religious events of Akhenaten's reign: the "Restoration Decree" of the boy king Tutankhamun.[28] Schlögl observed, however, that it asserted only that the temples were in ruins (read "closed"), not that the land was in economic or administrative crisis. The building program for Akhet-Aten was "a success of the first rank," and new temples had been constructed all over the country. The so-called new men had carried out their offices correctly.[29]

Jan Assmann, the leading historian of Atenism, suggests that "for the majority of Egyptians, the age of Amarna was one of destruction, persecution, suppression, and godlessness." His main evidence is Tutankhamun's "Restoration Stela." Amarna was "a dreadful aberration," a "traumatic experience."[30]

Joyce Tyldesley, a biographer of Nefertiti, agrees with Redford, although she undermines Redford's suggestion of "totalitarianism" which is also implied by Schlögl, by stating that "there appears to have been little if any bloodshed in defence of the old gods."[31] Marc Gabolde agrees: there was no dismantling of the judiciary, no persecution of individuals, no exploitation of the economy for the benefit of the autocrat and his circle, no reign of terror or violence. Tutankhamun's decree criticizes only religious policies, and does not mention economic or social problems.[32]

Nicholas Reeves has, nevertheless, reasserted the suggestion of dictatorship: "In seventeen years of dictatorial rule, dominated by the paranoia of an Amonist conspiracy, the king had brought the country and its people to the very brink of disaster."[33]

Such sentiments also infected Wolfgang Helck (1914–93), who begins with reference to "dictatorship"—as evidenced by "exiles" (*EA* 162) and "barbed wire watchtowers."[34] Helck's conclusion, however, bears no relationship to this bleak view of Akhenaten's reign: it was instead "an attempt to take a step on the way to a 'modern' world view, linked with freedom from the bonds of a tradition which had become incomprehensible."[35]

'Totalitarianism'

A clear pattern emerges from the early idealists to a more critical (albeit ambiguous) attitude, culminating by the 1980s in a very negative view, using words like 'totalitarian' and 'dictator.'

'Totalitarianism,' according to the *Shorter Oxford Dictionary*, is a policy that "permits no rival loyalties or parties." This is plainly a very modern concept, which ill fits the Bronze Age. And to a modern reader, there are further accretions of association: one thinks of Nazi Germany or Soviet Russia, with secret police, purges, mass executions, and genocide. One crucial aspect of this could perhaps still be applied to Akhenaten's Egypt: the most fundamental element of totalitarianism must be execution of opponents of the regime. The only requirement then is to name known victims of the 'regime.' None is known from Akhenaten's reign. There is none. The totally inappropriate term also ignores the power of the pharaoh at all high periods of Egyptian history. It is simply the product of an antihistorical desire to be sensational.

For those with eyes to see, there are, indeed, many facts about the reign of Akhenaten that disprove any such fantasies about 'totalitarianism.' The most striking is the matter of religious orthodoxy. The new theology was very clear, and it was monotheistic, with the usual corollary that other gods were anathema. In most such cases, orthodoxy is imposed through control of texts and especially the elevation of one text above all others. Modern scholars have named one Amarnan text the "Great Hymn," and even thought that it was written by Akhenaten himself. All of this is modern interpretation. There is, however, a so-called Shorter Hymn (again a modern name) that survives in no fewer than *five* versions, and all showing *endless* variants. This is a very lax way to impose religious orthodoxy.

Another major piece of evidence for the nature of life at Amarna is the plan of the city. There are clear differences in the size and form of houses, reflecting the social distinctions of the inhabitants. It is striking, however, that there is no physical separation of the classes. Simple houses abut the grander, indicating social interaction. The city also shows no sign of any 'master plan,' which is extraordinary considering that it was a newly created capital. A characteristic feature of totalitarian regimes is highly regulated and exhibitionist town planning.

The variation in the plans of the rock tombs for the leading courtiers, although rarely mentioned, further demonstrates the presence of the individual in Akhenaten's reign. This is all the more significant since the tombs were the gift of the king. It is also to be noted that no special measures were taken to conceal the tombs, suggesting "a high level of stability in the country during the Amarnan period, or at least in the new capital and its environs."[36]

What is known and what is not

It is amazing that so much fantasy is published about Amarna. One often hears that with ancient history the main problem is the lack of sources; we indubitably lack enough evidence to answer every question. Historians understand that this is simply a fact of life which has to be accepted. In the case of Amarna, however, we have a wealth of material:

1. the archaeological campaigns at Amarna from 1891, beginning with Petrie and predominantly by the British, but also the Germans;[37]
2. the corpus of the Amarna Letters;
3. detailed illustrations of the tombs of Amarna published in six volumes by Norman de Garis Davies, and of the Royal Tomb published by Geoffrey Martin in two;
4. the excavations at Thebes from 1925, which reveal Akhenaten's first five years; and
5. the hundreds of serious contributions in the most respected Egyptological journals of England, Germany, France, Belgium, Egypt, and America. Geoffrey Martin's splendid bibliography (1991) drew on nearly four hundred such journal articles.

It would be absurd, then, to claim that we do not have enough to occupy serious historians. There are, on the other hand, many basic matters about which we know little or nothing. It is this fundamental contradiction which lies at the root of the 'problem' of Amarna. One needs patience to master the enormous amount of material on some things, and control to confront our ignorance on others.

What we do *not* know is one of the least frequently broached matters. The American anthropologist Leslie White (1900–75) took an extreme view in 1948:

> The fact is that we know very little indeed about Ikhnaton as a political figure and virtually nothing about his personality and character. It is usually said that Amenhotep III was Ikhnaton's father, but Newberry asserts that this is merely an assumption: "this is nowhere asserted on any Egyptian inscription." Concerning the ancestry of other intimates of Ikhnaton—his wife, Nefertiti, his "beloved" coregent Smenkhkare, and his son-in-law and successor, Tutankhamun—"nothing whatever is definitely known" (Newberry). His age at the time of his accession has been much debated and is still uncertain. Evidence concerning his health and physical condition is so varied as to be virtually worthless. We do not know why he became estranged from his wife. We do not know how he met his death, whether from

natural causes or by violence. And, finally, we do not know where he was laid to rest. If, therefore, we do not have adequate information of this sort, data on Ikhnaton as a king, a political institution, how could we expect to have any reliable information pertaining to his personality and character? Indeed, do we have any facts at all on this subject?[38]

White went too far, but he was reacting against, in particular, Breasted and Arthur Weigall (1880–1934). He even needlessly added puzzles: Akhenaten's supposed separation from Nefertiti—orthodoxy at the time—and the place of Akhenaten's burial. In similarly exaggerated and paradoxical terms, Dominic Montserrat claimed that we cannot know "what Akhenaten himself actually believed," despite "voluminous records from the period."[39] Even William Murnane (1945–2000) wrote that "the individual remains hidden behind the carefully crafted persona."[40]

Of Nefertiti, Christiane Desroches-Noblecourt (1913–2011) asserted that "one cannot be sure . . . even of a single event in her life," except for her separation from the king and her move to the northern district of the town[41]—a 'fact' now, ironically, quite disproven. Dimitri Laboury has more recently made the fantastic assertion that we do not know what she looked like, because Rolf Krauss had "deconstructed" her famous Berlin bust and claimed that it was constructed according to an ideal graph: as if we had no other portrait of her, and as if the "mature Nefertiti" (fig. 85) were not the same person. For Dimitri Laboury, Nefertiti is no more than a personified function.[42]

What is not known at present with any certainty about Akhenaten:
- when he was born;
- anything about his childhood, or adolescence, or education;
- when his elder brother, the crown prince Thutmose, died;
- how old he was when he came to the throne;
- why he left Thebes; and
- how old he was when he died (but he ruled for seventeen years).

Of Nefertiti, we do not know at present for certain:
- where and when she was born (but she was Egyptian);
- who her parents were (although a consensus is growing);
- how she met Akhenaten; and
- when she died and at what age.

Of Kiya, Akhenaten's other known wife, we do not know fundamental matters, such as her origins, or when and how she died.

Of Smenkhkare, husband of the eldest princess, there is similarly no certainty as to his parents, when (or even if) he became coregent, or when and how he died.

Most of the above matters relate to the last five years of Akhenaten's reign. The last dated event belongs to Year 12. The fate of all the main actors and of Atenism itself lies shrouded in darkness.

The only dated events or documents of the reign are:

> Year 3: a letter from Kahun;[43]
> Year 4, II *3ḥt* 7: a legal case;[44]
> Year 4, III *3ḥt* 11: quarrying in the Wadi Hammamat;[45]
> Year 5, III *šmw* 19: letter from Gurob;[46]
> Year 5, IV *šmw* 13: the foundation of Amarna (the "Earlier Proc-lamation" on boundary stelae);[47]
> Year 6, IV *3ḥt* 13: the "Later Proclamation" at Amarna;[48]
> Year 8, I *prt* 8: the renewed oath to the above;[49]
> Year 8, IV *3ḥt* 30: the "Colophon" to the above;[50]
> Year 12, II *prt* 8: the 'durbar' (tomb of Huya);[51]
> Year 2 or 12: Nubian War;[52]
> Years 1–17: dockets.[53]

Some other vital matters—the dates of Akhenaten's accession and of his change of name—have been deduced by modern ingenuity, as we shall see. Another 'foundation-stone' in Amarnan chronology, however, is anything but that: the change of the name of the Aten from its Earlier to Later form. This has long been—and continues to be—automatically dated to Year 9, although more recently it has been placed by some scholars as late as Year 14. Yet another caution relates to material found at Thebes. This is usually automatically dated to somewhere in Years 1–5: nothing was later than that (but see pp. 51, 197, 202).

Canadian anthropologist Bruce Trigger (1937–2006) has drawn attention to one of the most fundamental gaps in our knowledge: our understanding of the reign is dominated by Amarna, with some additions from Thebes in the first five years. In the absence of data from much of

Egypt, definite conclusions regarding the king, his policies, and their success or failure cannot be reached with any confidence.[54]

The 'jigsaw'

One is used to viewing historical questions as a kind of jigsaw puzzle, in which one never has all the pieces. This is not the case with real jigsaws, where, unless someone has done something wicked, one knows that one has all the pieces, and that it is a matter of skill and patience to reconstruct the whole picture.

With the Amarnan jigsaw, there are many missing pieces, which makes putting the surviving pieces back together so much more difficult. Much more, however, is in play. Every now and again, someone offers a new, hitherto missing piece, which produces much excitement. The satisfaction is brief, however. Very soon someone else claims that the new piece has been quite misunderstood, or does not belong at all. Meanwhile, behind all this, others are busily working away at the pieces that do remain, trying to remove them from the picture or move them about into an entirely new position. To change the metaphor, it is as if historical evidence is like water running through one's fingers.

As examples of contested evidence, every family tree of the later Eighteenth Dynasty is different. One would think when one has *corpora delicti*—and we have many of them[55]—that modern methods of medical analysis to determine age at death and DNA analysis to determine relationships would solve many problems. To the contrary, despite the confident assertions of each new investigation, very little has gained universal approval (see further below).

Indeed, there is no statement in Amarnan studies which cannot be contradicted. A perfect example is that while almost everyone accepts that the smashing of Akhenaten's sarcophagus in the Royal Tomb was the action of Amunist fanatics, Gabolde asserts, to the contrary, that it "seems more plausible that smashing this monument into *such tiny pieces* [my emphasis] was a way of preventing any reuse, and hence it should be considered a pious act rather than offending one."[56]

He has, of course, undermined his own 'case' with his observation that the sarcophagus was smashed into "*tiny* pieces"; Martin notes that, "with few exceptions, none of the fragments is more than a few centimeters wide."[57] Who is more likely to have done this: supporters wanting simply to prevent its reuse, or fanatics wanting to obliterate every trace of the king? Gabolde's sole argument is that the sarcophagus of Akhenaten's mother, Tiye, was treated in the same way and this made "no sense." Fanatics do not concern themselves with sense; if they did, the fact that she was buried at Amarna proves that Tiye must have been a hated Atenist.

And so much vital evidence is fragmentary, for example, the so-called "Coregency Stela," which bears the cartouches of two kings, with the second pair recut over an earlier text. The question of recut inscriptions and reallocated objects, which is a continually recurring problem in Amarna, is nowhere more vividly illustrated than in the coffin and canopic jars of KV 55.

As though all this were not enough, there is something else which overshadows all the rest: *we were never meant to know anything about Akhenaten*. His enemies intended that his existence and his times were to be blotted out from history.

And yet, beyond all that, there are very special influences operating here. The art of Amarna is so extraordinary that it excites very contrary responses, from ecstasy to repulsion. That, however, is nothing compared to the religious question. The possibility that Akhenaten was a monotheist and a precursor by centuries of any earlier similar theology makes him the object of enormous theological controversy. The epithet 'heretic' is commonly applied to him—as if the Egyptians could have entertained any such concept.[58] Heresy is willful theological error by an inducted member of a religion, such as a baptized Catholic. This is only possible where doctrine has been defined by the authority of the Church. One cannot have heresy before one has orthodoxy, and then one requires institutions which enforce it and identify those who diverge and punish them. From theology, controversy then spills over into the whole nature of Egyptian society at this time; Akhenaten constantly mentioned *Maat* (good order), yet for some, then and now, he was the greatest overthrower of 'order' in Egyptian history, and his successors claimed to be responsible for a 'restoration.' Sides are constantly taken on all these matters by moderns.

Fantasy

Akhenaten and his time have been treated, as Helck rightly described it, after the fashion of historical novels.[59] No fantasy has been too extreme. Evidence has often been the last thing required. The historian is, however, bound by certain ironclad rules. One of the most fundamental is that the duty of professional standards applies equally, whether one's subject is someone living, who might bring a suit for libel, or someone who lived millennia ago.

We may single out three fantasies that have bedeviled Amarnan studies for decades. To my mind, without doubt, the most misleading was Percy Newberry's (1868–1949) reassignment in 1928 of two reliefs, understood since their discovery to show Akhenaten and Nefertiti, to Akhenaten and Smenkhkare, with overtones of a homosexual relationship. It was not until 1973 that a number of scholars in concert reclaimed these two reliefs and thus enabled our modern understanding of Nefertiti's importance.

The second most distracting episode in Amarnan studies, second only to the Newberry fantasy, was the claim by British excavators in the 1920s that Nefertiti had been disgraced. This was based on a total misreading of the archaeological record, corrected only in 1968 by Perepelkin, who read the erased name as that of Kiya.

A third major distraction, this time going back to Petrie, was the 'coregency debate,' which, not without precedent in the Eighteenth Dynasty, claimed that Akhenaten was coregent with his father, for anywhere between one and twelve years. The various theories were not cumulative evidence; each exclusively claimed to be right. The fact that almost twelve different answers could be given was surely an alarm signal, and Arielle Kozloff and Betsy Bryan made an illuminating observation: the supporters of the coregency were mostly art historians, whereas historians remained largely unconvinced.[60] The coregency theory dominated Amarnan scholarship for more than a century and is still held dear by a few researchers, but is now generally regarded by most historians as obsolete.

As John Wilson (1899–1976) warned, "scholars have difficulty maintaining their objectivity when they deal with the personalities of the Amarna period."[61] How, then, is one to make sense of Akhenaten and his reign? The most fundamental procedure of the historian is evaluation of sources. Those, of course, who are anxious about ancient historians not having enough remaining evidence easily overvalue what they have. Dearth of sources or superfluity makes no difference. Each source must be subjected to critical scrutiny. I cannot sufficiently express my amazement, for example, at the number of commentators who take as tendentious a text as Tutankhamun's "Restoration Stela"—the rewriting of history by the next regime—as straightforward evidence for what happened under Akhenaten.

There is one tried and true method for making sense of the most contested areas of history: historiography. It requires knowledge of the historical debate and patience to peruse it, analyze it, make sense of it, and present it. One has to sort the contributors into their various schools of interpretation: this makes clear the trajectory of the debate and puts it into historical perspective, so that we can understand why 'orthodox' exposition and interpretation were as they were at any given time. More important than that, however, as one goes, one must be eagle-eyed to collect any evidence that is offered. In this way, at the end, one has all the evidence that has been used by all the contributors, and that, gratifyingly, is bound to amount to more than any single one of them had. The historiographical method also makes one aware of the complexity of the possible interpretations, a matter often concealed by each author's desire to promote his or her own answers. One must also be alert to the main sources of that evidence, so that one can then make one's own check of it. In the case of Akhenaten, the main corpus of evidence is the excavations at Karnak and Amarna, which are available in more than half a dozen main works: by Petrie, Davies, Borchardt, Eric Peet, Henri Frankfort, John Pendlebury, Redford, and Barry Kemp.[62]

Above all that, however, one cannot maintain—as is constantly done with questions of Akhenaten's reign that have been controversial for more than a century—that there is a new and correct answer which suddenly trumps all previous answers. The likelihood of that is obviously slight. New evidence does appear from time to time, but experience shows that such novelties are frequently short-lived. All views and all evidence must be presented and analyzed. Only if one of them then has a greater degree of probability or plausibility should it be preferred, as every succeeding chapter will demonstrate. This may sound very unpromising, but, in fact, as the following pages will reveal, there are many occasions when such a preference may rationally be given. Its provisional nature must, however, at the same time be recognized.

Underlying the above method is a requisite philosophy. It springs from the last point and obviously causes great difficulty for many. Instead of claiming that one's own dogmatically asserted views are the only correct ones, one must retrace the historical debate on each question in order to distinguish the false trails, on the one hand, and, on the other, the paths that have turned out to be the most fruitful. In other words, one is ever watchful to give credit to scholars who have brought us to wherever we are at present. Historians, of all people, understand the debts that are owed to the past.

There is one misunderstanding that must be laid to rest. Historiography might seem to some simply a cataloguing of other people's 'opinions.' Nothing could be further from the truth. The investigator is in control at all times, sifting, categorizing, but most importantly organizing and accepting or rejecting: in short, reconstructing the debate and adjudicating. And what is demanded at every moment is the *evidence* on which the opinions are based. For the historian, sources are not 'icing on the cake' but the building blocks of history. They are either primary or secondary. The credibility of any secondary (modern) source depends entirely on the worth of the primary (ancient) sources quoted.

2 The Theban Years

THE EIGHTEENTH DYNASTY with its capital at Thebes, seat of the dynastic god Amun, was primarily a military monarchy, founded on the need to expel the Hyksos, who had occupied Lower Egypt. Its memorable kings had characteristically waged wars in Asia, not to mention Nubia, and had prided themselves on their physical prowess. That pattern had been broken by Thutmose IV, Akhenaten's grandfather, famous for his diplomacy with the Mitanni, and Amenhotep III,[1] his father, who was able to spend most of his long reign (thirty-eight years) in peace.[2] Little foreshadowed the upheaval that followed. Amenhotep IV began his religious revolution at Thebes, where he ruled for five years, then in his Year 5 founded a new capital in Middle Egypt and changed his name to the one by which the world now better knows him, Akhenaten.

The discovery of Akhenaten

The key to the long confusion in the nineteenth century over the place of Akhenaten in history is his passing over in the Egyptian king lists, which subsumed the Amarna period under Horemheb, so that historians were left only with the chronology of Manetho, a third-century BC high priest of Heliopolis.

Bonaparte's expedition and the accompanying scientific survey (1798), then the Franco-Tuscan expedition led by Jean-François Champollion

(1790–1832) and Ippolito Rosellini (1800–43) in 1828, could provide no historical background to the ruins of Amarna. The real 'discoverer' of Akhenaten was Nestor L'Hôte (1804–42). He spent thirty-five days copying at Amarna, early in 1839, and regarded "Bachn" as a usurper because of the obliteration of his name. His queen was "Nofrait," and his god "Atnra." L'Hôte positively identified the five cartouches of these three and devoted many pages to scenes in the tombs to throw light on the period. He placed Akhenaten's reign before that of "Horus" (Horemheb), perhaps even pre-Hyksos, or even pre-Menes.[3]

Richard Lepsius produced the first synthesis of the historical events of that time. His early version had Amenhotep III succeeded by his son "Horus," also leaving two other sons, Amenhotep IV, Tutankhamun, and a daughter, "Athotis." Amenhotep IV and Tutankhamun reigned during the life of "Horus" as rivals to him. "Bech-natenra" (Akhenaten) was at first assumed to be a woman, the wife and widow of Amenhotep IV. By 1851, however, Lepsius had realized that Amenhotep IV was the same as the king whose new name he rendered as "Bech-en-aten." He recognized the special cult of the sun disk, worshiped in open temples, and the obliteration, as he thought, of all other gods. The cult was revolutionary, but worship of the sun was fundamental in Egypt. Lepsius also copied the scenes in the tombs at Amarna and drew attention to their important evidence. He thought that Akhenaten had seven daughters (the eldest married to his successor), and that he ruled only twelve years. His two successors renounced the Aten cult but were not later recognized. It was "Horus" (that is, Horemheb) who was the first king of the time accepted by posterity.[4] Thanks to the genius of Lepsius, the modern understanding of Akhenaten had begun, but that did not mean the end of fantasy.

The founder of the Antiquities Service in Egypt, Auguste Mariette (1821–81), is notorious for his view, as expressed in 1855, that Akhenaten was a eunuch who had been captured and mutilated in the Nubian wars. This was, in fact, only a suggestion, to explain his portraiture.[5] As late as 1879, Heinrich Brugsch (1827–94) still held "Khu-n-Aten," a man of "unpleasing appearance" but "exalted notions," to be of nonroyal birth, because of his commoner mother—and a eunuch.[6] And in the same year, Villiers Stuart was still claiming "Khou-en-Aten" was merely a servant of Amenhotep III, but that he became king by marrying the pharaoh's daughter.[7]

Akhenaten's siblings

Akhenaten had an elder brother, Thutmose, who was the crown prince but predeceased his father, one of many princes of his dynasty who died early. His titles show him to have been Eldest King's Son (*s3-nsw smsw*) and Overseer of the Priests of Upper and Lower Egypt, High Priest of Ptah in Memphis, and *Sm*-priest of Ptah.

His attestations are numerous:
- a schist miller-shabti (Louvre E2749);
- the sarcophagus of his cat (from which the above titles come) (Cairo CG 5003);
- a miniature bier in schist (fig. 2);
- a relief with his father Amenhotep III from the first chapel of the Serapeum at Memphis.[8]

A whip from the tomb of Tutankhamun[9] has often been ascribed to him, but the only title on it other than King's Son, "Captain of the Troops," is not found on any certain monument of Akhenaten's brother and does not accord with his otherwise exclusively sacerdotal offices.

Amenhotep III had at least four and possibly five daughters. These were therefore Akhenaten's sisters:[10]

Fig. 2 Miniature bier-shabti of Prince Thutmose (Berlin VÄGM 112-97).

- Sitamun, many times called "King's Daughter"; also "Eldest King's Daughter," and several times "King's Wife" (alabaster vase, Cairo JE 18459). Her portrait is found on a chair (Cairo CG 51112) from the tomb of Yuya and Tjuiu (KV 46), her grandparents (fig. 3). She is shown in reliefs with her sisters Henuttaneb and Iset at the temple at Soleb in Upper Nubia.
- Henuttaneb, many times called "King's Daughter," but also possibly "King's Wife." She stands between the legs of her parents on the colossal group from Medinet Habu (fig. 4).
- Nebetta: on the right, in the same colossal family group. The name of a third daughter here, on the left, is unfortunately lost. It is often taken to be Iset.
- Iset: many times called "King's Daughter," but also "King's Wife" (a serpentine statue in a Dutch private collection). We have various representations, most notably this statue, where she is shown standing beside her father,[11] and with her sister

Fig. 3 Portrait of Sitamun on the back panel of her chair; from the tomb of her grandparents Yuya and Tjuiu (KV 46—Cairo CG 51113).

Fig. 4 Colossus of Amenhotep III and Queen Tiye, with three of their daughters, including Henuttaneb; from Medinet Habu, probably near the southwestern entrance to the king's memorial-temple complex, where it is likely to have stood (Cairo JE 33906).

Henuttaneb on a carnelian plaque (MMA 44.2.1),[12] and again with her sister on the Soleb temple reliefs. She, like Henuttaneb, is not heard of in Akhenaten's reign.

- Four unnamed daughters are shown together in the tomb of Kheruef (TT 192).[13]
- Baketaten, often taken to be the youngest daughter, is known only from the tomb of Huya, Tiye's steward (TA 1): she is shown with Tiye banqueting with the family of Akhenaten, with Tiye again facing Amenhotep III (fig. 61), and having her statue carved by the sculptor Iuti-inti (fig. 65).[14] Where her titles are given, she is "King's Bodily Daughter," not necessarily the present king (Akhenaten).[15]

Akhenaten's life before accession

History can be cruel. In the studio of Thutmose at Amarna, Ludwig Borchardt found a statue that he identified as being of Akhenaten as a child. It was reassembled from the pieces, only to be destroyed in the Second World War. Photographs survived, however, to be published by Marianne Eaton-Krauss in 1983.[16]

In a painting from tomb TT 226, the owner (probably the scribe Heqareshu) sits with four naked children on his lap, one of whom is the "King's Bodily Son, beloved of him," Akheperre (fig. 5).[17]

In the same tomb, Amenhotep III is shown enthroned with his mother, Mutemwia. Norman de Garis Davies drew attention to this painting in 1923. Previously, only one royal child had been shown on the lap. Now there were four, "a challenge to laughter." Davies considered that "The name of one of them (not the youngest) survives on a fragment as Akheper(u?)re; another may have been Thutmose, the heir who died young, and a third Akhenaton."[18] The tomb inscription was published by Davies in 1933,[19] although his identification of the children has been challenged as the surviving names suggest sons of Amenhotep II.[20] Dimitri Laboury took up this question of who may have been the essential tutor to the young prince: the owner of TT 226; the royal tutor Amenemopet; the vizier Aper-el; or the royal scribe Meryre.[21] There is, however, one Amarnan whose tomb inscriptions (TA 7) mention that he had served the Prince Akhenaten: Parennefer.[22]

Fig. 5. Four princes, including Akheperre, on the lap of their tutor in TT 226.

We know next to nothing of Akhenaten's life until his accession. The only inscriptional evidence is a wine docket from Amenhotep III's palace-temple complex at Malqata, in Western Thebes: "The King's Son Amenhotep."[23] Surmises have, however, been made. The rambling Malqata complex (fig. 6) had a number of "palaces": the southern (for Tiye?), the middle, and the northern; three "villas" (for the vizier, treasurer, and chief steward?); an audience pavilion; and to the north, a large temple of Amun with a festival hall.[24] William Hayes (1903–63) suggested that the middle palace was the home of Prince Amenhotep until the move to Amarna.[25] Heinrich Schäfer suggested that he was born at Malqata.[26]

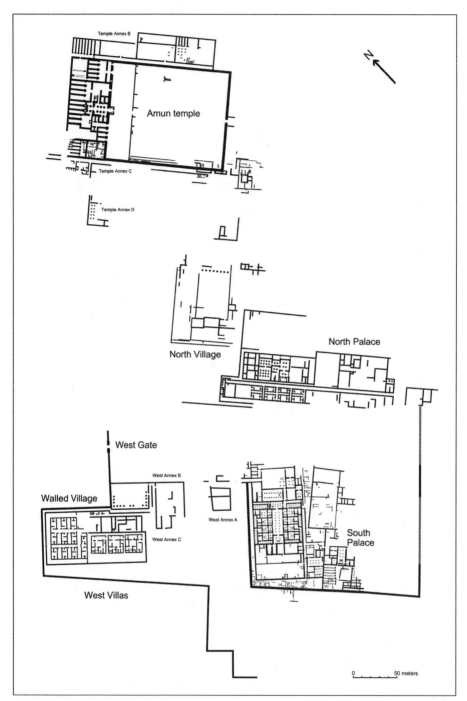

Temple Annex B

Amun temple

Temple Annex C

Temple Annex D

North Palace

North Village

West Gate

West Annex B

Walled Village

West Annex A

West Annex C

South Palace

West Villas

0   50 meters

Fig. 6. Plan of the Malqata palace-complex of Amenhotep III.

Cyril Aldred thought, however, that he was reared at Memphis, and came under the influence of the sun cults at nearby Heliopolis. He also would have known important officials of his father, such as Amenhotep, son of Hapu, administrator and scholar; his brother, also Amenhotep, high steward of Memphis; as well as Yuya and Tjuiu, his maternal grandparents, and the future king Ay.[27] Robert Hari (1922–88) also suggested that he was brought up by the priesthood of Re at Heliopolis.[28] Laboury, on the other hand, has denied any influence from Heliopolis.[29]

Amusing attempts have been made to fill the gaps. According to Arthur Weigall, he

> seems to have been a quiet, studious boy, whose thoughts wandered in fair places, searching for that happiness which his physical condition had denied to him. His nature was gentle; his heart overflowed with love. He delighted, it would seem, to walk in the gardens of the palace, to hear the birds singing, to watch the fish in the lake, to smell the flowers, to follow butterflies, to warm his small bones in the sunshine.[30]

Meanwhile, Akhenaten was, according to Donald Redford, "a man deemed ugly by the accepted standards of the day, secluded in the palace in his minority, certainly close to his mother, possibly ignored by his father, outshone by his brother and sisters, unsure of himself."[31]

What we can say with some certainty, however, is that his education would have included literacy, which would surely include acquaintance with the history and literature of his country, and the basic skills of a young king who, whatever his personal preferences, would be expected to be a military leader: handling of weapons and driving a chariot. It would not be going too far, unless his father jealously monopolized such matters, to add some acquaintance with the nature of Egypt's relations with her most powerful neighbors, with whom, after all, Egypt had enjoyed close diplomatic ties for some generations.

Coregency

The suggestion that Amenhotep III and IV shared the throne[32] goes back at least to Flinders Petrie (1853–1942), who in his history of Egypt in 1896 argued for an overlap of five years.[33] From then onwards, many scholars produced schemes involving some degree of overlap.[34] The most cogent documentation was perhaps produced by Herbert Fairman (1907–82) in 1951.[35] The proposal found its most passionate advocate in Aldred, who argued in 1959 and then in his biographies of 1968 and 1988 for a coregency of twelve years. Other lengths have also been proposed, all having different consequences for the broader historical picture of *both* kings' reigns.

Others have argued equally strongly against any overlap at all, with the majority of twenty-first-century Egyptologists agreeing that there was a simple direct succession between the kings.[36] For most opponents, the problem has been the reconciliation of the different artistic styles seen in the works of the two kings which, in the case of a coregency, would have been produced contemporaneously (although Raymond Johnson argues that they *do* work together[37]), and the bizarre situation of the radical turn to Atenism running alongside Amenhotep III's continued building in honor of Amun (particularly for those who place Amun's 'persecution' in the early or middle part of Akhenaten's reign). The theory of coregency has latterly been subjected to devastating critique; William Murnane's contribution was outstanding. He concluded: "Despite the impressive quantity of evidence mustered . . . none of it can be reckoned as convincing proof."[38] Laboury went further: "once much in fashion, now an Egyptological fiction."[39]

A key issue has been that no single piece of evidence adduced for *or* against the theory of coregency has won unconditional agreement, with criteria often treated in isolation, without regard for the consequences.

Accession

We have no direct record of Akhenaten's accession day—whether as sole or joint king—which marked the beginning of his regnal year-count. This is to be distinguished from the calendar year, which opened with the season of *3ḥt* (Inundation), followed by *prt* (winter) and *šmw* (summer). Murnane, however, made a brilliant but simple deduction:[40] the Amarna boundary stelae show that Year 8 included both an oath taken on I *prt* 8[41] and a 'colophon' (final statement), with a repeated oath, on IV *3ḥt* 30.[42] Murnane further noted that Boundary Stelae A and B show that these two events occurred *in that order*. The two events covered twelve complete months of a regnal (not calendar) year, with the exception of seven days. Akhenaten's regnal year must therefore have begun in I *prt* and extended to at least the end of IV *3ḥt*. The only days left unaccounted for are the first seven days of I *prt*. Akhenaten's accession must therefore have taken place in that first week. The year, according to the latest calculations, was around 1353.[43]

Akhenaten's accession was most likely at Thebes, the "Heliopolis of the South,"[44] although other suggestions have been Memphis[45] or Hermonthis (Armant).[46]

His first titulary reveals a man the world has completely forgotten. It ran as follows: Horus: "Strong Bull with two high feathers"; The Two Ladies: "Great in Kingship in Karnak"; Horus of Gold: "He who raises his crowns in Karnak"; Prenomen: "Beautiful are the appearances of Re– The sole one of Re"; Nomen: "Amenhotep, divine ruler of Thebes."

The Horus name follows that of his father: "Strong bull appearing in truth," but the Two Ladies and Horus of Gold names both link him with Karnak, the home of Amun, whereas Thutmose III and IV had stressed the stability of their reign in the Horus name, and Thutmose IV and Amenhotep III had been "Great of strength" with reference to Egypt's enemies in their Golden Horus name. The prenomen was traditionally a compound of Re. It is the stress on Karnak and the lack of slogans for the reign that are striking.

How old he was when he came to the throne we are not told. Suggestions have incredibly varied: "about ten,"[47] "eleven,"[48] "twelve,"[49] "thirteen to fifteen,"[50] "fifteen to sixteen,"[51] and "seventeen to eighteen"[52] have all been suggested, as well as, more commonly, "about twenty-one"[53] or "twenty-three."[54] These are all *guesses*. All we can say is that the higher end of the scale is more likely because his father had the second longest reign of the dynasty, almost forty years.

We have a number of representations of the young Amenhotep from the first years of his reign. First, there is a wooden statuette showing him wearing the *khepresh* (blue) crown (fig. 7). Second, we have a scene

Fig. 7. Wooden statue of the young Akhenaten (Berlin ÄM 21836).

Fig. 8. Amenhotep IV, followed by Queen Tiye, offering to Re-Horakhty and Maat on the lintel of the outer portico of the tomb-chapel of Kheruef (TT 192).

from the outer portico of the tomb of Kheruef (TT 192), who served with Amenhotep III and his son; some of the decoration of the main chapel can be dated to the former's first and third jubilees (Years 30, 33). In the portico, the younger king appears, named as Amenhotep, in traditional style, most notably on the lintel of the doorway of the outer vestibule of the tomb, with his mother Queen Tiye behind him, offering wine to Re-Horakhty and Maat, and incense to Atum and Hathor (fig. 8). There is no sign of Nefertiti. The scenes have therefore been dated to the first few months of his reign.[55]

The most famous scenes of the king in his earliest years are in the tomb of Vizier Ramose (TT 55), who also served both Amenhotep III and his son. The reliefs famously depict the last in two styles: traditional and Amarnan. On the southern side of the doorway in the western wall, in traditional style, he is enthroned, with the goddess Maat behind

Fig. 9. Amenhotep IV seated with Maat in the tomb-chapel of Ramose (TT55)..

him (fig. 9). The deceased Ramose appears four-fold, offering the king sacred objects and praying for him to gods; the second figure prays to the Aten under its earlier name. To the north of the doorway, he is shown in the Amarnan style (but still with the name Amenhotep), with the disk form of the Aten above, accompanied by Nefertiti and in a 'Window of Appearances'; the scene was carved perhaps three or four years later (fig. 10).

These two tombs offer some obvious suggestions about the earliest years of the reign. At his accession, the young king was quite mature—as one might well have expected from the long reign of his father. Three or four years later, he is married to Nefertiti—although the later ubiquitous daughters are nowhere to be seen, suggesting that none was yet born. Now the Aten is dominant, with the Earlier form of his name (for further evidence of the date of the marriage, see pp. 49, 52, 202).

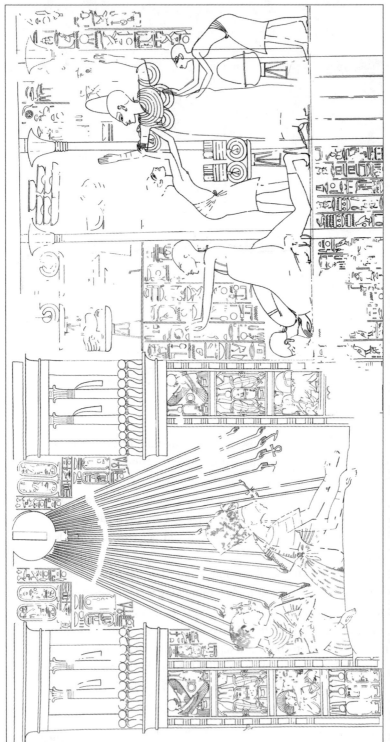

Fig. 10. Amenhotep IV and Nefertiti at the "Window of Appearances" in the tomb-chapel of Ramose.

Further evidence comes from Karnak, where he completed the work of his father at Pylon III by adding a porch, where he is shown in the traditional pose smiting his enemies. This work was left unfinished.[56]

Another early portrait is a relief at Gebel Silsila, 150 kilometers south of Thebes, accompanying a stela recording the extraction of stone for "the great *bnbn* [sacred stone] of Re-Horakhty" at Karnak. It has been very badly damaged, by both the Atenists and then the Amunists, but the figure of the king facing Amun-Re is still clear.[57] Further south, in Nubia, at Soleb, the young king completed his father's great jubilee temple by adding his figures again to its porch, on which he is shown being crowned by various deities, including Atum, Seth, and Horus, while he worships his deified father and Amun-Re.[58]

Vital evidence for the earliest years at Thebes is provided also by the Amarna Letters. Tushratta of Mitanni wrote to Queen Tiye following the death of Amenhotep III, calling her "mistress of Egypt," and complaining of the lack of precious greeting gifts. He asked Tiye to give Akhenaten a history of relations between the two powers, which she knew better than anyone else (*EA* 26; the same in 28 and 29). He does not mention Nefertiti, but there are generic references in other letters to "the rest of your wives," after mention of Tushratta's daughter Tadu-Kheba (*EA* 27, 28, 29). In the next letter, after greeting the king, he sends wishes to Tiye and a precious gift (*EA* 27; also 29). The reasonable inference to draw from these letters from Egypt's closest ally is that Tiye was at least still very powerful in Egypt as queen mother, if not as regent, as has been suggested by a number of writers.[59] It is also suggestive that an ally so well informed and sensitive in matters of such high protocol sent no gifts to Nefertiti at this point. Christiane Desroches-Noblecourt's interpretation of Maat in the Ramose scene as a representation of Tiye accords well with this interpretation.[60]

During his early years, the king presumably commissioned a tomb in the Valley of the Kings. Various scholars have suggested the unfinished WV 25, while others have suggested the beginning of WV 23, which later became the tomb of King Ay, to be that tomb.[61] The beginning of his memorial temple may have been what was later transformed into the rear section of the later Ramesseum.[62]

The destroyed Theban temple

In the aftermath of the Amarna age, Akhenaten's earliest temples, built at Thebes during his first five years, were demolished. Their stones, small sandstone blocks (52 cm long [a royal cubit] × 26 cm wide × 20 cm high),[63] often carved in relief and known then as "stone bricks"[64] and today as *talatat* (fig. 11), were used as foundations and filling in later buildings, particularly Pylons II, IX, and X (all built by Horemheb) (fig. 12). They were also used for the foundations of the Great Hypostyle Hall built by Rameses II as well as his pylon at Luxor.

Fig. 11. *Talatat*, as found in the filling of Pylon IX at Karnak.

Fig. 12. A *talatat* showing workers carrying the blocks and constructing with them.

These *talatat* were known to the early modern visitors to Thebes: Nestor L'Hôte and Émile Prisse d'Avennes (1807–79) in 1839 and Richard Lepsius in the mid-1840s.[65] Georges Legrain (1865–1917), Director of Works at Karnak from 1895 to 1917, extracted many such blocks during his restoration of Pylons IX and X. His work was continued by Maurice Pillet (1881–1964), Director of Works at Karnak from 1920 to 1925.[66] As early as the 1922/23 season, during work undertaken by Pillet to reinforce the columns, it was discovered that the foundations of the Hypostyle Hall were composed of *talatat*. Few, however, were decorated.[67]

Excavations at Karnak by Chevrier 1925–54

It was in 1925 that Henri Chevrier (1897–1974), Director of Works at Karnak from 1925 to 1954, began his clearance and restoration work at Thebes, which led to the recovery of the demolished Theban temples of Akhenaten, which were never meant to see the light of day again. Two statues of the king were found during drainage works around the main temple, and the next year a further nine were uncovered, in a row face down on the ground (fig. 13). They had each been on bases, thought to be backed by a pillar, and seemed to form part of a portico. Chevrier drew attention to the king's headdress: the *ḫ3t* (bag wig), surmounted by various crowns, notably one of four feathers, but also the double crown (fig. 14). He had found part of Akhenaten's *Gm(t)-p3-Itn* ("The Aten is found") temple (fig. 15).

Fig. 13. Royal statues found by Henri Chevrier in the *Gm(t)-p3-'Itn* at East Karnak in 1926; the 'bust' in the center of the photograph is now in the Luxor Museum.

During 1926/27, Chevrier found the southwestern corner of the building and many much more fragmentary statues with their heads detached. One of the finest was stolen from the site on a rest day, despite its considerable weight, but was later recovered. Chevrier then began to detect a court surrounded by Osirian statues of Akhenaten. After a year's break owing to lack of funds, work was resumed to the east and west during 1928/29, but with disappointing results because of greater destruction. These excavations required special funds to avoid encroaching on monies for restoration and consolidation. By 1929/30, expropriations of property to the east were needed; the western trench was therefore pushed north. Together with bases and heads, the largest statue of all appeared: "naked and asexual". Expropriations occupied two years, and excavations resumed in 1931/32: the line of statues was followed

Fig. 14. Colossus of Amenhotep IV wearing the *ḫ3t-* and double-crowns; found at the *Gm(t)-p3-'Itn* in June 1925 (Cairo JE 49529).

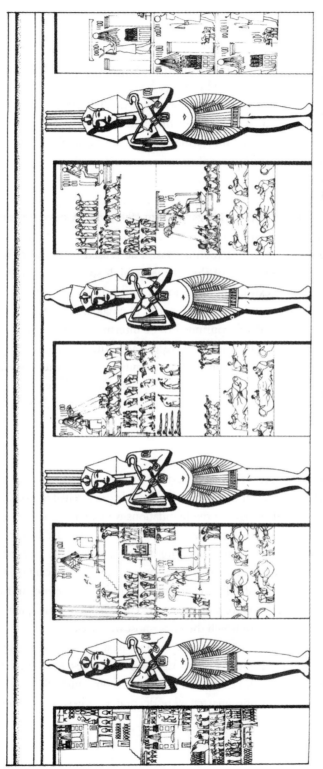

Fig. 15. Donald Redford's reconstruction of the southern colonnade of the *Gm(t)-p3-'Itn*. Recent studies suggest that the features identified by Redford and previous researchers as piers, against which the colossi stood, were actually the bases upon which the figures stood.

35

with more difficulty. Chevrier now had a locomotive to pull the wagons of the debris to the Nile, into which it was thrown. Work continued in 1932/33 until he was stopped by village houses once again, and therefore returned to the northern line of the western wall. Chevrier admitted that the work was becoming increasingly difficult. The 1935/36 season found a statue base to the east, indicating a whole series; work on the north found nothing.[68]

Pylon II

Systematic work on Pylon II began only in 1946, when Chevrier resumed work after the Second World War. This pylon, the work of Horemheb, had to be rebuilt from the foundations. The reused blocks were found in even the highest levels of the 25-meter-high structure. In 1948/49, 4,500 *talatat* were extracted, to be added to the 3,700 previously recovered from the Hypostyle Hall by Chevrier in circumstances that are only sketchily recorded. Work continued to be intermittent, owing to lack of funds, but another 4,000 *talatat* were extracted in 1952, and the work of classifying them was begun by two secondary-school teachers, André Hayler and Henri de Mazade. In sum, the pylon had included thirty-two courses of *talatat*, each of 770 stones, totaling more than 25,000, one-quarter of which were decorated.[69]

Pylon IX

In 1964, the Antiquities Service undertook massive works to save the western wing of Pylon IX, which had for many decades threatened total collapse. It was not a matter of repairs: the foundations were giving way because of movements in the subsoil, and the stones were being degraded by salt. The only solution was to dismantle the entire structure, rebuild the foundations, and then rebuild the monument. As well as restoring it to its original state, this would make it possible for the first time to study how the ancient Egyptians had built such massive gates. It was twenty-six meters high, made up of thirty-four courses, of which the uppermost were lacking.[70]

Talatat had for decades been identified in the area; work on the pylon, continued by the Centre Franco-Égyptien d'Études de Temples de Karnak (founded in 1967), revealed layer after layer—up to 800 per level, of which more than one-quarter were decorated. These were mapped,

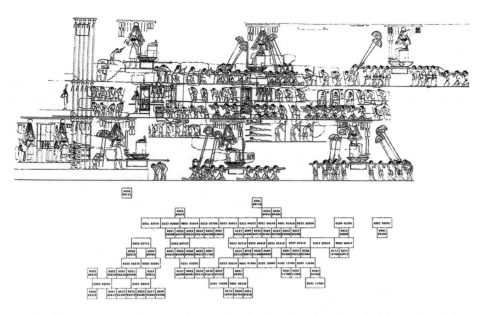

Fig. 16. A reconstructed scene using the Karnak *talatat*, including the underlying coding of the blocks that was used in this initial attempt at reconstructing scenes with the aid of a computer.

numbered, and extracted for study. The first attempts were also made to understand the fragmentary scenes, with the assistance of a team from the University of Pennsylvania in Philadelphia, led by Ray Smith (1897–1982), which led to the foundation of the Akhenaten Temple Project (fig. 16). Initial categorization of possible scenes showed the king being transported in a chariot or palanquin, worship of the Aten, the royal family, and temple staff. The British excavations at Amarna had revealed the complexity of the names of six different religious buildings there, but Serge Sauneron thought most blocks at Thebes came from the *Tni-mnw* ("Exalted are the monuments").[71]

Ramadan Sa'ad (1934–74) summed up the work on Pylon IX in 1967: between 1964 and 1967, 2,000 *talatat* had been found in the pylon, to be added to the 40,000 from Pylon II, the Hypostyle Hall, the temples of Amenhotep and of Khonsu, and Pylon X. As he stressed, these were but the decorated third of the blocks. The façade of Akhenaten's temple, as reconstructed by Sa'ad, showed him in the traditional scene of slaying enemies. The building had been finished by the time Akhenaten changed his name in Year 6 [*sic*], so almost all the cartouches had to be updated. There were also signs of the anti-Atenist 'restoration.'[72]

Sa'ad again summed up in 1976. The "Dismantling and Re-erecting the Ninth Pylon Project" had begun in 1963. Of the thirty-four courses, twenty-seven were dismantled, recovering 3,743 *talatat* (1,501 decorated), the scenes reconstructed depicting the *ḥb-sd* (jubilee: see below). Most of the king's cartouches had been changed from Amenhotep to Akhenaten, but the queen's name was in both the short (Nefertiti) and long (Neferneferuaten-Nefertiti) forms. There were few signs of the princesses.[73]

The Akhenaten Temple Project (1966)

The first report on the Akhenaten Temple Project appeared in 1973. By this time, 35,000 *talatat* had been photographed and computerized, but the actual matching of scenes was being undertaken by human observation. Fundamental questions were addressed, in particular what proportion of such decoration had survived? One simple test was reassuring: scenes showing the king or queen facing either right or left were roughly equal. Did the *talatat* come from one complex, or scattered buildings? The evidence pointed to the latter, some eight temples. How could one identify from which temple a block had come? Sometimes a temple is named.[74]

> Out of a total of 59 blocks on which the temple *Rwd-mnw* ["Sturdy are the monuments"] is mentioned, 47 come from either [Pylon IX] or Luxor. Out of a total of 20 blocks on which *Tni-mnw* ["Exalted are the monuments"] is mentioned 12 come from [Pylon IX] or Luxor. Conversely, 45 of the 56 talatat on which *Ḥwt-bnbn* ["Mansion of the benben"] occurs come from [Pylon II] or Hypostyle, and five of the six references to the *Sḥ-n-'Itn* ["Sunshade of the Aten"] emanate from the same area. Blocks of the scenes which depict the Jubilee come largely from the [Pylon II] and Hypostyle, while scenes of soldiers tend to predominate in [Pylon IX]. The provenience of stones from construction scenes is again [Pylon II] and Hypostyle, but *talatat* from chariot scenes are fairly evenly divided between [Pylon IX] and Hypostyle. The scenes in which Nefertiti is shown by herself come to a large extent from [Pylon II] and Hypostyle; in fact, 73% of all the blocks on which she is figured come

from that *locus*. In [Pylon IX] blocks, on the other hand, she plays a decidedly smaller role.[75]

It was also assumed that the materials from the demolished buildings were put into pylons close to their site (one would not transport such masses further than necessary).

Much more might be learned from the *talatat* about the layout and construction of particular temples. The *Tni-mnw* probably had a pylon and a line of at least three large roofless kiosks containing rectangular offering tables, as well as an aviary and a bakery. Nefertiti was depicted only in the first court. In scenes of worship, Akhenaten was accompanied by the high priest of the Aten and his own first prophet: the usual lector priest was strikingly absent. The king wore either the bag crown or the Red Crown. The presence of birds indicated a location south of the sacred lake. Names of the same type as *Tni-mnw* and *Rwd-mnw* persisted later in this area: remains of the former were found in the lower courses of Pylon IX, while the latter was found in the upper courses. At East Karnak, the structure found by Chevrier, Akhenaten's headwear featured the double crown, the quadruple feathers of Shu, and the Red Crown. The first and third are predominantly associated with the *Gm(t)-p3-'Itn* and the *Hb-sd*.

It seems, judging by the presence of his seals and scarabs, that Akhenaten continued to occupy his father's residence at Malqata. Yet in the *talatat*, the royal couple visited temples without crossing the river. The principal royal palace was therefore presumably on the eastern bank, west of Karnak. It was called "I am not far from him" (*sc.* Amun).

By the second preliminary report in 1975, Redford was able to define the "dispersal pattern" of the *talatat* and the individual nature of the decoration of each of the temples (see below). The major question, however, was: When did Akhenaten build at Thebes? A number of facts allow us confidently to answer that it was only in the first five years of his reign:

- only the Earlier form of the name of the Aten was found;
- almost exclusively the early form of the king's *nomen* (Amenhotep) was found;
- Nefertiti was shown with only one daughter 90 percent of the time (fig. 17), with two daughters 8 percent of the time, and with three only thrice;

Fig. 17. Nefertiti and Meryetaten on the reconstructed gateway of the *Hwt-bnbn* at Karnak. The king apparently never appears in this structure, which may have enclosed the 'single obelisk' of Thutmose IV, which lay west of the main Aten-complex at East Karnak.

- decorative motives matched those of the early tombs of Ramose and Parennefer;
- the royal iconography was very limited: for example, Akhenaten was shown worshiping, riding, walking, and occasionally eating.
- only the first *ḥb-sd* was mentioned.[76]

The first Akhenaten Temple Project volume appeared in 1976. Ray Smith, the man who inspired the whole undertaking, provided enormous technical detail, but major results on a broader scale deriving from the 35,000 *talatat* included the following: that the Karnak *talatat* were sandstone from Gebel Silsila; that offering tables appeared with great frequency, bearing Nefertiti's name; that the most frequent offering was to Maat; that there were many rectangular pillars from Pylon II bearing the figure of Nefertiti; that Nefertiti was associated with the *Ḥwt-'Itn* ("Mansion of the Aten"); and that she was always accompanied by a princess. In sum, the religious importance of Nefertiti was evident from the beginning of the reign. She apparently had a separate temple at Karnak, a fact that has "no close counterpart in Egyptian history." As for Akhenaten, he was more active building in stone for these first five years of his reign than he was at Amarna for the other twelve.[77] An impressive array of temples was revealed: the *Gm(t)-p3-'Itn*, the *Ḥwt-bnbn* ("Mansion of the Benben": a kind of obelisk) and the *Šḥ-n-'Itn* within it, the *Tni-mnw* and *Rwd-mnw*, a "Broad Hall," and the *Pr-'Itn* ("House of the Aten").[78] While Nefertiti was shown subordinate to Akhenaten in the *Tni-mnw* and *Rwd-mnw*, she was shown alone in the *Ḥwt-bnbn*. Most astonishing of all, Akhenaten was referred to on the *talatat* 329 times, but Nefertiti 564 times.[79]

Resumed excavations (1975)

With the Akhenaten Temple Project's matching of the *talatat* underway, in 1975 Redford and the University of Pennsylvania began excavations at East Karnak, looking for the sites of the Akhenaten temples. They began where Chevrier had found the colossi fifty years earlier.

The same area was again uncovered, revealing the southern outer mudbrick wall, with an inner sandstone wall five meters away, and the piers against which the colossal statues of Akhenaten had stood two meters in front of it. Most importantly, the name of this temple was confirmed as *Gm(t)-p3-'Itn*.

The temple here had been demolished down to the lowest course of the foundations under Horemheb, in whose Pylons II, IX, and X the remains of it and the other Aten-structures were found; a stamped jar handle naming Horemheb was found, in fact, in the *talatat* debris.[80] One hundred new *talatat* were discovered, of which almost half allowed themes of decoration to be recovered, focusing on the arrival of the royal party and jubilee ritual in the temple, a motif apparently associated exclusively with the *Gm(t)-p3-'Itn*.[81]

The excavations of 1979/80 discovered the wall of the *temenos* (precinct) of the temple, five meters away from the outside of the temple. The sequence of the later destruction could be reconstructed: the colossi were overthrown, and the roof of the colonnade behind them thrown down, then the *temenos* wall was fired and pushed in. The excavations attempted to locate the western line of the temple, but the destruction had been too thorough. One hundred meters north of the southwestern corner, traces of smaller pier bases were found and a wall of *talatat*, but it was uncertain if they belonged to the same temple. Attention then turned to the northern wall. Here paradoxically it was suggested that Chevrier, in one last attempt to find it, had in fact destroyed it. The northwestern corner seemed to be more than one hundred meters from the southwestern. The basic plan was taking shape.[82]

Redford's 1981/82 season was very important. He worked along the western wall of the temple, revealing that it was the same as the southern one: a wall of *talatat* behind rectangular piers and colossal statues of the king. This ceased about sixty meters north of the southwestern corner, where a monumental entrance to the temple was found: more than ten meters wide, flanked on both sides by walls that were in turn flanked by eight piers. The inner faces were decorated with scenes, but different from those on the south: courtiers and soldiers, probably associated with the royal entry to the temple. The search then continued for the northwestern corner, but it had not been reached after 140 meters.[83]

Redford summed up in 1984: the court of the *Gm(t)-p3-'Itn* was surrounded by a colonnade of piers, two meters square, seven meters high, against each of which had been a colossus of the king, wearing alternatively the feather crown of Shu and the double crown. From the ubiquity of the decoration, the main theme of the southern wall was the jubilee procession from the palace to the temple.[84] On the western wall the main themes were again processional and the king at table (feasting before and after the festival).

The whole temple could be understood as celebrating the king's jubilee. The gods and notables from all over Egypt were in attendance, the king visited all the gods, the coronation was reenacted, officials pledged allegiance, and of course the king ran the famous race, symbolizing his taking possession of all Egypt (presumably the festival for Upper Egypt was depicted on the southern wall, and that for Lower Egypt on the northern). At the end of each day was feasting, and Akhenaten and Nefertiti appeared at the 'Window of Appearances.' Taxes were levied all over Egypt and wealth diverted from other temples.[85]

During the thirteenth to fifteenth campaigns (1987–89), the northwestern corner of the *Gm(t)-p3-'Itn* was found, which at last established the width of the temple. The entrance had already been found on the western side. The statuary here survived in pitiful fragments, in comparison with the colossi found by Chevrier on the southern side. The destruction had been much more ruthless. The same was true of the northern side. All *talatat*, piers, and statues had been removed.

As finally revealed, the *Gm(t)-p3-'Itn* was 216 meters wide and more than 600 meters long, comprising a series of open courts. The *talatat* showed an open court with roofless shrines. They would traditionally have held the various deities of whom the king asked permission to continue to rule; now they were empty, open to the sky.[86] The perimeter wall was two meters thick and possibly nine meters high, and decorated with reliefs that were protected by a colonnade of piers. On the south side, in front of these piers were giant statues of the king in sandstone. On the north side, between the piers were set life-size statues of the king in red quartzite. A relief from the tomb of Akhenaten's butler Parennefer (TT 188) showed that the eastern side was dominated by an altar to Re-Horakhty.[87] Laboury calculated that there would have been two hundred colossal statues, each seven meters tall. The main court could have held a hundred thousand people. The building was more palace in his opinion than temple, with its 'Window of Appearances' for audiences.[88]

The colossi

There are now some thirty-five identifiable colossi.[89] In 2010, Arielle Kozloff noted that the colossi showed signs of having been extensively recut, suggesting that they might have been modified from statues originally made for Amenhotep III.[90] Raymond Johnson pointed out, however, that the recutting could just as well have been of images made for Akhenaten before the change to the Amarnan style.[91]

They have mostly been interpreted as representing a deity, albeit with the features of the king: suggestions have included the Aten,[92] Hapi,[93] Osiris,[94] and the king in connection with Osiris and the Sed festival. Three types of headdresses are found on the colossi: the headcloth (*nms*) with four ostrich plumes, the *nms* with the double crown on top, and the bag wig (*ḫ3t*) surmounted by a small double crown. The figures have their feet together and arms crossed and hold a crook and flail. This was the old pose of Osiris. The same was indicated by the pillars against which the statues were placed. The three types of statues have been suggested as representing three stages in the perpetual renewal of the strength of the king.[95]

Rita Freed has focused on the crowns worn by Akhenaten.[96] He was shown, she concluded, in both a traditional and a new style. The *Gm(t)-p3-'Itn* statues have him with crossed arms, crook, and flail = Osiris; with a double crown = Atum; with a feather crown = Shu; and a tall crown = Tefnut. Johnson suggested that the last three were meant to invoke the triad of Aten, Akhenaten, and Nefertiti. Johnson also emphasized the feather crowns, pointing to Shu, who was male and female in one, with a female counterpart Tefnut. "In these statues Amenhotep IV and Nefertiti are one entity, and perhaps we err in trying to distinguish one from the other."[97]

Wolfhart Westendorf made a powerful case for the king's identification here with the Aten.[98] The Karnak statues with the symbols of royalty recall Osirid statues, as found in the portico of the temple of Rameses III at Karnak. The standard dogma on kingship in ancient Egypt held the king to be the son of Re but also the son of Osiris, with whom the king was reunited on death. Under Westendorf's view, Akhenaten will have adapted this theology at Karnak, where Osiris was replaced by the Aten, with the facial features of the king.

The depiction of the Aten would be to emphasize one divine quality: he was the original god, and that deity was usually androgynous. The Aten was self-created[99] and replaced Re-Atum in this role. As the latter had created Shu and Tefnut, so Akhenaten and Nefertiti identified with these deities.[100] The Aten was both mother and father of all his creation,[101] but more often the former role is stressed.[102] Most creator deities are shown as male (Atum, Amun, Ptah, Osiris) or female (Neith, Isis, Mut), but as early as the Old Kingdom, the Inundation (Hapi) is both man and woman, and Amenhotep III appeared in this guise.[103] The Amarna dogma reversed these roles: Nun had been father of Re; now the Aten was the creator of the Inundation. The king as his son could appear as the Inundation, and indeed adopted a loincloth. The exaggerated abdomen could then represent not only the fertility god but also the maternal body. The pelvis and thigh of the Aten statues have the appearance of being feminine.

Christian Leblanc put the case for Osiris. For him, the colossi formed part of a well-known series of Osirid royal statues backed by a pillar, known from as early as the Middle Kingdom (for example, Mentuhotep III at Armant, Senwosret I, Thutmose I at Karnak, Hatshepsut at Deir al-Bahari, Thutmose III at Karnak, Amenhotep III from Western Thebes, Rameses II at Luxor and Abu Simbel, and Rameses III at Karnak and Medinet Habu, as well as individual statues now in museums). Leblanc divided them into five classes according to dress (mummiform, kilt, and so on) and headdress (the grouping is not chronological, so that developments cannot be traced). The religious significance of the statues was thus made clear, as was the fact that Osiris, a most fundamental Egyptian deity, still played a very prominent role during Akhenaten's first five years.[104]

One may compare the distortions of the colossi to the effect on the modern mind of landscapes transformed by the Impressionists or the human body deconstructed by the Cubists. There is a growing consensus, indeed, that the colossi represent essentially an artistic convention. Edna Russmann described them as "deliberately unrealistic," depicting a new concept of kingship; Claude Vandersleyen called them "an artistic concept"; and Erik Hornung spoke of "a manneristic distortion of reality."[105] Furthermore, Valérie Angenot has emphasized—as others had noted—that these figures, being colossal, were never meant to be seen face to face, but only from below. The sculptors made allowances for parallax distortion.[106] Seen from this correct perspective, the figures appear physically much more normal, but at the same time more imposing.

The asexual colossus

One colossus discovered by Chevrier in 1929/30 (fig. 18) was described from the outset as "naked and asexual."[107] This was accepted almost without demur for a half century until John Harris in 1977 offered a dramatic solution: it was not an image of Akhenaten, but of Nefertiti.

Fig. 18. The "asexual" colossus, found at the *Gm(t)-p3-'Itn* during 1929/30 (Cairo JE 55938).

Harris drew attention to the fact that most of the Karnak statues are anonymous; in only a few cases, the names of Amenhotep IV are preserved on the belt. Furthermore, the headdress of the "asexual" figure differs from the mass of the figures in having its crown fitted directly onto the head, rather than on top of an interposing *nms* or *ḫ3t* hair-covering. On the eight other examples of this arrangement (seven at Karnak and Louvre E.27112), the crown seems to be the double crown.[108] It is interesting that Akhenaten himself rarely wore this, or the false beard. All 'directly-crowned' colossi except for the 'asexual' one have been broken into pieces, and all but the Louvre example have had their features defaced, Harris noted, in contrast to the vast majority of colossi, whose features have been untouched.[109] It has been noticed at Karnak that Nefertiti is a particular object of attack. That these figures are female is suggested by Schäfer's "neck criterion": Nefertiti's neck is convex at the back.[110]

Vandersleyen stressed that the 'naked' statue is otherwise unique: it is hardly characteristic of anything. It thus makes more sense as a *clothed* woman than a *naked* man—and it was indeed clothed: the junctures on the thighs and abdomen and the points of the breasts are all masked by clothing, rather than truly naked.[111]

There are a number of problems with the Nefertiti thesis. This statue is unique in the *Gm(t)-p3-'Itn* temple: why is there only one representation of the queen in such a mode? Second, the features are unmistakably Akhenaten's, while there is no indication that Nefertiti bore kingly attributes while still only King's Chief Wife. Third, vital female characteristics of the art of this period are lacking, notably emphasis on the pubic mound.[112] Could the king be here represented as a god, embodying both female and male characteristics, but lacking the most vital of the latter? There is one obvious candidate: Osiris, whose body, lovingly restored by Isis, lacked the genitals. A further consideration may be that the god Aten was asexual.[113]

There have been many other interpretations. Westendorf suggested it might be a statue of the god Hapi,[114] who was ambiguous in sexual appearance; Gay Robins agreed. All depictions of Akhenaten in relief abandon the earlier male fashion of the kilt, which itself naturally conceals the genitals. He was always shown with his two thighs meeting just below the exaggerated abdomen, in other words asexually. Robins therefore interpreted the asexual colossus as the king as a fecundity figure, comparable to Hapi.[115] Johnson suggested the "self-generating Atum-Re."[116]

Julia Samson (1910–2002) thought traces of a kilt could be easily added: a curving ridge on the abdomen and then the kilt carved onto the upper legs.[117] Winfried Barta saw the "sexless" colossus as Aten in the form of Kamutef, the bull, relying on parallels with Bat in the *Story of the Two Brothers*.[118] Redford rejected the interpretation of the primordial hermaphrodite god Yati or Kamutef, albeit in the stance of Osiris, because an 'Urgott' was contrary to all Akhenaten's thinking; but that the asexuality was "not intended to be of significance" will not stand.[119]

Lise Manniche suggested, on the other hand, that if Nefertiti was indeed represented, then the triad of Atum, Shu (Akhenaten), and Tefnut (Nefertiti) could be present, representing the daily solar cycle of the young sun Shu, the older sun Atum, and the womb (Tefnut/Hathor) from which the sun was reborn.[120]

Pylon IX post-1967

The further work on Pylon IX carried out after 1967 by the Centre Franco-Égyptien extracted thousands more *talatat* that provided invaluable evidence about the temples and their financing.[121] Coming mostly from the *Tni-mnw* and *Rwd-mnw*, they showed Akhenaten drinking, washing his hands, dressing, and being censed, as well as port scenes, massacres of enemies, and the 'Hathor dance' (part of the *ḥb-sd*).

Of great importance are the lists of sanctuaries paying taxes, about thirty in each of Lower, Middle, and Upper Egypt. That of Lower Egypt is the best preserved, and contributors included Horus of Athribis, Thoth of Hermopolis, Osiris of Busiris, Isis of Hebyt, Sekhmet of Eset, Mut of *Bwy-nṯrw*, Sekhmet of Khasy, Re of *Ḥwt-wrt* (Heliopolis), Hathor of *'Im3w* and of Sekhet-Re (Abusir?), and Horus of Sile. Donations included metals, clothing, and food. Taxation of religious property was not unprecedented, but was usually paid to the treasury. The innovation was the payment for one cult and a fixed amount from all other sanctuaries.

The *talatat* from Pylon IX have revealed more than sixty blocks showing dancers. These derive from a scene on the model of tableaux in the tomb of Kheruef under Amenhotep III, showing the 'Hathor dance' celebrating the union of Hathor and Re, a festival of the harvest in the Middle Kingdom and the *Ḥb-sd* in the New Kingdom.[122] This was probably true also for Akhenaten in the earliest years of his reign. If this scene was part of the new theology, then presumably Nefertiti took the role of Hathor.[123]

The *talatat* also showed the importance of the royal bed in the palace, to which the Aten extended his rays.[124] The king and queen were even shown going to bed. The closest Egyptian art had approached this previously are theogamy scenes (most famously, Hatshepsut's conception at Deir al-Bahari).

The problem of the *talatat* was always the same: how to reconstruct the original scenes. In 1984, Robert Vergnieux began a new program to attempt this. By that time, 12,450 *talatat* had been found from one pylon. He devised an electronic index for 6,700 of them, and as a result, after a decade's work, he was able to use 2,000 to reassemble 150 scenes.[125] The most important new evidence derived from what had been the *Tni-mnw*, a sanctuary with a 'Window of Appearances,' and the *Rwd-mnw*, which Vergnieux took to be a royal residence: the reconstructed scenes in the main show worship and ritual. Redford was able to go further: assuming that the themes of the decoration indicate the purpose of a building, these two "seem to have been given over to domestic occupancy and food preparation." He identified both of them, indeed, as extensions to the palace.[126]

Pylon X

Jean-Luc Chappaz analyzed Akhenaten's earliest building at Karnak, as revealed by the Franco-Egyptian excavations.[127] Akhenaten finished Pylon III of his father and demonstrated that he was still an 'Amunist.' Before Year 4, he had built a structure dedicated to Re-Horakhty, some blocks of which were found inside Pylon X—including blocks rather larger than the later *talatat*—and which were known to the early nineteenth-century travelers and investigators (figs. 19 and 20). Chappaz analyzed more than 140 blocks. The structure's original location and its name were unknown, but he suggested the "Great Benben of Re-Horakhty." The only god was Re-Horakhty, bearing the epithets that soon turned into the didactic name of the Aten. Other gods were named, admittedly, but only in stereotyped formulae. The king was shown in traditional guise: White Crown, Red Crown, and Blue Crown. His name had usually been recut as Akhenaten. He offered incense, bread, wine, and meat. There was no sign of Nefertiti, who first seemed to appear in Year 3/4, suggesting perhaps

Fig. 19. Amenhotep IV back to back with Re-Horakhty-Aten; found by Lepsius at Karnak Pylon X (Berlin ÄM 2072).

Fig. 20. Perhaps the earliest "classic" depiction of the Aten-globe, with the lower parts of the god's cartouches visible. The king (with his name later altered from Amenhotep to Akhenaten) is shown in a transitional style between the 'classical' and the 'revolutionary'; another early find from Pylon X at Karnak (Louvre E.13482*ter*).

that this was the time of her marriage. The texts already emphasized the filial relationship of the king to his god. The structure was completed by Year 4 and apparently remained in use until Year 6.

South of Pylon X is an avenue of now ram-headed sphinxes, leading toward the temple of Mut and inscribed for Tutankhamun. Claude Traunecker has noted, however, that they originally represented Akhenaten and Nefertiti.[128]

Texts and names

The sandstone quarry at Gebel Silsila records the commission to a military figure whose name began with "Amun" to carry out works from Elephantine to Gambehdet (the length of Egypt), and to quarry sandstone to make the *bnbn*-stone of Horakhty under the name of "Light which is in the Aten" in Karnak.[129]

As noted above, inscriptions show that temples, royal estates, and municipalities throughout Egypt were taxed to provide for the "House of the Aten in southern Heliopolis." They provided gold, silver, bronze, incense, cloth, wine, oil, honey, and animals.[130]

The upkeep of the new temples of Akhenaten was certainly expensive: the subordinates in the House of the Aten in Karnak numbered 3,622 people, mostly specified as northerners.[131] The religious staff included the Greatest of Seers of the Aten in the House of the Aten, God's Fathers, and lay priests, as well as the Overseer of the Treasury of the House of the Aten, Scribes of Storehouses, an Overseer of Herds, and a Chief Beekeeper.[132]

More than half a dozen temples are named, although their relationship to each other is quite uncertain. The main temple is the *Pr-'Itn*. Within this was the *Gm(t)-p3-'Itn* and within this were the *Ḥwt-bnbn* and the *Sḥ-'Itn*. We also hear continuously of the *Rwd-mnw* and the *Tni-mnw*.[133] A new approach was offered by Marianne Doresse, who matched the names of Akhenaten's early structures with the building materials and compared their names with buildings known later at Amarna.[134]

Sandstone

1. The *Gm(t)-p3-'Itn*—also the name of the main temple at Amarna and of the Nubian site of Kawa.
2. *Ḥwt-bnbn m Gm(t)-p3-'Itn*—paralleled at Amarna.
3. *Tni-mnw n 'Itn r nḥḥ*—found only at Thebes.
4. *Rwd-mnw n 'Itn r nḥḥ*—found also at Amarna, near the *Pr-'Itn*.

Doresse suggested that the presence of the name Amenhotep (IV), sometimes chiseled out, dated these buildings to before Year 4 (but see below). Sometimes, however, the name was Akhenaten, showing that work continued, but since there was no trace of the Later form of the Aten name, work stopped by the end of Year 8—or Year 12 (see chapter 4).

Limestone and granite

1. *Ḥ'y m 3ḫt n 'Itn* ('He who rejoices in the horizon of Aten'; fig. 21), and granite altars from it.
2. *M33rw mḥty n p3 'Itn* ("Northern viewing place of the Aten," mentioned on a block from Pylon II in connection with a lake)—found at Amarna, and using the Later form of the name of the Aten: perhaps a kiosk.

The sandstone four are now accepted as Akhenaten's temples at Karnak,[135] but the limestone block naming the *Ḥ'y m 3ḫt n 'Itn* may have come from Memphis.[136]

Redford dated the buildings by the number of princesses shown: Meryetaten appeared in the *Gm(t)-p3-'Itn*; by the time of the *Ḥwt-bnbn*, Meketaten had been born, and he dated this to Year 4; Ankhesenpaaten was probably born by Year 5, before Akhenaten left Thebes.

The temples served different functions, to judge by the surviving fragments of decoration: the *Tni-mnw* featured domestic activities, such as bread- and wine-making; the *Rwd-mnw* showed cult scenes in roofless kiosks, with Akhenaten and the court riding out to open-air offerings, and foreign dignitaries being presented; a military escort always seemed to be present. The *Ḥwt-bnbn* was connected with the primeval hill at Heliopolis, where Re created the universe. The word *bnbn* was written with the determinative of an obelisk, most likely recalling the obelisk of Akhenaten's grandfather Thutmose IV at the eastern end of the main Karnak complex, dedicated to Horakhty.[137] Here, Nefertiti and Mery-etaten offer to Aten; there was apparently no sign of the king. The *Gm(t)-p3-'Itn* was associated overwhelmingly with the *ḥb-sd*.

Where were these temples located? Redford very logically suggested that they were close to where their dismantled building blocks were found. *Tni-mnw* and *Rwd-mnw* blocks come from Pylon IX, middle and lowest courses respectively, suggesting a southern location, while those of the *Ḥwt-bnbn* come from mainly Pylon II and the Hypostyle Hall respectively, as did those of the *Gm(t)-p3-'Itn*. This might suggest a northern location, although the location of the *Gm(t)-p3-'Itn* is known for certain to be well to the east.[138]

The cult

Redford noted that the *talatat* showed Akhenaten accompanied by the Great Seer, the Lector Priest, and the First Prophet of the King when going to the *Gm(t)-p3-'Itn*; by the first and third of these at the *Tni-mnw*; and by only the first at the *Rwd-mnw*. He was shown alone at the kiosk of offering.[139]

Sayed Tawfik (1936–90) attempted to uncover the evidence for the religious ceremonial in these temples. Was it radically different from the traditional service? The priesthood remained the same: the *talatat* mention the Chief Seer *(wr m33w)*, the same as the chief priest of Re at Heliopolis.

That part of the traditional daily ritual concerned with the image of the god was, of course, no longer possible, because there was no image of the Aten. The rest of the ritual, however, was very similar: the "offering of Maat." The *talatat* show Amenhotep and Nefertiti with an offering table presenting items, including Maat, to the Aten. Akhenaten "lives on Maat" and Aten "is satisfied with Maat." Purificatory libations of water were poured; purification was made also with incense. The Aten was then presented with various objects, such as collars or pectorals, oils and ointments. There was a final offering with 'utterances' of natron, incense, and water.

As Tawfik concluded, the main problem was that these rituals had been devised for the worship of deities represented by statues, but the Aten was immaterial. The visual evidence, however, confirms that all these offerings were made nonetheless.[140]

The jubilee(s)

The famous limestone relief in the Fitzwilliam Museum (fig. 21) was first published by Francis Griffith in 1918. He recognized it as a jubilee scene. On the left, Akhenaten (originally Amenhotep, but with the name later updated) wears a White Crown and stands before an altar of offerings, hands uplifted to the Aten. The god's titles are in the Earlier form, and he is "rejoicing in the horizon of the Aten." On the right, the king wears the short festival cloak and again the White Crown. Behind him is the High Priest of Neferkheperure, in front two other priests, one a chief lector. The inscription states that the scene is in Southern On (which Griffith understood to be Hermonthis, a little south of Thebes, rather than Thebes itself).[141]

Fig. 21. Akkenaten (name altered from its Amenhotep form) at his *Hb-sd*, worshiping at an altar and surrounded by priests; perhaps from Memphis, the Gayer-Anderson relief (Fitzwilliam EGA.2300.1943).

Schäfer in 1919 sharpened the analysis, noting that the original inscription bore the name Amenhotep. He also connected the Gebel Silsila inscription with the *ḥb-sd*, stressed the presence of the human-handed disk of the Aten, and suggested its introduction at this time. Like Griffith, Schäfer took the Southern On to be Hermonthis as the location of the scene. The relief showed Amarnan artistic characteristics in a "mild" form.[142]

Aldred collected reliefs of the Aten offering *w3s* scepters, which he took to be related to the *ḥb-sd*. In the Fitzwilliam piece, the original name of Amenhotep had been recut as Akhenaten; the king, moreover, is by himself. In others, the name was not recut, and he was accompanied by Nefertiti and their daughters. The *ḥb-sd* was seemingly celebrated also by the Aten: for an immortal god to renew his reign, however, seems, incongruous.[143]

Crucial to dating the jubilee(s) is the tomb of Ramose, where on the western wall a doorway shows two different styles (figs. 9 and 10). On the south side is a traditional scene, but on the north is the new Atenist style. In the former, Re-Horakhty has his name without cartouches; in the latter, the Aten shines on king and queen (no daughter is shown). This change coincided, Aldred suggested, with the first jubilee. The distribution of rewards from the 'Window of Appearances' was also suggested as having originated with the first *ḥb-sd*.

Jan Assmann stressed the importance of the jubilee to the establishment of Atenism. Akhenaten created two "Houses of Rejoicing of the Aten-distinguished-in-Heb-Seds."[144] For Assmann, the epithet of the Aten as "Festival-Celebrating" marked his proclamation as "over-king" (Überkönig), the "House of Rejoicing" being the stage for the god's (and king's) *ḥb-sd*.[145]

Redford went further:

All the evidence militates in favor of the kaleidoscope of revolutionary changes associated with Akhenaten's program having taken place at his jubilee, or in anticipation thereof. This includes the new style of art, the new, outlandish representation of the king, the first steps in overt iconoclasm, the introduction of the Disk as an icon, and the enclosing of the didactic name in cartouches.[146]

Talatat were also invented at this time, and the enlarged *Pr-'Itn* became the *Gm(t)-p3-'Itn*, complete with statues, altars, and shrines.

The *ḥb-sd* was held here, as shown by the scenes on the *talatat* from this location that are analyzed by Redford.[147] Over many days, the king left the palace and proceeded to the temple. He, the queen, and princesses were carried in palanquins. Crowds lined the route. The courts of the temple were full of kiosks containing altars. The king went from kiosk to kiosk, making offerings and pouring libations. Redford identified the three priests in the relief: the chief priest of the sun god, the lector priest holding a papyrus setting out the ritual, and a personal priest carrying the king's sandals. On the return each evening to the palace, the king and queen are shown feasting, while musicians, both Egyptian women and Hittite men, play for them.[148]

The most exhaustive study of the festival at Thebes is by Jocelyn Gohary. She concluded that:

- there was only one *ḥb-sd* of Akhenaten (as Amenhotep IV) at Karnak;
- there was no evidence that the Aten was a co-celebrant;
- there was no evidence that this festival coincided with any of Amenhotep III's *ḥb-sd*s;
- the festival scenes have been recovered from Pylon II and the Hypostyle Hall;
- the style of the art was transitional, rather than the developed Amarnan one;
- there were two main types of scenes: a palanquin procession, and an offering to the Aten in kiosks;
- the traditional *ḥb-sd* showed offerings to various deities; now they were made only to the Aten, which was therefore done in multiple kiosks;
- Nefertiti was shown only in the palanquin scenes;
- no daughters were shown;[149] and
- closely connected with the temple in the festival was the palace to the west, associated with daily feasting by both the court and the common people.[150]

Controversy remains regarding the date of the *ḥb-sd* at Karnak. Redford dated it to Year 3—or to the second anniversary of Akhenaten's accession; Eric Uphill placed it in Year 6.[151] The obvious question is what the young king was doing celebrating at the beginning of his reign a festival normally only held after thirty years. John Darnell and Colleen Manassa make the attractive suggestion that he was incorporating his father's reign into his own, thus following on from Amenhotep III's third jubilee in his Year 37 (probably just over a year before his death).[152]

Akhenaten certainly stated his intention to celebrate a jubilee also at Amarna,[153] but modern scholarship has turned against it. Aldred attributed to such a second festival a scene in the tomb of Parennefer at Amarna (TA 7): Akhenaten wears the *3tf*-crown and is seated under a baldachin.[154] Aldred first placed this putative jubilee in Year 9, linking it with the change in the Aten's names and its epithet from "in Heb-sed" to "Lord of Heb-seds," positing even a third festival within a span of nine years. By the time of his 1968 biography of Akhenaten, Aldred was caught in a trap, defending vigorously a coregency of Amenhotep III and his son for twelve years and arguing for the contemporaneity of their festivals, thus placing Akhenaten's in his own Years 3, 7, and 10.[155] Uphill agreed that Akhenaten celebrated a second festival at Amarna in Year 9.[156] It was customary for a king to celebrate this festival subsequent to the first at approximately three-year intervals, but there was no sign of any further one in Year 12 or 15. By the second edition of his biography, Aldred was of the view that Akhenaten had celebrated only one jubilee, in Year 3.[157] Redford oscillated: there was no evidence for any further festival at Amarna—or perhaps there was another in Year 9.[158] Nicholas Reeves hinted at "a theoretical scheme of repeated celebrations at el-Amarna," but explained no further.[159] Laboury accepted that there was only one, at Karnak.[160] It must be confessed that this appetite for anniversaries was not unique: Thutmose III held four in twelve years, Rameses II celebrated fourteen.[161]

The king's change of name

The king was still called Amenhotep as late as the Gurob letter: Year 5, III *šmw* 19.[162] He had changed his name to Akhenaten as early as the carving of the first boundary stelae at Amarna: Year 5, IV *šmw* 13.[163] Only twenty-four days separated these two dates. The change was therefore in the middle of Year 5.[164]

His full new titulary was as follows: Horus: "Beloved of Aten"; Two Ladies: "Great of kingship in Akhet-Aten"; Horus of Gold:

"Who raises up the name of Aten"; King of Upper and Lower Egypt: "Neferkheperure-Waenre" ("Beautiful are the appearances of Re-The only one of Re"); Son of Re: "Akhenaten."[165] The stress has thus shifted completely from a traditional focus in his original names to the Aten.

Translations of the king's new throne name have varied over the years. The difficult element is the first: *3ḫ*. Suggestions have included: "(Aten is) satisfied" (Breasted); "Serviceable to (the Aten)" (Gardiner); "Effective spirit (of the Aten)" (Aldred).[166]

The meaning of Akhenaten's name has been fully revealed by the studies of Gertie Englund and Florence Friedman, relying on texts such as, "I am your [the Aten's] son who is *effective* for you and who exalts your name" and "son of eternity, who came forth from the Aten, *effective* for him who is effective for him," which stress the interdependence of the king and his god. An apparently unique variant of the early form of the name of the Aten replaced "Shu" [i.e., "sunlight"] with "*3ḫ*," implying the equivalence of the two. Akhenaten could thus be "the sunlight" of his father, the Aten. There was finally a potential connection between *3ḫ* and *3ḫt* ("horizon"), a wordplay that goes back to the Pyramid Texts (Spells 158 a–d, 585a). Friedman suggested that scenes of the king and queen facing each other with the Aten centered above them formed an analogue of the horizon from which the Aten rises.[167]

A final issue regarding the name of the king is that certain German scholars have argued that the standard vocalization of the name of the god, "Aten," is mistaken, and that it should rather be written as "Jati."[168] The king's name would then therefore be "Akhenjati," the queen's "Nafteta." It seems safe to predict that these will not displace the traditional forms, concealing as they do the underlying structure as seen in the hieroglyphs.

Akhenaten's pathology

Not the least fascinating aspect of the historiography of Akhenaten is his physical condition and appearance. Since the nineteenth century, those who understand nothing of art have been fascinated by Akhenaten's physical representation, have understood it literally, and have therefore been sure that there is a medical diagnosis to be made. No attempt will be made to chart and catalogue every such theory. The endless contradictory diagnoses should be enough to convince anyone that obviously

Fig. 22. The king's figure from what was originally a dyad of the king and queen, presumably Akhenaten and Nefertiti, although no texts survive (Louvre N.831).

this is a false trail. It will suffice to mention the two syndromes that have gained more adherents than others: Fröhlich's and Marfan's.

The former is named after the Austrian pharmacologist Alfred Fröhlich (1871–1953). Its symptoms as described in a current textbook of pathology are stunting of growth, obesity (feminine distribution of fat), arrested sexual development, mental retardation, and decreased production of growth and other pituitary hormones.[169] It is obvious that little of this can be applied to Akhenaten. In adults, one of the main symptoms is inability to produce children. The acrobatics indulged in to explain Akhenaten's six daughters defy belief: Aldred, for example, suggested that they were Amenhotep III's children.[170]

Marfan's Syndrome is named after the French pediatrician Antoine Marfan (1858–1942). Symptoms include slender bones, long face, arachnodactyly, spinal deformities, pigeon chest, a wide pelvis, and visual impairment. The usual cause of death is cardiovascular weakness. A prominent recent supporter of this diagnosis is Alwyn Burridge, who recognized a complication: "If Akhenaten had Marfan's Syndrome, he was most likely blind for most of his adult life."[171]

There are a number of facts that make the literal interpretation of Akhenaten's physiology improbable, if not impossible.

First, in the tomb of Ramose at Thebes, dated about Year 30 of Amenhotep III, Akhenaten is depicted in two ways: alongside Maat with normal physiology; but also alongside the Aten and Nefertiti, while still Amenhotep IV, with 'Amarnan' anatomy. That the same person could be shown realistically in two such different ways about the same time is impossible.

Second, there are many portraits of the king with normal physiology: for example, the well-known yellow steatite seated statue in the Louvre (fig. 22); or holding an offering table, from Amarna house O49.14.[172] To account for this, there are theories of 'early' and 'late' styles, the earlier more 'extreme.'

Third, the 'exaggerated' anatomy is shared by not only his family, but also members of his entourage. This could not possibly be the case in fact; these must be examples of artistic distortion, or fashion.

Fourth, admittedly an argument based on omission, the Amarna Letters make no reference to any illness suffered by Akhenaten. None of Akhenaten's siblings, moreover, is known to have had any deformity.[173]

3 Akhet-Aten: "The Horizon of the Aten"

Foundation

The best-documented events in Akhenaten's reign are, appropriately, those associated with the foundation of Akhet-Aten, modern Tell el-Amarna. This fact derives from the survival of the boundary stelae, fifteen of them known to date.[1] They reveal much about the mentality of Akhenaten.

Their texts give four dates:

Year 5, IV *prt* 13: the foundation of the city;

Year 6, IV *prt* 13: the first anniversary;

Year 8, I *prt* 8: repetition of the oath of Year 6, when inspecting the stelae; and

Year 8, IV *3ḫt* 30: another oath on establishing boundary stelae.[2]

The stelae are of three types:

i. simply a tablet with text in a niche, without statuary (X and M), at the northern and southern limits on the east bank;

ii. the niche has been widened to include statues on the left: Akhenaten and Nefertiti and two daughters (A, H, J, and R); these are all at the extremities of the site (fig. 23);

iii. there are statues on *both* sides (B, N, P, Q, S, U, V, and K—fig. 24): since this type has the "repetition of the oath," they

Fig. 23. Amarna Boundary Stela R, at Tuna el-Gebel.

belong to Year 8. Some stelae of this third type have a third princess (P, Q, and U). Latest of all is B because it (like A from the second type) has an added colophon.

Stela S had been found and copied by Prisse d'Avennes's companion George Lloyd ('of Brnestyn' – 1815–43) at the beginning of the 1840s, who also drew A and P. Richard Lepsius discovered K, M, N, and R in 1845, Flinders Petrie found B, F, J, L, P, and V in 1892, and Percy Newberry located Q in 1893. The *editio princeps* was by Norman de Garis Davies in 1908,[3] with a modern edition by William Murnane and Charles van Siclen in 1993. Stela H was found by Helen Fenwick during 2005/6.[4]

Fig. 24. Amarna Boundary Stele S, in the southeastern part of the city, as seen early in the twentieth century; it has now been largely destroyed.

What has been called the "Early Proclamation" (the city's foundation text) is represented on stelae X and M, the latter of which deteriorated early on and was replaced by K. Akhenaten appears with his new name, the narrative telling of his arrival at Akhet-Aten in his great electrum chariot. The site was chosen because it was the "place of the primeval event," that is, the creation of life, and the "horizon" where the Aten's "circuit comes into being." Rich offerings (bread, beer, cattle, fowl, wine, fruits, and incense) were made to the Aten. Akhenaten then summoned "the royal companions, the great ones of the palace, the supervisors of the guard, the overseers of works, the officials, and all the court." He announced that the Aten desired a monument and emphasized two things: that it was the king alone who was told this, and that the site had no buildings and had belonged to no deity or king. It was to be a memorial to either him or Nefertiti. The courtiers replied with total approval, praising both the king and the god. This is a variation on the common motif of the king's council, from which he seeks advice that he generally does not follow.[5]

Akhenaten offered his own short hymn to the Aten before returning to the city. He promised not to go past the southern or northern stelae. The most interesting part of the text follows: "Nor shall the King's Chief Wife say to me, 'Look, there is a nice place for Akhet-Aten some place else,' nor shall I listen to her." The same applied to all officials, although it is surely harder to imagine any of them daring to say any such thing.

Vital for the understanding of the topography of the new city is the following list of buildings which Akhenaten stated that it was his intent to construct:

> At Akhet-Aten in this place shall I make the House of Aten [the Great Temple] for the Aten, my father.
>
> At Akhet-Aten in this place shall I make the Mansion of Aten [the Small Temple] for the Aten, my father.
>
> At Akhet-Aten in this place shall I make the sunshade of the [King's Chief] Wife [Neferneferuaten-Nefertiti] for the Aten, my father.
>
> In the "Island of the Aten, whose jubilees are distinguished" [the central city?] at Akhet-Aten in this place shall I make the "House of Rejoicing" for the Aten, my father.

In the "Island of the Aten, whose jubilees are distinguished" at Akhet-Aten in this place shall I make the "House of Rejoicing in [Akhet]-Aten" for the Aten, my father.

At Akhet-Aten in this place shall I make all revenues that [are] in [the entire land] to belong to the Aten, my father.

At Akhet-Aten in this place shall I make oblations overflowing for the Aten, my father.

[And] at Akhet-Aten in this place shall I make for myself the residence of Pharaoh, l.p.h., (and) I shall make the residence of the King's Chief Wife.[6]

The list ends with the Royal Tomb, which was to be not only for Akhenaten, but also for Nefertiti and their daughter Meryetaten. And it should be noted that Akhenaten recognized that he might die away from the city: there is no suggestion that he will be a prisoner or recluse here for the rest of his life.[7] There is to be a tomb also for the Mnervis Bull (the sacred bull of Re)[8] and for the chief priest of the Aten and other priests.

From this point, unfortunately, the text is very damaged, precisely where it deals with intriguing matters. Something terrible is stated to have been heard—something worse than anything heard during Akhenaten's first four years, or under Amenhotep III or Thutmose IV (his father and grandfather), worse than anything heard by any king of the White Crown. It is hard to make any sense of this, especially as a motive for the founding of the new city. What could possibly have been so 'offensive' that it required such an unprecedented and costly action? Kings had been assassinated, but capitals had not been moved.

This reference to the terrible things heard is generally taken to refer to opposition by the Amunists (for example, rejection of Atenist doctrine) or disputes with the priests of Amun.[9] Cyril Aldred, by contrast, has argued that there is no evidence that Akhenaten quarreled with the priesthood of Amun or left Thebes "in a mood of bitter resentment." Priesthood and kingship were "indissolubly linked": the kings had built up the cult of Amun and could therefore take its wealth away again, and they appointed the priests. Aldred immediately admitted, however, that in the redistribution of wealth to the Aten, Amun would have suffered most.[10]

Wolfgang Helck had earlier suggested that the reference was to the opposition by the administrative class to the move to the new capital. Donald Redford took the "things heard" to be simply "vocal and unremitting opposition to his projects," and declared that it all bespeaks "an underlying lack of confidence."[11] Helck and Aldred thought that a rumor had circulated that there would be no tombs for courtiers.[12] Murnane noted that this section does indeed follow the section on the new burial arrangements. It would have been a heavy blow to all those employed in Theban cemeteries. James Hoffmeier would go no further than something 'evil' *(bin)* or something 'offensive' *(mr)*.[13] Some have suggested something as serious as "counter movements" *(Gegenbewegungen)* of the "traditionalists," or even an attempt to assassinate Akhenaten.[14]

Agnes Cabrol, on the other hand, thought that the argument related to foreign relations: the next reference is to Nubia.[15]

On the choice of site, Aldred offered an invaluable insight. Sailing down the river, he observed that the plain formed a bay, with the wadi in the center—which leads to the Royal Tomb—forming a "natural silhouette" of the *3ht* (horizon) hieroglyph (fig. 25). From this the Aten appeared every day, and to it the king flew on his death.[16] This has stimulated Hoffmeier to make the overlooked but attractive suggestion that the foundation of the new capital was the result of some sort of theophany experienced by Akhenaten.[17]

Fig. 25. Small Aten temple, with the dip in the cliffs marking the entrance to the Royal Wadi to the right. This may have been seen as a natural *3ht* (horizon) hieroglyph.

An attempt has been made to calculate this fundamental date in Akhenaten's reign: the foundation of Akhet-Aten, as recorded in the boundary stelae. Ronald Wells suggested that the "foundation day" on stelae M, X, and K—IV *prt* 13 in Year 5—would have corresponded with the appearance of the sun to the east, exactly in the center of the opening of the Royal Wadi, as observed from the axis of what became the Small Aten Temple. Taking into account the known problems of the Egyptian calendar, Wells calculated Year 5 as 1351 BC and the actual day in the Gregorian calendar as 20 February.

Murnane, the expert on the boundary stelae, also reconsidered the damaged texts of the stelae that specified the exact location of the foundation ceremony: "in front of the mountain of Akhet-Aten," namely the Royal Wadi. The location would therefore be the "Chapel Royal," beside the Royal Residence.[18] The two contributions are thus complementary.

The discovery of Amarna

The first Europeans to note the site that was to become known as Tell el-Amarna came there in the early eighteenth century. The Jesuit Claude Sicard (1677–1726) copied boundary stela A as early as November 1714.[19] Bonaparte's expedition mapped the ruins of the city in 1798, but did not apparently notice the rock tombs and other features of the cliffs behind; Edme Jomard (1777–1862) described in the resulting *Description de l'Égypte* the great sandy plain, surrounded on three sides by mountains, the site of a "large city" to be found on no map, of which scarcely the foundations survived. He noted the many brick houses, the gates, the main street. He paid much attention to the Great Temple, its pylons still seven meters high, but could not guess its purpose. Opposite was another large building: palace, temple, fortress, or grain store?[20] The tombs were first recorded by John Gardner Wilkinson (1797–1875) in 1824. In his opinion, their reliefs were:

> of a very peculiar style. . . . Some have supposed that the kings whose names were found here belong to the dynasty of the shepherds, but their era does not agree with the date of the sculptures. They may, however, have been later invaders, and there is reason to believe that they made a change in the religion . . . which would agree with the

erasure of the names. From their features it is evident they were not Egyptians . . . the peculiar mode of worshipping and representing the Sun argues that their religion differed from the Egyptian.[21]

The Franco-Tuscan expedition led by Jean-François Champollion and Ippolito Rosellini made a brief stop in November 1828. The two leaders' notes are short: the city was Psinaula, not Wilkinson's Alabastron. "We traversed the whole city," stated Champollion, noting the streets and the temple (not a grain store, as Jomard had suggested).[22]

Nestor L'Hôte spent thirty-five days copying at Amarna in February 1839. He gave the first detailed description of the decoration in some six tombs that were accessible: he emphasized the richness of the decoration, such as scenes of driving to the temple, of rewards, and in the temple and palace. He noted the streets and northern suburb.[23] Robert Hay (1799–1863) also visited the area and copied the tombs in 1827.

The first extensive survey was carried out by the Prussian expedition under Richard Lepsius, which visited Amarna 19–21 September 1843 on its way upriver and 7–14 June 1845 on its return.[24] Lepsius's letters from 1843 show that he already knew that the rulers here were "antagonistic kings of the Eighteenth Dynasty." By the second visit in 1845, the tombs were assigned to the "fourth Amenophis, that royal Puritan who persecuted all the gods of Egypt and would only permit the worship of the Sun's disc."[25] The twelve volumes of plates of the great *Denkmäler* illustrating the expedition's findings appeared between 1849 and 1858; those illustrating Amarna occur in the sixth volume (part of section III) with a selection of scenes in the "northern tombs 1, 2, 3, 4, 6 and 7," and "southern tombs 1–3" (now numbered TA 6, 5, 4, 3, 2, 1, 25, 8, and 7 respectively), as well as two boundary stelae (N and K). The text meant to accompany these plates, drawn from Lepsius's journal and notes, did not, however, appear until 1904,[26] long after Flinders Petrie's excavations began the first modern uncovering of the city.

Petrie's excavations 1891–92

The first modern excavation was conducted as a single season (November 1891–May 1892) by Flinders Petrie (fig. 26), who was assisted by Howard Carter (1874–1939), Francis Llewellyn Griffith (1862–1934),

Fig. 26. William Matthew Flinders Petrie (1855–1942).

and Archibald Sayce (1845–1933).[27] Why should interest have been shown in Amarna precisely at this time? It was four years since the discovery of the Amarna Letters.

The plain was "one of the most perfect sites that is possible for a great town."[28] Petrie's excavations concentrated on the Great Palace. Every stone of the walls had been removed, but Petrie traced the foundation trenches, noting to the south a great hall of 542 brick pillars surrounded by a double wall and covering an area of 130 × 71 meters. With his keen eye for architectural history, Petrie declared that such great pillared halls were previously unknown and that this was the prototype of the Hypostyle Hall at Karnak. To the north, another four halls contained forty pillars each. In total, here were more than seven hundred pillars, made of mudbrick and plastered in white. One small hall contained many wine and oil jars, dated to Year 2, which is presumed to be of Tutankhamun: this, Petrie argued, showed that the site had been abandoned to become a storage depot.[29]

Beyond the bridge across the north–south main road of the city (the so-called Royal Road, a name it retains in modern Arabic: Sikkat el-Sultan) and to the north, an open court contained finely ornamented and painted floors, high-quality stonework, and glazed decoration. The many "sleeping cubicles" opening off suggested to Petrie a queen's pavilion or harem.[30]

Decorative elements caught his eye: "it is remarkable how well the artists of Akhetaten succeeded with the horse." And he was struck that "great inscriptions intended to be seen from a distance on the palace walls were blazoned out in gorgeous colored glazes set in the white limestone."[31]

The pavements are probably the best-remembered aspect of Petrie's excavations. The main one was preserved by having tapioca water applied to it by Petrie using his finger, over a total area of some three hundred square meters. Protective roofs were then erected, and raised boardwalks were installed to give access to visitors. The scenes showed the royal family (fig. 27), bound captives, tanks of fish, plants and animals, and bouquets of lotus. Shortly after Petrie's clearance, a local farmer, enraged at the damage to his fields by the visitors, hacked the painstakingly preserved paintings to pieces (another version of the story attributes the destruction to jealousy regarding tips paid to the guards). The sections sent to England alone survive (now in the Ashmolean Museum, Oxford).[32]

Fig. 27. Part of a fresco of the royal family from the King's House, showing two princesses, probably Neferneferuaten-tasherit and Neferneferure (Ashmolean AM1893.1.41).

From the largest house (his no. 13),[33] opposite the Great Palace, a wall fresco showing Akhenaten, Nefertiti, and the princesses was detached by cutting away the bricks at the back, then lowering the painting into a frame and coating the back with mud.

Petrie searched the rubbish heaps and found imported Aegean pottery (from Rhodes and Cyprus) and locally made glass. He also noted where the Amarna tablets were found in the 1880s (his no. 19, now the "Records' Office"), in the southwest. He lamented that allegedly only half of those found had been preserved: it was believed that many had been ground to dust while being carried on donkeys. Petrie meticulously cleared for sixty meters around where they were found to be sure that no tablets had been missed.

The first evidence appeared for the religious observances of the inhabitants of the city of the Aten: amulets and pendants of Osiris, Shu, Hathor, Re, Maat, Bes, Taweret, and Hapi indicated that traditional deities were by no means excluded. Griffith studied dockets on wine jars and found that the king was known as Amenhotep IV until Year 5 and

Fig. 28. Ludwig Borchardt (1863–1938), in 1903.

that he reigned for seventeen years (his highest year known had previously been the twelfth).[34]

In his report on the season, Petrie included a summary of his conclusions, most of which would serve as the basis for understanding and interpreting Amarnan history for many years.[35] Key points, some of which highlighted contemporary theories, included these: Amenhotep IV and Akhenaten were the same person; Akhenaten was not a female-male transvestite, nor was he a eunuch; he came to the throne aged twelve years under the tutelage of Tiye; Smenkhkare was coregent, sometimes with the epithet "beloved of Neferkheperure/Waenre"; Smenkhkare was then Akhenaten's independent successor for two or three years and was himself succeeded by Tutankhamun, who was succeeded by Ay.

The German Oriental Society excavations: Borchardt 1907–14

After Petrie's departure, no substantive work was done in the city for another seventeen years, although in that period Davies undertook the epigraphic documentation of the boundary stelae and of the private tomb chapels in the cliffs to the east.

Ludwig Borchardt (fig. 28) then conducted a preliminary survey during 1–20 January 1907 before beginning substantive work in 1911, after completing his work at Abusir. He worked in the name of the Deutsche Orient-Gesellschaft (German Oriental Society), founded by James Simon (1851–1932), who paid 30,000 marks for each season. With Borchardt were Hans Abel (1883–1927), the architects Uvo Hölscher (1878–1963) and later Georg Möller (1876–1921), and the engineer Dietrich Marckus.

The Germans were to concentrate on houses, of which 530 were cleared over four seasons. A major innovation was the system of grids—two hundred square meters, identified by letters west to east and numbers north to south—which would be the basis for identifying houses and all other structures at the site.

The 1911 season lasted from January until 15 April. The expedition house at L50.9 was constructed in 1908 on the remains of an ancient one; it was also later used by the Egypt Exploration Society.[36] Work began on the eastern edge in squares L49–O51, clearing about eighty houses.

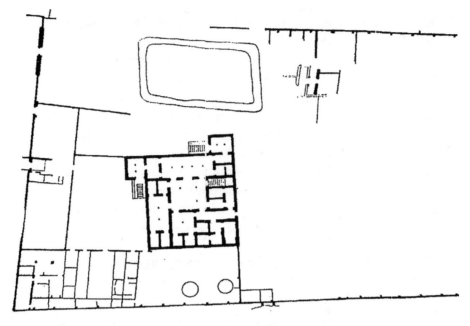

Fig. 29. The house of Pawah, High Priest of Re (O49.1).

Although 250 men were employed, work was slow. Borchardt concentrated on the street sixty meters wide, running southeast to northwest, parallel to the Nile, and instantly identified what remains a key feature of the city: the houses of the different social classes were all mixed together. Rich and poor lived alongside each other.

Borchardt's system in these preliminary reports was to focus on a few examples of houses. The largest (O49.1), 75 × 125 meters, was that of the High Priest of the temple of Re, Pawah (fig. 29).

The second campaign lasted from 9 November 1911 until 28 March 1912. There were now three architects instead of two, so that a new studio had to be built. Borchardt made two major discoveries this year, concerning the pre- and post-Amarnan period: pre-Akhenaten levels were uncovered (although these were slight and remain undated), but the houses and palace or temple of late Ramesside period show that the city continued to be occupied, even though rich officials left under Horemheb.

Domestic features were a focus this year: the water supply was shown to rely on wells, with a laborious system of steps down to the top of the shaft between two and two and a half meters below ground, where water was raised by a *shaduf*. Great care was taken to drain away any overflow from the water jugs to prevent unhealthy stagnation.[37] Tremendous work had been undertaken to establish gardens in the desert by bringing in fertile soil, which fortunately allowed garden beds still to be distinguished.

Major additions to archaeological evidence in this year's campaign were sculptures, mostly of the king, but also the famous unfinished relief showing Nefertiti pouring wine for her husband (fig. 83).[38]

The third season lasted from November 1912 until March 1913. The staff was new: the on-site director Breith, the architects Hollander and Honroth,[39] and the archaeologist Hermann Ranke (1878–1953). The aerial photography was undertaken by Major Paul Timme (d. 1928).

"High Priest Street" (as the Germans dubbed it, after his house) could be followed for two kilometers from M51 in the south to S42 in the north; it was forty-five meters wide. Borchardt emphasized again that the site was not virgin: predynastic wavy-handled cylindrical vases had been found, and post-Amarnan evidence included a coffin of the Twentieth Dynasty. The overall picture did not change this year, but a clearer contrast emerged between main and minor streets; one of the latter, two meters wide, led from Q47.9 to Q46.2. The house of the overseer of cattle of the Aten, or the "Christmas House" (Q46.1), measured 76 × 60 meters, and had to the north a garden of 1,700 square meters, entered by a large pylon to the east, leading to a pool and garden kiosk (figs. 30, 31). Borchardt was still interested in sanitation: Q47.1 showed that waste was collected in huge earthenware vessels (a kind of cesspool).

A painted stela from Q47.16 showed Akhenaten and Nefertiti with three daughters, the eldest standing between her parents, with Akhenaten handing her an earring.[40] The most sensational find of this third season, however, was the studio of the sculptor Thutmose (P47.1–3) (figs. 32, 33). Finds included many statues and busts of Akhenaten and Nefertiti, as well as portraits of (presumably) leading inhabitants of the city, most spectacularly, the famous bust of Nefertiti (fig. 80) and the statue of her as a mature woman (fig. 85).[41]

The division of finds with the Cairo Museum was made on 20 January 1913, and the site was closed on 15 March of the same year.

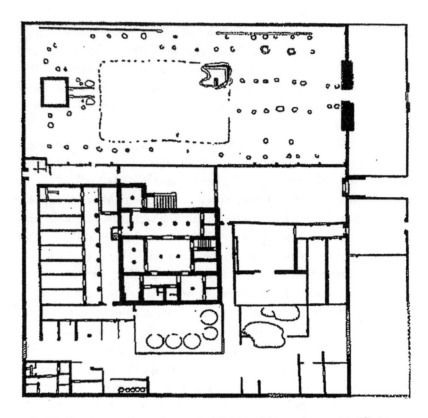

Fig. 30. The house of an Overseer of Cattle of Aten—Borchardt's "Christmas House" (Q46.1).

Fig. 31. The ruins of the "Christmas House" in the twenty-first century.

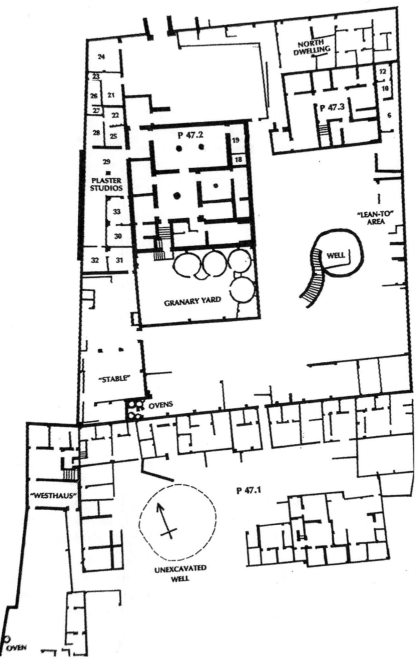

Fig. 32. The house of the sculptor Thutmose (P47.1-3).

Fig. 33. The ruins of the house of the sculptor Thutmose.

What turned out to be the last season, 1913–14, centered on the estates adjoining the studio of Thutmose. Borchardt commented on the fact that along the nearby wadi there was a difference in the levels of the houses of four and a half meters, inferring that torrents had swept away most of the houses here.

He estimated the full area of the ancient city to be seven kilometers north to south, but only one and a half wide. The planning was beginning to become clear: the south–north main street parallel to the river, with parallel streets to the east and smaller connecting cross-streets. Outside the city were desert paths that connected the tombs and boundary stelae.

The grandest house to be excavated was that of General Ramose (P47.19). The season's success was capped by the discovery in December 1913 of two more Amarna Letters (*EA* 359, 379), but they are a grammatical and a literary text.

The account closed with an expression of dismay at the outbreak of war that rendered the work of "body and soul" so "unimportant and insignificant" and the hope that it might be resumed with peace. That was not to be.[42]

John Pendlebury (1904–41), a later director of excavations at the site, was very critical of the German work:

Thanks to the fact that the Germans have only published their results in a most inadequate preliminary form, the objects which they found can only be regarded as so much loot from random excavations and the scientific knowledge acquired during the course of the work must be considered as lost.[43]

These preliminary and summary reports may seem disappointing, but Jacobus Janssen stressed their "high quality." And, as he noted, Borchardt's notebooks, twenty and sixty years later, allowed Herbert Ricke to publish important studies of Amarna as a city.[44]

Barry Kemp, another later director, and Salvatore Garfi praised the Germans for persevering with less lucrative areas, with the result that "Their demonstration that the pattern of housing remained more or less the same across a width of some 700m . . . is of enormous value in forming a general picture of the city as a whole."[45]

The Egypt Exploration Society: Peet and Woolley, 1921–22

After the First World War, the concession at Tell el-Amarna was granted to the British. In 1921, the excavations were directed by Thomas Eric Peet (1882–1934) (fig. 34), and in 1922 by Leonard Woolley (1880–1960) (fig. 35), the same year in which he began his famous discoveries at Ur in Mesopotamia.[46]

Special attention was devoted to town planning, and the German grid system devised by Timme was continued, as were some street names. Main streets running north–south were identified: High Priest Street (the German name), Street A (160 meters wide: surely deserving a more individual name), and Sekket al-Sultan (Royal Street, the main one).

The houses that were uncovered varied enormously. The "ideal of the good Amarnan house," in the view of the excavators, was that of the vizier Nakht (K50.1), 30 m × 26 m, consisting of thirty rooms (fig. 36). A middle house was O49.23, 12 m square with a dozen rooms, while a poor house was N50.16, 7 m × 10 m with eight rooms.[47] All houses were built of unbaked mudbrick, with stone for the thresholds and frames of outer doors and for the bases of columns in richer houses. Flooring in poor houses was mud plaster, in richer ones whitewashed or painted plaster.

Fig. 34. Thomas Eric Peet (1882–1934).

Fig. 35. (Sir) Leonard Woolley (1880–1960).

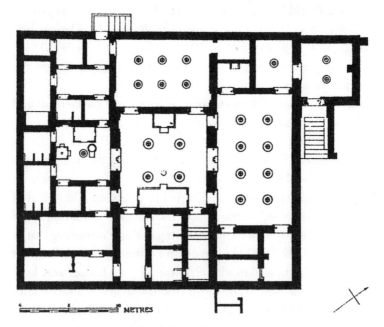

Fig. 36. The house of the vizier Nakht (K50.1).

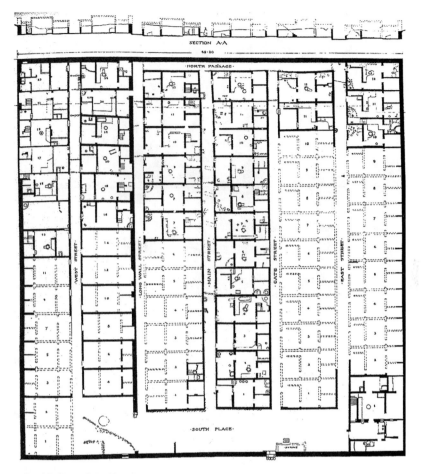

Fig. 37. Plan of the Eastern Village.

Two underlying and persistent categories of evidence were revealed: the presence of Mycenaean ware, and the continuing worship of the old gods—Isis, Horus, Taweret, and most frequently Bes.

The eastern village (fig. 37) was identified as the home of the tomb builders, with their cemetery in the next wadi to the north and the shrines or chapels immediately outside the village wall. The village was regularly planned: all houses were of equal size, 10 m × 5 m. The entrance was on the south side, with the overseer's house in the southeastern corner. The blocks were divided by north–south streets. All houses were identical: an

Fig. 38. Eastern Village: reconstruction of Chapel 525.

entrance hall, a living room, and two smaller back rooms—a bedroom and kitchen. Stairs led to a flat roof.

Not to be confused with the rock tombs for important people are the tomb chapels (fig. 38), consisting of an outer court, inner court, and shrine, with a burial shaft. No trace of human remains was found.

Apart from houses and the workers' village, Peet paid attention to the Maru-Aten (*M3rw-'Itn*, "Viewing place of the Aten") (fig. 39), containing lakes, gardens, and buildings. This was originally identified as a royal pleasure resort, an interpretation now long since discarded. The Maru-Aten was thought to reveal vital evidence regarding the fate of Nefertiti: a queen's name had been almost everywhere erased and replaced by that of Meryetaten, and the queen's features had also been recut. Peet identified the expunged queen as Nefertiti, creating a misunderstanding that was to have disastrous results for almost half a century.

A major contribution to our understanding of the Maru-Aten was made in 1956 by the architectural historian Alexander Badawy (1913–86). He adduced as comparative evidence the ancient description of the "Maru" constructed for Amun by Amenhotep III at Western Thebes:

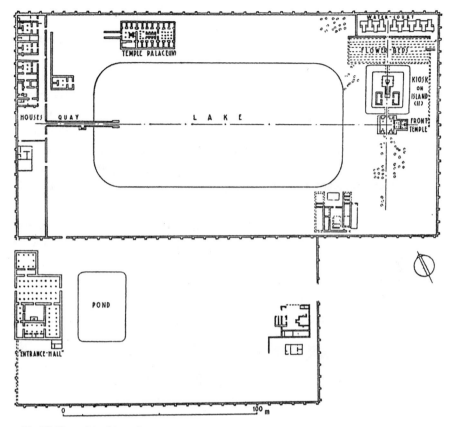

Fig. 39. Plan of the Maru-Aten.

a place of flourishing for my father at his beautiful feast. I created a
great temple in the midst like Re when he rises in the horizon. It is
planted with all flowers; how beautiful is Nun (the primeval water)
in his pool at every season; more is its wine than water, like a full
Nile, born of the lord of Eternity. Many are the gods of the place,
the import of all countries is received, much tribute is brought here
before my father, being the offering of all lands.[48]

This accords very closely with the buildings in the "Maru" at Amarna.
The northeastern complex seems to have been the viewing area. The kiosk
on the island may have been a 'Sunshade' and the 'front temple' contained
the 'Window of Appearance.' In the northwestern corner is a 'temple palace,'

where many dockets from offerings were found. It was thus not a "royal pleasure resort," as Peet described it, but a structure for ritual purposes.

Griffith and Newton 1923–25

Following Woolley's shift to the excavations at Ur in Mesopotamia, the direction passed first to Francis Llewelyn Griffith, then to Francis Newton (1878–1924), who was taken ill on site and died of encephalitis at Asyut. Other members of the team were Thomas Whittemore (1871–1950), Stephen Glanville (1900–56), Walter Emery (1903–71), Rosalind Moss (1900–90), Duncan Greenlees (1899–1966), and H.B. Clark.

The House of Panehsy, Chief Servitor of the Aten (T41), was discovered, with the famous stela showing Amenhotep III and Tiye (fig. 40). One hundred and fifty houses in the south along High Priest Street were then excavated, to link up with the area excavated by the Germans.

The most important focus, however, was the North Palace (fig. 41, 42), in the North City, away from the residential quarters in the center that had hitherto been the focus of excavation. Its heavy external walls

Fig. 40. Amenhotep III and Tiye from the house of Panehsy (BM EA 57399).

were two meters wide and preserved up to two meters high. The main entrance was on the west side, facing the river. Everywhere Meryetaten's name was found replacing an earlier name—which gave rise to further baleful theories, compounded by the finding of rings with the names of Nefertiti and Tutankhamun. The area contained water courts, gardens, living quarters, a hypostyle hall, and a throne room. Indifference and haste in the construction, according to the excavators, were found everywhere, but the frescoes were as fine as any others found in the city.[49]

In their later survey of Amarna, Kemp and Garfi summed up the North City as the "main residence for the royal family and for an intimate circle of court officials." It consisted of a palace, but not a temple, and a residential area marked by "the unusual degree of coherence and regularity of the core group of large houses."[50] Further excavations showed that it measured 115 m × 148 m, oriented east to west, with the entrance on the west, opposite the throne room, which had a large basin in the middle. It included accommodation for staff and servants, animal houses, and a small chapel.[51]

Fig. 41. The North Palace.

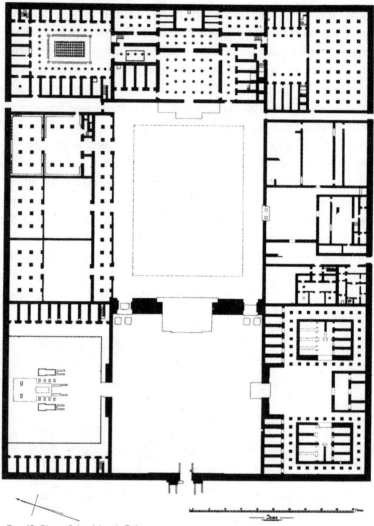

Fig. 42. Plan of the North Palace.

Frankfort and Pendlebury 1926–31

The teams comprised Henri Frankfort (1897–1954) (fig. 43), Henriette Frankfort (his wife, née Groenewegen), Stephen Glanville, H.B. Clark (architect), Seton Lloyd (architect, 1902–96), Alan Shorter (1905–38), John Pendlebury (fig. 44) and his wife Hilda, Hilary Waddington (architect, 1903–89), (?) Burnett, Mary Chubb (1903–2003), Ralph Lavers

Fig. 43. Henri Frankfort (1897–1954).　　Fig. 44. John Pendlebury (1904–1941).

(architect, 1907–69), Herbert ("Tommy") Fairman (1907–82), and Stephen Sherman.[52]

Work concentrated on the northern suburb, a later extension of the city; some houses, indeed, were constructed after the city had ceased to be the capital. The large estates bordering the main roads were laid out first. T36.11 was the most sumptuous house. Between "East Road" and "West Road" were very poor quarters, perhaps for the temple workers. The northwestern quarter was identified as "mercantile," with magazines where boats landed after crossing from the west bank. It was declared that apart from this area, "Akhetaten lacked a sound economic basis as a city."[53] T36.36 belonged to a Mycenaean merchant (the leg of a tripod bore a Mycenaean face). Much Late Helladic III pottery was found in the central-western and southwestern quarters. Important evidence for dating was provided by the numerous faience rings, among which those of Akhenaten are usually equaled by those of Smenkhkare, but exceeded by those of Tutankhamun.

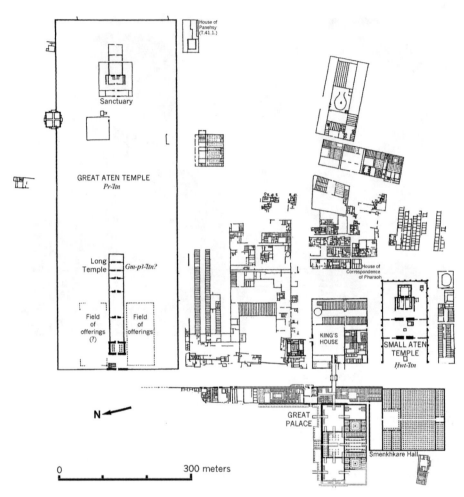

House of
Panehsy
(T.41.1.)

Sanctuary

GREAT ATEN TEMPLE
Pr-Itn

Long
Temple   *Gm-pꜣ-Itn?*

Field
of
offerings
(?)

Field
of
offerings

House of
Correspondence
of Pharaoh

KING'S
HOUSE

SMALL ATEN
TEMPLE
Ḥwt-Itn

N

GREAT
PALACE

Smenkhkare Hall

0   300 meters

Fig. 45. Plan of the Central City.

Pendlebury 1931–36

Pendlebury's team comprised himself and his wife Hilda, Charles Orwell
Brasch, Mary Chubb, Margaret Drower (1911–2012), Fairman (the
epigrapher), Lavers, Sherman and Mrs. Sherman, and Waddington and
Mrs. Waddington. These campaigns focused on the Central City (figs.
45, 46), previously worked by Petrie (the Palace, Royal Estate, Records
Office, and Sanctuary of the Great Temple) and Frankfort (the Sanctuary, Hall of Foreign Tribute, and House of Panehsy).

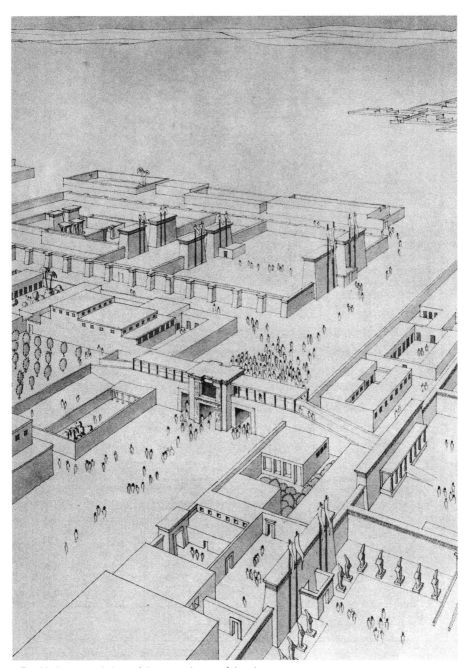

Fig. 46. A restored view of the central part of the city.

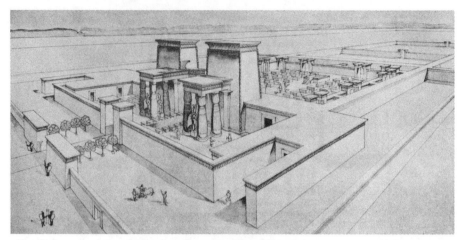

Fig. 47. A restored view of the sanctuary of the Great Temple.

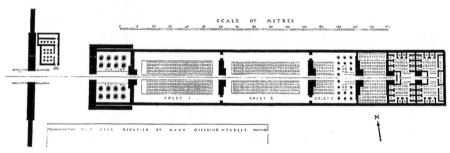

GREAT TEMPLE: RESTORED PLAN OF PER-ḤAI AND GEM-ATEN

Fig. 48. Restored plan of the Great Temple.

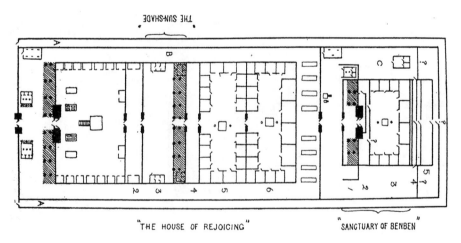

Fig. 49. The Great Temple: the House of Rejoicing and the House of the Benben.

At the *Great Temple* (figs. 47–49) the main entrance was located in the middle of the western wall, leading into a rectangular court. On the east–west axis, another door led into a larger three-sided court, but access to the sanctuary was only along the main axis. Paper restoration was facilitated by the reliefs showing the building in many tombs (see below).[54]

The ruins of the *Hall of Foreign Tribute* (fig. 50) were found to be very damaged. Eight flights of stairs led to elevated platforms on all four sides. This was identified with the scene in the tomb of Huya (TA 1), which shows the 'durbar,' and the inscription names the "Great Throne Room of Akhenaten for receiving the imposts of every land." Akhenaten and Nefertiti are shown seated on the northern platform, while the tribute is loaded on the other three.[55]

The official residence of Panehsy, Chief Servitor of the Aten (R44.2), was cleared.[56] His private house was in the city (T41).

The longest part of the third volume of the excavation reports was devoted to the *Great Palace* (fig. 51).[57] It extended seven hundred meters

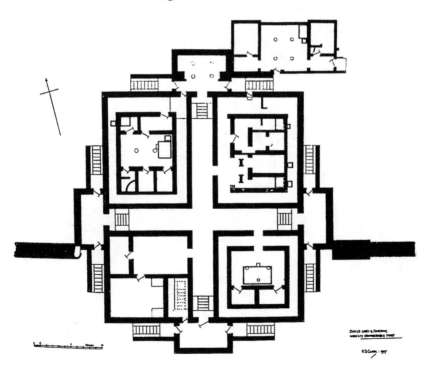

Fig. 50. Restored plan of the Hall of Foreign Tribute.

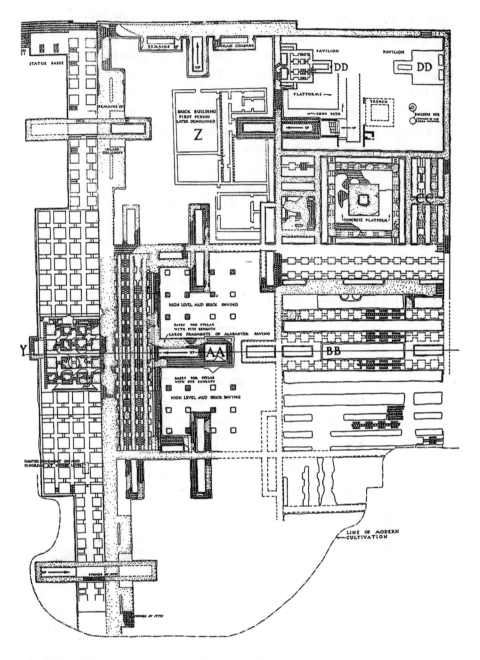

Fig. 51. The "State Apartments" of the Great Palace (east at top).

Akhet-Aten: "The Horizon of the Aten"

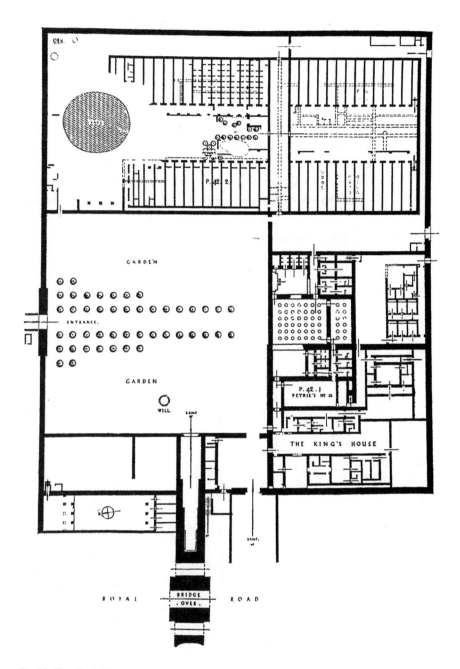

Fig. 52. The King's House.

along the western side of Royal Street, and occupied the whole space down to the river. It was divided into private quarters and state apartments. The former, in brick, were for servants, the harem, and magazines; the latter included the *Wbn-'Itn* ("Aten Shines"), the 'Broad Hall' (both in stone), and the "Coronation Hall" for Smenkhkare (bricks bear his name). These apartments were, noted the excavators, "the largest secular building in the ancient world," and the only one in Egypt constructed of stone. The plan was quite innovative. "Whence came the idea we cannot say."[58] Pendlebury's antipathy to Akhenaten precluded his thinking of an obvious answer.

Other important clearances included the *Royal Estate*, more commonly known as the "King's House" (fig. 52), the private residence of the king, across Royal Street, which Petrie had already entered.[59] Fran Weatherhead suggested in 1993 that the complex in the middle of the southern section was a throne room.[60] Kemp has now posited that this house was perhaps really the office of the vizier (Nakht, who lived at

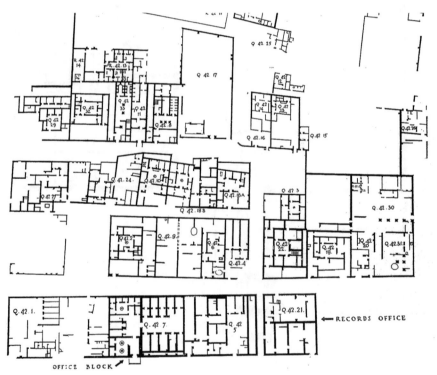

Fig. 53. The area of the Records Office (Q42.21).

K50.1, and whose tomb was TA 12). One-third of the building was storerooms.[61] Next door, to the south, was the Small Temple, or 'Chapel Royal,' measuring 110 m × 190 m.[62]

Apart from the temples and palace, excavation work was devoted to the most famous building in Amarna, the *"Records Office"* (fig. 53), with the "Foreign Office" on the western side. At the southern end, the excavators placed the Bureau for the Correspondence of the Pharaoh: the Amarna Letters had been found in the main room to the east. To the south, more than seventy houses (Q43) were cleared, while on the extreme eastern edge of the city the police and military headquarters were found.[63]

The Egypt Exploration Society excavations resumed

After a pause of half a century, the Egypt Exploration Society returned to Amarna under Barry Kemp in 1977 (the permit passed to the Amarna Trust in 2008). Following two years of survey, excavation recommenced in 1979.[64] As Kemp himself has emphasized, the purpose of the excavations changed completely in the 1970s, from revealing the structure of the city to reconstructing its life. The work has been much less sensational than before; there has been a great deal of reworking of old material, but techniques earlier unknown have also been employed. Major gaps in our understanding of the capital have in consequence been filled.

Most of the buildings in the city were of mudbrick, but stone was also used. The obvious question was the location of the quarries. The limestone came from the "Quarry of Queen Tiye" at Amarna and from Deir al-Bersha, 15 kilometers to the north; sandstone from Gebel Silsila, 450 kilometers to the south; red granite from Aswan, on the southern border; quartzite also from Aswan and Gebel Ahmar, near Cairo, 270 kilometers north; basalt and dolerite from Gebel al-Teir al-Bahari, 60 kilometers north; and alabaster (or travertine) from Hatnub, 16 kilometers east.[65]

Important work was resumed on understanding the Great Temple. Kemp divided the *temenos* or sacred area (300 m × 800 m—most of which was empty) into three equal areas from the entrance (west to east): the *Gm(t)-p3-'Itn*; the open middle area; and the Sanctuary. Kemp later preferred to call the first the "Long Temple," with a colonnade in front, then six courts with another colonnade between the third and fourth of them. They contained the remains of the bases of nearly eight hundred offering tables. The middle space (230 m × 270 m) was the puzzle: perhaps it was for large festivals and huge crowds. The Sanctuary, 30 m × 47 m, was 340 meters behind the Long Temple. To the southeast, the House of Panehsy, Superintendent of Cattle, was associated with great quantities of animal bones, while closer to the southwestern corner were large bakeries (one hundred ovens). There was a clear distinction between the 150 stone offering tables in the sanctuary and the 920 brick offering tables outside the southwestern corner. The latter would seem to indicate some popular participation in the rituals.[66]

Further discoveries about the history of the building were made in 2014. There were two levels: an earlier and a later temple, the latter perhaps dated about Year 12. The earlier had only a mud floor, and its architectural elements, even royal statuary, had been treated as rubble in the rebuilding. This second phase included a huge colonnade, but most importantly, it had buried the great fields of offering tables and seemed to feature platforms surrounded by basins.[67]

Excavation at the Small Temple was resumed in 1987. The work revealed hitherto overlooked phases in its construction, the first of which was simply a brick altar, until a more grandiose sanctuary could be built farther back. It was also noted that there had originally been open ground between this temple and the river, before the "Coronation Hall" was built.[68]

Further work on the Great Palace clarified that the entrance was on the north side, whereby one entered the huge courtyard (the "Broad Hall"), 160 meters square, with red granite statues of Akhenaten and Nefertiti and other family members in front of limestone walls with colored scenes. Kemp suggested that the purpose of this huge space was for the assembly of large crowds and for feasts, because there followed three areas to the south, the central one of which was a hall of state with a throne room connected to the great court by a 'Window of Appearances.'[69]

Given the previous excavators' poor opinion of the quality of the building, one of the most important of Kemp's observations is about the "exceptional care devoted to the finish. This is visible in the faience moldings and tiles, the inlaid hieroglyphs carved from separate pieces of hard stone, the stelae and balustrades in travertine, the inlaid and gilded columns in a variety of plant forms. The building would have been ablaze with color and shiny surfaces and the dull glitter of gold leaf."[70]

The Northern Riverside Palace was identified as the main royal residence, two and a half kilometers from the Great Palace. It had a gateway toward the south side and was enclosed in a battlemented wall. Most of it has, however, been eroded by the river, save for a northern fragment. "There is nowhere in the center of the city where one can seriously imagine the royal family permanently residing," Kemp observed. The basic feature of the city is the 'Royal Avenue,' forty meters wide, linking the North Riverside Palace to the Maru-Aten in the south. This explains why Amarnan art features the royal family traveling in chariots, which would have made no sense if the king had to travel only within the central city. The ordinary population of the city lived in the northern and southern suburbs (the vizier Nakht lived in the south), so that the central city "may have been largely deserted at night."[71]

The most famous single location in the city is the 'Window of Appearances.' It could not, Kemp realized, be where the earlier excavators placed it: on a bridge between the "King's House" and the "House of Rejoicing." The kiosk was on a podium, with a balustrade and ramps. Rewards for officials would not be given publicly in a street. They would have taken place rather in an inner court of the palace (Ricke) or the Northern Palace (Whittemore).[72] Kemp noted that this window is shown in some ten tomb reliefs, but survives in only one example, that of Rameses III at Medinet Habu.[73] He proposed to locate the window in the northeastern corner of the "King's House" in the "Royal Estate," opposite the great garden courtyard with the northern entrance, through which the official who was to be honored would have approached.[74]

The Society had cleared in the 1930s only some thirty-seven houses in the Workmen's Village;[75] it was reexcavated between 1970 and 1986. The village was square (seventy meters) and walled and comprised seventy-two houses. The inhabitants seem to have been mainly laborers who excavated the tombs; perhaps the artists who decorated them lived in the main city. The villagers grew their own food and raised animals: here were found growing pots and animal pens, and perhaps abattoirs—bones suggest pigs. There may also have been a small police contingent, perhaps twenty men. Not to be overlooked was the evidence for painting, even in this most basic residential compound. The village was marked, however, in Kemp's words, by "the bleakness of the environment and the necessity to import all water and most foodstuffs."[76]

The chapels of mud brick were also reexamined and new ones cleared, notably the "Main Chapel" to the east of the village: two halls (the walls of the outer lined with benches), then a sanctuary with three shrines, oriented west to east. The structure of the chapels showed marked uniformity, but also provided evidence for different religious practices in the various family groups that used each one. Kemp judged that "for people living in the tightly packed village, the chapels offered a periodic escape to a more salubrious setting."[77]

William Stevenson Smith (1907–69) put the Workmen's Village in context: "We have here again one of those projects on a united plan with a repetition of the individual structures such as in the Middle Kingdom town of Kahun and the artisans' village at Deir el-Medina."[78]

Important new ground was cleared in Q48.4 in 1987. This area was, in fact, connected with the Workmen's Village. It was first used for pottery and jewelry manufacturing before becoming a domestic area. Both these phases dated to the reign of Tutankhamun, providing vital evidence for the post-Akhenaten occupation at Amarna.[79]

Without doubt, however, the most exciting new discovery, beginning in 2003, has been the cemeteries of ordinary Amarnans. Only notables' tombs had previously been known. Southeast of TA 25 (Ay), the bones of seventy bodies were discovered: fifty-three adults, fourteen aged between five and seventeen years, and three infants. For the first time, we are face to face with ordinary Amarnans. Kemp observed that "life for the common residents of Amarna appears to have been satisfactory, with no extremes of work or stress."[80] Appearances can be deceiving. Further analysis showed that anemia rates for children were as high as 23 percent, indicating "a significant problem with diet and iron deficiency."[81] The proportion of infants is unexpectedly small (30 percent would be normal), suggesting that they were buried elsewhere. And later analysis of the adult remains revealed that only 13 percent were over thirty-five years of age, indicating now "conditions of high stress."[82]

Excavation proper began in 2006, revealing some three thousand bodies. Most of them had been brutally robbed shortly after burial, resulting in severe disarticulation. They seem to have been buried in an extended position. Some were covered with matting, others were in "stick coffins" (strips of wood bound with rope). Two grave stelae were discovered, but they were without inscription. One grave was a vaulted brick chamber. By the fourth season in 2009, the excavation reached lower levels with more wooden coffins and stelae, suggesting greater affluence. There were many more infant burials, while the average age at death was early thirties, with few older than fifty years.[83]

Second to the cemeteries in importance as a new discovery was a stone village to the east of the southern city, already noticed in the 1970s. It is uncertain whether it was a military outpost or a village for tomb workers. It was an enclosure that measured 67 m × 80 m. Perhaps it supplied food for workers in the desert, but some people certainly lived here. It was also linked to stone quarrying.[84]

Important advances have been made concerning our understanding of the economy of the city. An 'industrial quarter' has been revealed south of the Small Temple (O45.1). The Amarna Glass Project is investigating this. Kilns were found here and reconstructed to answer the question of whether the Amarnans were simply molding glass or making it: the latter requires temperatures of 1,100 degrees Celsius. Experiments showed that this temperature was easily reached. This area also produced pottery and faience.

Modern scientific techniques can also be employed to analyze ancient crops and vegetation; thousands of fragments of textiles; charcoal, to discover the original species of wood; and animal bones, of which sheep, goats, deer, pigs, horses, and dogs have been identified; and to identify sources of disease, notably the housefly, which is the spreader of much contagion.

The tombs

The tomb chapels in the eastern hills, one group in the north and the other in the south (figs. 54, 55), were, as noted above, first studied by L'Hôte, Hay, and Lepsius. Some, however, especially in the southern group, were found to be largely untouched when they were surveyed during the 1880s and 1890s, and published in 1903 by Urbain Bouriant (1849–1903), Georges Legrain, and Gustave Jéquier (1864–1946). They also gave valuable historical notes: TA 13 had been opened by Robert Hay in 1830, and TA 9, 10, and 14 discovered by Bouriant in 1883. TA

Fig. 54. The Northern Tombs at Amarna.

Fig. 55. The Southern Tombs at Amarna.

11 was discovered and cleared by Gaston Maspero and Bouriant in the same year. TA 12, 23, and 24 were discovered by Alexandre Barsanti (1858–1917) in 1892.

The rock tombs were finally comprehensively copied in exemplary fashion by Norman de Garis Davies (fig. 56), and published in six volumes, 1903–1908. Tribute must here be paid to years of backbreaking work, requiring the highest skill and providing the dossier of the single most important archaeological source for the site. These painted reliefs

Fig. 56. Norman de Garis Davies (1865–1941).

have been vulnerable to damage since the Amunist reaction, and not least in modern times; Davies's copies allow us now to view them as they were more than a century ago. Davies recorded eighteen tombs, all six from the northern series (TA 1–6) and twelve from the southern (TA 7–14, 16, 19, 23, and 25). The Amarnan tombs, Davies observed, revealed a striking innovation: "The king's figure, family and retinue dominate everything." It is difficult even to distinguish the deceased, the tomb's owner. This was, however, perhaps because Akhenaten had bestowed these tombs on favorites—a costly gift. The wife of the deceased usually does not appear, and never his children, which is a major departure for Egyptian tombs.[85]

There was a change in the plan of the tombs between the two cemeteries. In the south, the tomb was either small with a narrow transverse chamber (the "small T-shaped" as Davies called it), or a long corridor, or a spacious columned hall. In the later northern tombs, there were some of the small T-shaped and several corridor-style, but the majority used the hall reduced to two or four columns.[86]

The southern group of tombs seemed to be the earlier foundation; the inception of the northern ones was dated by Davies to Years 8 and 9, based on the presence of the Later form of the Aten's name, the detailed plans of the Aten temple, the new plan of the palace, the showing of the deceased rather than the king in the doorway, and the absence of Nefertiti's sister, Mutnedjmet.[87]

Finally, Davies identified a significant feature: there were only a few stock designs for the decorations of these tombs; for example, the tombs of Ahmose, Pentju, Panehsy, and Meryre i were very similar in decoration.[88] Dimitri Laboury added another observation: none of the tombs seems to have been finished. And forty-three in total was far from sufficient for all the important officials of the city. It seems that many must have made arrangements to be buried elsewhere, perhaps in their ancestral cemeteries.[89]

Chronology of the tombs

Davies declared that the only firm criterion for dating the tombs was the number of the princesses in the reliefs.

The tombs show:

one daughter: tombs of Mahu (TA 9) and Ramose (TA 11);
two daughters: Any (TA 23);
three daughters: Ipy (TA 10), Ay (TA 25), Tutu (TA 8), Ahmose (TA 3), and Pentju (TA 5);
three or four daughters: Panehsy (TA 6);
four daughters: Meryre i (TA 4) and Huya (TA 1);
five or six daughters: Meryre ii (TA 2).

He suggested that the first three daughters were born in Years 4, 6, and 8. This would fit the position of the tombs: the northern cemetery (tombs 1–6) is later in date. It would also fit the form of the Aten name: the Later form was dated by Davies to Year 10, and the Earlier is invariable in the southern tombs.[90]

There are various cautions. In the tomb of Huya (TA 1), which includes the 'durbar' of Year 12, two daughters are shown in the banquet scene with Queen Tiye, while four seem to be in the 'durbar,' and in the famous 'double family' scene. Yet all six princesses are shown in the other 'durbar' scene, in the tomb of Meryre ii (TA 2) (fig. 57). In the tomb of Mahu (TA 9), a southern tomb which uses the Later form of the Aten name, the royal family is shown sacrificing at an altar, with only Meryetaten present. Davies suggested that this was due to lack of space.[91]

In the tomb of Panehsy (TA 6), similarly, scenes on the entrance portal show three princesses, while those further inside show four.[92] This could perhaps be accounted for by the progression of the tomb's decoration.

Jean Capart noticed another important caution: if the daughters appeared on monuments from their birth, they would have been babies in cradles, but they are immediately shown as little women.[93] In any case,

Fig. 57. Akhenaten and Nefertiti, with all six princesses depicted behind them; from the durbar scene in the tomb-chapel of Meryre ii (TA 2).

the dates of the princesses' births have been much contested. We do not understand the criteria for the way they are shown in the tombs. In sum, we cannot reliably date the tombs this way.

The royal family in the tomb decoration

There are six main themes:

1. The royal family worshiping the Aten. This is shown in eight tombs: TA 4, 6, 7, 8, 9, 10, 14, and 25 (fig. 58).[94]
2. Royal visits to temple (fig. 59). This is shown in five tombs: TA 1, 3, 4, 5, and 6.[95]

Apropos of this very impressive theme in Amarnan decoration, Kemp pondered "to what extent the royal family did live and move as a single unit, and if any of them ever remained still for very long, or was always about to leave for somewhere else, for another elaborate station along a corridor of travel, forever the object of attention in a highly structured lifestyle."[96]

Laboury offered theological insights: Egyptian cities were designed for processions of the gods. Amarna was designed for processing by Akhenaten. Aten moved from east to west, but the king moved from north to south, as Amun at Thebes, except that the god's bark was replaced by the more mobile chariot.[97] He then went too far in suggesting that the main activity of the royal family seemed to be religious ritual[98]—forgetting that these scenes came from tombs, where religious scenes would be most appropriate.

The military escort in TA 4 is interesting: four men and a sergeant, then six men with axe and spear and a sergeant with a baton, and above them Nubian, Semite, Libyan, and Egyptian standard-bearers (fig. 60). Syrians, Nubians, and Libyans also appear in TA 4. Adolf Erman (1854–1937) saw sinister conditions behind the fact that the royal bodyguard was formed of Nubians and Asiatics.[99] It is far from exclusively so, and these foreigners may simply be representing a 'universalist' ideology of Atenism.

3. Domestic scenes in the palace (fig. 61). This is shown in four tombs: TA 1, 2, 3, and 5.[100]
4. The 'Tribute of the Nations,' or 'durbar,' in Year 12 (fig. 62). This is shown only in the two northernmost tombs: TA 1 and 2.[101]

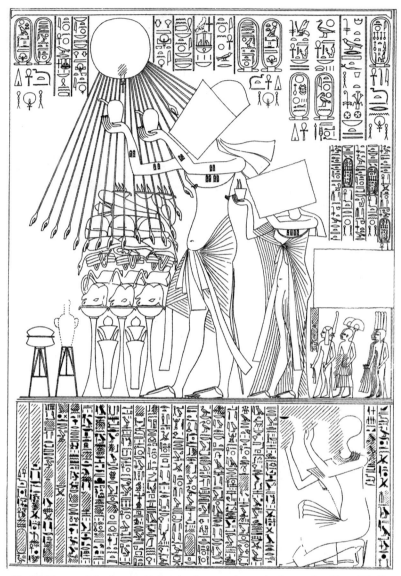

Fig. 58. The royal family worshiping the Aten, as shown in the tomb of Tutu (TA 8).

In the tomb of Huya (TA 1), tribute is specified as coming from Kharu (Syria), Kush (Nubia), and the islands; the tribute from the north is chariots and vases; from the south, slaves, skins, gold rings, ivory, spices, and animals. In the tomb of Meryre ii (TA 2), southern tribute includes metal,

Fig. 59. Akhenaten, Nefertiti, and four princesses driving to the temple, as shown in the tomb-chapel of Meryre i (TA 4).

Fig. 60. The military escort, in the tomb of Meryre i (TA 4).

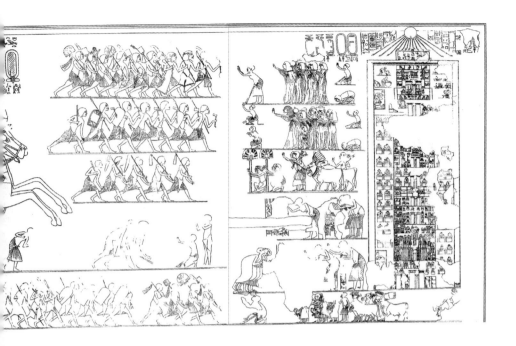

Fig. 61. Akhenaten, Nefertiti, Meryetaten, and another daughter banqueting with Queen Tiye and Baketaten in the tomb-chapel of Huya (TA 1).

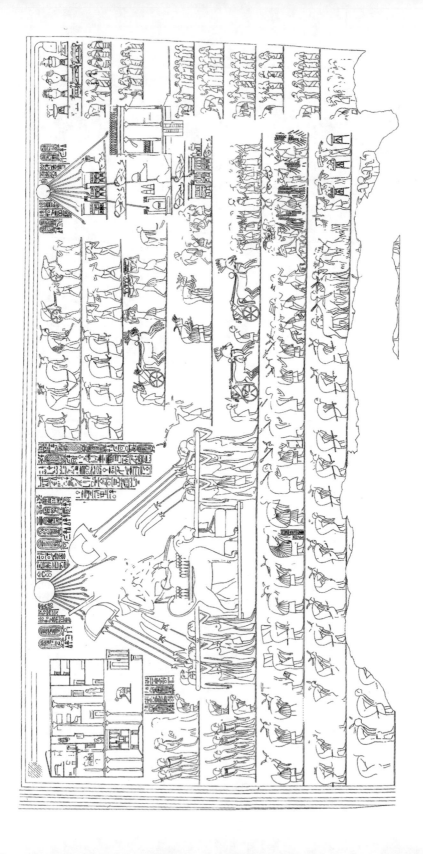

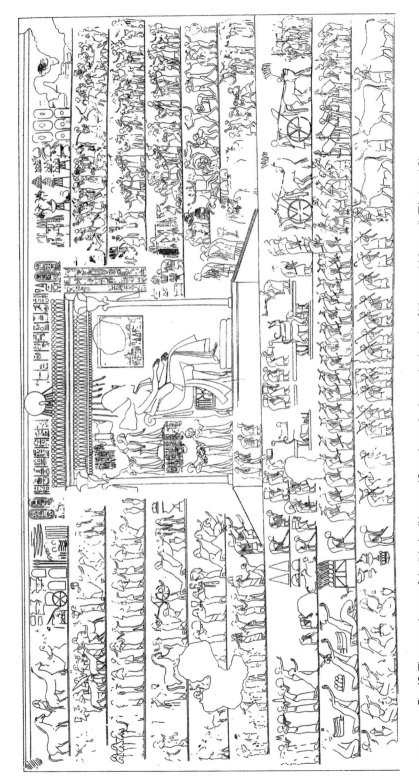

Fig. 62. The two phases of the "durbar" in year 12, as shown in the tomb-chapels of Huya and Meryre ii (TA 1 and 2).

109

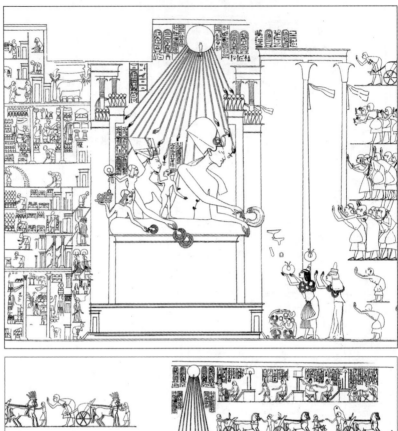

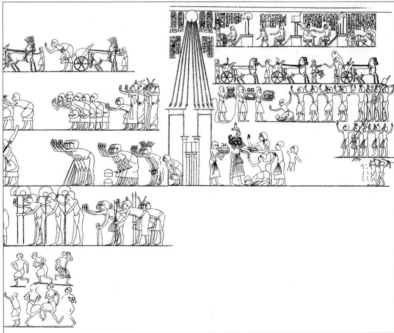

Fig. 63. Akhenaten, Nefertiti, Meryetaten, Maketaten and Ankhesenpaaten reward Ay; tomb-chapel of Ay (TA 25).

Fig. 64. Dancers at the reward of Ay.

gold, arms, ivory, animals, and slaves; northern tribute includes arms, slaves, ivory, and animals, together with calves and grain or incense from Punt, Libyans with ostrich eggs, and Hittites (?) wearing pigtails with metalwork.

This 'durbar' has been interpreted in diametrically different ways: as a celebration of the marriage of Ay and Tey (Gaston Maspero); the accession of Akhenaten after twelve years of coregency (Aldred); the arrival of Aziru, the treacherous ruler of Amurru, summoned to Egypt (Redford); the ephemeral victory in the recapture of Sumuru (Eleanore Bille-de-Mot); a victorious Nubian war (Alan Schulman, John Darnell, and Colleen Manassa); even Nefertiti's elevation as coregent (Joann Fletcher); or the completion of the new capital (Aidan Dodson).[102] Whatever else it shows, it is, as James Allen described it, "the last clear view we have of the Amarna Period before the accession of Tutankhamun."[103]

    5. Rewards for courtiers (figs. 63, 64). This is shown, not unexpectedly, in no fewer than eight tombs: TA 2, 4, 5, 6, 7, 8, 9, and 25.[104]

What is important is the political and artistic influence of Amarna. As Redford noted, these scenes of reward were "in a style which was to become stereotyped for three and a half centuries."[105]

      6. Investiture in office. This is obviously a special honor, shown in only three tombs: the installation of Meryre i as High Priest (TA 4), of Huya as steward of Queen Tiye (TA 1), and of Tutu as chief servitor of Akhenaten in the temple of the Aten (TA 8).[106]

There are also unique scenes found in only one tomb, for example: an artist at work—Iuta in his workshop putting the last touches of paint to a statue of Baketaten (TA 1) (fig. 65), and in the same tomb, the funeral scene (fig. 66: the mummy of Huya is shown as Osiris); or Akhenaten, Nefertiti, and Meryetaten in a chariot going to inspect the defenses (TA 9), and in the same tomb a scene illustrating the policing of the capital, with Mahu drawing supplies for the guards, and the arrest of malefactors.[107]

Fig. 65. The sculptor Iuta finishing a statue of princess Baketaten in the tomb of Huya.

In Amarnan tombs, the deceased is depicted less frequently than the royal family, who are generally shown worshiping the Aten or making visits to the temple. They are also shown banqueting, exactly as in pre- and post-Amarnan tombs where the deceased was always shown being nourished in the afterlife. The deceased is most often shown being rewarded by the king, although even these scenes seem to be more a celebration of the royal family than of the dead. This also appears to have been an honor granted for exceptional merit, since only one-third of the courtiers' tombs have such scenes. Even rarer is the depiction of appointment to office—in only three cases. The tombs' owners describe their cemetery as "the place of the favored ones" no fewer than four times.[108]

Akhenaten's detractors can, of course, find support for their theories even here. That all the tombs are unfinished, Nicholas Reeves declared, was evidence of "financial mismanagement."[109]

Fig. 66. The Osirian funeral of Huya.

What have excavations revealed of the conditions of the inhabitants?

Estimates of the population have varied wildly: from approximately twenty-five thousand persons (Kemp); twenty to fifty thousand (Reeves); forty-five thousand (Joyce Tyldesley); forty-five to fifty thousand (Laboury); and fifty to one hundred thousand (Janssen).[110]

The publication in 1980 by Herbert Ricke of Borchardt's notes on the houses at Amarna allowed much more detailed analysis of the housing. Christian Tietze divided the houses into categories according to area, plan, thickness of wall, and so on. He discerned a three-fold social structure: more than half the population lived in small houses (an average of forty-six square meters), one-third in middle-sized ones, and the rest in houses of remarkable size (between eight and twenty rooms): these last were for the religious, military, and administrative people closest to the king.[111] It is also striking that alongside the remarkable variation in the size of the houses, there is an uncharacteristic uninterrupted progression from most modest to most opulent.[112] The luxury of the royal quarters is undoubted, but equally luxurious was the housing of the upper classes in general. Grand houses could cover up to eight hundred square meters, in contrast to workers' quarters comprising three rooms and fifteen square meters. The city certainly revealed Egyptian skills at this time in understanding of water supply and sewerage.

Tietze was able to elucidate another matter fundamental in the Egyptian climate: insulation. Houses had a central living area, complemented by rooms on one, two, three, or four sides: the more sides on which there were rooms, the more comfortable the living area would be. Domestic planning, however, was more sophisticated than mere number of rooms: the more rooms there were, the thicker the walls tended to be, and so the cooler or warmer the house. Walls varied in thickness: between 14 and 18 centimeters (54 percent of the walls discovered), between 30 and 38 centimeters (37 percent), and the significantly greater thickness of 49–118 centimeters (fewer than 10 percent). Overall, however, one can infer that living conditions in the city were comfortable.

The daily religious ritual may have been a boon for the population. Kemp has raised the question of the city's food supply, noting that "the two Aten temples acted as giant food supplies." Atenism bred, in fact, "an obsession with victuals." On the northern side of the Great Temple was an abattoir, and on the south a gigantic bakery. Priests, officials, and employees of the temple were certainly fed by it—but it is most likely that the temples also provided food to the public on a large scale.[113]

It is paradoxical, despite the fundamental contribution of tomb art to our understanding, that, without the contents of any tomb, we have no information on the condition at death of the upper classes (it has even been suggested that their tombs were unfinished and unoccupied). Workers' graves, on the other hand, show very simple burials, and a low life expectancy.

There are other very important matters to be broached. We may not know the number of inhabitants, but how did they come to Amarna? Reginald Engelbach (1899–1946) long ago suggested that the nobles would have been loath to leave their Theban estates: "Some compulsion is indicated, or fears for their personal safety."[114] Much more sinister views have recently been aired. According to Tyldesley, "The military and armed police who had been so prominent at Thebes maintained their high profile at Amarna." Was this, we may ask, to keep "foreigners" [sic] out, or citizens in? "It would not be too surprising if some resented their enforced seclusion in the king's model city." This is shortly after Tyldesley admitted that "Akhenaten seems to have resisted the temptation to regulate the private lives of his citizens."[115] Reeves wrote of a "groveling populace . . . kept in check by large numbers of police with batons, and *their* loyalty has been bought by the favors bestowed from the 'Window of Appearances' upon their commanders and those charged with the execution of the royal will."[116] Bouriant and his colleagues a century earlier had noted the presence of the police at Amarna, but they offered an innocent explanation: the king was preoccupied with protection of caravans.[117] The real answer, however, is suggested by the city's second most basic feature: it was open on all sides. The fact that it lay spread out, unwalled on open ground, is very revealing of the nature of this society. The only boundary, in fact, was the stelae.[118]

Archaeological details and statistics bring us into only indirect contact with the ordinary inhabitants of Amarna. The famous nonroyal portraits from the studio of Thutmose presumably represent better-off Amarnans. Where are the 'ordinary' Amarnans? One relief shows a herdsman (fig. 67). He watches over a grazing goat. His thick hair is cut short, and he

Fig. 67. An Amarna herdsman (Brooklyn L.71.8.1).

Fig. 68. Two chatting guardsmen (Brooklyn 61.195.2).

is unshaven (for whom would he shave?). He wears only a cloth around his lower body, and his abdomen is somewhat distended (evidence of poor diet?). He has a herding stick in his right hand, and another stick over his shoulder carrying a jar which probably contained his only sustenance. Another shows two palace employees—guards—wearing the

Fig. 69. A family group (MMA 11.150.21).

more formal Nubian wig. They are chatting (fig. 68). These are men engaged in their occupations. What of family life? A man in the center is flanked by his son and grandchild against a plinth in a standard pose (fig. 69). They seem dignified and content (Aldred, however, found them "morose"[119]). A more relaxed scene is of a banquet (from house R44.2),

Fig. 70. Stela with a banquet scene; from Amarna, outside house R44.2 (San Diego 14881).

not one of the well-known royal ones, but of modest inhabitants. Such private stelae are rare. Two men (Yaya and Menna) are seated, being greeted and served wine by two women (Shety and Mery) wearing "perfume cones" (fig. 70). Further fascinating evidence of relaxation is toys. They illustrate also the Amarnans' interest in monkeys or baboons: six ride in a boat, one plays a harp, a mother carries a young one on her back, and—most intriguing—a monkey drives a chariot in what could be taken to be a satire on royal driving (fig. 71).

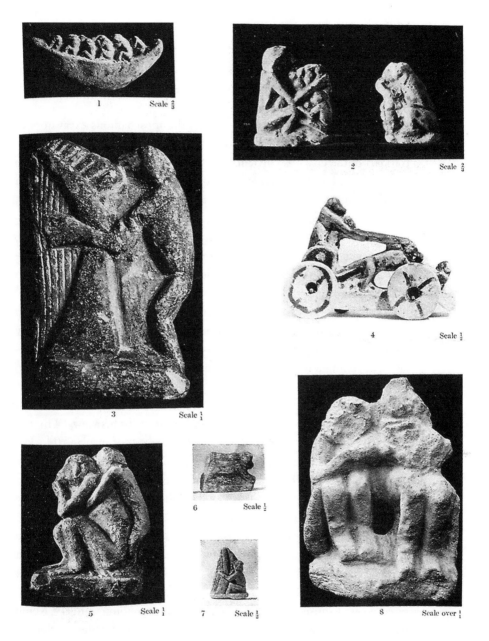

Fig. 71. Toys from Amarna: six monkeys in a boat; a monkey playing the harp; a monkey riding in a chariot; a mother-monkey carrying her young on her back.

What does the city tell us about Akhenaten?

The "Early Proclamation" indicates that the basic concept of the city and almost certainly its major features were determined by the king himself. He must, however, have been assisted by architects, although none are named.

On the planning of the city, one of the most famous excavators at Amarna, Pendlebury, was paradoxically impressed, noting that "the central part of the city was particularly well laid out. The various blocks are self-contained and are divided up by streets as straight as an Egyptian could be expected to make them."[120]

Kemp, on the other hand, remained unimpressed as his excavations progressed: "A royal decision had been made to create a new city, exemplifying a new creed. . . . Yet on this occasion no one sought the satisfaction . . . of translating a grandiose, even megalomaniac vision into bricks and mortar."[121] "For a city laid out on a virgin site with a relatively even surface, and built as an expression of a visionary king attempting to create a new order, the residential parts of the city have a surprisingly inconsequential layout."[122] Amarna is "essentially a replicated mud village containing a few isolated monuments built with little thought as to their contribution to the overall urban effect."[123]

Janssen did detect a plan, albeit a broad one: the city consists of two residential zones separated by an "official center." In his view, "There is no trace of a master grid or of a prior marking out of insulae" (blocks). The various housing densities, furthermore, are striking. "Clusters of closely packed small houses mix almost indiscriminately with larger houses which, because of their walled enclosures, are more widely spaced."[124] It was Borchardt who first drew this fundamental matter to our attention.[125] The most important thing to deduce is that Akhenaten did not impose social segregation. Laboury offered an explanation. Just as the leading figures in the city were dependent on the king, so the lower classes were in turn dependent on their superiors, and their houses clustered around those of the better off, forming economic units.[126] Kemp put it in another way: important people chose a place for their residence that gave them some space from their peers, and then that space was settled by their dependents. The distinction at Amarna, therefore, was not between rich and poor, but between the royal family and everyone else.[127]

An early criticism was that the city lacked an 'economic base,' but evidence is increasingly coming to light of manufacturing areas. It must also be remembered that the city's connection to the Nile is now hidden under the cultivation.

Many have made much of the "haste" with which the city was built. The lack of uniformity in the blocks of houses, James Baikie averred, showed the "haste with which the city was run up." There was also no distinction between residential and commercial quarters. That was not, however, the whole story. The basic material may have been the humblest mud brick, but the decoration was brilliant: there were even painted pavements.[128]

Pendlebury was more direct:

The frantic haste attending the 'running up' of this mushroom city is everywhere in evidence. Instead of finely-cut masonry, rubble was used with a thin stone facing. Mud brick was whitewashed to look like limestone. The number of skilled craftsmen was not sufficient and practically untrained men were set to carve the inscriptions, as we can see from the rough hieroglyphs in plaster which had to be used as models for every letter by the illiterate workmen.[129]

Alan Gardiner and Redford agreed: "workmanship everywhere is shoddy"; the buildings were "hastily designed and assembled . . . as in all the construction undertaken during [Akhenaten's] reign."[130]

The haste has been exaggerated. Reeves suggested that the building took three to four years. The city was fully functional certainly by Year 9.[131] Tietze offered a very positive assessment: "Amarna is an example of how Egyptian society had the capacity to fulfil large and complicated economic plans in a short time with great efficiency."[132] And not to be forgotten, as Laboury noted, was the way in which desert had been converted into green and watered land.[133]

One special feature of the city might be very revealing of Akhenaten. It has long been claimed that many of Akhenaten's favorites seem to be 'new men' or parvenus. Erman stated that those buried at Amarna were not "the great men who had served under the old regime, but . . . the creatures of the new king."[134] Gardiner was particularly interested in this matter, but he meant only that these officials had not accompanied

Akhenaten from Thebes. He further makes the remarkable statement that few of them ever attained high positions, and then lists a
large number of offices, giving very few names: the vizier (Nakht),
the mayor (Neferkhepru-her-sekheper), priests (unnamed—not even
Meryre i, High Priest), overseers of the royal harem, the chief physician
(Pentju), the army commander (Pa-aten-em-heb), the commander of
cavalry (Ay), and chief of police (Mahu). He concluded with the strange
statement that "Of really exalted station was only the overseer of the
treasury" (Sutau).[135]

Redford agreed that the incidence of "new men" was higher under
Akhenaten than otherwise in the Eighteenth Dynasty. He inferred this
from the very personal formula of investiture[136] and a change from "genuine reward to unmerited favor,"[137] and drew hasty conclusions from
the parvenu status of these men: Akhenaten "may well have lacked the
ability to judge character."[138] Baudouin van de Walle (1901–88) more
logically explained the reliance on "new men" as a possible reaction to
the unsuitability, or unwillingness, of the old aristocracy to adhere to
the new cult.[139]

There are, indeed, officials who admit that they were raised from
humble circumstances. May says: "I was a poor man on both my father's
and my mother's side—but the ruler built me up."[140] This is confirmed in
the view of some by the "Restoration Inscription" of Tutankhamun: he
installed lay priests and higher clergy from among the officials of their
cities, each one being the "son-of-a-man" whose name was known.[141]

The vital question is how innovative these claims are, and how far
they are to be believed. Aldred comes to our rescue:

> During his reign Amenophis III was served by loyal and competent
> officials whom he rewarded with valuable gifts, including gold deco-
> rations and magnificent tombs in Western Thebes. Foremost among
> his henchmen was Amenophis son of a certain Hapu, a man of no
> account, so we are asked to believe.[142]

Amenhotep III's high steward in Memphis, treasurer and overseer
of the Double Granary, Amenhotep, also claimed that his parents were
humble in origin. Aldred then revealed the truth: these "new men" of

Akhenaten were, in fact, the sons of his father's officials. Their statements were conventional flattery, "no more than a polite acknowledgment that he had appointed them to their posts."[143]

There have also been claims that Akhenaten held his officials in a servile position, with much 'bowing and scraping.' Maanakhtef, for example, stated that he hoped to kiss the ground in the king's presence every day, because he was his slave.[144] Redford put all this in context. The advice to officials that they should obey and depend on the king is timeless in Egypt: Ptahhotep in the Fifth Dynasty, Sehetepibre in the Twelfth Dynasty, and Any in the New Kingdom will serve as examples.[145]

There have, finally, been claims that Amarna was designed simply to allow the king to live in his own totally isolated world unconnected with reality. Assmann painted a very depressing picture indeed: many other kings had changed their residence, but now it was "the shrinking of the royal domain, which previously had filled the whole horizon of the Thutmosid empire from Nubia to Syria and now remained limited to a couple of square kilometers on the edge of the desert." For the next fifteen [sic] years, he led a "shadowy existence," which Tutankhamun—a nine-year-old boy—described as "the sickness of the land."[146] The idea that Amarna was an isolated and even insulated city is disproven by the importance of, for example, Memphis at this time, where a number of officeholders are known.[147]

It is Kemp, the director of the modern excavations, however, who has stressed the single most revealing feature of the city in connection with the king, something quite extraordinary: here, there was "nothing grandiose, nothing megalomaniac."[148] That insight was confirmed by Erich Hornung regarding the Royal Tomb, where the king "opposed the steady enlargement and the propensity for the gigantic, which triumphed in the funerary temples of his father."[149]

Let there be no doubt, however, about one thing: the foundation of Akhet-Aten sent shock waves through Egypt. This was not merely another royal foundation, of which there had been so many. It was a new capital, dedicated to one deity alone, where only the king, his family, and presumably adherents of the new religion would live, uncontaminated by any undesirable religious or political influences. The rest of the country, its cities, and its deities, must have felt rejected and abandoned.

A Postscript to Frankfort's Work at Amarna

Henri Frankfort left Amarna in 1929, invited by James Henry Breasted to direct the Oriental Institute Iraq expedition, where he made his name. *"My Dear Miss Ransom . . .": Letters between Caroline Ransom Williams and James Henry Breasted, 1898–1935,*[150] throws new light on the end of the Egypt Exploration Society excavations at Amarna under Frankfort. Breasted explained what happened:

> In the first place, the autocratic methods of [Pierre] Lacau [Director of the Antiquities Service 1914–36] have very seriously damaged Frankfort; in the second place, the depleted treasury of the Egyptian Exploration Society; in the third place, the embarrassing situation of the Institute in the matter of scientific-executive personnel. It is exceedingly difficult to find men of good scientific competence combined with average business ability to manage a field expedition.[151]

He went on to say that Alan Gardiner was "very much depressed" about the epigraphic work of the EES, and Breasted thought of sending them Ugo Hölscher, the master at Medinet Habu. Ransom revealed that Frankfort had asked her to find American support for the excavation at Amarna. He estimated that it would take seven years to finish the excavation, at 3,000 pounds sterling per annum.[152] Breasted replied that he did not think that the English should have taken the work away from the Germans. Gardiner was urging the EES to pull out. Breasted admitted that "nothing would suit me better than for the Institute to continue the job."[153]

4 The Cult of the Aten

The so-called "Great Hymn" to the Aten—a modern title given to a text found in the tomb of Ay (TA 25)—is the longest text relating to the Aten that has survived:

> Beautifully you appear from the horizon of heaven, O living Aten
> who initiates life—
> For you are risen from the eastern horizon and have filled every
> land with your beauty;
> For you are fair, great, dazzling and high over every land,
> And your rays enclose the lands to the limit of all you have made;
> 5   For you are Re, having reached their limit and subdued them <for>
> your beloved son;
> For although you are far away, your rays are upon the earth and you
> are perceived.
> When your movements vanish and you set in the western horizon,
> The land is in darkness, in the manner of death.
> (People), they lie in bed-chambers, heads covered up, and one eye
> does not see its fellow.
> 10   All their property might be robbed, although it is under their heads,
> and they do not realize it.
> Every lion is out of its den, all creeping things bite.

Darkness gathers, the land is silent.
The one who made them is set in his horizon.
(But) the land grows bright when you are risen from the horizon,
15 Shining in the orb (the Aten) in the daytime, you push back the
         darkness and give forth your rays.
The Two Lands are in a festival of light—
Awake and standing on legs, for you have lifted them up:
Their limbs are cleansed and wearing clothes,
Their arms are in adoration at your appearing.
20 The whole land, they do their work.
All flocks are content with their pasturage,
Trees and grasses flourish,
Birds are flown from their nests, their wings adoring your *ka*;
All small cattle prance upon their legs.
25 All that fly up and alight, they live when you rise for them.
Ships go downstream, and upstream as well, every road being open
         at your appearance.
Fish upon the river leap up in front of you, and your rays are (even)
         inside the Great Green (sea).
(O you) who bring into living foetuses in women,
Who make fluid in people,
30 Who give life to the son in his mother's womb, and calm him by
         stopping his tears;
Nurse in the womb, who give breath to animate all he makes
When it descends from the womb to breathe on the day it is born—
You open his mouth completely and make what he needs.
When the chick is in the egg, speaking in the shell,
35 You give him breath within it to cause him to live;
And when you have made his appointed time for him, so that he
         may break himself out of the egg,
He comes out of the egg to speak at his appointed time and goes on
         his two legs when he comes out of it.
How manifold it is, what you have made, although mysterious in the
         face (of humanity),
O sole god, without another beside him!
40 You create the earth according to your wish, being alone—

People, all large and small animals,

All things which are on earth, which go on legs, which rise up and
fly by means of their wings,

The foreign countries of Kharu [Palestine and Syria] and Kush
[Nubia], (and) the land of Egypt.

You set every man in his place, you make their requirements, each
one having his food and the reckoning of his lifetime. Their
tongues differ in speech, their natures likewise. Their skins are
distinct, for you have made foreigners to be distinct.

45   You make the inundation from the underworld.

And you bring it to (the place) you wish in order to cause the subjects to live,

Inasmuch as you made them for yourself, their lord entirely, who is
wearied with them.

The lord of every land, who rises for them,

The orb of the daytime (the Aten), whose awesomeness is great!

50   (As for) all distant countries, you make their life;

You have granted an inundation in heaven, that it might come down
for them

And make torrents upon the mountains, like the Great Green, to
soak their fields with what suits them.

How functional are your plans, O lord of continuity!

An inundation in heaven, which is for the foreigners (and) for all
foreign flocks which go on legs;

55   (And) an inundation when it comes from the underworld for the
Tilled Land [i.e., Egypt],

While your rays nurse every field:

When you rise, they live and flourish for you.

You make the seasons in order to develop all you make:

The Growing season to cool them, and heat so that they might feel
you.

60   You made heaven far away just to rise in it, to see all you make,

Being unique and risen in your aspects of being as 'the living Aten'—
manifest, shining, far (yet) near.

You make millions of developments from yourself, (you who are) a
oneness: cities, towns, fields, the path of the river.

Every eye observes you in relation to them, for you are the Aten of
the daytime above the earth (?),
When you have gone, nobody can exist.
65 You create their faces so that you might not see [your]self [as] the
only (thing) which you made.

You are in my heart, and there is none who knows you except your
son Neferkheprure-Waenre,
For you make him aware of your plans and your strength.
The land develops through your action, just as you made them [that
is, people]:
When you have risen they live, (but) when you set they die. You are
lifetime in your (very) limbs, and one lives by means of you.
70 Until you set, (all) eyes are upon your beauty (but) all work is put
aside when you set on the western side.
(You) who rise and make [all creation] grow for the king, (as for)
everyone who hurries about on foot since you founded the land,
You raise them up for your son, who issued from your limbs, the
King of Upper and Lower Egypt, who lives on Maat,
The Lord of the Two Lands, Neferkheprure-[Waenre],
Son of Re, who lives on Maat, Lord of Crowns, Akhenaten, long in
his lifetime;
75 (And) the King's Chief Wife, his beloved, the Lady of the Two
Lands, Neferneferuaten-Nefertiti—may she live and be young
forever continually.[1]

The original 'prose' text is in thirteen columns on a wall of Ay's
tomb. It is conventional in translations to adopt this more 'poetic' form;
the line count relates to this and is merely for convenience of reference.
The main structure is clear:
  - the celebration of the rising sun (lines 1–6);
  - the dangers when the sun sets (7–13);
  - the return to daylight (14–27), and its effect on the land,
    nature, and even shipping;
  - the Aten as the source of all life (28–37);
  - the Aten, unique, the creator, the universal organizer and

controller especially of water and the seasons in Egypt and abroad (38–65);

- no one knows the Aten save the king, his son, and all creation is raised up by him and his queen (66–75).

Who was the author of this famous text? There is one obvious candidate: Akhenaten himself.[2]

Evaluations have varied greatly. For James Breasted, this was "a veritable gospel of the beauty of light."[3] William Hayes, in contrast, considered it to be "hardly more than a lyrical meditation on the manifestation of God in nature"—as though that were a cliché in the fourteenth century BC.[4] Donald Redford admitted the "deep-seated wonder at the beauty of the sun and its power in nature," but claimed that the Aten shows "no compassion to his creatures" because he represented "divine kingship, projected into the heavens."[5]

James Allen showed the complexity of the "Great Hymn." He identified five themes: 1. light animates all things; 2. light creates all things; 3. light sustains all things, even the inundation; 4. light controls the cycle of life: the seasons and the inundation; and 5. the king holds a privileged position. As the king's new name stated, he was "effective for the Aten." He thus replaced "the traditional images of the gods as the medium for human contact with the divine."

There are many references to the Aten's creation of the universe, but far more important is the recreation of the world every day. The focus of devotion was the light; hence the emphasis on the visible, tangible reality (cf. Amun the "Hidden").[6]

Jan Assmann identified the changes, comparing the Aten hymn with the many other solar hymns. In the first section, the Aten was shown at morning, noon, and night (lines 1–27). The traditional sun hymn showed the sun in "a very complex cosmic drama," the triumph of life, order, and justice over death, rebellion, and injustice, reflecting human life. Now the Aten was above all this: simply the life-giving god. The noon phase traditionally represented the triumph of the sun over the evil Apophis. In the Aten hymn, the sun's rays brought all lands to obey the king. There was no more cosmic foe, no more political conflict. Most innovative of all, the nocturnal phase had totally abandoned the sun's descent into the netherworld. Mythical imagery was replaced by visible reality: light and darkness. With the return to morning, great detail was devoted to depicting the awakening, not only of humankind, but also of all nature, which worshiped the sun.

The second part of the hymn dealt with creation (lines 28–55). Past was replaced by present, cosmogony by "embryogony" in Assmann's terminology. Assmann suggested that the cosmopolitanism and universalism represented the new Late Bronze Age phenomenon of the *oikoumene*, the inhabited world.

The third part was centered on "becoming" (lines 56 following): the celestial transformation of the Aten and his terrestrial transformations. They were the visible world. The Aten both looked down on the whole world and was seen by it. Light created everything, including time, even eyes. This led to the king—and it is significant that almost all Eighteenth Dynasty kings had "the manifestation of Re" (Kheperu-Re) as their prenomina. There was an inversion of the traditional theology, where seeing the gods was reserved for the dead, while knowing them was required of everyone. Now everyone saw the Aten (at least in the day), but only the king *knew* him.

If the Aten created both light and time (an idea that went back to the Middle Kingdom), then everything could be related to him. God was nature, but in an anthropocentric way, which at the end of the hymn became pharaoh-centric.

Assmann summed up with a paradox: Akhenaten's "explanation of the world as nature is, above all, an act of iconoclastic destruction, of negating the world's religious significance."[7]

James Hoffmeier has shown that philology is also revealing. The most common verbs relate to rising and shining and creating, while the chief epithets are "living" or "causing to live."[8]

There is also the so-called Shorter Hymn to the Aten found in five tombs, those of Any (TA 23), Ipy (TA 10), Mahu (TA 9), Meryre i (TA 1), and Tutu (TA 8).[9] These are all earlier southern tombs, except for that of Meryre. The copies of Tutu and Ipy include the Early form of the Aten's name in their preamble, while the other three have the Later form. All texts vary in detail, that in the tomb of Tutu diverging most radically from the others. A major methodological error has been to take the version in the tomb of Meryre i as the 'standard'—presumably because he was the high priest—and proceed to construct a 'composite version' based on all five.[10] In this way a text is presented which *never existed*. Even worse has been the next step, the presentation of this artificial version as the *Ur-Text*! In this way most vital evidence about the cult is destroyed before our eyes. A synchronized version of these complicated texts runs as follows:[11]

You appear beautifully, O living Aten, lord of eternity [*Tutu substitutes for this clause "O [my] (divine and royal) father, O living Aten who ordains life"*] dazzling, fair, powerful [*Ipy and Meryre i substitute "bright" here for the last*]. The love of you is great and extensive. Your rays reach the eyes of all you created [*Any, Meryre i, Ipy, and Mahu substitute, "Your rays are pervasive (?) for everyone." The version in Tutu's tomb is damaged but clearly differs from the rest: "[they] being your bright hue"*], and your bright hue receives all hearts [*Tutu probably had "the love [of you fills all lands with] your [life]"(?)*] when you have filled the Two Lands with love of you, O august god [*Meryre i substitutes "good ruler"*] who constructed himself by himself—maker of every land, creator of what is on it: namely, people, all sorts of long- and short-horned cattle [*thus Meryre i and Any; the others have "herds and all sorts of short-horned cattle"*], all trees and what grows on the ground—they live when you rise for them [*Tutu substitutes: "They [live] (as) your rays shine for them"*]. You are the mother and father of all you make. When you rise, their eyes see by means of you [*All four versions in Mahu's tomb end here, and they diverge both from copies in other tombs and from one another. All four copies in this tomb end with: "For the ka of the chief of the Medjay of (or in) Akhet-Aten, Mahu, justified (or may he live again)"*]. When your rays have illuminated [*Tutu's version diverges here ("when your rays have illuminated your [. . .]") and omits the following two and a half clauses*] the entire land, all heart(s) rejoice at seeing you [*Any has "the entire land is in joy and rejoicing at seeing you," and so on*] manifest as their lord. When you set in the western horizon of heaven, they repose in the fashion of those who are dead, heads covered, noses obstructed, until the occurrence of your rising at dawn from the eastern horizon of heaven. Their arms are in adoration of your *ka*:

when you have revived all hearts with your beauty, one lives; and when you give forth your rays, every land is in festival [*Tutu adds "and provisioned when you illuminate it"*]. Singing, chanting, and joyful shouting are in the courtyard of the Mansion of the Benben and (in) every temple [*Meryre i substitutes "every sunshade"*] in Akhet-Aten, the place of truth in which you have become content [*Thus Ipy and Tutu; Any and Meryre i substitute "(and) every place in which you are content"*]. Food and provisions lie within it, while your son is pure in doing what you praise.

O Aten, who lives in his appearances! All that you make is dancing in front of you, and as for your august son [*Meryre i omits the preceding clause; and Tutu omits "august"*], his heart exults with joy, O living Aten, who is born in the sky daily [*Thus Tutu; Meryre omits this clause and the last; Ipy and Any have "who is content in the sky"*], that he might give birth to his august son, Waenre, just like himself [*Tutu again omits "august" and substitutes "who issued from his body" for "Waenre"*], without ceasing—the son of Re who raises up his beauty, Neferkheprure-Waenre. [*Meryre ends here with "without ceasing forever"*]

I am your son, who is effective for you and raises up your name. Your might and your power are established [*Any: "firm"*] in my heart. You are the living Aten: continuity is your image, for you made the distant sky in order to rise in it and see all you make—while you are one, but with millions of lives in you, in order to make them live. The breath of life penetrates into noses when your rays are seen [*Tutu: "Breath enters into noses when you give yourself to them"*]. All sorts of flowers are continually alive; growing on the ground and made to flourish, because of your rising; they grow drunk at the sight of you [*Any's text ends here*], while all sorts of cattle are prancing [*Ipy's text ends; Tutu's version continues almost to the end*] on their legs. Birds which were in the nest are aloft in joy, their wings which were folded are spread out in adoration to the living Aten, the one who makes them all.

These texts reveal more than twenty variants, some of them major, in a rather short hymn. The importance of these variations should be obvious to all. In most religions, sacred texts are exactly that: the word of the deity or of his prophet. Not a word is to be tampered with. Here, however, it seems that even in the tombs of the highest members of the Amarnan bureaucracy a 'personal' version of what was presumably one basic text—since the five versions agree in the main—could be set up in one's tomb. There is obviously no possibility of explaining these variations as the fault of carelessness by scribe or copyist.

If this is accepted, we have a vital piece of evidence for religious and intellectual freedom under the reign of Akhenaten.[12] Rarely, however, have ancient sacred texts been manipulated so wantonly by modern scholarship to produce a text that never was.

We also have any number of simple prayers to the Aten: by Amenemopet, scribe and overseer of field workers during Years 1 to 5;[13] by Parennefer, royal cupbearer, in his Theban tomb (TT 188);[14] by May, fan-bearer to the king, from his Amarnan tomb (TA 14);[15] and by Meryre i, High Priest of the Aten, from his tomb at Amarna (TA 4).[16]

Norman de Garis Davies found the hymns in the tombs so carelessly constructed that they made little apparent sense. For him, the results were "tediously alike in sentiment and phraseology": the Royal Hymn was "plagiarized and mutilated."[17]

It is widely accepted that the author of the "Great Hymn" was Akhenaten himself. There is, indeed, another text by the king that has been little noticed on Boundary Stela K:

As lives my father the Hor-Aten,
The beautiful living Aten who began life and ordains life,
My Father who is with me among [. . .] in his journey,
My rampart of millions of cubits,
My reminder of continuity,
My witness to eternal things,
The one who constructed himself with his own two hands, no craft knowing him;
The one who makes guidance by rising and setting every day without cease, in the sky or on earth, while (all) eyes behold him;
Who has no [equal] when he has filled the land with his rays, causing every face to live;

The one at whom my eyes are sated, seeing him risen daily when
he rises in this house of the Aten in Akhet-Aten, having filled it
utterly with himself, with his fair and loving rays.[18]

The king also makes clear his relationship to the Aten on the later
boundary stelae:

The Good God, only one of Re *(Waenre)* whose beauty the Aten
created,
Truly effective on behalf of the one who made him, who satisfies
him with what pleases his *ka*,
Who does effective things for the one who fashioned him,
Who administers the land for the one who placed him on his throne
and provisions his house forever with countless hundreds of
thousands of things,
Who lifts up the Aten and magnifies his name, causing the land to
belong to the one who made it.[19]

Akhenaten's position in the cult, however, is described in the Amar-
nan tombs with great variation. In them, he is identified with the Aten
(TA 1), but he is also Hapi and Shu;[20] he is like the Aten (TA 9), he is the
son of the Aten, he is "the sole living god";[21] he lives on Maat (TA 2).
There was obviously, as in the Shorter Hymn, great latitude in theology.
The tombs also reveal the different worldly concerns of their owners: for
Huya (TA 1) Akhenaten is essentially the "creator of officialdom."

Representing the Aten

One preliminary matter of great importance is the shape of the Aten
following its transformation from a falcon-headed man to its abstract
form with rays ending in hands. It is traditionally always referred to,
by convention, as the 'sun disk' (and will be here), but a few scholars
have argued for the fact that the Aten was a *globe*: Christiane Desroches-
Noblecourt always called it so. A brief defense of the notion was offered
by Claude Vandersleyen, relying especially on a balustrade sculpture
where the Aten's shape is deeply cut away;[22] Davies had already noticed
this.[23] Another such illustration comes from the Royal Tomb (fig. 72).

Fig. 72. Relief showing Akhenaten, Nefertiti, Meryetaten, and Maketaten worshiping the Aten; from Amarna Royal Tomb, chamber 4 (Cairo JE 54517).

The Aten dominates most Amarnan scenes where one or both of the royal couple are present. The disk usually wears only a uraeus, but some-times also has its own *ankh*. One of the earliest, the early *ḥb-sd* relief (fig. 19) shows *ʿnḫ* and *ḥqꜣ* signs attached to the disk. Another early block, which shows the Aten in its falcon-headed form, also has a sun disk with no rays, but has *ʿnḫ* signs hooked onto the disk. At Amarna, the tombs

Fig. 73. Akhenaten and Nefertiti offering to the Aten in the tomb-chapel of Ipy (TA 10); the Aten's rays embrace the offerings piled up for him.

of the courtiers give us the basic repertoire of scenes incorporating the rayed disk. There are royal offering scenes, where the Aten usually touches the offerings—perhaps as a sign of acceptance, as well as extending life to the rulers (fig. 73).[24] In the first of these, very unusually, the Aten wears a double pectoral.

In visits to the temple, many more of the rays end in hands, to protect the temple itself,[25] touching the frame of the scene and offerings[26] or the pylon and offering tables.[27]

In the scenes of rewards from the 'Window of Appearances,' the Aten is at the top of the picture (fig. 63).[28] Scenes of reward without the 'window' also feature the presiding Aten.[29] Royal chariot riders are protected by the Aten (fig. 59).[30] In one case both king and queen each have their own disk; in another the rays enclose the couple in an arc and seem to include the horse.[31] The Aten is present at the 'durbar' (fig.

62) and presides over the boundary stelae. Finally, the Aten is depicted in intimate family scenes of eating, both in the tombs (fig. 61)[32] and on stelae from private houses.[33]

Strange to say, there are a number of occasions where the Aten does not seem to extend life also to Nefertiti,[34] although here we must be cautious, for the portraits are often damaged. There are cases where Akhenaten also misses out,[35] but in offering scenes, he is often holding equipment awkwardly so as to block any access to the *ʿnḫ*. The extended rays of the Aten are usually a symmetrical triangle, but not in offering scenes, where the tables must also be covered. Apart from the king and queen, the *ʿnḫ* was offered to Amenhotep III and Tiye (fig. 40), but not to the royal princesses or Kiya.

As to the nature of the disk-icon, in Alan Gardiner's view, Akhenaten did "everything in his power" to rid the Aten of "anthropomorphic associations"—but it was impossible: the sun had rays that ended in hands; he was described as 'mother' and 'father' and Akhenaten was his 'son.'[36] Erik Hornung drew attention to the "restrictive iconography" of the god: "the many hands, the life-sign, and the Uraeus remain the sole attributes of the Aten."[37]

The Egyptians were used to anthropomorphic deities: human forms, although often with animal heads. Even in this case, they shared eyes and mouth with humans. The Aten, in contrast, was simply a disk (or orb). The irony is that this is the most basic outline of a face, but it completely lacked all associated features. As the sun it had only rays, which extended in straight lines: this was the only means of communication with mankind. And then, only in the most special circumstances—in the presence of the king and queen—the rays developed hands. The Aten was thus, at one and the same time, sensible to all of mankind, by its heat, and yet paradoxically inaccessible.

The Names of the Aten

The Aten's names had two developed forms, both written in twin cartouches, although embryonic forms lacked this feature; our understanding of them continues to depend heavily on the research of Battiscombe Gunn (1883–1950).[38] The Earlier and Later forms could be translated respectively as follows:[39]

The living Re-Horakhty, who rejoices in the horizon in his name Shu/sunshine who/which is in the Aten.[40]

The living Re, ruler of the horizon, who rejoices in the horizon in his name of Re/light which comes in the Aten.

The Aten is unique among Egyptian deities in having twin cartouches, like a king (figs. 72, 73). Indeed, his reign and Akhenaten's were considered contemporaneous: the 'durbar' is dated to Year 12 of both the Aten and Akhenaten.[41] As to when the Aten's name was first placed in cartouches, it certainly took place before the change from the falcon-headed form to that of the disk;[42] Dimitri Laboury has suggested early in Year 4.[43]

The crucial changes between the Earlier and Later forms are the replacement of reference to "Re-Horakhty" by simply "Re" in the first cartouche, and the replacement of "Shu/sunshine" in the second by "Re/light." In addition, one of the god's accompanying epithets changes from "in jubilee" to "lord of jubilees."

A fundamental question is the date of the change, in particular because it has been used continually as a criterion for dating. Gunn calculated that it occurred no earlier than the middle of Year 8 and no later than Year 9, perhaps in connection with a second jubilee.[44] Year 9 therefore became the canonical date, used as an automatically accepted terminus *ante/post quem* for various events and persons.

It was Kurt Sethe (1869–1934) in 1921 who set out the basic argument for such a date by noting that Neferneferuaten-tasherit was not shown on Boundary Stela A, of Year 8, suggesting that she had not been born until after this—but not much later, since all six daughters are shown in the Meryre ii-version of the 'durbar' scene of Year 12. Since the Earlier form of the Aten's name accompanies scenes in the tomb of Panehsy, where the eldest three daughters are shown, but the Later form when Neferneferuaten-tasherit had joined them,[45] Sethe connected the change in name, therefore, with the birth of this fourth princess. At the same time Sethe admitted that there is no attention in art to the princesses' relative ages and proportions.[46] Herbert Fairman reconsidered the question and concluded that Year 9 "still seems to be approximately correct."[47] Cyril Aldred would not be more precise than dating the change to "somewhere" between Year 8 and Year 12—but perhaps Year 9, for him the putative third jubilee of the Aten.[48] Redford also accepted Year 9.[49]

One of the few to challenge Year 9 as the dividing line has been Marc Gabolde, who has pointed out that the Year 12 scenes in the tombs of Huya and Meryre ii may not actually have been carved that very year, and that the Later form there might simply be what was current at the time of carving, not necessarily in Year 12. He also identified a "Middle" form of the Aten's name, apparently found only in the Royal Tomb, in which the cartouches were changed to the Later type, but retained the Early epithet of "in jubilee," rather than "lord of jubilees." The one room E in fact contained *all three* forms. He also saw an interesting corroboration. Proportions suggested the same date for the change: at Amarna, the Earlier form accounts for 64 percent of occurrences, the "Later" for only 36 percent, suggesting that the "Later" form was used in the last third of the time: from about Year 12![50] Laboury, using the same evidence, suggested Year 14 for the name change.[51] Suffice to say, the old certainty of dating the change to Year 9 and using it for dating everything else is now open to serious doubt.

John Bennett argued that *itn* was a common noun (the physical sun), not a name: the name of the actual sun god was Re. He thus proposed that the *itn* at the end of the second cartouche of both Earlier and Later forms should be read as a concrete solar phenomenon, rather than the name of a god. He would thus prefer to translate them respectively as "-who rejoices in the horizon in his role of sunshine" and "-who rejoices in the horizon in his role of the sunbeams." Bennett also suggested that the change of name—to state that the sun god was now a "ruler"—was to allow the king to invoke his god's aid in his struggle against increasing opposition.[52]

The development of Atenism

The early history of the Aten, as shown by the tombs at Thebes, was discussed by Davies in 1923. A key monument was the tomb of Kheruef (TT 192), steward of Tiye, the outer vestibule of which dates from Akhenaten's early reign.[53] A lintel shows him (as Amenhotep IV) and his mother worshiping the gods. The king is called "image of the sun-god of Edfu" and offers incense to Atum and Hathor on the right, and Re-Horakhty and Maat (fig. 8) on the left. On the rear wall, Kheruef offers a prayer to the sun. On the south side of the vestibule, Akhenaten offers

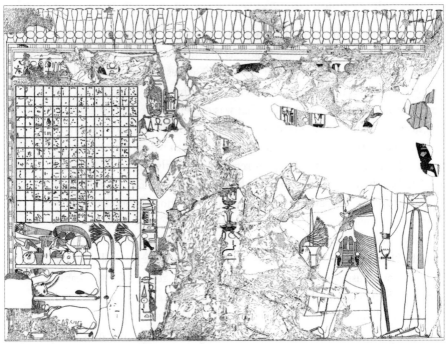

Fig. 74. South wall of the portico of Kheruef's TT 192. The right half shows a largely destroyed figure of Amenhotep IV offering to Amenhotep III, accompanied by Tiye, and the left another figure of the younger king reciting a hymn to Re-Horakhty in the form of a word-square.

to Re-Horakhty and Amenhotep III (fig. 74), and opposite Kheruef addresses the underworld gods. Davies noted "the greatly increased pretensions of the king, one of the less attractive features of the revolution": he has replaced the deceased as the focus of attention.

In the tomb of Parennefer (TT 188), the Royal Cup Bearer, the lintel is similar to that in TT 192, with the king offering to a seated Re-Horakhty. On the western façade, however, the Aten in disk form appears above an altar and the king, possibly with a queen behind him. The Aten and its rays also appear above the enthroned king and queen on the back wall of the transverse hall of the chapel. The tomb of Ramose (TT 55) has a similar mix of 'traditional' and Amarnan depictions. Davies noted the survival of Osiris in TT 188 and 192, leading him unconsciously to undermine his earlier judgments of Akhenaten's 'despotism': the survival of the old gods shows "how reticent and diplomatic Akhenaten was"!

He now commented on Akhenaten's and Nefertiti's "apparent affability towards their people."[54]

There have been various attempts to set out the development of the Aten, building on these depictions and other material. Aldred considered the earliest stages, during the first two years of Akhenaten's reign, to be:

- the increasing importance of Re-Horakhty (the lintel of the tomb of Kheruef, the lintel of the tomb of Parennefer);
- Re-Horakhty is given a 'didactic' name (the Aten), but not a cartouche (Gebel Silsila stela; figs. 19 and 21);
- the Aten subsumes Re-Horakhty;
- the names of the Aten are enclosed in two cartouches (for example, figs. 20, 72).[55] The god has become also a pharaoh;[56]
- the Aten becomes a sun disk, with a uraeus, 'nḥ, and rays ending in hands (e.g., figs. 20, 57–59).
- the Aten sometimes also holds a w3s scepter (e.g., fig. 21); this change was apparently connected with the ḥb-sd, the Aten sometimes holding the "jubilee" sign (fig. 20).[57]

Redford, relying on the evidence of the Theban *talatat*, offered a more complicated development of Atenism even at Thebes, which he divided into three stages:

Early stage
Akhenaten's innovation is the association of the Aten with Re-Horakhty: "the august god of the primordial moment," "the creator of all that is," and "he who brightens the land with his beauty." The stress was on his primordial existence, his role as creator, and his sunlight. Altars were set up at sites from Memphis to the Delta.[58]

Intermediate stage
The Berlin relief (fig. 19) shows the falcon-headed god on the left, while on the right (often unnoticed), above the king's head, is the lower curve of the sun disk with uraei supporting large 'nḥ signs on either side of three smaller 'nḥ signs without visible means of support. The god's name is here written without cartouches, but the falcon-headed Re-Horakhty is sometimes found with two cartouches, perhaps by Year 4 (figs. 75, 76; blocks from Pylon X).

Fig. 75. The stela of Kia, with the Aten shown as a falcon-headed man, but with double cartouches (Edinburgh A.1956.347).

Fig. 76. The falcon-headed Aten in a graffito at Aswan, once again with twin cartouches.

Final stage

The falcon-headed god is replaced by adding sun's rays with human hands to the disk (fig. 20). This has cartouches and an epithet is added to them: "who is in jubilee, lord of heaven and earth." The disk is henceforth *above* the king, not in front, so that the king becomes the focus of attention. The reference to jubilee suggests that this development is connected with the first *ḥb-sd*.[59]

The daily cult

Archaeologists are trained to study the remains of buildings and attempt their theoretical (sometimes actual) reconstruction. A much harder task is to recreate the life that was lived in them. The most imposing building at Amarna, its very *raison d'être*, was the Great Temple, of which we now have the outline. What, however, happened here every day, and what was different from the standard solar ritual? Few scholars have attempted an answer.

Outside the precinct wall of the temple on the southeast, Flinders Petrie found a dump with many pans of red pottery containing resin and charcoal. Typical of his attention to the smallest details, he interpreted these as pans used for burning incense in the temple.[60] The scholar who has contributed most, however, is the specialist in religion, Aylward Blackman (1883–1956), who attempted in 1922 to recreate the Amarnan liturgy. Using the tomb reliefs, he deduced that worship of the Aten consisted mainly of offerings of food, drink, and flowers; the burning of incense; the pouring of libations; and the chanting of hymns; where the princesses are shown, they are rattling *sistra*.[61] The central difference was the absence of a cult image: there could be no anointing, so unguents were simply held up to the sky.

The crucial question is what part, if any, was played by the general population in the worship? Blackman argued for their participation, bringing animals for sacrifice and flowers as offerings.[62] Barry Kemp was able to go further, suggesting the presence not merely of "a hand-picked entourage," but real crowds. The evidence is the reference to "singing, chanting, and joyful shouting," the large spaces in front of the Great and the Small Temples, and the width of the gateways, between six and eight meters.[63]

The Aten and the royal family

Akhenaten was the chief priest of the Aten, his "First Prophet."[64] As such, he was the intermediary between the Aten and mankind; the king was the only mortal, Aldred asserted, entitled to have contact with the Aten. "There was but one god and Akhenaten was his prophet."[65] But if Akhenaten's relationship with the Aten was so special, there is one great puzzle: the Aten always holds out the sign of life also to the nostrils of Nefertiti.

The famous triad of gods in the Eighteenth Dynasty, Amun, Mut, and Khons, was replaced, according to Aldred, by Akhenaten, Nefertiti, and Meryetaten. This explains the importance of family life in Atenism.[66] Davies saw another possible new triad: the Aten, Akhenaten, and Nefertiti: "a strange anticipation of Christian Trinitarian worship in its more popular form" (!) which suggested that "the faith of Akhenaten was more than a personal eccentricity or a freak in religious thought."[67] Allen extended this even further: the old Ennead was replaced by the Aten, Akhenaten, and Nefertiti—and their six daughters.[68] The main problem with this view is that all six daughters are very rarely seen. Female deities were certainly absent, replaced by Nefertiti, as Hornung saw.[69]

There is no evidence that Akhenaten himself was worshiped as a god in the formal hymns to the Aten, as distinct from shorter prayers. The former refer to the king as the *son* of the Aten, whatever the flattery and adulation which the courtiers offered the king.[70] The very foundation of Atenism was the divine filiation of Aten and Akhenaten. This was, at the same time, a very traditional theme in Egyptian religion and politics: the king had always been the "son of Re," and the Eighteenth Dynasty had paid special attention to theogamy as a justification for rule. Atenism developed the divine filiation into a "cosmic phenomenon"; the Aten produced himself every day, and thus gave birth to his son, who was his image.[71] Hornung pointed out, however, that there "was no longer any dialogue between king and god, in contrast to the conversation of king and god which was a standard motif of earlier Egyptian art."[72] One of the features of Amarnan texts is the reference to the "teaching" (*sb3yt*) of the king.[73] This has commonly been understood as some crude ideology inflicted on Akhenaten's subjects, but Assmann has argued that this was a result of the fact that the Aten was, in contrast to all other Egyptian deities, *mute*. The word of the gods had previously been conveyed not only through the priesthood, but also by the gods themselves, especially in public appearances and in 'conversation' with the king. Although there was a priesthood of the Aten, Akhenaten was his son, and he therefore was the main interpreter of the divine.[74]

There has been considerable attention to the evolution in Egypt of 'personal piety'—prayers addressed by an individual direct to a deity without the intermediation of priests and the like—and its relationship to Atenism. Breasted thought that this type of prayer originated then,[75] but Georges Posener (1906–88) found many examples of pre-Amarnan piety on *ostraka* from Sheikh Abd al-Qurna: thanking gods for restoring sight or curing an illness, or adopting a god as a protector.[76]

Both Amarnan 'loyalty' and personal piety can be treated as literary phenomena, but this is a superficial approach, as Assmann showed.[77] A characteristic Amarnan text is found in the tomb of Ay: "worship the king, unique like the Aten, without another who is great except him, and he will grant you a lifetime in tranquility, with food and provisions which are his to give."[78] Or the tomb of May: "the one who listens to your teaching . . . shall be sated with seeing you and shall reach old age."[79] These 'beatitudes' are an Amarnan invention. 'Hearing' the king will result in well-being, old age, favor, honor, burial equipment, and eternal memory.

Universalism

There has been much controversy about whether the cult of the Aten had a universalist quality. Some have rejected it outright. Jaroslav Černý declared that on his monuments Akhenaten shows no concern for non-Egyptians.[80] Gardiner declared that the texts lend little support for a desire by Akhenaten to found a universalist religion: his interests were "almost parochial."[81]

Others have declared that, if there is a universal element, there is nothing that is new. James Baikie accepted universalism, but declared it to be a consequence of the conquests of the Thutmosids. The cult was derived from the only "non-local" aspect of the old religion: Re. Atenism therefore "had its roots deep down in the ancient Egyptian faith": that universalism was already present in the stela of Suti and Hor; in contrast, it was not present in the Shorter Hymn.[82] John Wilson noted that universalism was also a quality of Amun, adding the hymn to Amun-Re from the time of Amenhotep II.[83]

Others have drawn stronger contrasts. H.M. Stewart commented that

Contrary to what one might suppose from the study of the few
well-known hymns of the pre-Amarneh period, the contrast between
the Aten specimens and their precursors is on the whole very
marked. The emphasis on the universalist ideas is by no means comparable, and in matters of expression there are remarkably few literal
parallels. While recognising the Atenists' debt to the orthodox cult,
one might stress the perception and imagination which found there
much [*sic*] revolutionary potentialities.[84]

If one wishes to understand the difference between the views of the world
under Atenism and under Amunism, one only has to compare the "Hymn
of Victory" of Amun to Thutmose III.[85] Amun's promise to the king reads:

I give you valor and *victory* over all foreign countries; I set the glory
of you and *the fear of you* in all lands, *the terror of you* as far as the four
supports of heaven. I magnify *the awe of you* in all bodies. I set the
battle cry of your majesty throughout the Nine Bows. [Egypt's enemies].
    The great ones of *all foreign countries are gathered together in your
grasp.* I stretch out my own arms, and I tie them up for you; *I bind
the barbarians* of Nubia by ten-thousands and thousands, the northerners by hundred-thousands *as living captives.* I cause your *opponents
to fall beneath your sandals*, so that you crush the quarrelsome and
the disaffected of heart, according as I have commended to you the
earth in its length and its breadth, so that westerners and easterners
are under your oversight.
    You tread all foreign countries, your heart glad [my emphases].

The stress is on military domination, fear, and terror—the complete
opposite of Amarnan values. The only universalism is violence. Most striking of all, whereas the Aten gives life to all, Amun boasts, concerning the
enemies of the king, that he has "cut off their nostrils from the breath of life."
    Others see a contradiction. For Hornung, the Aten "is not a national,
but a universal god; he could be accepted by all humanity. . . . But Akhenaten
remains an Egyptian pharaoh, not a prophet for all the world."[86]

Most Egyptologists, however, have accepted the presence of a new universalism in Atenism. Breasted stated that the symbol of the Aten "was capable of practical introduction in the many different nations making up the empire, and could be understood by any intelligent foreigner."[87] Adolf Erman stressed that the "Great Hymn" considered "all men as children of the Aten."[88] John Foster (1920–2011) stated bluntly, "the Aten is universal."[89] For Hoffmeier the Aten was "lord of every land."[90]

Arthur Weigall offered a telling insight from art: "It is particularly noticeable that the groups of miserable captives which one sees in all such scenes of other periods, with their arms bound in agonising positions and their knees giving way under them, are entirely absent from the representations of Akhenaten's ceremonies."[91]

Frederick Giles accepted the motivation of Atenism as being "the accepted integration of diverse territorial possessions by imposing a common religion," and offered the Roman parallel of first the imperial cult and then Christianity.[92] As Assmann put it: "In contrast to earlier texts, the Hymn does not equate the world with Egypt, but understands it as embracing many lands and peoples, who differ in skin color, language and conditions of life."[93]

For many of these scholars, the "Great Hymn" is the vital evidence. In it, the Aten's rays extend over his whole creation (lines 2–5); he has created the whole earth, people, all animals large and small, all legged and winged creatures, including the east (Kharu) and south (Kush) (40–43); he creates life for all distant countries, even those who received their inundation from heaven (50–52). This is markedly different from Amun, the patron of Egyptian imperialism. Only once is that kind of concept hinted at: the Aten has subdued the world for his son (5). The evidence of the hymn can, in fact, be borne out by numerous references to the Aten. "The flat land, the hill countries and the islands of the sea" bring tribute to "the maker of their lives"; "you illuminate every land with your beauty"; the "maker of every land"; "when you give forth your rays, every land is in festival"; "when you cross the sky in peace, the entire world calls out to your face."[94]

The visual counterpart to this text is the scene in the Royal Tomb at Amarna (Room *alpha*, wall B), showing foreigners worshiping the Aten (fig. 77).[95] And there is a seldom-cited Amarna Letter, from Abdi-Milki

Fig. 77. Foreigners worshiping the Aten in room *alpha* in the Royal Tomb at Amarna.

of Tyre (*EA* 147): "My Lord is the Sun who comes forth over all lands day by day, according to the way of being of the Sun, his gracious father, who gives life by his sweet breath and returns with the north wind; who establishes the entire land in peace, by the power of his arm."

Iconoclasm

One of the most discussed features of Atenism is the antipathy toward other deities, even to the point of obliterating their names in existing monuments and texts. Helmut Brunner (1913–97) painted a dramatic picture:

> He sent out troops who ravaged all ancient monuments throughout the land seeking the hated name, to obliterate it with chisel blows. High obelisks were reached by scaffolding, hundreds of years old graves were opened, all temple walls were scoured, even the old reports of the Foreign Office, letters written in cuneiform by near eastern states rummaged through, and all portraits of Amun and words that contained his name obliterated.[96]

Aldred described a campaign "carried out with great thoroughness from one end of the kingdom to the other" that attacked objects varying in size from scarabs to temples. He went so far as to suggest that it was proof of the king's "mental collapse"![97] Redford wrote of a "widespread and thorough" iconoclasm and "an army of hatchetmen." Amun was anathematized and his temples closed. This was "a monotheism that would brook no divine manifestations."[98]

Sheer imagination can take one even further. Eleanore Bille-de-Mot asserted: "We are told nothing of what happened to Amun's priests; but we may presume that they were pitilessly hunted down, banished, reduced to servitude."[99] This is what Reeves called the "terror." He wrote of "paranoia" and "streets filled with pharaoh's soldiers." What is the evidence? Manetho writing on the Hyksos.[100]

What has not, however, ever been pointed out is that *we know absolutely nothing about the identity of the agents, or their numbers, or the instructions which they were given!* Particular antagonism was shown to Amun, excised everywhere, even in royal names.[101] Referring to the Theban tombs, Davies declared it "entertaining" to see that the Amun of the name Amunhotep (IV) remained uninjured in all the tombs of the "Atenists," although it was obliterated in the name of Akhenaten's father![102] In the tomb of of Kheruef (TT 192), the names only of Amun and the plural "gods" (ntrw) have been erased, but not the names of other deities, and not the king's cartouches.[103] The name of Amun was removed even from the tip of Hatshepsut's obelisk at Karnak—because this kind of monument was especially associated with the sun.[104] And in Nubia, at Amenhotep III's temple at Soleb, where Akhenaten also appears, most of the old gods' names are respected. Amun is the target.[105]

Re was the great solar god. The alliance between the Aten at Amarna and Re at Heliopolis and Memphis continued to be strong.[106] It seems that Amun excited most special opposition where he was associated with Re, such as on the upper terrace at Deir al-Bahari. Other gods "with no solar pretensions" escaped erasure.[107] Baikie, as always, had insights: the names of the two youngest princesses were compounded with Re, in contrast to the first four, whose names all included the Aten. This suggested "a modification of the bitter intolerance of the middle period."[108] Sayed Tawfik went so far as to suggest that the Aten was simply Re by another name. One of Akhenaten's names was Waenre; his younger daughters had names compounded with Re, as did many officials and priests. Pawah was "Greatest of the Seers of the Aten in the house of Re."[109] The tomb of May (TA 14) refers to Akhet-Aten "within which is the sustenance of Re."[110] The tomb of Ay (TA 25) is most interesting: "may you see Re at the morning when he rises on the eastern horizon, and may you see the Aten when he sets in the western horizon."[111] The important question that then arises is why Akhenaten chose a separate name for his solar god. Tawfik suggested that the priesthood of Re, like that of Amun, had become too powerful. This rather contradicts his evidence for its close association with the Aten.[112] There are, in fact, two extraordinary and unnoticed references to Re, which support Tawfik's case: "Akhet-Aten, the beautiful place you made for Re," and "Akhet-Aten, which Re made to be given to his son."[113]

The other most important deity was Osiris. Alexandre Moret used the example of the Hymn to Osiris by Amenmose, Overseer of Flocks, to test the extent of excisions.[114] The "Amun" of the donor's name has been hammered out, but the names of all the other gods are untouched.[115]

Ludwig Borchardt noted the prevalence at Amarna of figures of baboons, the animal sacred to Thoth, a god whose center was at nearby Hermopolis. Atenism apparently "was not at all opposed" to the cult of this god.[116] Marianne Eaton-Krauss noted that in Tutankhamun's "Restoration Stela" only two gods are mentioned: Amun and Ptah; the latter's name was damaged only in the Theban area. And in the great Theban complex of the temples of Amun, Montu, and Mut, only 50 percent of private statues were defaced.[117]

Aidan Dodson suggested that the erasures of the word *nṯrw* may not have been the result of objections to the concept of multiple gods, but rather the result of Akhenaten's objection to Amun's claim to be "King of the Gods"—something intolerable to the all-powerful Aten; the erasures were intended to nullify that epithet, rather than deny the existence of the broader pantheon.[118]

Gabolde, who offered very detailed documentation, played down the extent of this aspect of Atenism. The action was originally directed only at Amun. That god's name suffered the main force. There was no attack on Osiris at Abydos or the gods of Memphis. There was nothing like the army of hammerers commonly imagined.[119]

A crucial matter is the date of these attacks on rivals to the Aten. Tawfik pointed out that the blocks from Akhenaten's Karnak temple mention a priest of Selqet, Hathor, and Mut, as well as the plural "gods."[120] Redford dated the dispatch of agents to hack out the name of Amun to Year 5,[121] while Gabolde suggested that the action began in Year 6.[122] Laboury drew attention to the survival of the hierarchy of Amun as late as Year 4, when the high priest was helping build the domain of the Aten![123] He therefore suggested Years 5/6.[124] Reeves dated the "terror" to Year 10.[125] Aldred suggested that the serious iconoclasm occurred toward the end of the reign, no earlier than Year 15. An important piece of evidence is the shrine made for Tiye by Akhenaten, which bore both the Later form of the name of the Aten and also the Amun-featuring nomen of Amenhotep III (of which the Amun element was later erased). On the basis of the god's name, the construction of the shrine was dated at the earliest to Year 9[126] or even after Year 12. Dodson also argued that the persecution of Amun began late in the reign, adding an apparent Amun-foundation of Smenkhkare who, he argued, died about Year 13/14, well within Akhenaten's reign.[127] The conclusion to be drawn is obvious: *we do not know the answer.* One thing, however, is sure: in Year 5, the steward of Memphis reported to his king that the offerings to all the deities in Memphis had been made![128]

Personal names at Amarna also reveal paradoxes. One of the vine-dressers recorded on a wine-jar docket was named Amenemhet; there were also the scribe Amenemopet; Ptahmay, chief maker of gold leaf in the House of the Aten; Thutmose, the chief sculptor at Amarna; and Thutmose, Viceroy of Nubia.[129] The general Ramose, in contrast, had changed his name from Ptahmose when he served under Amenhotep III.[130] Meryneith similarly changed his name to Meryre.

It has, furthermore, frequently been noted that the iconoclasm was very careless.[131] The evidence for this is somewhat bizarre—for example, that the excisions at Karnak were far from complete. It could hardly have been otherwise at a temple of this size. The strangeness of this matter is shown by the extraordinary explanations which have been offered: that the campaign may not have been on the orders of Akhenaten, but is rather to be attributed to fanatics protected by some high court official, or initiated toward the end of the reign by 'purists,' horrified at the idea of a rapprochement with Amun! It has also been suggested that the operators were illiterate: they cut out not only the bilateral sign *mn* in Amun, but the *mn* in "to remain." *Mwt* (mother) was also mistaken on occasion for the ideogram of the goddess Mut.[132]

The hacking out of names is one thing. What of the cults and temples of the gods whose names were defaced? Few have bothered to raise this question. Ronald Leprohon uses as evidence the "Restoration Stela" of Tutankhamun, which asserts that "the temples and cities of the gods and goddesses, starting from Elephantine as far as the Delta marshes . . . were fallen into decay and their shrines were fallen into ruin, having become mere mounds overgrown with grass. Their sanctuaries were like something that has not come into being and their buildings were a footpath."[133] Redford pointed to the *talatat* texts which show that early on in Karnak over 13,000 workers were employed on the temple building, including many identified as being from Lower Egypt.[134] On the basic question whether the temples were closed down or simply left to rot, Hoffmeier stressed the enormous diversion of resources involved in the building of the vast temple at Karnak and the new capital. This would, in effect, have starved the other temples of resources.[135]

We must be on guard against mere propaganda, but the statements here seem specific. Even in the Theban years, temple revenues began to be dominated by Aten: "The revenues of every god are measured in *oipe*, but for the Aten, one measures in heaps."[136] Kemp, however, properly described the "Restoration Stela" as "tendentious, even malicious."[137] He cited the mention of an Amun-foundation in Year 3 of Neferneferu-aten,[138] which he took as falling before Tutankhamun's accession, and also the functioning of the temple of Horus at Buhen in Akhenaten's reign,[139] although there is no evidence for any antipathy toward Horus. It is highly ironic that the temples of Akhenaten's predecessors have survived while his have been totally demolished!

What one most requires is a little historical context. Destruction of the monuments (and therefore the memory and existence in the afterlife) of predecessors was commonplace in Egypt. An outstanding example is the tomb of Rekhmire, vizier to Thutmose III and Amenhotep II (TT 100). His memory has been completely destroyed. His face was almost universally obliterated, even where it is very high and a ladder must have been needed. The author of this was Amenhotep II. Davies described the Atenists as "still more thorough," but their aim was not the man, but the names of Amun, Mut, Karnak, the word "gods," and the leopard skin of the priests.[140]

Most infamous of all was the treatment of Hatshepsut by Thutmose III. Almost every mention of the queen was hacked from the walls of Deir al-Bahari and the forest of statues in the colonnade was smashed and buried in the vast pit dug in the causeway.[141] The colossi and sphinxes from the temple were brutally defaced, even by fire, and the features battered, and then they were smashed into fragments: "every conceivable indignity had been heaped on the likenesses of the fallen queen."[142] A striking example of the parallels is provided by Gebel Silsila, where most of the chapels suffered this double defacement.[143]

From Amarna and the sequel comes an instructive contrast. In the tomb of Ramose (TT 55), in the 'traditional scene' (fig. 9), the name Amenhotep (IV) was not touched by the Atenists. The Amunists, however, defaced the cartouches of the Aten and cut through his rays, and destroyed the cartouches of Amenhotep and Nefertiti in the Amarnan scene.[144]

The afterlife

Amarnan texts are full of references to the dead. Early in the reign, Ptah-may, chief maker of gold leaf of the House of the Aten, asked for offerings of "all good and pure things": bread, beer, cool water, oxen, fowl, wine, incense, and milk, and all sorts of fresh plants. The dead asked the Aten to give them breath in order to see the god every day and to breathe the fragrant north wind. The titles "justified" and Osiris were still used.[145]

In an important study, Etienne Drioton examined three funer-ary monuments of the period.[146] The shabti of Lady Py made much of "breathing the north wind."[147] This doctrine of the breezes went back to at least the time of Thutmose III.[148] In the Amarnan context it was now necessary for the reawakening of the deceased after the night, when living and dead alike slept. The stela of Panehsy in the Louvre showed the deceased before a table of offerings under the Aten. Both the disk and the king are called "my god." Horakhty is called "Lord of Eternity" (*nb ḏt*), a title of Osiris.[149] The stela served the same purpose as previously the false door in the tomb. The earliest monument of the three, a lintel of Hatiay, still shows Osiris.[150]

At the other end of the spectrum was the prayer of Akhenaten for his own mother on the shrine he made for her: "When the Aten appears in his horizon, his rays lift you up at dawn in order to see him every day. May you live on the *ka* of the living Aten, may you breathe the air with finest incense."[151]

The fullest idea of the afterlife under the Aten, however, is given by Ay:[152]

Be adored when you rise in the horizon, O Aten! You [Ay] shall
not cease from seeing Re. Open your [eyes] to see him. When you
pray to him, may he listen to what you say. The breath of life, may
it enter your nose. Raise yourself up on your right side, so that you
may place yourself on your left side. May your *ba* [soul] be glad on
the highland. May the children of your house make offerings for
you (of) bread, beer, water, and breath for your *ka*. May you stride
through the gates of the underworld. May you see Re at dawn at his
appearance in the eastern horizon; and may you see the Aten at his
setting in the western horizon of heaven. May you be given offerings and provisions from the offering-trough of the House of the

Aten. May you be given incense and libation from the "staircase of the living one," the Aten. It is the king, the Aten's son, who decrees it to you continually. May you receive all that comes forth in his presence every day, without ceasing. May you receive all gifts in the necropolis when your *ba* rests in your tomb. May your *ba* not be opposed in what it wants, but be content with the daily offerings—(with) the intelligence lasting and the heart in its proper position beside the lord of continuity. May your name be pronounced every day continually forever, as is done for an excellent favorite like you! For the *ka* of the one whose favors are enduring in the presence of the Lord of the Two Lands, the Father of the God Ay, justified.

This picture contains two fundamental ideas: that the deceased would see Re/the Aten during the day, and would receive offerings/libations. Ay's tomb uses the Earlier form of the Aten name. Similar concepts are found in the tombs of Meryre i, Pentju, Tutu,[153] and Tiye's steward Huya, which uses the Later form of the Aten name. According to the last:

'May you [the Aten] cause me to be continually in the place of favor, in my tomb of justification; (and as for) my *ba*, may it come forth to see your rays and receive nourishment from its offerings. May one be summoned by name and come at the voice. May I partake of the things which issue [from the presence, that I might eat *shenes*-loaves, *bit*-pastry, offering loaves, jugs <of beer>, roasted meat, hot food, cool water, wine, milk, everything which issues [from the Mansion of the Aten in Akhet-Aten].' For the *ka* of the favorite of the Lord of the Two Lands, the overseer of the royal quarters, treasurer, steward in the house of the King's [Chief Wife Tiye, Huya, justified].[154]

Funerals, of course, remained important. It is Ay again who gives a description, in traditional terms: "May you be united with your place of eternity, and may your mansion of eternity receive you, with oxen dragging you and a lector priest in front of you, purifying the catafalque with milk."

It is often stated that there is only one depiction of a funeral in the Amarnan tombs, in that of Tiye's steward Huya (fig. 66). The deceased stands behind offerings on which a priest pours libations, with mourners around:

May a "boon the king gives" offering be made for you, consisting of your bread and the beer of your house. May libation be made to you of water from your pool, and may there [be] brought [to you fruit(?)] from your trees. May invocation be made for you [with the] ritual (?) of Aten. May you be offered *pat*-cakes upon the offering table on behalf of your *ka* [every day], and may your name be remembered: the overseer of the royal [quarters], the overseer of the double treasury, Huya, justified.[155]

The deceased wears the traditional Osirian beard.[156]

It is not true that Huya's is the only funeral depicted at Amarna. Even more striking is the funeral of Akhenaten and Nefertiti's (three?) daughters in the Royal Tomb, where the parents are shown in grief before their biers (figs. 104, 105).[157] As Gabolde observes, however, these reliefs show that the only two elements of traditional funerary rites retained were the lamentation over the unmummified body, and the statue of the deceased.[158]

Other important evidence is provided by the same tomb, which contained shabtis, but without any summons to work as in traditional ones. There were scarabs, but they did not beg for mercy from Osiris. The most striking innovation of this tomb, however, is shown on the corners of Akhenaten's sarcophagus, where the place of the four traditional protective goddesses was taken by Nefertiti (fig. 102).

The graves of the ordinary Amarnians have only recently become known. Excavations by the Egypt Exploration Society and Amarna Trust from 2005 have at last revealed their cemeteries, southeast of the tomb of Ay. The burials show various signs of affluence: the body covered with matting, or in a 'stick' coffin or a wooden one. Some had a stela, but they have no inscriptions. There is, therefore, apart from their simplicity, no evidence of popular thoughts about the afterlife.

Outside Amarna, there is little evidence. At Thebes the coffin of Hatiay, Overseer of Granaries of the Temple of the Aten, is completely traditional.[159] At Deir al-Medina, the burials of Setau and three female relatives are Osirian, with the exception of the woman Taat, whose coffin has only references to her family, perhaps explained by the fact that she died at Amarna and was later transferred here.[160]

In general, Robert Hari writes of "a silence—which seems to have been organized around death," and of an "illogicality": there is an indifference affected toward death in the texts, "a negative element in the creation of Aten." The word "death" *(mwt)* appears, indeed, but twice in the Amarnan texts: in the "Great Hymn," referring to the world being dead when the Aten sets (lines 8, 69). Death is therefore like night; in that case, as Hari stressed, after death there is also an awakening. Akhenaten had stripped away all the old Osirian mythology, but retained the mummy and the *ka*. It was a spiritual religion that stopped short.[161]

Hornung stated that the hereafter "simply did not exist anymore." Both living and dead are awakened each morning by the Aten: "All the world is thus oriented to the East, while the West, the realm of the dead since time immemorial, has fallen into oblivion." The deceased receive their offerings in the temple at Amarna. Hornung went so far as to suggest that those who died away from that city were "bereft of any connection with the Aten."[162]

Brunner's judgment was that Akhenaten did not succeed in creating a credible relationship between his god and the dark sides of life, especially death and overcoming it.[163] Davies long before had made a momentous suggestion: "The failure of Atenism to present any vivid and detailed hopes for the future life . . . may have been a main cause of its final failure."[164]

Atenism and ethics

Wilson, who came from a strong Christian background, firmly rejected any ethical content in Atenism:

> Akh-en-Aton's faith was intellectual rather than ethical; its strong emotional content derived from the fervor of the discoverer and convert, who rejected past forms and preached new forms. The conviction of right and wrong was not ethical, but was a passionate reiteration that the new was right and the old was wrong. Aton's blessings were primarily physical; he made and sustained life. The worshipper was called upon to render gratitude for that life, but was in no text called upon to render to the god an upright and ethically correct life in his social relations or in his innermost heart. The

universalism of the Aton could have carried the implication that all men are equal under the god and should be so treated, but such a logical conclusion is strikingly absent from the texts.

Connected with this was the famous/notorious question of a possible influence on the Hebrews. Wilson argued against this on practical grounds: none of them could have known about this cult, which was so limited in time and space. The question then arises of how to explain the oft-claimed similarities between the "Great Hymn" and Psalm 104. In a curious piece of explanation, Wilson suggested that while Atenism was a cult of a "fleeting and superficial nature," it drew on religious ideas that preceded it, ideas that also survived it, and these are the sources of any Egyptian influence on the Hebrews.[165] This is remarkably similar to the stance of Ronald Williams: the hymn is half a millennium earlier than the psalm, and belongs to an anathematized religion, but "just as the Aten hymn itself owed much to the earlier hymns to Amun-Re, so later Egyptian sun-hymns incorporated ideas and phrases from that of Akhenaten."[166] A recent lengthy study by a Biblical scholar, James Hoffmeier, declared the similarities to be "banal" and the means of influence difficult.[167]

Hayes was curt: Atenism contained "little or no ethical content."[168] Gardiner also declared that there was a "complete lack of ethical teaching." He attributed this in good part to the elimination of Osiris.[169] Assmann noted that immortality and justice were two religious ideas "absolutely crucial for the Egyptians and conspicuous by their complete absence from Akhenaten's hymn. . . . Truth and justice were now identical with the will of the king and his teachings." God had previously stood by the needy and oppressed on earth; now he was only light and time.[170]

Baikie had earlier approached the question in his own way: he detected no ethical content in the two Aten hymns, but admitted that we have too little material to know. He offered the devastating comment that the text so often compared to these hymns, Psalm 104, was equally devoid.[171]

It is strange that no one could remember what one of the most famous scholars had stated in 1912. Breasted admitted that it was "remarkable" that there was so little reference to ethical matters, but it was "inconceivable that the Amarna movement should have rejected the highly developed ethics of Heliopolis." It placed, moreover, endless emphasis on Maat.[172]

Weigall added an insightful observation: "One may search the inscriptions in vain for any reference to a malignant power, to vengeance, to jealousy, or to hatred."[173]

Baudouin van de Walle drew attention to texts that can only refer to the moral doctrines of Atenism. Ay was "true-hearted to the one who confided in him," but more importantly "one who abandoned falsehood in order to do Maat." May, the King's Fan-bearer, described himself as "one who was straightforward on behalf of the Lord of the Two Lands and effective for his lord who placed Maat in my body and detestation of falsehood." And Tutu, the chamberlain, stated: "Maat makes her abode in me: I am not rapacious, I do not do evil, I do nothing which your son (the king) hates." "My voice is not loud in the king's house. I do not swagger in the palace, I do not receive the reward of wrongdoing in order to repress Maat falsely, but I do what is righteous to the king. I act only in accordance to what he decrees as my charge." "I made no concealment with respect to any case of wrongdoing in any business of his Person when I was chief spokesman of the entire land." Even more directly, Ay declared that he was a "righteous one devoid of wrong doing," and Tutu laid down a challenge: "no instance of any wickedness of mine can be found."[174]

Predecessors of Atenism

As early as 1924, Walter Wolf (1900–73) directed our attention to two earlier texts: the "Hymn to Amun-Re" and the "Hymn of the architects Suti and Hor."[175] The former, which dates to around the time of Amenhotep II, is remarkable testimony to Amun's ability to subsume all other deities: principally Re, but also Min, Horus, and Khepri. It is an unashamed celebration of Egypt's imperial position at the time: "Far reaching of stride, presiding over Upper Egypt, Lord of the Madjoi and ruler of Punt." He is celebrated as the creator god, taking over from Atum-Re: "father of the gods, who made mankind and created the beasts." Amun is awesome: "The lord of fear, great of dread, rich in might, terrible of appearances"; "he extends his arms to whom he loves, but his enemy is consumed by flame."

In the middle of this hymn, however, is embedded a hymn to the sun:

The love of you is spread throughout the Two Lands,
When your rays shine forth in the eyes.

The good of the people is your arising;
The cattle grow languid when you shine.
The love of you is in the southern sky;
The sweetness of you is in the northern sky.
The beauty of you carries away hearts;
The love of you makes arms languid;
Your beautiful form relaxes the hands;
And hearts are forgetful at the sight of you.
You are the sole one, who made [all] that is,
[The] solitary sole [one], who made what exists,
From whose eyes mankind came forth,
And upon whose mouth the gods came into being.
He who made herbage [for] the cattle,
And the fruit tree for mankind,
Who made that (on which) the fish in the river may live,
And the birds soaring in the sky,
He who gives breath to that which is in the egg,
Gives life to the son of the slug,
And makes that on which gnats may live,
And worms and flies in like manner;
Who supplies the needs of the mice in their holes,
And gives life to flying things in every tree.
Hail, to you, who did all this!
Solitary sole one, with many hands.[176]

The prefiguring of Amarna is remarkable. The second major text seen as a forerunner of Atenism is the Hymn of Suti and Hor, two architects who served Amenhotep III.[177] It begins "Praising Amun," but it praises Re, who takes in the falcon Horus, the scarab beetle Kheper, and the creators Khnum and Amun. At the end he is called "the sole lord," but Wilson pointed out that in the surrounding scenes, Suti and Hor worship a whole host of other gods![178]

The terms of the praise of Re are again important as a forerunner of Atenism:

Hail to you, sun-disk of the daytime, creator of all and maker of their living! Great falcon, bright of plumage, scarab beetle who has elevated himself, self-created, who was not born! Horus, the first-born in the midst of the sky-goddess, for whom they make jubilation at rising, as well as at his setting! The fashioner of that which the soil produces, the Khnum and Amun of mankind. He who seizes upon the Two Lands, (from) great to small. A mother of profit to gods and men; a patient craftsman, greatly wearying (himself) as their maker, without number; valiant herdsman, driving his cattle, their refuge and the maker of their living.

In light of this, Gardiner went so far as to declare that the "Great Hymn" "contains little that had not been said in earlier hymns to the sun god."[179]

Gerhard Fecht, for his part, demonstrated the careful construction of the architects' hymn in symmetrical and matching strophes ("a literary masterpiece") and its importance in religious history ("an early form of the Amarna dogma"). The elevation of the Aten entailed the subordination of Horus. Amun is mentioned after Khnum so as not to be taken as a sun god (Amun-Re). He is in the poem only as an aspect of the Aten, like Khnum, often shown ram-headed. Ptah (unnamed) is also present as "the patient craftsman." Finally, the king appears as the herdsman. The three sun gods and three creator gods are thus all subordinated to the Aten, with whom the king has a special relationship.

In the continuation of this hymn, again the sun-disk *(itn)* is referred to in its pre-Amarnan sense. At the end, a claim is made to universalism ("every land"). The morning (Khepri) and midday (Re-Horakhty) sun are celebrated, but the setting sun (Atum) is not mentioned, although it had been mentioned in the first hymn to Re.

Fecht, however, called attention to the vital differences between this hymn and the Amarnan theology: Re has the surname Khepri (in the morning), and he makes the night voyage; the god is not given cartouches; the king is mentioned, but not yet given his later importance; Shu is absent. At the same time, the various creator gods are subordinate to the Aten. Nut is "demythologized" and there is an "affront" to Amun-Re, but it is not aggressive. The abolition of the old posthumous world was the great "weakness" of the Amarnan cult. It is significant that this stela ends with a "death text" which links with the second part of the hymn to Re, and the god's nightly journey followed by rebirth. Amun is mentioned, but separated from Re. Fecht found this so striking that he suggested that it had to have the support of a high authority.[180]

Alexandre Piankoff (1897–1966) pointed to other earlier Eighteenth Dynasty religious texts: the funerary Book of Amduat ("that which is in the Underworld") and the Litany of Re, first found during the reign of Thutmose III.[181] These texts celebrated Re as the creator god, who appeared under seventy-five names of the other gods ("his form is that of each god"). The Aten was simply his visible manifestation. Each night when Re "set," he traveled in a boat beneath the earth, to be reborn each morning in the east, undergoing many transformations and gaining in strength.[182]

The evidence has, in fact, been accumulating for years that the Aten—as an entity, but not necessarily a god—was part of Egyptian religion at least as far back as the Middle Kingdom. This evidence has been well known since the beginning of the twentieth century.

An *itn* appears in the Coffin Texts of the Middle Kingdom as the disk in which a god (usually Re) resides. The disk is also commonly associated with sunshine *(i3ḥw)*. Less commonly, the disk may have been a deity. In the Story of Sinuhe, at the death of Amenemhat I, "the king was united with the *itn*, returning to him who begat him." To his successor Senwosret belongs "what the *itn* encircles daily," stressing the universal domination of the king. The king's splendor, furthermore, is likened to the shining of the *itn*: "he (Amenemhat III) is the one who brightens the Two Lands more than the *itn*."[183] The *itn* is also a symbol of victory in battle, associated with Sekhmet and Hathor.[184] Similar examples are numerous from the earlier Eighteenth Dynasty.[185]

In 1931, Alan Shorter (1905–38) published a commemorative scarab of Thutmose IV.[186] Its text, as translated more recently by Betsy Bryan, runs as follows:

> The chiefs of Naharin bearing their revenue espy Menkheperure proceeding from his house. They hear his voice like the son of Nut, his bow being in his hand like the son of Shu's successors (?). As to when he extends himself in order to fight, the *itn* (?) being before him, he destroys the mountain countries, trampling the desert countries, treading to Naharin and to Karoy in order to cause that the foreign countries should be like *rekhyt* [according to] the control of the *itn* (?), forever.[187]

This text was described by Shorter as "of the first historical importance" because it made sense of the scattered references to Thutmose IV at Amarna, and was evidence that the Aten was already in existence and worshiped as a god of battles.[188] Like other crucial Amarnan evidence, however, this text is now suspect. The scarab itself has been subjected to chemical tests and found genuine, but the language of the text raises concerns: the unadorned king's prenomen, his residence, and the writing of the alleged name of the Aten. Is it a genuine scarab, with an unreliable inscription?

Undoubted mention of the *itn* is common by the reign of Amenhotep III.[189] While the collection of evidence is impressive, it must nonetheless be placed in context. The main god of Amenhotep III was Amun: the king was his son, Amun was the source of his victories, the god had a barge, and the king's mortuary temple in Western Thebes was dedicated to him.[190]

While the word *itn* is on occasion found with a divine determinative as far back as Thutmose I, there is no sign of any formal cult of the Aten prior to the death of Amenhotep III.[191]

A special note is required about a supposed temple of the Aten at Thebes under Amenhotep III. The originator of this fancy was Stephen Glanville, when he published an inscription on a box naming Penbury "Scribe of the Treasury of the Temple of the Aten."[192] There was no mention of a king's name, but Glanville nonetheless assigned the inscription to Amenhotep III. He reasoned that a temple of the Aten could not be later than Akhenaten, but neither could it belong to his reign because it mentioned Amun—in a personal name. It should therefore be dated to Amenhotep III. This "evidence" took in even Wilson,[193] but Murnane dated the text to Tutankhamun,[194] although, as noted above, 'Amun' names are still known during the early years of Akhenaten.

It has thus become accepted that much in the Amarnan sun cult had precedents. The essential differences between the traditional sun cult and that of Amarna are, however, of much greater significance.[195] Re traditionally crossed the sky in his bark and was depicted in many guises and associated with many other deities. Tendencies to division and unity were in opposition—but there was no trace of mankind. All older forms of the sun cult—Re, Khepre, Atum, and Horakhty—were now abandoned, although Horakhty lingered in the didactic name of the Aten until the shift to its Later form. For the first time a god's name was put in two cartouches, like a king's. Nothing was known about the Aten before his enthronement: everything about him was encapsulated in the double name, and after Year 4, he appeared only as a rayed sun disk.

The old and the new

The scholar who has made the most sustained contribution here is Assmann, and his views have modified over time. He began by making a very strong case for the great distinction between the pre-Amarnan cult of the sun and its form under Akhenaten. In the former, the basic event was Re's journey across the sky, under so many forms and names, and his nightly journey until rebirth, accompanied by so many other deities, expressing the complementarity of Egyptian religious belief. Assmann suggested that the exclusivity of the Amarnan version was such a drastic change that it could properly be called a "heresy" (but see p. 12).

From Year 4, all animal and human forms of deity were banished, and the god was represented only by a disk with rays ending in hands. The light of the sun had never been worshiped before. It replaced anthropomorphic representation of deity and all forms of symbolic representation, and could not be given sculpted form. There were no more conversations between god and king: the Aten never spoke. The god of light was, in fact, a king, with cartouches. He reigned "with and over the king." The created world became nature. Was a religion possible, however, without a personal link between god and man? In the Aten cult, the king incorporated the god in personal relations with mankind.[196]

These thoughts could be developed further. The Amarnan religion was a real revolution because it contradicted the classical cults in various ways: the old duality was abolished, and there was no more opposition to the sun god in his nightly course. There was no need to maintain the world any more. The Aten was singular.

The old relationship between cosmic and social order was replaced by a unified universe with man as partner of divine action. Maat disappeared from the cosmos and became 'truth' rather than 'justice' in society. The king was son of, and coregent with, the Aten.

Assmann saw a theme that pointed in this same direction in the stress on divine intention and action in the reign of Hatshepsut (the Punt expedition, the divine birth at Deir al-Bahari).[197] Piety, in short, replaced the

Middle Kingdom virtue of wisdom, and divine will replaced unchange-able cosmic cycles and the justice (Maat) underpinning social life, as in the teaching of Amenemopet, two generations later.[198] Even the king relied on divine favor, primarily through piety.[199] Another fundamental change was the loss of religious festivals. These were crucial to all Egyptians for their social identity, based on allegiance to a town and its deity.[200]

More recently, however, Assmann has attempted to show the Amarnan solar cult more as a phase in a long development. He assembled the enor-mous number of solar texts from the Old Kingdom to the Empire and was able to distinguish a number of phases: "traditional" solar religion going back to the Old Kingdom; a "new solar theology" beginning with Amen-hotep III, independent of the Amarna cult, which would have developed even if Amarna had not occurred; and the post-Amarnan and Ramesid texts which continued uninterruptedly from the pre-Amarnan ones.

Assmann went so far as to describe the "new solar theology" as having "considerable influences" on Amarnan religion, but it was not itself influenced by Amarna. In this case, Amarna appears as a momentary dead end, an offshoot of a much more sustained religious development. The influence of Amarna, he posited, is seen paradoxically in the response of the Theban cult of Amun, which in Ramesid times became "pantheistic." What made the Amarnan religion "heretical" was its intolerance and its theology of kingship.[201]

Hornung also acknowledged the combination of revolution and tra-dition. The revolution "expressed itself for the most part in conventional forms": the Aten was worshiped under Thutmose IV and Amenhotep III, and the change of capital was nothing new. Akhenaten's changes, how-ever, were "intolerable" to the Egyptians: the replacement of "mythical statement by rational statement, many-valued logic by two-valued logic, and the gods by God." Akhenaten was not a visionary, but a "methodical rationalist," a virtuoso manipulator of the power of institutions. And the changes were made gradually: from henotheism, to syncretism, to mono-theism by Year 9 [sic]. Myth was abolished, and Akhenaten became the sole intermediary to whom the Egyptians prayed. The one and the many were no longer complementary but mutually exclusive. "The change in logic is surely the intellectual core of this revolution, which for a few years anticipated Western modes of thought."[202]

Brunner emphasized further contrasts. In the first place, in classical Egyptian religion, the gods were powerful, but ambiguous. They could be dangerous or helpful. They had "two faces." Akhenaten's single god, by contrast, was "only good": his love was manifest in society and nature. Secondly, nature, which Egyptians regarded as "harsh and sober," with everything having its unsentimental place, was now the source for knowing god and the proof that even the smallest part of nature was under his care.[203]

No one has summed up better than Redford—admittedly from an unsympathetic stance—the differences between the old religion and Atenism:

> No mythology surrounds his god; apart from a brief period at the beginning of his reign, no anthropomorphic depiction is permitted. The rich potential of mythological symbolism in art, cult, and magic can no longer be realised, as it is everywhere interdicted. Thus, the ever-growing and creative thought of an intelligent polytheism is repressed. The subtle and profound syncretism of Egyptian religion which produced the Memphite Theology is viewed with suspicion and hostility; Akhenaten's god does not absorb; he excludes and annihilates! No truth can come from anyone but the king; no teaching but his is to be accepted. The multifarious and mysterious world of the Beyond, so central to Egyptian religious lore, is swept away at a stroke. There is no further need for the age-old tradition of the mortuary cult, for the welfare of the deceased depends only on hearkening to the king's teaching. The complexity of the cultus, depending as it does on actualized myth and its symbols, becomes the thing of the past. No cultic acts beyond the simple offering are permitted. Gone are the elaborate temples where such cultic acts were carried on. Gone, too, are the cult images, the focal points of those cults. The multiplicity of divine names and the concept of divine forms as a sequence of voluntary or necessary modes of existence are both foreign to Akhenaten; the only designation of the deity that is tolerated is the time-honored solar one, which has, however, been reduced to the status of a mere epithet.[204]

Was Atenism monotheism?

The most important question of all regarding the Amarnan religion is obviously whether it was "monotheism," in the sense understood by Judaism, Christianity, and Islam. Flinders Petrie did not commit himself, but was enthusiastic. He described Atenism as an "express appreciation of the power of the radiant energy of the sun . . . a truly philosophic view . . . which anticipated the course of thought by some thousands of years."[205]

The classification of Atenism as "henotheism" (belief in and worship of a single god while accepting the existence or possible existence of other deities) has understandably been attractive. Davies described Atenism as "little more than a beautifully expressed and humanized henotheism."[206] For Laboury, the texts claim primacy for the Aten, not uniqueness, although he also wrote of "a visceral rejection of all other deities" and suggested that the epithet "living" for the Aten implied that all other gods were dead.[207]

Wilson described the cult not as monotheism, but as syncretism (the combining of different, often contradictory beliefs). It was not monotheism because Akhenaten also was a god.[208] Siegfried Morenz (1914–70) identified a trinity: Akhenaten was "in no sense an advocate of simple monotheism"; his cult was rather a "trinitarian formulation": Re-Horakhty, Shu, and the Aten. Morenz was fundamentally unsympathetic, writing of "theologians hammering out these sophistries."[209]

The overwhelming majority of scholars, however, accept Akhenaten's monotheism—albeit not without qualification. The first to propose this was Alfred Wiedemann (1856–1936) in 1884.[210] In Breasted's view the Aten was "the sole god."[211] For Gardiner, it was "a genuine monotheism."[212] Redford declared it "unabashedly monotheistic."[213] For Hari, "there can be no doubt: we have here for the first time in the history of humanity the establishment of a monotheistic religion."[214] Assmann was equally emphatic: Akhenaten was "the first founder of a monotheistic religion in the history of mankind." Assmann pointed out, however, a vital distinction between the monotheism of Akhenaten and the later Mosaic monotheism. The former was not a redemptive religion, appealing to a soul and alienating its believers from the world; it incorporated its followers into the world.[215] Foster was eloquent: "Aten is one. He is a unity, the only deity, the lord of the universe."[216] Hoffmeier stressed that the word "unique" *(w')*, applied to gods since the Old Kingdom, now indicated monotheism.[217]

Evaluations of this monotheism could vary. Louis Zabkar (1914–94) declared that "the theological axiom, 'There is no god but God' is the highest achievement of the Amarna movement."[218] Hayes accepted that it was monotheism, but "it was not of great significance to the history of the world religion," because worship was confined to the royal family.[219] For Aldred it was monotheism—but "nothing revolutionary . . . an austere . . . unyielding monotheism," which in the form of attack on Amun, he suggested, "may reflect a mental collapse"![220]

Redford's work at Thebes made him more aware of Atenism's development. The *Gm(t)-p3-'Itn* was polytheistic because this temple was used for the *Ḥb-sd*: Horus, the Souls of Nekhen, the Souls of Pe, jackals, scorpions, Selqet, Geb, even Amun, and 'the gods' were all present. Outside Thebes in these Years 1 to 5, the other gods continued to appear. After that time, however, he took the view that "the Sun-disk was unique and supreme over all the universe, the only god there was."[221] Hornung upheld Atenism's monotheism very vigorously, but dated its full acceptance to Year 9.[222]

What else, however, but monotheism can one call a religion which speaks of its god as "sole god, without another beside him" ("Great Hymn," line 39)?

Motives

Now that the characteristics of Atenism have been elucidated, we can ask a further important question. What were the motives for Akhenaten's religious revolution? Fate has once again dealt us a miserable hand. The speech Akhenaten gave about religion in the early part of his reign in Thebes is mostly too damaged to give any sense.[223] All we can see is a reference to something falling into ruin (temples?), the king asserting his religious knowledge,[224] and special mention of the unique solar creator god.

It has long been suggested that Atenism was an attempt to break the exclusiveness and power of the cult of Amun. Moret in 1908 was representative of his time: "To sever the relations between the state and the sacerdotal class, who administer the official religion, has proved an arduous task in any country and in any age." He pointed to the power of the priests of Amun—the god who sponsored the expulsion of the Hyksos and the growth of the empire—including the part they allegedly played in the upheavals in the time of Hatshepsut: "The high priests of Amun had concocted these intrigues, by turn giving and withdrawing their support. They had thus become, in very truth, the governors of the palace." He gave as examples Hapuseneb under Hatshepsut, and Ptahmose, high priest of Amun and vizier under Amenhotep III.[225]

Drioton and Vandier concurred with the theory of an attack on Amunism.[226] Wilson admitted that the Eighteenth Dynasty had greatly increased the power of the priesthood.[227] Hayes suggested that Atenism was "an act of religious fanaticism," not a political act, because priests were appointed and removed by the king at will—but he then admitted that a "clash" with the priesthood led to the move to Amarna.[228] Redford agreed that the "single most striking feature" of Egyptian religion in the early years of the Eighteenth Dynasty was the predominance of Amun. Asian campaigns had seen unprecedented wealth flowing into Egypt: the god seemed to be a safe guardian. This new wealth was accompanied by an explosion in the number of temple administrators, but we unfortunately know little of the high priests under Amenhotep III. Although he was known as "the hidden one," Amun associated with, and took over the function of, many other gods, especially Re, Horakhty-Atum, and Ptah.[229]

Reeves argued for a clear pattern of religious dependence during the Eighteenth Dynasty:[230] Hatshepsut and Thutmose III both relied on Amun, claiming him as their divine father.[231] On the other hand, Thutmose IV, Akhenaten's grandfather, claimed on his "Dream Stela" between the paws of the Sphinx at Giza to owe his throne to Horemakhet of Heliopolis.[232] Officials under Thutmose IV and Amenhotep III were no longer priests of Amun. Hari argued that Amenhotep III had reasserted the right to nominate the high priest of Amun.[233] Assmann rejected any clash between king and priesthood, as in Egypt the temples were "organs of the state." He then admitted that such conflicts in the late Twentieth Dynasty caused the end of the New Kingdom.[234]

Aldred proposed modifications: First, he suggested the main conflict had not been with Amun, but with Osiris, in ideas of the hereafter.[235] Atenism did away completely with the journey of the soul to the west, the judgment, and—for those who passed—the blessed life in the Field of

Reeds. Aldred claimed that there was no evidence for conflict with Amun before the move to Amarna, which was undertaken simply to give the Aten a home, like every other deity (but the king went with him!). The boundary stelae gave no evidence for any quarrel (although they are broken at precisely the point where Akhenaten is explaining some great distress). Second, he argued that the whole idea of a church–state quarrel was an invention of the nineteenth century. As the king gave wealth and power to gods, so he could take them away. And the Atenist revolution certainly redistributed the wealth. Aldred then rather undermined his whole argument by admitting that it was wealthy Amun of Thebes who suffered most: on the "restoration," Tutankhamun could allegedly find no priests![236]

Political motives have also been put forward. Redford stated that for Akhenaten, the Aten was simply "the hypostasis (underlying substance) of divine kingship, a pale reflection of his own on earth, projected heavenwards." Having been installed on the throne by the Aten, he was simply adapting his predecessors' exploitation of Amun for the same purpose![237] Redford also offered an intriguing variation on the political theme. He described a model of kingship, when Akhenaten came to the throne, under which a Thutmosid monarch

> signalized his function by daring plans that always came to fruition, he performed feats of strength renowned the world over. He was pious and wise: he kept up the cults and worshipped his ancestors, and instructed his subjects in what they should do. But if this persona was his native inheritance, he also donned a guise forced on him from outside. He now wore the mantle of a king of kings who had to deal with monarchs of equal rank whom native mythology would never credit.

Akhenaten rejected all this: "it [was] certain that he either could not, or chose not to, fulfil them [these roles] *in toto*." He attempted therefore to strengthen his position by the relationship with the Aten. This was an unprecedented "intellectual union," but the new form of monarchy failed: "mythology and empire" could not be discarded.[238]

Redford also fell back on Freudian explanation. Unlike his father, Akhenaten did not identify himself with the Aten: he was created by him, and given kingship by him, but by remaining apart he was avoiding "passivity"—and following his father: "One of the subconscious factors motivating the young man was a fixation with a father-image"![239]

In sum, at the risk of confusing the descriptive with the prescriptive, or, as some would claim, seeing the past through an Enlightenment filter, three facts seem unassailable: the most powerful god in Egypt before Akhenaten was Amun; the main object of the king's attack was Amun; and the losses to Amun must have been catastrophic. It is inconceivable that Akhenaten was not aware of these matters.

Aten temples outside Amarna

The earliest temples to the Aten[240] had been built in the first five years of the reign at Karnak (see chapter 2). The finding at Gurob in the Fayoum[241] of the pedestal of a family statue of Akhenaten and Nefertiti and their three eldest daughters led Labib Habachi (1906–84) to posit that there had been a temple there called, like the Small Temple at Amarna, "The Mansion of the Aten in Akhet-Aten."[242]

Habachi assembled evidence for a temple of the Aten at Heliopolis, where Charles Wilbour had found an inscription, which Gaston Maspero published, naming the temple "Elevating Re in Heliopolis."[243] It had also long been known that reliefs from this temple were embedded in the wall of the Hakim mosque in Cairo. Habachi gathered some seventeen fragments, although none was very revealing. He also republished the most important sources, including a large stela of red quarzite, originally published by Pierre Lacau in 1909.[244]

A close relationship between Amarna and Heliopolis should not surprise us.[245] The Mnervis bull of Re was to be interred in the new capital, the chief priest of the Aten was "Chief Seer" (as at Heliopolis), and the most sacred part of the Aten temple at Amarna was the "House of the Ben-ben," as at Heliopolis. Amarna jar sealings also refer to "The House of the Aten in Heliopolis."[246]

What is important is that the temple of Re also continued to exist: the important Amarnan official May (TA 14) counted among his offices "Overseer of cattle in the House of Re in Heliopolis";[247] it is also mentioned on wine-jar dockets.[248] The high priest there might have been Pawah: "Greatest of Seers of the Aten in the House of Re."[249] Beatrix

Löhr suggested that this temple might have been the only one that escaped the persecution of the other gods. There may also have been another temple of the Aten at Heliopolis called "Amenhotep is the exalter of the Aten."[250]

Another temple of the Aten was at Memphis.[251] Many wine-jar dockets mention the temple from Year 8 onwards. Löhr was able to list many pieces of evidence, mainly from Petrie's excavations,[252] which she suggested came from a structure to the south or southeast of the Ptah temple. The whole complex was called the "House of the Aten." A block from Pylon IX at Karnak lists offerings to the Aten from Memphis to Tell Balamun (that is, from the southern to the northern borders of Lower Egypt),[253] while a number of temple officials are also recorded: Ipy, the Scribe and Fan-bearer; Meryneith (later Meryre), Manager of the Temple; Huy, Mercantile Agent of the Temple of the Aten; and Ptah-may, Goldsmith in the Temple of the Aten.[254]

More than twenty years later, Jaromir Malek revised the question of the location of this temple. Reinterpreting Löhr's evidence, he noted that, in contrast to the tens of thousands of *talatat* from other sites, only seventeen items of any kind were known to have certainly come from the temple of the Aten at Memphis. The provenance was known for fifteen of these: most came from Rameses's temple of Ptah, but three came from Kom al-Qala, and their nature suggests that they were found there. Malek therefore relocated Akhenaten's temple of the Aten to the southeast of the temple of Ptah.[255]

At Hermopolis Magna, opposite Amarna, *talatat* have been found in pylons of Rameses II, but no solid evidence for a temple (most have assumed that the blocks came from Amarna as building material for reuse). At Asyut, one hundred kilometers south of Amarna, there was a small temple called "Firm is the Life of the Aten."[256]

Evidence for Akhenaten's building was also found Akhmim, 190 kilometers south of Amarna,[257] the town of origin of Yuya and Tjuiu, Tiye, and perhaps Ay and Nefertiti, where a temple to the Aten might therefore be expected. The remains took the form of reused limestone blocks much larger than *talatat*, with remains of scenes showing worship of the Aten by Akhenaten and Nefertiti. It has been suggested that the demolished building belonged to the early years of Akhenaten's reign because the loaves on the offering table are shown in profile, and because of the material and size of the blocks. The latter may, however, be due simply to the fact that they came from a local quarry.

From Abydos, 250 kilometers south of Amarna, the Pennsylvania–Yale excavations recovered twenty-six *talatat*, seven with reliefs, perhaps suggesting a small shrine,[258] although it remains unclear how far *talatat* from demolitions at Amarna and Karnak may have been distributed for reuse. At Armant, a little south of Thebes, Eduard Naville (1844–1926) found the fragment of an inscription suggesting an Aten temple here.[259]

As early as 1902, Breasted drew attention to the existence of a city of *Pr-gm-'Itn*, in Nubia, recorded by the fifth-century BC Nubian king Nastesen.[260] Breasted suggested that it lay at Sesebi just north of the Third Cataract; he also posited the existence of a similar city in Palestine. Later, however, Francis Griffith's excavations at Kawa, south of the Third Cataract, from 1930 to 1936, showed that *Pr-gm-'Itn* (originally *Gm-p3-'Itn*) was located there. Laming Macadam was definite: "Of Akhenaten . . . no trace whatsoever has been found at Gem Aten." He suggested, on the basis of a scarab, that the city might instead have been founded by Amenhotep III,[261] but the earliest structure at Kawa is actually of the reign of Tutankhamun.[262]

Sesebi was then excavated by Blackman in 1936–37.[263] It was a fortified city lying between the Second and Third Cataracts, founded in the early Eighteenth Dynasty. In the northwest were three contiguous temples facing east, of which the foundation deposits named Amenhotep IV. The central temple had a crypt decorated with reliefs of Akhenaten seated with Geb, Shu, Osiris(?), Atum, and the deified Amenhotep III.[264]

Twenty-first-century excavations have revealed further Nubian constructions of Akhenaten, both built of *talatat*. A temple was constructed at Kerma-Dukki Gel, using the Earlier form of the Aten name; this was discovered by Charles Bonnet.[265] Work by Timothy Kendall at Gebel Barkal, the Nubian center of the Amun cult, has revealed that (uninscribed) *talatat* had been used in the original construction of temple B500 (the Great Temple of Amun), and thus the temple could be attributed to Akhenaten (fig. 78).[266]

After listing all but the last two Nubian sites, Hari asserted: "it will be agreed that this is very little."[267] Assmann went much further. He dismissed most of the blocks at sites other than Amarna, Karnak, and Heliopolis as

Fig. 78. *Talatat* in the foundations of the original phase of temple B500 at Gebel Barkal.

"strays," moved by later generations for reuse: "The world of the Tuthmo-sids from Nubia to Syria shrank to two square kilometers of desert. Aten was worshipped in only one place: from the 'real' Amarna period, the only other temple was Re in Heliopolis."[268] Evidence is, however, continually increasing. The most recent finds are at Tell al-Borg, ten kilometers east of the Suez Canal, where Hoffmeier's excavations have revealed that *talatat* blocks have been reused to make a cistern, a moat, and a Ramesid fort and gate, and that the moat was filled in at the end of the Eighteenth Dynasty with limestone decorations suitable for a temple.[269]

Bruce Trigger stated, more than thirty years ago, that we know very little about the cult of the Aten outside of Thebes and Amarna, in fact, of only a few temples elsewhere in Egypt and the Egyptian empire. There are, indeed, many questions that we cannot answer: How was the Aten cult spread? What happened to the traditional local cults? Was Atenism predominantly a court cult?[270]

Reception

According to Breasted, the cult was incomprehensible to the people.[271] Gardiner suggested that it had "likely never penetrated deeply into the consciousness of the masses," citing as evidence the continuation of previous worship among the inhabitants of the Workmen's Village.[272] Heinrich Schäfer agreed that the cult completely lacked a popular base. Its "misfortune" was that it was the work of a very small circle of the enlightened. Akhenaten was surrounded by flatterers, and the teaching, in Schäfer's view, was "not very clearly conceived."[273]

Wolf stated that the Amarnan dogma, originally a "secret" of the Heliopolitan priesthood, could not appeal to the masses. Indeed, monotheism offended them. With the founding of the new capital and the creation of new art, "with every step Akhenaten distanced himself more and more from what was truly Egyptian," and this unpopularity was "the rock on which the whole work must shatter." Wolf qualified this, however, by admitting that there was something that spoke to the time: the sun was the creator god, and there was an awareness of the world outside Egypt.[274]

Erman asserted that the new form of the sun god must have been more comprehensible than a falcon-headed man, but then went on to identify "weakness and incomprehension" in the cult because the god appeared in three forms: the sun, a king with cartouches, and the king himself.[275]

Hari argued that Atenism was confined to Amarna. He dismissed the temple at Heliopolis, while at Nefrusy (fifteen kilometers from Amarna) two mayors (Iuny and his son Mahu) dedicated statues to Khnum and Thoth.[276] In Thebes, the temple of Amun continued and tombs still used Osirian rites.[277] He also listed the many traditional deities still venerated at Amarna—Bes,[278] Taweret, Hathor, Sobek, Isis, Thoth, Ptah, Horus, even Amun—as evidenced not only by amulets, but also inscriptions on the walls of houses, even in the Royal Tomb and two chapels to Shed and Isis.[279]

Further fascinating evidence has come to light from the Workmen's Village, where people continued to worship Thoth, Isis, Wepwawet, and Amun—valued helps to survival in a dangerous world, as Kemp put it. The most common design on finger rings was the *Wedjat* (well-being) eye of Horus, and the cobra goddess Retenutet gave protection against insect infestation of grain stores: these last two were found even in the House of Panehsy, the chief priest! Bes and Taweret (fig. 79) were protectors of

Fig. 79. The persistence of the worship of Taweret at Amarna; stela from house N49.21 in the Main City (Cincinatti 1921.279).

childbirth, and Hathor protected people living in remote or desert areas. Kemp also noted that medicine, for all its pragmatism, could not disregard traditional elements such as "confrontation of demonic powers."[280]

There is also evidence that is rarely cited: correspondence. Of Ramose, the unguent preparer for Meryetaten, two letters survive, although badly damaged.[281] He wrote to his brother and his sister, calling upon the Aten as part of the normal greeting to bless them and to give him good advice, thus showing some penetration by Atenism into daily life.

Foster, however, summed up the view of most scholars: "It is probable that worship of the Aten was essentially limited to the city of Akhet-Aten and its inhabitants. . . . Atenism also was probably limited to court circles and, at most, many of the citizens of Akhet-Aten."[282]

According to most modern analysts, therefore, Atenism was a failure. The evidence is, of course, more complicated. Only Davies made a grudging argument that some had accepted the new cult, though they seem to have done so only under duress: "It must have been by the adhesion of the smaller officials and the passive backing of the mass of the population that the king could invade every tomb and temple in the land and brutally force their helpless inmates to a dumb acquiescence in his creed."[283]

Baikie argued both sides before settling for indifference: "Atenism was, from start to finish, almost exclusively a court religion." There was, however, a growing gulf between "the official faith of the empire" (Amunism) and the common people, otherwise Atenism could not have had what he called an "easy triumph": there is no record of any struggles, although "they may have been bitter enough"; there was no "single overt movement in opposition to the royal will." The people saw Amun go and the Aten come with the same indifference with which, a few years later, they saw the Aten vanish and the old god return.[284]

Joyce Tyldesley did not see any problem, on the one hand, in the suppression of major cults:

Most Egyptians worshipped a highly personal mixture of regional deities and family-based cults, with a heavy emphasis on the spirits responsible for pregnancy and childbirth, supplemented with strong doses of superstition and magic. The absence of the great state gods may therefore not have been a problem for the majority of the population, although they would certainly have missed the great festivals and processions which had so far provided regular breaks in their otherwise monotonous lives.

The nature of the Aten, on the other hand, she judged as unattractive: "he was both asexual and androgynous, had no anthropomorphic association and, by his very nature as sole creator, could have no spouse" (although the same could be said of Atum). There was "no comforting mother-wife goddess," there was no "divine domesticity," which made the gods comprehensible and loved by ordinary people.

She rightly cautions, nevertheless, against too facile an interpretation of the well-documented persistence at Amarna of popular cults such as those of Bes and Taweret: "As far as we can tell, no steps were taken to hide these images and we must assume that Bes and his friends were acceptable to Akhenaten"—being outside the list of proscribed major deities. This evidence rather takes the wind out of the sails of those who have mocked Akhenaten as being unable to rid the people of superstition.[285]

Reeves stressed that the people missed the old religious calendar and the many traditional gods who protected aspects of their lives. We may well be surprised to learn, forty pages later, that he asserts that reluctance to abandon Atenism—temples continued to function up and down the country—was the principal reason for the condemnation not only of Akhenaten but also of his successors down to Ay.[286]

Fascinating insight into popular religious belief and practice is afforded by the many private shabtis of the period, subject of an excellent study by Geoffrey Martin. He was able to list nearly forty examples, falling into five categories (here rearranged for our purposes). His fourth class was uninscribed; his first class bore only an owner's name and title (like the shabtis of the king). His third class, the largest (twenty-five of them), still retained the standard formula for such statuettes from Spell 6 of the Book of the Dead:

O thou shabti, if Osiris N is counted off to do any work that is wont to be done yonder in the god's domain—lo, obstacles have been set up for him yonder—as a man to his duties, thou art charged with all these tasks that are wont to be done yonder, to cultivate the fields, to irrigate the shores, to transport sand of the west or the east. "I will do them; here am I" thou shalt say.[287]

His fifth class has a purely Atenist formula:

A boon which the King gives to the living Aten, who illuminates every land with his beauty. May he grant the sweet breeze of the north wind. . . . (then follows a list of desired offerings, which varied, but included cool water, wine, milk, beer, cakes, fresh herbs, and incense for the *ka* of the deceased).

His second class, finally, has a formula which combines Atenist and traditional:

Breathe the sweet breeze of the north wind which comes forth from the sky upon the hand of the living Aten. Your body is protected, your heart is glad. No harm shall happen to your body, because you are sound. Your flesh will not decay. You will follow the Aten (from the moment) when he appears in the morning until he sets in life. There shall be water for your heart, bread for your stomach, and clothing to cover your body. O shabti, if you are counted off, if you are called, and if you are reckoned, "I shall do it; here I am," shall you say. It is the only one truly favored of Waenre (Akhenaten), N, may (s)he live.

This last category is the most interesting. Here are the essentials of Atenism: the deceased was completely protected and nourished and accompanied the Aten throughout the day. Then, however, suddenly the formula reverts to the Osirian version: the shabti answers any call. The only trouble is the lack of any explanation for the source of this call or what the shabti was to do! In sum, the shabtis confirm the evidence from other sources, such as popular cults, that there was amid the general population a range of responses to Atenism, from acceptance to syncretism. Martin suggested that the continuation of the shabti is "not altogether astonishing," but that their continuation in Osirid guise is remarkable. It is the contradiction that is striking: a hankering after the Osirid cult when the Osirid underworld had disappeared and the basic purpose of the shabti had therefore been abolished. From this we may argue, as Martin does, that Osiris was not a deity specially persecuted. We may also claim it as evidence for the survival of older cults, supposedly now irrelevant. Martin also drew attention to the fine quality of the shabtis, equaling that of any period.[288]

A vital part of the evidence for the popular reaction to the cult of the

Aten beyond the royal family had been known since the excavation of the official House of Panehsy (R44.2) in 1926, but it was not until 1989 that Salima Ikram highlighted its import. Excavators had not taken great notice of domestic shrines, but she was able to catalogue eighteen simple shrines, fourteen more complex shrines, three mini-temples, two altars, and nine other miscellaneous shrines and chapels. They are admittedly found only in larger, more luxurious houses, and she interprets the private chapels as a means of obtaining access to the Aten, albeit via the royal family, who are represented on the surviving cult stelae. The shrines thus attest to the willingness of at least the more affluent inhabitants of the new capital to adopt the new cult.[289]

Not to be overlooked are the unsuspected long-term effects of Atenism, as identified by Giles:

> It should be stressed, however, that the decline of the Aton cult did not result in the triumph of Amun, since even though Atenism disappeared as a popular religion—though probably not as an article of worship—Amunism never recovered the preeminent position it had enjoyed during the first three-quarters of the Eighteenth Dynasty. The kings from Horemheb onward had their main royal residence in Lower Egypt, Thebes ceasing to be the major administrative headquarters of the government, and becoming only a religious center.[290]

In the last analysis, what must be stressed above all else is the revolution that Atenism represented for Egypt. Polytheism suddenly became monotheism. The nature of deity changed in a positive way: instead of gods both beneficent and baleful, there was only a good god. There was, however, no more mythology: There were no stories associated with the Aten. There was no more hereafter. Both the living and the dead slept at night and went forth by day. The image of the new god was the most disquieting and unsympathetic element. The traditional gods had a strange hybrid form: they had animal heads, but they were at least half human. The Aten, by contrast, was a face-like, but at the same time face-less, disk, with only hands at the end of his rays. And communication was impossible: he was mute and deaf. The shock of the new royal religion must have been indescribable.

Fig. 80. The Berlin bust of Nefertiti (ÄM 21300).

5 Two Queens

THE SINGLE BEST-KNOWN image of the Amarna period is the bust of Nefertiti, found by the Germans in 1912 and now in Berlin (fig. 80). It dominates in our minds over the many striking portraits of her husband, and even the image of the boy king Tutankhamun and his queen, discovered in sensational circumstances in 1922.

Portraiture of the Egyptian queens has always been memorable: the wonderful depictions of Menkaure and Khamerernebty;[1] Montjuhotep II's wife Kawit;[2] and then the women of the Eighteenth Dynasty: Tetisherit, Ahhotep, and Ahmes-Nefertiry, "a succession of particularly forceful consorts"[3] who were important at the inception of the dynasty; Hatshepsut ruling in her own right; and most immediately the unforgettable Tiye, Akhenaten's own mother, always beside her husband, although the royal harem was pullulating with lesser wives, many of them princesses from allied foreign countries. The position of Nefertiti should not, therefore, come as a surprise, but the real level of her importance has been revealed only in recent years.

Nefertiti
Nefertiti's parents
Nefertiti's origins have naturally been of special interest. Absence of royal blood seems implicit in her lack of the title *s3t-nsw* (King's Daughter)

that was *de rigueur* for princesses of the blood—although this has not deterred everyone from proposing such a background. Urbain Bouriant, for example, suggested in 1885 that she was the daughter of Amenhotep III and Tiye, and that Akhenaten's marriage to her was his way to the throne.[4] A variation on this first view is that Nefertiti was a daughter of Amenhotep III by a lesser wife[5] or a daughter of Amenhotep III and one of his sisters.[6] At any rate, for such scholars she was a sister of Akhenaten.[7]

Then with the discovery of the Amarna Letters in 1887 and the attention given to Tadu-Kheba, Tushratta's daughter and member of Amenhotep III's harem, many wanted to equate Nefertiti with this foreign Mitannian princess, who therefore changed her name when she came to Egypt—and Nefertiti does mean "A beautiful lady has come."[8] Nefertiti's sister Mutnedjmet (fig. 81), on the other hand, was never thought to be a foreigner, the Mitannian princess is never referred to in the letters by other than her native name, and Nefertiti had an Egyptian "nurse."[9] Alan Gardiner therefore concluded that Nefertiti was not

a foreigner, but he did not go further.[10] As late as 1966, however, Eleanore Bille-de-Mot continued to maintain the identity with Tadukhepa, based on the meaning of 'Nefertiti,' Tushratta's failure to mention any queen other than Tiye, Nefertiti's "Asian" headdress, and her "ethnic type."[11]

The third obvious category, Egyptian but not of royal birth (as implied by her titulary), was proposed by Georges Legrain in 1903.[12] As John Wilson remarked, "If her name at birth or at marriage was Nefertiti, this was a common enough name in the New Kingdom, and had no exceptional significance."[13]

The whole debate was transformed two years later by Ludwig Borchardt, who argued that the title *it-nṯr* (Father of the God [the king]—to be distinguished from a similar priestly title) could mean not only his real father,[14] but also his father-in-law.[15] Akhenaten's Commander of Cavalry, Ay,

Fig. 81. Nefertiti's sister Mutnedjmet, as shown in the tomb of Parennefer (TA 7).

the man who would later be king, held this very title and thus could have been Nefertiti's father. Borchardt showed that the title had had this possible meaning since the Old Kingdom, and had for some years suggested that Ay was

Akhenaten's father-in-law. This would have remained speculation, he admitted, but for the discovery of the tomb of Yuya and Tjuiu, the parents of Queen Tiye, where Yuya was called "Father of the God," thus apparently confirming the continuing use of the title in this sense in the late Eighteenth Dynasty.

Norman de Garis Davies adopted Borchardt's position, but considering that Nefertiti's titles indicated that she was the "royal heiress," carrying the right to the throne, in accordance with then-contemporary theory,[16] he complicated the situation by making Ay's wife, Tey, also an heiress, and then speculated that Queen Tiye had taken her name (essentially the same as Tey's) "to conceal her non-royal birth."[17] On the other hand, Keith Seele (1898–1971) dismissed Borchardt's 'theory' as "impossible to affirm or deny."[18]

Borchardt's proposal was modified by Moses Worms, who stressed that Ay's wife Tey, unlike Tjuiu, was never called "Mother of the King's Chief Wife," but rather the nurse of Nefertiti.[19] He thus made Tey Ay's second wife;[20] Nefertiti's mother was therefore his first wife.[21] Aidan Dodson suggested that Nefertiti's mother might have been the Lady Iuy, who seems to have been the mother of Ay's son, Nakhtmin.[22]

If this reconstruction is correct, a remarkable parallel exists between father and son, Amenhotep III and Akhenaten. Both married non-royal wives who became politically very important, and whose fathers were both commanders of the royal cavalry. There would be no difficulty in the crown prince meeting such a young woman, given her father's importance at court and contacts between the two families. As Worms suggested, their mothers may also have had important court positions.

The whole question was reopened by Helmut Brunner in 1961. He showed that there are cases where the title "Father of the God" indicates a tutor's role.[23] Brunner thus suggested that Ay was simply tutor to Akhenaten and therefore played a leading role in the religious revolution (it being fitting that the "Great Hymn" was inscribed in his tomb), and also then under Tutankhamun. He had used this double position to claim the throne, but he brought the title into disrepute, so that it was not subsequently used.[24]

While the majority view has tended toward the Borchardt/Worms solution, for a long time no potentially definitive data were available.

The implications of such emerging data, derived from the genetic examination of mummies, will be considered below.

The bust of Nefertiti

The most famous single work of art from Amarna is the painted bust of the queen (fig. 80), with its beautiful colors, its obvious celebration of her beauty, and the missing left eye.[25] It was allegedly found on 6 December 1912 in Thutmose's workshop (P47.2), room 19. To the inattentive, she is absent in the text of Borchardt's preliminary report of that campaign. Unflagging alertness, however, reveals an almost unrecognizable small illustration.[26] It shows only the face, and that in profile.

There is more. At the end of the year's report, Borchardt noted that the division took place on 20 January 1913, but that the campaign did not finally close until 16 March. The intervening time was taken up, in part, with the packing of the finds, "this time very long." He revealed, moreover, that according to a new Egyptian ministerial decree, the division had been very rigorous: exactly half to the Germans and half to the Egyptians. In this case, incredibly, the finds from the workshop of Thutmose were not divided: as Borchardt put it, they were not "rendered scientifically completely worthless through senseless division." He judged this to be "a masterly achievement" of the museum officials entrusted with the division.[27]

The first publication of the masterwork was not, in fact, until ten years later in 1923: *Porträts der Königin Nofret-ete*, when more questions were left unanswered than answered. This lavish folio publication was devoted to two pieces, the outstanding finds of 1912: the Nefertiti bust; and the Cairo relief (JE 44865), a representation of Akhenaten and Nefertiti *en famille* with three daughters, to which the first twenty-nine pages were devoted. The bust was discussed on only the last ten pages. One could thus be forgiven for thinking that Borchardt wished to give the impression that the Cairo Museum received the better half of the division, yet in this case, the title of the book is both completely misleading, and draws attention back, paradoxically, to the bust.

Borchardt thanked, above all, Dr. James Simon, the founder of the German Oriental Society and financier of the excavations (p. 73, above), who, as the concession holder, formally received the bust at the division of finds. After it was seen at the museum for one day, he kept the bust in his house for some time before he lent everything to the Berlin Ägyptisches Museum, and finally donated it there on 7 July 1920.

Borchardt's judgment on the value of the bust was enthusiastic. He quoted an (unnamed) art expert: it is "the Egyptian art work most full of life."[28] In his journal, he admitted that he had enthused: "It is useless to describe it: see it!" Even colored photographs could not show how lifelike and delicate it was. He alluded to art historians who even gave it a high place in *world* art. How, then, was it given to the German excavators? How, also, was the bust so little damaged? Portraits of Akhenaten found a few feet away had been smashed (for example, Berlin ÄM 21360).[29] Borchardt suggested that Nefertiti survived on a shelf in the narrow room, until that collapsed, and she fell forward onto the soft ground.[30]

In 1968 the Ägyptisches Museum (West Berlin) published a beautiful booklet on the bust by Rudolf Anthes (1896–1985). It contains a valuable technical description, a historical essay on the Amarna period, and a history of the bust. His most particular contribution to the puzzle is the suggestion that when the division was made, "the sympathetic understanding of the Egyptian official representatives ensured that the discoveries in the model workshop were so divided that those works of art which were recognized as models or patterns were given in their entirety to the excavators." The 'proof' that Nefertiti's bust is a 'studio model' is the fact that only one eye had been inserted.[31]

The full story of what happened was revealed only in 1987 through the research of Rolf Krauss. He highlighted disturbing omissions in Borchardt's account, most notably that the excavations on 6 December 1912 were being visited by Prince Johann Georg of Saxony and his wife Princess Maria Immaculata of Bourbon-Sicily, as well as other princesses.[32] The prince was an enthusiastic photographer, and his photographs of the newly discovered bust are invaluable.[33] This led to stories that the discovery had been stage-managed for their benefit, even that the bust was a fake. Its genuineness has, however, been proven by manifold tests on material and coloring.

Of one important matter we may be certain: Borchardt urged the board of the Oriental Society to secrecy over the finds because of his fears over the division with the museum.[34] That division occurred on 20

January 1913. Before 1914, finds from an excavation had been divided into two equal parts, with the Egyptian government having first choice.[35] On this occasion, Gaston Maspero, Director General of Antiquities, was represented by an inspector, Gustave Lefebvre (1879–1957). In that division, the bust went to the Germans. The obvious question is, how did the Antiquities Service forego such a masterwork? One reason, according to Borchardt, was that Lefebvre was an epigrapher and papyrologist, not interested in art. Another is that his superior, Maspero, was generous in such divisions, and the "complex of finds" from the sculptor's workshop was not divided.[36] It would later be claimed that Borchardt had somehow disguised the true value of the bust. This stemmed principally from Lefebvre's hesitant recollections: he *thought* that the bust must have been shown to him. His version certainly aimed to exonerate himself and inculpate Borchardt.[37]

Borchardt himself had in fact provided an explanation. On the first page of his 1923 publication, he singled out the relief and the bust as the two outstanding pieces, works of the first rank, found in 1912/13: one therefore went to Cairo, the other to Berlin. This would suggest that the division was equal and thus fair,[38] but, as usual, it simply raises a further question and only increases the puzzle. Borchardt, as we have seen, emphasized the sense of not dividing the finds from Thutmose's studio. It was not, then, simply a matter of the bust, but of what was obviously the most exciting collection of portraits ever discovered in the whole history of Egyptian archaeology. Why, then, did they not *all* go to Cairo?

In Borchardt's report of the year's finds, he was at pains throughout to stress that what had been found was Thutmose's workshop *(Werkstatt)*, and that the individual pieces were "models" *(Bildhauermodellen)*. Each one is labeled "Modelmaske," whether in plaster or painted limestone. One does not need to imagine any subterfuge to achieve the export, if the Antiquities Service was brought around to accept this interpretation. The Nefertiti bust must, admittedly, have presented a problem: it is labeled "finished state of the model portrait of the queen"![39]

Although the bust soon came to the Ägyptisches Museum, and despite Borchardt's extraordinarily high estimate of it, it was at his wish that it was not at first displayed. It was not until 1918 that the director of the museum, Heinrich Schäfer, persuaded Simon (still technically the owner) to allow the bust to be exhibited. Borchardt was faced with a *fait accompli*. To the German chancellery, Borchardt then revealed that the "greatest strictness" had been enjoined on the Egyptians in the division, but that the Germans had been helped by the allocation to the Americans of a very important piece: the Menkaure dyad, which went to Boston.[40] This had provoked the British—at that time the administrators of Egypt—through the then Consul General, Lord Kitchener, to promise that such things would not happen again. Borchardt feared that exhibition of the bust would lead to stricter controls on excavation and division of finds. Schäfer demanded that the bust be included in the Amarna exhibit at the museum, but this did not happen. He persevered, however, having the sculptress Tina Haim make stone replicas and the artist Clara Siemens make a series of drawings of the Amarna finds, including the bust, with text by Grethe Guterbock-Auer. Then came Borchardt's own essay.[41]

The reaction from Cairo was swift. The new Director-General of Antiquities, Pierre Lacau, demanded the return of the bust. Egypt had no legal claim, Lacau admitted, but a moral one. When Borchardt applied for a license to resume excavation in 1925, it was refused. Lacau began, however, to speak of recompense for the return of the bust. A standing statue of Ranefer (Old Kingdom—CG 18 or 19) eventually came to be mentioned. Public opinion in Germany hardened.

The campaign to return the bust was led by none other than Schäfer. He considered that the Ägyptisches Museum would be enriched by the proposed exchange, since he valued the Ranefer statues very highly. He frankly rated the art of the Old Kingdom far above that of Amarna, which for him was "decadent"—despite the attention he paid it! There was, besides, antagonism between Schäfer and Borchardt on personal and academic grounds (such as judgments in art history and claims that Schäfer had been duped by fakes).[42] The Nazis came to power in 1933, and Adolf Hitler famously forbade the exchange in 1935.[43]

Nefertiti's crowns [44]

On the bust, Nefertiti wears what has come to be seen as her trademark headdress: the flat-topped crown.[44] It is shown on *talatat* dating as early as the Theban years,[45] and on Boundary Stelae R and Q from Amarna she wears the same crown.[46] On Stela N it is topped by a solar disk and plumes.[47] She also wears this crown in domestic scenes from Amarna (for example Berlin ÄM 14145 and Cairo JE 44865). Akhenaten usually wears the Blue Crown, and Nefertiti's crown has been seen as being the feminine counterpart.[48]

The flat-topped crown is also found with goddesses, such as Anukis, in Nubia, but it is not known before the Middle Kingdom. Earl Ertman interprets this crown as a king's and as a sign of deification: it was never worn by the princesses.[49] Tiye wears a similar crown at her temple from Sedeinga in Nubia, and it is also found as the headdress of Asiatic goddesses.[50]

At Thebes, Nefertiti also wore the Hathor crown, with cow horns, disk, and plumes (fig. 17, as had Tiye);[51] she continued to do so at Amarna (figs. 23, 24, 72),[52] even with horns, disk, and plumes on top of her own crown.[53] A 'cap crown' (a close-fitting cap which follows the shape of the head) is also found at Amarna, and seems to be worn especially when performing ritual acts.[54] Dorothea Arnold has suggested that most representations of this crown date from after Years 9 to 12.[55] The *atef* (*3tf*) crown is also worn at Amarna by both Nefertiti and Akhenaten.[56] On other uses of royal headwear by Nefertiti (see below, p. 194).

Nefertiti's wigs

The queen is also found with a number of other head coverings. The so-called 'Nubian' wig[57] was first described by Georges Daressy (1864–1938) in 1910 as seen on the canopic jars from KV 55 (fig. 89):

> Short behind, where it leaves the neck uncovered, it gradually
> lengthens, and ends in two points touching the clavicles, falling
> straight down the sides of the face, which it encloses, hiding the
> ears. It is divided into a number of small coils that fall vertically
> from the top of the head, except in front, where the hair is cut short,
> and forms three rows on the forehead and on the sides of the face,
> where the locks are arranged obliquely, and end in an arrangement
> of five rows, diminishing in length one above the other.[58]

Cyril Aldred returned to this wig half a century later. He referred to it as "valanced," but "the salient feature" was that it was cut up at the back to reveal the nape of the neck (in contrast to the standard Nubian wig).[59] Both were Eighteenth Dynasty fashions, and its inspiration was judged to be military.[60] It was regularly worn by Nefertiti in various Theban contexts,[61] but was infrequently depicted at Amarna (fig. 61).[62] This wig was also worn by Tiye and by Ankhesenamun.[63]

Nefertiti also wore the *khat* (*h3t*) "bag wig," hitherto restricted in use to the king and the tutelary goddesses, although it was worn also by Tiye. Nefertiti wears it frequently, not as a sign of equality with her husband, but to symbolize her substitution for those goddesses.[64]

While it has been claimed that there was no relationship between Nefertiti's headdress and her activities,[65] representations in the Amarna tomb chapels suggest a pattern: the flat-topped crown is the preferred ceremonial headdress, especially in scenes of worship and reward, but also when driving; within the palace, however, on more relaxed occasions and especially while banqueting, a wig was preferred.

Nefertiti's position and importance

From the beginning, Nefertiti's exceptional status in relation to her husband (and to most earlier queens) was noted. Arthur Weigall, as early as 1922, identified the key: "in opposition to all tradition, the queen is shown upon the same scale of size and importance as that of her husband."[66] Aylward Blackman also commented that

> the El-Amarna reliefs nearly always depict the queen as acting in exactly the same capacity as the king in the temple service. Together they burn incense, pour out libation, elevate trays of offerings, offer flowers or unguent, or consecrate an oblation with the *ḥrp*-baton. Or again, while the king burns incense the queen presents an offering or makes libation, or while he makes libation she burns incense, or while he presents an offering she prepares to perform the act of consecration.[67]

In the publication in 1923 of the British excavations at Amarna, Eric Peet and Leonard Woolley, however, claimed that there was evidence for the queen's disgrace some time after Year 12 (see below). The most baleful contribution to understanding the later career of Nefertiti—and indeed the last half decade of Akhenaten's reign and its immediate aftermath—came in 1928. Percy Newberry then made the first concerted

Fig. 82. The stela of Pay, showing a naked man and woman in an affectionate pose. Both wear kingly crowns, but the fact that there are only three (blank) cartouches—apart from the double twin cartouches at the top of the Aten—shows that the woman has not yet transitioned to full pharaonic status. Although originally, and now once again, understood by the majority of scholars as representing Akhenaten and Nefertiti, for many years it was regarded as attesting to homosexual relations between Akhenaten and Smenkhkare (Berlin ÄM 17813).

attempt to assemble the evidence for the mysterious coregent Smenkhkare. In so doing, he attempted to reassign two important reliefs.

The first was the stela of Pay (fig. 82), showing two naked blue-crowned figures in an affectionate pose. The three cartouches that accompanied them were all, unfortunately, empty. The scene was first taken to represent Akhenaten and Nefertiti,[68] but after Newberry's attention had been drawn to the stela by Howard Carter, he reinterpreted it as

Fig. 83. Another unfinished and uninscribed stela from O49.1, almost certainly showing Nefertiti pouring wine for Akhenaten, although the absence of even blank cartouches makes it impossible to be certain if Nefertiti is yet Neferneferuaten. However, on the basis of her crown, she is now clearly of kingly status (Berlin ÄM 20716).

two kings, on the basis that both wore crowns. They were thus identified as Akhenaten and Smenkhkare, and Newberry went on to suggest parallels between them and the Roman emperor Hadrian and his favorite Antinous. Newberry also recalled that Peet and Woolley's excavations at Amarna had revealed, as they believed, the erasure of Nefertiti's name and its replacement by that of Meryetaten. Newberry did not himself choose between the two possibilities, that the queen had died or that she had been 'disgraced.'[69]

The new interpretation of the stela was universally adopted. Schäfer, for example, changed his mind, admitting that he had taken the second figure to be Nefertiti until Newberry "proved" otherwise.[70] It must be recorded that Walter Wolf instantly rejected Newberry's homosexual interpretation as romance rather than history.[71] Many others were less skeptical, and the homosexuality of the two kings became a 'fact.'[72]

The same reidentification was also applied to another unfinished stela, found in house O49.1 in 1911/12 and representing a seated king wearing the *nms* crown, for whom a drink is being poured by an individual wearing a Blue Crown (fig. 83). As with the stela of Pay, it was first taken to show Akhenaten and Nefertiti; but then Newberry switched to interpret the figures to be Akhenaten and Smenkhkare;[73] they have also occasionally been seen as Amenhotep III and Akhenaten during the putative coregency.

Newberry's interpretation of these two stelae held sway for almost half a century. The year 1973 was a turning point, however, with contributions by John Harris, Julia Samson, Sayed Tawfik, and John Wilson. Regarding the stela of Pay, Harris pointed out what had been manifestly evident since the stela was found: that the Aten is at the top, with two pairs of cartouches, while the two royal figures have only three cartouches between them, so that they could not be two kings, but must be a king and a queen.[74] The iconography supports this: the figure on the left has breasts and has her arm around the other, and the shape of the necks indicates a man and a woman (a criterion which none other than Schäfer had identified in 1918: Akhenaten's neck was shown as concave, Nefertiti's as convex).

In the wine-pouring scene, the physique of the right-hand figure again suggests a woman. Nefertiti can, in fact, be seen in this very pose in the tomb of Meryre ii—evidence that had been available to everyone since 1905.[75]

Harris's reassignment of these reliefs to Nefertiti was a vital step. The woman—identified as Nefertiti—was shown on both wearing the Blue Crown, which Harris says "appears to have been symbolic of coronation, and so became the royal crown par excellence."[76]

The reassigned reliefs were tied in with other evidence from the *talatat* known since the 1920s, which revealed Nefertiti's place in the new religion. One of them refers to the Aten "residing in the *Ḥwt-bnbn* in the

Gm(t)-p3-'Itn of Queen Nefertiti." Tawfik took this to be a Mansion of the Sacred Stone *Ḥwt-bnbn* belonging to the queen, "either as a divine person praying to Aton or being worshipped herself." He noted that of the forty-eight references to the *Ḥwt-bnbn*, eleven are connected with Nefertiti.[77]

In the Karnak temple was a pillared courtyard in the *Gm(t)-p3-'Itn* in the *Pr-'Itn*, where only the queen is shown, sometimes with her two eldest daughters, but not with the king. Again, Karnak blocks mention the *Šh-n-'Itn* (Sunshade of the Aten), which is also associated—according to the evidence we have—only with Nefertiti.[78] Nefertiti's name or figure is, in fact, almost twice as frequent as the king's on the Karnak *talatat*; this may be explained, however, by the fact that a large proportion of the surviving *talatat* came from the *Ḥwt-bnbn*, which was particularly associated with her.[79] Wilson drew particular attention to the fact that the Karnak *talatat* from Pylon II often show Nefertiti alone worshiping the Aten; this, as he most acutely noted, contradicts Akhenaten's claim that he alone knew the Aten. "Nefertiti also knew the Aten."[80] Tawfik, building on an insight of Davies's, noted that when she was given the additional name 'Neferneferuaten,' although the other hieroglyphs are written facing in the same direction as the queen, the name of the Aten is written facing backwards, toward her: "an extraordinary honor. . . . Even her gifted husband did not enjoy this eye-catching relation to the god."[81]

Highly significant also was the observation by Michel Malaise in 1981 that the Aten, as well as offering the *'nh*-sign, also often extends the *w3s*-sign (scepter) not only to Akhenaten but also to Nefertiti.[82]

Harris also drew attention to the device in three tomb reliefs representing the king and queen by "duplicate outline,"[83] indicating "virtually equal status"[84] (figs. 57, 62).

In the same year, Wilson cited other evidence that had been known for some years: Nefertiti was shown both at Karnak and at Amarna in the traditional role of the pharaoh clubbing enemies. "Such scenes . . . are elsewhere restricted to kings or gods" (fig. 84).[85] Tawfik noted another scene of this type from Luxor temple. There also seemed to be four shrines showing Nefertiti stabbing an enemy and, as a sphinx, trampling one. Tawfik went so far as to call her a "queen goddess."[86]

Beyond the political and religious evidence for Nefertiti's importance, a quite separate question, often confused with this, is whether she

Fig. 84. Nefertiti smiting enemies; from block from Hermopolis (MFA 63.260).

196   Two Queens

was worshiped as a goddess. Tawfik and Wilson have been the two main proponents of this idea. Tawfik published a remarkable *talatat* with the name of Nefertiti between the names of the Aten above *rekhyt* birds, *nb*-signs, and stars: this symbolized the adoration by all subjects of the Aten and the queen.[87] He also pointed out her position at the corners of her husband's sarcophagus (fig. 102), replacing the traditional four protecting goddesses in the Royal Tomb.[88] This is conclusive evidence that she was worshiped as a goddess.

Wilson added further evidence. The "Great Hymn" to the Aten opens with the adoration of the god, of Akhenaten, and of Nefertiti. "No distinction is made among these three powers, except for the order in which they are named. All three are to be worshipped." And the Amarnan tombs contain prayers of the deceased asking benefits of the Aten, Akhenaten, and Nefertiti: "the queen may be asked for the same benefits as the god or the king."[89]

Nefertiti's names and possible status as coregent

'Nefertiti' was presumably the queen's birth name, associated with her especially at Thebes, but this 'short name' made no reference to the Aten.[90] This lack was remedied by the 'longer name,' Neferneferuaten ("Beautiful are the beauties of the Aten"), which appeared in Year 5 on boundary stelae at Amarna, apparently after the birth of Meketaten.[91] The logical time for the change, therefore, would seem to have been at the same time as Akhenaten took his new name: the move to the city of the Aten. The 'longer name' was also found at Thebes, but this is presumably in contexts carved in and after Year 5.

A further major development was the appearance of the name 'Neferneferuaten' (not followed by 'Nefertiti') as a kingly nomen, with the prenomen 'Ankhkheperure [Living are the manifestations of Re], beloved of Waenre [part of Akhenaten's prenomen].' Many items from the tomb of Tutankhamun bear (or once bore) this pair of cartouches, including the canopic coffinettes,[92] some of the gold bands that surrounded Tutankhamun's mummy,[93] a bow,[94] bracelets,[95] a pectoral,[96] and a fragment of a box, where the two cartouches appeared along with the names of Akhenaten and Meryetaten.[97] The simple cartouche 'Ankhkheperure,' however, appears as the throne name of a king named in the second cartouche as 'Smenkhkare,' a juxtaposition that would lead to decades of historical confusion.

As the culmination of his 1973 studies, Harris suggested that Nefertiti had been not only a quasi-kingly queen, but also a fully fledged female monarch, noting the existence of finger rings bearing the prenomen Ankhkheperure incorporating a feminine ending (t): 'Ankhetkheperure.'[98] On this basis, King Neferneferuaten was seen to be a woman—and judged to be none other than Nefertiti, bolstered by Harris's reinterpretation of the Berlin Pay stela. Harris followed Newberry, however, in assuming that there was only one Ankhkheperure, declaring that Nefertiti had later changed her nomen to Smenkhkare.[99] The only problem with this is that it requires identifying the only known representation of Smenkhkare (fig. 91) as the figure of a woman, which does not make sense given that the image is accompanied by what appears unequivocally to be Smenkhkare's wife—Meryetaten.

A second identification of queen Ankh(et)kheperure was favored by Krauss, who argued in 1976 that she was Akhenaten's eldest daughter Meryetaten, whom he believed to be his wife and then widow. He relied essentially on Manetho, who stated in the third century BC that Akhenaten was succeeded by a daughter/wife "Akencheres," whom he equated with Ankhetkheperure. Krauss found evidence to support this theory in the prominent role she played in the Amarna Letters (*EA* 155).[100] This view is ingenious, but it has not gained acceptance because it relies on such a late source and considers so little of the evidence.

James Allen cut the Gordian knot in 1991 by at last separating Neferneferuaten from Smenkhkare. Although Neferneferuaten shared her core prenomen, Ankhkheperure, with Smenkhkare, all the prenomina that were unequivocally associated with the name Neferneferuaten always incorporated an epithet which referred to Akhenaten, as did most nomina; Smenkhkare's prenomen was always, in contrast, 'plain.'[101]

Marc Gabolde accepted this distinction, but, following Krauss, he preferred Meryetaten as the future Neferneferuaten.[102] To the various objects of Neferneferuaten found in the tomb of Tutankhamun, he now added a "heavy-breasted" figure on a leopard.[103] He also drew attention to a hitherto unnoticed epithet found within some examples of Neferneferuaten's nomen: *3ḫt-n-ḥ(i).s*, "Effective for her husband."[104]

Neferneferuaten's gender was thus proven beyond doubt. This revelation prompted the reexamination of other Neferneferuaten cartouches, which revealed that the epithet which had been read on, for instance, a stela from Amarna (the so-called "Coregency Stela," fig. 95) and on canopic coffinettes of Tutankhamun as "mery-Akhenaten" was a phantom: all epithets were actually *3ḫt-n-ḥ(i).s*.[105]

In favor of identifying Neferneferuaten with Meryetaten, Gabolde cited some gold plaques that included the prenomen Ankhkheperure-meryaten (and the nomen Neferneferuaten-heqa ['the ruler']); he understood the epithet to refer to Princess Meryetaten, despite the lack of the feminine ending. He believed the Amarna Letters to be crucial evidence, especially *EA* 11, where the Babylonian king speaks of "Mayati" (presumably an Akkadian writing of "Meryetaten) as Akhenaten's "mistress of the house."[106] This clearly does not mean "king," however, and there have been arguments about whether this title is actually associated with Mayati, whose name is mentioned next.[107]

A major obstacle to Gabolde's interpretation is a box belonging to Tutankhamun which lists Akhenaten, Neferneferuaten, and Meryetaten (as a King's Wife) with every appearance of their being separate individuals. If Gabolde is right that Neferneferuaten is also Meryetaten, then either she appears in two guises alongside herself, or she has *three* cartouches! This is unparalleled. Gabolde suggested Hatshepsut as a precedent, but she never used three cartouches at once. Gabolde's underlying motive is that, having repeatedly asserted that Kiya had returned to Mitanni and that Nefertiti was dead, he is left with only Meryetaten as a candidate for Neferneferuaten.

Allen made a third suggestion about Neferneferuaten's identity when he revisited the question in 2006. He ruled out Nefertiti on the basis of Christian Loeben's suggestion that her shabti showed that she had died while still only a queen (see below). Relying on Manetho, as Krauss did, to search for a daughter of Akhenaten, Allen next considered Meryetaten, but she also was ruled out on the basis of the "Tutankhamun box-fragment." Allen then argued that the "primary element" in the nomen remained constant before and after accession, leaving as his only candidate the *fourth* daughter, Neferneferuaten-tasherit! He thus made her Akhenaten's coregent and wife, from whom he hoped for a son. To make this work, the date of the princess's birth had to be moved back from the usually assumed Year 8 to make her thirteen by Year 16/17, with Neferneferuaten's known three years' reign extended after Akhenaten's death, rather than being dated to Years 15–17, as Allen had previously argued.[108]

Dodson, however, accepted that Neferneferuaten was indeed Nefertiti. Her epithet $3ht-n-h(i).s$ and the fact that Nefertiti had long also used the name Neferneferuaten, combined with her long-term importance, make it difficult to conceive an alternative.[109] On the aforementioned "Coregency Stela," the twin cartouches of Neferneferuaten replaced the single cartouche of Nefertiti, suggesting that the latter had been transformed into the former; it is unfortunate that Nefertiti's figure is not preserved on the stela, so we will never know if this was altered as well. The Pay stela, meanwhile, shows that she wore a king's crown while still using a queen's single cartouche, which suggests that she began fulfilling the role some time before acquiring a prenomen. Accordingly, she could have been shown thus on the "Coregency Stela," which was probably carved late in the reign of Akhenaten, since it appears to include only two daughters.

Another piece of evidence pointing to Nefertiti as Neferneferuaten was presented by Raymond Johnson in 2015. He showed that a head in Hannover had originally been carved as one of Nefertiti wearing her flat-topped crown, but had subsequently been altered so that the figure wore a Blue Crown, a change difficult to explain except by her promotion from queen to king.[110]

On the career of Neferneferuaten, and more detail on some of the above evidence, see chapter 7.

Nefertiti's daughters

Nefertiti bore Akhenaten six daughters: Meryetaten, Meketaten, Ankhesenpaaten, Neferneferuaten-tasherit, Neferneferure, and Setepenre (fig. 57). This is the sequence in which they were born, but can anything be discovered concerning their dates of birth?

One of the earliest and best discussions is by Davies, who tried to use their appearances in the tombs to date their births. He deduced that the first three daughters were born in Years 4, 6, and 8 respectively.[111]

There are, however, a number of cautions here. The same tomb may show different numbers of daughters in different scenes, with the number possibly determined by the available space. When he turned to the boundary stelae, Davies was on firmer ground. On Stela K of Year 5, only Meryetaten is mentioned in the text, but alongside her portrait that of Meketaten's has been added. On Stelae A and B of Year 6, only these two daughters originally appeared, but Ankhesenpaaten was subsequently added.[112]

The *talatat* from the dismantled Theban temple of Years 1–5 showed Nefertiti with one daughter (Meryetaten) in 90 percent of cases; with two (adding Meketaten) in 8 percent; and with three (adding Ankhesenpaaten) in only three cases. On this evidence, Donald Redford argued that Meketaten was born in or before Year 4 and that Ankhesenpaaten was born very shortly before the move to Amarna.[113] The birth of the eldest daughter, Meryetaten, he strangely assigned to the "earliest months" of the reign, on the basis that she is shown as at least a toddler in all reliefs.[114]

Redford provided a most revealing table of the appearance of the daughters in the Amarnan tombs and also the Hermopolis *talatat*. He detected a "pattern of three daughters" in the tombs, and alerted us to fundamental unknowns: Were the daughters shown as soon as they were born, or only when they were old enough to appear in public? Were all daughters alive at any time necessarily shown? Did the availability of space on the surface being carved play any part? What weight is to be given to signs of physical maturity?[115] He was nevertheless willing to suggest that the three youngest daughters were born at Amarna, probably by Year 10, but since they are rarely shown, they may have died in childhood.[116]

Dimitri Laboury dated the births as follows: Meryetaten, Year 5; Meketaten, Year 6; Ankhesenpaaten, Year 8; Neferneferuaten-tasherit, Year 9; Neferneferure, Year 10; and Setepenre, Year 11. Meketaten was buried, apparently after Year 12, in room *gamma* of the Royal Tomb, where her parents are shown with three surviving daughters (fig. 105). Laboury and Dodson suggested that the last two daughters were buried in room *alpha*,[117] so that by the visit of Queen Tiye to Amarna only two were left.[118]

William Murnane set out the complicated evidence most logically. The boundary stelae are clear: the "Earlier Proclamation" of Year 5 refers to, and originally showed, only Meryetaten. To stela K, Meketaten was then added: she was born between mid-Year 5 and early Year 6. Then to stelae A, B, F, Q, and V Ankhesenpaaten was added; she was born, therefore, between late Year 7 and mid-Year 8.[119] This evidence seems, however, to be contradicted by carvings from Karnak, where as many as three daughters are shown, presumably before Year 5. This is a dilemma. Murnane preferred the evidence of the stelae, where we can apparently see the daughters being added as the stelae were 'updated.' It seems inconceivable that only Meryetaten would be mentioned in the detailed burial arrangements on the "Earlier Proclamation" if other daughters were alive in Year 5, given that provision was made for priests of the Aten and even animals. And there is a simple solution for the Karnak *talatat*: there is in fact no reason to assume, as is often done, that the Theban temples were totally and suddenly abandoned; construction and decoration probably continued at least during Years 6 to 8, when the second and third daughters could have been included.

The chronology that emerges is a little strange. If Akhenaten were married at the latest shortly after he came to the throne, he and Nefertiti would have had only one daughter by Year 5, but then another five within the next seven years. The most obvious deduction is that they were married a year or so before the birth of Meryetaten.[120]

Father–daughter marriages?

A bombshell was dropped in 1938, when Brunner published *talatat* from Hermopolis referring to "the King's Daughter of his Body, Ankhesenpaaten, born of the King's Daughter Born of his Body, Ankhesenpaaten . . . Neferkheperure."[121] Here were two princesses of the same name, one Akhenaten's well-known third daughter, the other her daughter, both born of the king's body. Attempts to suggest that the father was the elder Ankhesenpaaten's husband Tutankhamun will not work by reason of his age and the fact that here alone as his queen she would lack the title "King's Chief Wife." The solution suggested by Brunner is that at the end of his reign Akhenaten married his own daughter. There are parallels in Amenhotep III's marriage with Sitamun and Rameses II's marriages with at least two of his daughters, although in the latter cases the women all received the title King's Wife.[122]

Wilson countered that Ankhesenpaaten did not appear on the boundary stelae of Year 6, so she could not be a mother until the end of the reign, eleven years later.[123] Redford argued that the text was simply a misunderstanding of the three-generational formula to identify the granddaughter: "king's daughter of his body, whom he loves [NAME], born of king's daughter of his body, whom he loves, born of the great king's wife Nefertiti."[124]

A much more exhaustive discussion was offered by Christine Meyer. She began by noting Yuri Perepelkin's view that by their father's last year, no daughter was old enough to bear a child; she was also skeptical that princesses should name children after themselves. Meyer noted that both of the daughters in question married a successor and that, most importantly, the two texts used to claim Akhenaten as father of his own granddaughters were all recut, all originally having shown Kiya and her daughter, except for single blocks from Amarna[125] and Thebes[126]—but both these were fragmentary and relied on restorations: they could as easily refer to Akhenaten's third, fourth, or fifth daughters.[127]

As a perfect example of the circularity of Amarnan scholarship, Edward Wente reopened the whole question in 1980. For him, Ankhesenpaaten-tasherit and Meryetaten-tasherit were indeed daughters of their grandfather.[128] He further argued, on the basis of the apparent maturity of a *talatat* representation of Meryetaten,[129] that she married her father *prior* to his change of name and could also have borne her daughter before this point, making her at least twelve years old by Year 4/5![130] Ankhesenpaaten was nevertheless thought to have been born in Year 3/4. The ages do not make sense.

One suggestion was that the 'problem' princesses were the daughters of Kiya, but Allen showed in 2006 that this was not possible, since they replaced Kiya's daughter in a number of scenes. In addition, although the majority of monuments recarved to include these two younger princesses showed the Later form of the Aten name, approximately a third used the Earlier one, thus ruling out Smenkhkare and Tutankhamun as fathers. Allen went so far as to suggest that Meryetaten died in childbirth, and that the father was Akhenaten, who had already produced a daughter by her, whom he identified as the problematic nursing figure on wall A in room *gamma* in the Royal Tomb. Allen suggested that all three elder daughters became their father's sexual partner at thirteen. Meryetaten's daughter, he argued, was born "not much later" than the end of Year 12. Allen therefore dated Meryetaten's birth before Akhenaten came to the throne. Meketaten's appearance for the first time in the "Later Proclamation" of Year 6 was, he argued, not related to her birth, but rather celebrating her weaning. The fourth daughter, Neferneferuaten-tasherit, allegedly married to Akhenaten in Year 16–17, had to have been born around Year 3, five years earlier than usually assumed. In all this, Allen assumed a "thirteen years rule" for the earliest age at which a girl could be married.[131] Ages are being constantly manipulated.

Murnane was uncertain about the paternity of Meryetaten-tasherit and Ankhesenpaaten, suggesting that the title "King's Daughter" for these two granddaughters of Akhenaten and Nefertiti was simply a claim to direct descent during a possible power struggle between them and Kiya and her daughter.[132]

Apart from these putative father–daughter marriages, it is now a matter of historical curiosity that early historians of Egypt believed that the then-newly discovered Amarna Letters showed that the eldest daughter, Meryetaten, was married to the son of Burnaburiash of Babylon.[133] The letter in question (*EA* 10, line 48) in fact mentions a necklace as a "greeting gift" for Meryetaten, but says nothing about marriage. Such a marriage of an Egyptian princess with a foreign king was unheard of, although foreign princesses are regularly found in the Egyptian royal harem.

Did Akhenaten have sons?

Ever since the discovery of the tomb of Tutankhamun in 1922, many scholars have suggested that he was the son of Akhenaten.[134] A key piece of evidence was the identification of a pair of *talatat* from Hermopolis that together named the "King's Son of his Body, his Beloved, Tutankhaten" and a "King's Daughter of his Body, Praised by the Lord of the Two Lands [. . .]aten."[135] On the one hand, they clearly labeled a scene showing the prince and a princess (almost certainly his future wife Ankhesenpaaten), and the context makes it difficult to doubt that they were siblings and thus offspring of Akhenaten. On the other hand, it has been asked why the future Tutankhamun was not more on show during his father's reign. This is mostly accounted for by the fact that he was the son of a minor wife, although occasionally Nefertiti has been accepted as his mother.[136] It has also been pointed out, however, that royal sons are all but invisible on the monuments before the Nineteenth Dynasty (in contrast to daughters), and therefore that the lack of representations of any sons of Akhenaten may say nothing about whether any existed.[137]

The fate of Nefertiti
Nefertiti was disgraced

No fewer than four answers have been put forward over the past century as to the fate of the queen. Until 1923, the question had not been asked, but when the 1921/22 excavations at Amarna were published, Peet and Woolley had disturbing findings to report, which threw "a new and unexpected light upon the domestic life which (Akhenaten) paraded with such insistence." Describing their work at the Maru-Aten, they wrote of the "monotonous uniformity" of inscriptions and art—except that "here, as nowhere else, the queen's name has in nearly every case been carefully erased and that of her eldest daughter, Meryt-aten, written in palimpsest upon the stone, her distinctive attributes have been blotted out with cement, her features re-cut and her head enlarged into the exaggerated skull of the Princess Royal."

Here was obviously a problem to be solved. "Nefertiti, if alive, could hardly have agreed to so public an affront, nor would her death have been seized upon by so devoted a husband as an occasion to obliterate her memorials." There seemed only one explanation: "are we to suppose that things were not so happy as they seemed in the royal household, and that a quarrel so serious as to lose the queen her position put an end to the idyll which had long been the standing theme of the court artists?"[138]

Battiscombe Gunn treated the inscriptions separately and revisited the problem. Either Nefertiti had died or she had fallen into disgrace. He admitted that "the evidence which would justify us in choosing between these alternatives is lacking"—but he nevertheless inclined to the latter. Her "disgrace or retirement" had to be after Year 12, given her presence at the 'durbar' in that year.[139]

And yet all was not as it should have been. It was admitted that the queen's name had been erased in the Maru-Aten "in *nearly* every case" (my italics). Parts of the name and title of Nefertiti were found undefaced in the Entrance Hall of the Maru-Aten twenty-one times: her name and title were mostly left untouched on the blocks; on the columns "her" inscriptions were "roughly erased."[140] If Nefertiti had been "disgraced," surely her name and titles would have been effaced everywhere at Amarna.

Five years later Newberry linked his proposal for "intimate relations" between Akhenaten and Smenkhkare with Nefertiti's apparent disgrace and replacement by Meryetaten. It all seemed to fit, and the queen's "fall" became all but canonical—but explanations differed. Stephen Glanville, following the lead of the Amarna excavation reports, wrote of conclusive proof of Nefertiti's "disgrace" from the evidence of the Maru-Aten and her displacement by Smenkhkare. He also followed Henri Frankfort's suggestion (in an unpublished lecture) that the pivotal event was in Year 12, when Tiye came to Amarna with her steward Huya in "a final effort on their part to rouse the king to a more active foreign policy," Nefertiti having been responsible for "the hopelessly laissez-faire policy in Syria."[141]

Others followed Newberry more closely with a sexual explanation, based on his false identifications of the "Akhenaten and Smenkhkare" stelae.[142] For others the motive was religious. For Davies, Nefertiti was a *traitor* to Atenism. For Pendlebury and Seele, Nefertiti was disgraced and banished for *loyalty* to Atenism at a time when her husband was moving toward rapprochement with tradition.[143]

Few protested. One was James Baikie:

The Egypt Exploration Society's excavators have most unkindly and ungraciously tried to insinuate a serpent into this little Eden in the shape of a suggestion that the absence of Queen Nefertiti from the fragmentary inscriptions which have been recovered from Maru-Aten points to domestic trouble in the royal family, and to the breaking up of that idyllic love and unity of which so many pictures have survived. Surely such a suggestion is an entirely unnecessary outrage upon our feelings, and upon the memory of a couple whose mutual affection must often have been the only stay of their hearts in sore trouble. Akhenaten has had to bear enough blame, living and dead, without saddling him, almost gratuitously, with that of having quarrelled with his beautiful wife. It surely needs more than the mere absence of Nefertiti's name, of the reasons for which we know absolutely nothing, to overweigh the mass of solid evidence which points to a happiness in wedded love not often enjoyed in royal unions; and until some weightier testimony is forthcoming from the Devil's advocate we may continue to believe that as Akhenaten and Nefertiti were lovely and pleasant in their lives, so they were not divided, till the end.[144]

The disgrace theory was sunk with three shots. First, in 1968, Yuri Perepelkin noted that in the Maru-Aten, Princess Meryetaten stands behind her father, instead of behind her mother as was usual. Moreover, while elsewhere she was usually shown as a young girl, despite her actual age, here she was depicted as a woman. No reference was made to her mother. Her name was, indeed, written over another erased name, but as for the date of the replacement, Meryetaten was still a princess so had not yet become Smenkhkare's queen: she had no cartouche or uraeus. That was the vital clue: if these had been modified portraits of Nefertiti, she would have worn a uraeus (two, in fact).[145] Perepelkin then recognized that the phrases in the palimpsest texts recalled those of the gilded coffin from KV 55. And part of the original inscription gave the erased lady the title *ḥmt-mrryt-'3t* ("Greatly Beloved Wife"), a unique form never used for Nefertiti, whose titulary also did not include her husband's name, which had been present here. Perepelkin assumed that models of standard inscriptions had been made for workmen to follow, and such discarded models had, indeed, been found south of the estate wall: "Wife beloved of one . . . of the King of Upper and Lower Egypt . . . who will live to all eternity, Kiya."[146] These titles corresponded with those on her calcite pot in New York, making it clear that the original owner of the Maru-Aten was *not* Nefertiti, but a hitherto shadowy second wife of Akhenaten: Kiya.

The second blow to the disgrace theory was Harris's 1973 recovery for Nefertiti of the two Berlin stelae. The third was evidence known since the 1930s' reconstruction of Akhenaten's sarcophagus, but stressed by Tawfik in 1973 and Geoffrey Martin in 1974, that Nefertiti replaced the four traditional tutelary goddesses at its four corners.

Something more, known since 1912, can be added against the theory of Nefertiti's disappearance or disgrace. If Borchardt's reconstruction of the history of the famous Berlin bust is correct, this stood in the sculptor's workshop from whatever time it was made—presumably in Akhenaten's reign—and through the early years of Tutankhamun in Amarna until the city was abandoned and fell into ruin. It is unthinkable that this stunning portrait of a woman disgraced about Year 12 could have survived untouched for another decade.

Nefertiti died in the reign of Akhenaten

Aldred argued that Nefertiti died shortly after her daughter Meketaten, and was buried in the Royal Tomb. There was no evidence, he claimed, for her fanaticism for Atenism and banishment, or for her survival into the reign of Tutankhamun. Aldred also noted a fragmentary shabti in the Brooklyn Museum (see below).[147]

Wolfgang Helck denounced the way in which Nefertiti's fall from favor had become accepted as a fact, creating such total fictions as the idea of the royal family divided into factions: Nefertiti and Tutankhaten against Akhenaten and Smenkhkare. He had not, however, been able to consider Perepelkin's evidence, so that he still believed that it was Nefertiti who was replaced by Meryetaten in the Maru-Aten. He knew, however, that there was no evidence that Nefertiti had been outlawed; he suggested that she had in fact simply died and been replaced as "owner" of the Maru-Aten by her daughter, still a princess.

The date of her death was the crux, and for that the wine labels seemed important. The last ones known to name her, at that time, were dated to Years 10 and 11, but wine from an unnamed queen's estate continued through Years 13 to 17. Helck's interpretation was that after a royal person's death, his or her estate lost his or her name, but could continue. He therefore suggested that Nefertiti died after Meketaten, perhaps in Year 13.[148]

Joyce Tyldesley tried to bridge the old and the new on the basis that the last recorded appearance of Nefertiti was at the funeral of Meketaten, which she dated to Year 14 or 15. The only problem here is that there is no such firm date for this crucial event, especially as this 'date' becomes, some pages later, the linchpin of a statement that Nefertiti was replaced as queen by her eldest daughter Meryetaten, because she was "by now either dead or in semi-retirement."[149]

Gabolde, followed by Laboury, has asserted that Nefertiti died as late as a "few months" before Akhenaten.[150] They offer no evidence for this vital date. That she had *died* is proven for them by a number of facts: that there is a shabti of her (see below); that "Nefertiti's nurse" is not among the titles of Ay's wife Tey listed on a box in Berlin;[151] that the titles of Meryetaten and Ankhesenpaaten do not mention her when their names and titles replace those of Kiya; and that Nefertiti's name had been erased on statue bases of these daughters. They also emphasized an apparent reference in the Amarna Letters (*EA* 11) to Meryetaten as "mistress of the house," which they interpret to be an allusion to her taking over her mother's role on her demise. They suggest that a further piece of evidence for Nefertiti's 'absence' before the death of Akhenaten is the inscription on the box fragment from the tomb of Tutankhamun, which names Akhenaten, Neferneferuaten, and Meryetaten but, conspicuously, not Nefertiti. The emerging view of most other specialists in the period is, however, that she is indeed present in this text—as King Neferneferuaten.

Akhenaten and Nefertiti died together

In the authoritative *Lexikon der Aegyptologie*, Emma Brunner-Traut states: "The end of Nefertiti is shrouded in darkness: she and her husband were presumably murdered." The associated footnote offers no evidence for this assertion.[152]

Nefertiti survived her husband

One of the first to suggest that Nefertiti outlived Akhenaten was John Pendlebury in 1935. He believed that Nefertiti had been disgraced and retired to the Northern Palace with Tutankhamun, where she lived on until Tutankhamun's Year 3, whereupon he returned to Thebes.[153] This is very similar to the reconstruction by Redford: when Akhenaten appointed Smenkhkare coregent about Year 15 or 16, Nefertiti had to leave Amarna.[154] On his death a year or two later, she returned, championing Tutankhamun. Her death about his Year 3 signaled the abandonment of Amarna. Perepelkin agreed.[155] Redford later added evidence from the Hermopolis *talatat*: Nefertiti is shown with a granddaughter and the wish "may she live," indicating that she lived long enough to have grand-children (Meryetaten-tasherit and Ankhesenpaaten-tasherit). In the case of Ankhesenpaaten, she was born at the earliest in Year 5, so could not have had children herself until the very end of her father's reign. Nefertiti was therefore still alive at this time.[156]

In 1973, as we have already seen, Harris and Samson proposed a startling theory: Queen Neferneferuaten-Nefertiti became King Ankhkheperure Neferneferuaten, who became King Ankhkheperure Smenkhkare. The mystery of her disappearance was thus solved: she had assumed a new name and status.[157] According to Samson: "At (Akhenaten's) death, until the succession of Tutankhamun, she would have been the obvious royal and divine ruler in the interregnum."[158]

The wine-jar dockets were reconsidered by Krauss, who set out a table showing that Nefertiti's estate is last mentioned in the surviving dockets in Year 11, while the estate of the (unnamed) queen is found until Year 17, the last of the reign.[159] It had been Gunn's suggestion that the wine jars of the unnamed queen belonged to the queen *ex officio*, or a queen other than Nefertiti.[160] Helck's idea[161] that the anonymous estate of the queen signaled Nefertiti's demise is disproved by the fact that this category is known as early as Year 11, and she was alive at the 'durbar' the next year. There is also a possible (but by no means agreed) docket of "Lady Kiya" in Year 11. She, however, was never called queen but "Great Beloved Wife." The queen's estate in Year 17 was therefore Nefertiti's. Krauss argued that what consigned Nefertiti to oblivion after Akhenaten's death was the fact that she had not produced a male heir, and so lost the title of queen or King's Mother.[162]

The last vital piece of evidence to prove that King Ankh(et)kheperure Neferneferuaten was a woman was provided by a brilliant piece of detective work by Gabolde in 1998. He discovered something previously unnoticed: While it had long been known that various items in Tutankhamun's tomb (canopic coffinettes, pectorals, and so on) had been taken over from Neferneferuaten, an epithet within some of the latter's palimpsest cartouches had been wrongly read as "mery-Akhenaten." Gabolde's analysis showed that the epithet was actually "*3ḫt-n-ḥỉ.s*," that is, "effective for her husband." This made it absolutely certain that Neferneferuaten was a woman.

While Gabolde preferred to identify Neferneferuaten with Meryetaten, Dodson noted that most of Neferneferuaten's other known cartouche epithets associated her with Akhenaten, making it difficult for him to doubt that Akhenaten was the said "husband." He thus accepted that Nefertiti became coregent of Akhenaten as Neferneferuaten, but as *successor* of Smenkhkare, who had ruled only for a year or so about Year 13 or 14. He then argued that she went on directly to become coregent of Tutankhamun, the Year 3 in the graffito of Pawah being a year the two rulers shared. In the end, she either died or was deposed.[163]

Other crucial evidence remained unnoticed for decades. Aldred saw that if Nefertiti had predeceased Akhenaten, her portraits would not have been kept in the workshop of Thutmose.[164] In 1999 Marianne Luban drew attention to the standing limestone statue of Nefertiti, found by the Germans in the studio of Thutmose in 1912 (fig. 85). This was, she suggested, that of a woman aged forty years at the bare minimum.[165]

She could not possibly, in that case, have 'disappeared' by Year 12. The portrait could date at the latest from Year 3 of Tutankhamun, when Amarna was abandoned—and probably even earlier. If Nefertiti was forty then, she would have been about twenty when Akhenaten came to the throne. There is no cast-iron rule that he had to be the same age as her, but it is more likely than not. In that case, his age at accession is at the latter end of the proposed time span (early twenties), and he was in his late thirties when he died (as has

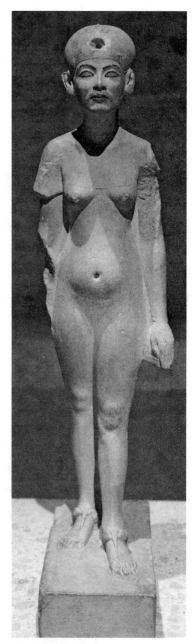

Fig. 85. The so-called "mature Nefertiti," from the studio of Thutmose (Berlin ÄM 21263).

usually been argued). Furthermore, Nefertiti wears a cap crown with the uraeus on her brow, which is anything but the insignia of a disgraced or supplanted queen. It must be noted, however, that, estimating the age of a stylized piece of sculpture is notoriously subjective.[166]

Left to the very end, deliberately, because it demonstrates the way in which a single new discovery can nullify decades of debate, is a new text first published in 2012. In the limestone quarries of Deir Abu Hinnis, at Bersha, ten kilometers north of Amarna on the same side of the Nile, and exploited at that time, was found a graffito of *Queen* Nefertiti dated to III *ꜣḫt* 15 in Year 16 of Akhenaten![167] One of the most ephemeral genres of sources, comprising a few words, thus overturned volumes of now utterly obsolete argument. Nefertiti's survival of Akhenaten is now almost certain. For those accepting the equation of Nefertiti with King Neferneferuaten, it also delays her assumption of full titles to the very last months of Akhenaten's reign (in any case before his death, given evidence of the Tutankhamun box fragment and the "Coregency Stela."

Burial

The original plan after the move to Akhet-Aten was for Nefertiti to be buried with her husband in the Royal Tomb.[168] Of material prepared for such a burial, the lower section of a shabti now in Brooklyn was published by Aldred in 1968,[169] but in 1986 Christian Loeben published a reconstruction incorporating an upper section, long held by the Louvre (fig. 86).[170] Loeben's reconstruction of the text (there is a gap between the two fragments) ran as follows: "The Princess, Great One in the Palace, blessed one of [the King of Upper and Lower Egypt, Neferkheperure-Waenre, son of Re Akhenaten, may he have a long life]; the King's Chief Wife Neferneferuaten-Nefertiti, may she live always and for eternity."[171] Loeben thus argued that Nefertiti had died as Akhenaten's queen and must have been buried in the Royal Tomb. Aldred reinforced this by asserting that royal shabtis were made during the embalming period (although without offering any evidence for this statement).[172]

Krauss, however, noted that there is no sign of Nefertiti's burial in the Royal Tomb at Amarna. As for Loeben's shabti, Krauss stated that this raised a whole series of questions about "provenance, epigraphy, and function." Her titles, the reconstruction of the scepter and flail, and the mention of Akhenaten were, in his view, not convincing. That she is called "King's Wife" was no evidence, he argued, that she died before Akhenaten: shabtis could be prepared long before burial.[173] The evidence of the shabti was, therefore, entirely indecisive. As Marianne Eaton-Krauss cautioned: "the existence of this piece documents only that a funerary outfit was prepared for the queen during her husband's lifetime. When she died is another matter."[174]

Fig. 86. Upper fragment of a shabti of Nefertiti (Louvre AF.9904).

Nefertiti's mummy

Two candidates have been proposed to be Nefertiti's remains, both found in a side-chamber of KV 35, the tomb of Amenhotep II, which was discovered by Victor Loret (1859–1946), Director of the Antiquities Service, in 1898. They were found with a third body, a male youth, which is still in the tomb (fig. 87).[175] The female bodies, always known as the "Elder Lady" and the "Younger Lady," were moved to Cairo in 2010.[176]

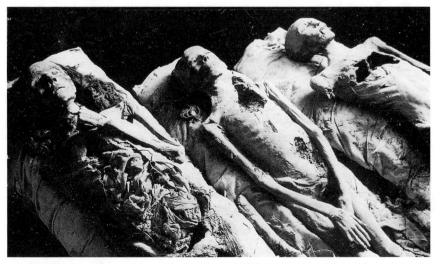

Fig. 87. The three mummies in a side-chamber of KV35: the "Elder Lady," the "Young Prince," and the "Younger Lady."

The "Elder Lady"

This mummy was identified as Queen Tiye in 1978 through a comparison of its hair with the lock of hair labeled as Queen Tiye's in the tomb of Tutankhamun.[177] Renata Germer challenged this identification, noting that the quoted skull measurements were unconvincing because the control group consisted of eleven women of uncertain identity spanning a period of over four hundred years! She also considered the hair samples to be unconvincing, again because of the lack of a satisfactory control group. Finally, she pointed to blood tests: Yuya and Tjuiu were both A$_2$ while the Elder Lady was O^5; she thus could be their child, but this was not a certainty.[178]

X-ray evidence suggests, moreover, that the mummy is of a woman aged about thirty. That would be far too young for Tiye: she was probably married as a young woman to Amenhotep III, who ruled for nearly forty years, and whom she survived for at least twelve years. It should, however, be noted that the calculation of the ages of the royal mummies is notoriously uncertain, with many apparently securely identified bodies being far too young.[179] The identification with Tiye has nevertheless been revived by Zahi Hawass on the basis of DNA data, which, as noted above, appears to support the possibility that the Elder Lady was a child of Yuya and Tjuiu.[180]

Susan James, on the other hand, has argued—on the basis of subjective analysis of a number of traits—that the mummy was Nefertiti's, explaining away the hair evidence as a gift to Tiye's original tomb at Amarna from her daughter-in-law.[181]

The "Younger Lady"

The idea that this mummy (fig. 88) might be Nefertiti was apparently first suggested by Marianne Luban in 1999. Her arguments were as follows: the unusual shape of the cranium suggested that she was a member of the Amarnan family; the bone structure was similar to the busts of Nefertiti: a slender neck, beautiful jawline, and the unbroken line of the nose from the brow; she had a shaved head, such as some claimed Nefertiti might have needed to wear her tall crown; she had double pierced ears; and the facial measurements were comparable with sculptures identified as Nefertiti. Luban did, however, admit that the mummy's

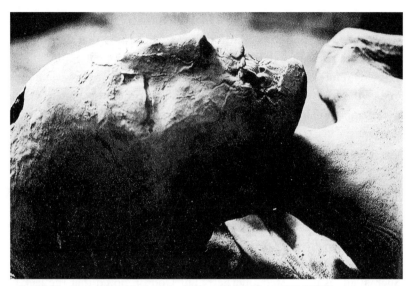
Fig. 88. The face of the "Younger Lady" from KV35 (Cairo CG 61072)..

left arm alongside the body does not correspond to what is generally regarded as "the queenly attitude."[182]

Apparently unaware of Luban's study, Joann Fletcher announced in 2003 her "discovery" that Nefertiti's mummy was the Younger Lady, using almost the same arguments, adding a claim that the body had been associated with a "Nubian" wig and that a depression on the brow suggested a brow band.[183]

Susan James countered these arguments: the Nubian wig may not have belonged to the mummy, and in any case it was not exclusive to Nefertiti and was worn as early as the court of Amenhotep III; there is no evidence that Nefertiti's head was shaved, or that, indeed, it had to be to wear her famous flat-topped crown; double ear piercing was not exclusive to Nefertiti and her daughters: Tiye's mother Tjuiu has it; tight-fitting brow bands were not exclusive to royalty; and the evidence of the mummy's arms had been seriously mishandled.[184] The right one is missing, but a detached and flexed right arm was found together with the three bodies in this chamber.[185] Argument about the owner is irrelevant. The mummy's left arm is still attached and rests on the thigh—and it is that arm which should be flexed if she were a queen!

In 2010, an analysis of the DNA of these mummies (and others attributed to the period) was interpreted as suggesting that the Younger Lady was a sister of Akhenaten and mother of Tutankhamun by him.[186] Gabolde refuted this three years later, noting that such a sister cannot be one of the four otherwise known, and also that the same genetic result would apply if Tutankhamun were the offspring of three generations of first-cousin marriages.[187] If the long-standing speculation that Neferiti was a daughter of Ay, that Ay was a brother of Queen Tiye, and that the mother of Amenhotep III, Mutemwia, might have been a sister of Yuya were correct,[188] this would be exactly the situation if Akhenaten and Nefertiti were Tutankhamun's parents—thus suggesting that the Younger Lady was indeed Nefertiti. The one 'new' relationship genetically required by such a conclusion would be that Nefertiti's mother could not have been either Iuy or Tey, but a sister of Amenhotep III. Such a lady is unattested anywhere, but Dodson noted that the lack of any data on Ay prior to the move to Amarna makes the concept perhaps less unlikely than a previously unknown sister-wife of Akhenaten.[189]

Many scholars remain skeptical regarding these DNA studies,[190] making it unlikely that conclusions derived from them will find general acceptance in the immediate future.

The fate of Nefertiti has been one of the most intriguing of all Amarnan questions. Suffice to say that in the last century a total revolution has taken place. Once suggested to have been a queen disgraced two-thirds of the way through her husband's reign, she is now thought sure to have outlived her husband and to have attained the rank of coregent, if not pharaoh in her own right.

Kiya

After decades during which Akhenaten's monogamy with Nefertiti had become an Egyptological 'fact,' another wife of Akhenaten was restored to history in 1959. William Hayes mentioned a little unguent jar (MMA 20.2.11), four and a half inches high, with an inscription giving the names of the Aten, the king, and "the titulary of an apparently hitherto unknown member of the latter's harim," the Greatly Beloved Wife, Kiya. Hayes declared that her name suggested a foreign origin.[191] The jar was not then illustrated, but an image of a companion piece was provided by

Herbert Fairman in 1961, with a copy of the hieroglyphic text: "The Greatly Beloved wife of the King of Upper and Lower Egypt, who lives on Truth, Lord of the Two Lands Neferkheperure-waenre, the goodly child of the living the Aten, who shall be living for ever and ever, Kia."[192]

The scholar who attempted to bring Kiya back to life was Perepelkin in 1968. He reconsidered all the evidence that had been accumulated since Newberry's discussion of Smenkhkare in 1928: the stela of Pay, the unfinished relief of a king pouring wine for Akhenaten (figs. 82, 83), a block from Memphis, a broken stela from Amarna, and several reliefs from Hermopolis. The second figure in the first two reliefs would soon be mostly attributed back to Nefertiti, but Perepelkin suggested that the attributes and clothing did not suit her. He also noted that one of the Hermopolis reliefs mentioning Ankhesenpaaten-tasherit retained traces of the original name of the mother, Kiya, and must therefore have originally been a representation of the latter. Perepelkin argued that Kiya was also the

Fig. 89. One of the canopic jars from KV 55 (MMA 30.8.54).

original owner of the coffin and the canopic jars in KV 55 (fig. 89). Kiya's distinguishing feature was her large round earrings (fig. 90). She had never borne the conventional queen's title, her name was never written in a cartouche, and she did not wear a uraeus. Her title, ḥmt-mrryt-ʿ3t ("Greatly Beloved Wife"), differed fundamentally from Nefertiti's conventional ḥmt-nsw-wrt "King's Chief Wife."[193]

Fig. 90. Section of a scene of Akhenaten and Kiya sacrificing birds, with its two blocks recently reunited by Raymond Johnson. Kiya's portrait (with exceptionally large earrings) and label-text were reworked for Meryetaten; from Ashmumein (MMA 1985.328.2+Ny Carslberg ÆIN 1775).

She was mostly shown with a daughter worshiping the Aten, behind Akhenaten, but the Aten did not extend an 'nḥ-sign to her. She had her own "sunshade" in the Great Temple and a southern estate, the Maru-Aten, "bristling" with references to her. The Northern Palace similarly showed a queen's name,[194] and not Nefertiti's, because the epithet desiring longevity, "may she live," was not elaborate enough ("may she live to all eternity"). This palace was taken by Perepelkin to be "the permanent retreat" of Akhenaten and Kiya. He further claimed that Kiya's name could be restored on two wine-jar dockets: of Years 11 and 16.[195]

According to Perepelkin, "Kia's star rose to a considerable height as the years passed toward the later part of the pharaoh's reign."[196] She finally became coregent, later modified to "semi-pharaoh,"[197] wearing the Blue Crown, holding a scepter, and wearing a "sporran," but she only ever had one cartouche. Her elevation was placed in Year 16 or 17, based on Perepelkin's belief that the two unfinished Berlin stelae were representations of Kiya, rather than Smenkhkare or Nefertiti.[198]

Kiya was pharaoh only for "a short period of time." As for her fate, her name was replaced by that of Meryetaten—who was not yet a queen but still only a princess. The Northern Palace and Maru-Aten estate were renamed for Meryetaten, Kiya's sunshade was reassigned to Ankhesenpaaten, and even her coffin and canopic jars were taken over.[199]

Despite what has subsequently been seen as an "over evaluation" of Kiya's career, Perepelkin's epoch-making contribution was to recover Kiya in the recut inscriptions of the Maru-Aten and the Northern Palace at Amarna, and in the coffin and canopic jars of KV 55.[200]

Harris was then able to list six places where Kiya's names occur: the two cosmetic jars (with her full title); two blocks from the Maru-Aten; a block from Hermopolis; and a strip of wood from a box or pen case,[201] as well as four doubtful cases. Her full title was given on the calcite vases, and Harris agreed with Perepelkin that this accorded with the inscription on the coffin in KV 55. At Maru-Aten and Hermopolis, the texts were all palimpsests.[202]

Nicholas Reeves identified six more texts from the reserve collections of the British Museum, of which the more important are an offering table with a short titulary, and three column fragments from the North Palace, where her name was usurped by Meryetaten. Only Akhenaten and Nefertiti were otherwise honored by offering tables.[203]

Work had also progressed on identifying her portraits, recut for the Amarnan princesses.[204] She wore no uraeus, but might wear a distinctive wig, which bared both the brow and the back of the head.

Rainer Hanke (1929–2001) reexamined the changed portraits found on some blocks from Hermopolis, where the head and hair of a woman had been altered. The changes had been made only where the woman originally wore a wig (either the pointed Nubian or the curled one), not a crown. The replacement figure was shown to have a shaved forehead and back of head, and now wore a side-lock.[205] In one striking example, a smaller head was made into the larger one of an unidentified queen wearing a crown.[206]

Eaton-Krauss suggested that there should also be statues of Kiya from Amarna, because they are shown in reliefs. She suggested two possible examples: the head of a statuette and the so-called "kissing king."[207]

This matter of Kiya's appearance especially interested Krauss:[208] the only reasonably sure portrait in the round was the lids from the KV 55 canopic jars.[209] He now attributed to her a relief from Hermopolis, usurped by Meryetaten,[210] and a quartzite head from the studio of Thutmose.[211]

Raymond Johnson has recently dramatically added to our understanding of Kiya by reexamining Hermopolis *talatat*. He showed that the famous profile adjoins the unique scene of Akhenaten offering a duck to the Aten (fig. 90), so that she is associated with him in that worship. He also has suggested that traditional scenes can be reconstructed of her with Akhenaten hunting in the marshes.[212]

The period of Kiya's importance has been understood by most scholars to be after Year 12, especially those who assumed that Nefertiti must have been dead, or had suffered some other fate by that time. Kiya's monuments are, however, associated with both the Earlier and Later forms of the name of the Aten,[213] traditionally dated before and after Year 9. She therefore may have had a much longer role.

Her importance is attested by the considerable number of texts now known to be hers. There are, however, certainly no traces of Kiya at Thebes; she is not shown in any tomb relief and is associated with only three buildings at Amarna: the sunshades of Maru-Aten, the *Pr-ḥʿ* (House of Rejoicing), and a chapel therein. She is, of course, found on many of the Hermopolis *talatat*, along with her now nameless daughter, but the nature and exact former location of the structures represented by those blocks remain uncertain. Her image, titles, and name have in all cases been replaced in reliefs by those of Akhenaten's daughters—mainly by Meryetaten, but sometimes by Ankhesenpaaten.

As for the date of her disappearance and/or death, it seems to have been later than Meketaten's death, because her monuments were taken over only by Meryetaten and Ankhesenpaaten. Jacobus van Dijk therefore suggested around Year 12, her last definite dated monument being the wine-jar docket of Year 11, while a block from Hermopolis (on which she is replaced by Ankhesenpaaten) gives her the epithet *nḫt ḫprš* (Victorious War Crown),[214] which van Dijk referred to the Nubian campaign of that year.[215] Gabolde, however, dated her disappearance as late as Year 16 on the basis of a restored wine docket: "[Year . . .] 6 the Noble Lady [Kiya]."

Concerning her fate, fantasy dominates: According to Helck, after the failure of her Hittite overtures (see below) she was murdered by the supporters of Meryetaten and Ankhesenpaaten and her body flung into the Nile.[216] According to Tyldesley she died giving birth to Tutankhamun.[217] According to Fletcher, Nefertiti engineered her death.[218] Gabolde proposed proscription, *damnatio memoriae*, disgrace, and repudiation (she fell from favor after the Hittite defeat of the Mitanni), but concluded with the assertion that she simply returned to Mitanni. Laboury agreed.[219]

It has become fashionable to suggest that Kiya was the mother of Tutankhamun.[220] She is, however, shown with only a single daughter, rather undermining the principal argument for this proposed relationship: that Nefertiti is shown only with daughters, and thus cannot have been Tutankhamun's mother!

In sum, since 1959 a remarkable thing has happened: an important figure, another wife of Akhenaten, has been restored to history. She is now well known from a long list of her possessions and of the places associated with her at Amarna, and her portrait is now easily recognizable. She has recently been widely accepted as Mitannian, perhaps the famous Tadu-Kheba, the Mitannian princess in the harem of Amenhotep III.[221]

The Hittite letter

The Hittite Annals of Suppuliliumas tell a sensational story. On the death of Pharaoh Bibkhururiyas (variant Nibkururiyas),[222] his widow "Dakhamunzu" wrote to the Hittite king seeking a Hittite prince as husband; he was at length sent, but was then killed.[223] Walter Federn showed in 1960 that Dakhamunzu was not a name, but a title: a transcription of *t3 ḥmt nsw*, "the King's Wife."[224]

No fewer than four candidates have been put forward as "Dakhamunzu."

Nefertiti

Some have thought that the Hittite form of the the king's name was a version of Neferkheperure (Akhenaten): the widow was therefore Nefertiti. Redford championed this view. In the Hittite annals, immediately before the queen's request, Suppuliliumas had sent Lupakku and Tarkhunta-zalma to attack Amka.[225] In *EA* 170, Hittite troops under Lupakku had captured Amqu; the letter was addressed to Aziru of the Amurru. Redford argued for the identity of events here, which the letter shows cannot be as late as the death of Tutankhamun.

For Redford, the omission of the second Hittite commander in the letter was not a problem. He dismissed the name Nibkhururiyas (Tutankhamun) as a mistake (!), and he argued that the chronology fits perfectly: the Hittite king Suppuliliumus died six years after Akhenaten, while by the time of Tutankhamun's death, his son Mursilis was in his second year.[226]

Kenneth Kitchen's review was devastating: "if philology is to have any meaning at all the Hittite form could only be the name of Tutankhamun." He noted that Redford had defined a choice between two things: either *EA* 170 did not refer to the same attack on Amqu as the Hittite annals, or the king's name was a mistake, and he adopted the latter. "Alas, Redford chooses the wrong alternative." Kitchen furthermore knocked away Redford's main historical support: it was a "methodological error" to treat "the hypothesis of the identity of campaigns in *EA* 170 and the Hittite texts as if it were the absolute certainty that it is assuredly not." And there were historical difficulties. Even if Smenkhkare were not alive when Akhenaten died, Tutankhamun was obviously a candidate. And Nefertiti was no longer the gateway to the throne; that was Meryetaten or Ankhesenpaaten.[227]

Nefertiti has continued, however, to be considered by some scholars as the queen in question, particularly after Robert Stempel identified a certain

"Armaya," mentioned in a fragmentary Hittite text, with Horemheb, the regent of Tutankhamun; the result is that Suppiluliumas I would have died before Tutankhamun.[228] As Dodson has pointed out, however, while "Armaya" might indeed be a Hittite writing of "Horemheb," the latter is a sufficiently common name to make it impossible to rely on the equation with the regent, particularly in view of its wide-ranging implications.[229]

Kiya

There has been one champion of Kiya as author of the letter: Helck. As early as 1981, he dismissed Krauss's view that the author was Meryetaten, because she was a royal daughter, not a widow (on his reading of Smenkhkare's chronology), and because when the Hittite plan failed, that woman would not survive, but Meryetaten did and became queen. Kiya's name and portrait were replaced by those of Meryetaten and the latter even took her coffin and canopic jars for her husband.[230]

Twenty years later, Helck argued that even if the late king referred to in the annals is written Nibhururiya, *b*, *p*, and *f* in cuneiform are interchangeable. The scribe might have mistaken the name of a more recent king for an earlier one (NeferkheperuRe), that is, Akhenaten. Linguistics, therefore, could not solve the problem; one must turn to historical considerations.

For Helck, the negotiations over the Hittite husband took one and a half years, but Tutankhamun was buried after seventy days and Ay was already king, so that the royal widow could not offer the throne to a Hittite prince. Dakhamunzu thus could not be Meryetaten: her husband Smenkhkare (Ankhkhepererure) would be in cuneiform "Anshururiya." Meryetaten became First Lady under Akhenaten (*EA* 155), and Burnaburiash distinguishes her from the "Mistress of the House" (*EA* 11), who is Kiya. The letter writer therefore was Kiya.[231]

Meryetaten

Krauss attempted a third identification. He asserted that philologically the name of the Egyptian king in the Hittite annals could be either Akhenaten or Tutankhamun: philology, it was again agreed, could not solve the puzzle. For him, however, the Hittite war occurred at the end of Akhenaten's reign (*EA* 170), so he was the king mentioned.[232] The war with the Hittites will have broken out in Akhenaten's Year 16, when

Suppuliliumas attacked the Mitanni and conquered Qadesh, establishing Aitaqami as king there. The following year (his last), Akhenaten attacked Qadesh after Aitaqami attacked Amqu. Relying on the evidence of Manetho that a daughter of the king succeeded Akhenaten, Krauss identified her name, Akencheres, as a version of Ankh(et)kheperure, who for him was Meryetaten. Hermann Schlögl agreed with Krauss.[233]

Rolf Hachmann also accepted the identity of events in the Hittite annals and in *EA* 170, arguing that the queen could not be Ankhesenamun, because there was allegedly no question of Ay not succeeding. The queen could thus only be Meryetaten, the daughter and *wife* of Akhenaten. On the failure of the Hittite overture, she then married Smenkhkare, but did not survive his reign.[234]

Gabolde was also of the view that the queen was Meryetaten. The Egyptians had attacked Qadesh and the Hittites attacked Amqu. It was then that the letter was written. Then Carchemish was captured. These events he tried to pin down, relying on a reexamination of *EA* 43 by Pinhas Artzi, which indicated that some ruler had been assassinated by his son, but that Suppuliliumas had rewarded someone by making his sons his sons-in-law, one of whom would become king. This very peculiar situation would accord with the assassination of Tushratta of the Mitanni by his son, and the installation as vassal king there of Suppuliliumas's son-in-law Kiliteshshub. The siege of Carchemish took place at this time, which was the end of Akhenaten's reign or under Ankhetkheperure Neferneferuaten, whom Gabolde identified with Meryetaten.[235]

The main problem with every one of Nefertiti, Kiya, or Meryetaten is that none of them could say there was no son—because Tutankhaten was unequivocally alive. Yet the Hittites accepted the claim, even after sending an envoy to investigate. To escape this inconsistency, Gabolde claimed that we have not read the text carefully enough, and he turned it into a harem drama. The letter was entirely duplicitous: the Egyptians were frightened by the Hittite advance, and the queen took the amazing step of turning to the enemy simply in order to trick them into sending her a prince as hostage. Laboury followed Gabolde and tried to answer the main objection by claiming that Tutankhaten was being hidden at Akhmim.[236] This, of course, tied in with Gabolde's view that Smenkhkare was, in fact, the Hittite prince.

Ankhesenamun

The dead king in the Hittite annals has most commonly been identified as Nebkheperure (Tutankhamun); the widow was therefore Ankhesenamun.[237] Problems have, however, been pointed out.

From the floral evidence, the king was buried in March/April, but the Hittite annals show that the king in question died in August/September.[238] The negotiations took some six months, yet traditionally the embalming process for a king took seventy days, and by the time of the funeral Ay had become king: the fresco in the tomb shows him officiating at the occasion. Some have gone so far, in attempting to circumvent this inconvenient fact, as to claim that Ay was king only in an acting capacity.[239] More importantly, the seventy-day period for embalming can be questioned: it is a generalization, and there is no evidence that it necessarily applied in this case. Trevor Bryce accepted the evidence of both the Hittite annals (date of death) and the floral evidence (date of burial) and posited that the throne was left vacant for some months.[240] Dodson also accepted an interregnum and suggested that, had a successor already been appointed (rendering the negotiations deceitful), the Hittite envoys would have known it.[241]

In conclusion: we have a letter to the Hittites, and we have Hittite sources with which to compare it, but the cuneiform version of the dead pharaoh's name is not agreed, and the widowed queen is referred to by title, not by name. One of the most extraordinary documents in Egyptian history remains inscrutable.

6 An Empire Lost?

Who 'lost' the Egyptian 'empire'?

The domination of Egypt by the Hyksos at the end of the Middle Kingdom and their expulsion at the beginning of the New Kingdom was a defining episode in Egyptian history. This foreign domination (albeit restricted to Lower Egypt) was a national shame that deeply affected the mentality of the Egyptians of the Eighteenth Dynasty and underlay first the expulsion of the Hyksos from the national boundaries and next, more importantly, their pursuit into Asia. The result was the creation of an Egyptian 'empire,' primarily the work of Thutmose III. Egyptian texts, known since the nineteenth century, gave the victors' account, with the expected pride in success.

This picture was completely transformed by the discovery of the Amarna Letters, which appeared to show a collapse of that empire during the reigns of Amenhotep III and Akhenaten. The modern assessment of the latter as ruler of an empire outside Egypt has thus been almost universally negative. James Breasted, for instance, declared that "he was not fit to cope with a situation demanding an aggressive man of affairs and a skilled military leader."[1]

The potent influence of contemporary events on many such judgments is demonstrated by the remarks of Henry Hall in 1921. Akhenaten let the empire go, not because of

225

mere indolence, but apparently a conscientious pacifism, a new phenomenon in the history of human thought. Akhenaten was an artist
and a philosopher, who lived, or aspired to live, *au dessus du combat* on
a plane higher than that of the contending forces of his world. . . . Yet
this young man, whom we may believe to have been animated by
the purest and most elevated of motives, succeeded by his obstinate
doctrinaire love of peace in causing far more misery in his world than
half a dozen elderly militarists could have done. It is the usual tragedy
of such men as he, the usual catastrophe when a philosopher rules,
whether his philosophy takes the form of pacifism or any other doctrine. We can hardly doubt that Syria and Palestine were far happier
under the *pax aegyptia* of Amenophis III than during the lawless chaos
which was allowed to supervene by the well-meant inaction of his son.

So the appeals for help went unanswered. "Akhenaten was too busy
imposing the 'doctrine' on his unwilling subjects and in designing new
decorations for the tombs of his faithful followers."[2] Here are all the
agonizing conflicts of the Great War and its aftermath played out more
than three millennia earlier. Akhenaten's supposed pacifism, however, ill
accords with the Amarna Letter Hall quoted (*EA* 162).

John Pendlebury expressed himself in similar terms in 1935: "It seems
obvious to us now that a display of force would have saved untold misery."
Queen Tiye came to Amarna in Year 12. "She well knew what was hap-
pening in the empire." It was she who "stirred" Akhenaten to stage the
"durbar." Pendlebury thought that it was "quite possible" that most of the
"tribute" had to be manufactured on the spot. The history of Asia during
Akhenaten's reign made sorry reading. Pendlebury listed the events: Tushratta, king of Mitanni and Egypt's ally, was killed; his son Mattiwaza called
in the Hittites; Aziru of the Amorites captured the coastal towns of Syria
and Phoenicia; and Rib-Hadda of Byblos, "one of the most loyal and
lovable characters," was driven out by pro-Hittite factions. In sum, "the
work of centuries was undone." His effort to place the blame squarely on
Akhenaten was, however, completely demolished by the careless admission
that perhaps the empire was lost through Nefertiti's "womanish policy."[3]

John Wilson identified no fewer than five stages in the "disintegra-
tion" of the Egyptian empire, although the first two admittedly dated to

the reign of Amenhotep III. First, the Syrian princes broke away; second, the Amurru under Abdi-Ashirta and Aziru created a separate state in northern Syria, in alliance with the Hittites; third, Suppuliliumas and the Hittites took Syria and conquered the Mitanni; fourth, Phoenicia was lost, and Labayu of Shakmu with the Habiru established himself in Palestine; fifth, the garrisons were withdrawn.[4]

The crisis is vividly recreated by Cyril Aldred. Late in the reign of Amenhotep III, the Hittite vassals joined the Mitanni and sacked the Hittite capital. The Hittites seemed finished, but a young king, Suppuliliumas, took power in a coup and the situation was soon reversed. The vassals wavered. This was about Year 12.

> The moment was therefore ripe for a parade of force by the Pharaoh in person. At the head of his chariotry and infantry, with his Nubian shock-troops, archers and auxiliaries, he ought to have taken the field, suppressed the overtly rebellious, replaced those who were plotting treachery, rounded up some of the local footpads and Bedouin, encouraged the waverers, rewarded the faithful, and removed to the Egyptian court the sons of those whose reliability was not wholly assured. The campaign could have been concluded with a grand hunt in the chief trouble spot to exhibit the prowesss of the Pharaoh.

This all sounds so simple. Could this considerable program have been accomplished? More to the point, even if it had, would any lasting solution have been achieved? A page further on, Aldred admitted that such an expedition would have led to an armed clash with the Hittites, and that punitive measures *were* taken: Aziru was summoned to Egypt, and Labayu was killed in a skirmish. "Forces and supplies were obviously being marshalled for a serious Asiatic expedition at the end of Akhenaten's reign; and indeed such a campaign in the region of Gezer [Gazru] may have been mounted." Akhenaten therefore was certainly no pacifist.[5]

Donald Redford offered a more nuanced interpretation. He distinguished the south and the east as the two main areas of Egyptian interest. In Nubia, foreign policy was "pursued with determination and intelligence" (colonies, temples, Nubian troops used as garrisons in the east, and an expedition under viceroy Thutmose), while in the east Akhenaten's hesitancy and lack of foresight lost him the initiative. . . . A recluse with a single fixation, pharaoh was apt to grow tired of the extended periods of concentration necessary to pursue a consistent foreign policy. Having to deal and bargain with people unnerved him; for he was essentially a timorous man. His only irrevocable resolve pertained to his cultic program, not to his treatment of his territorial vassals.[6]

One can instantly see here the fundamental contradictions: the man of short attention span who could pursue a sound policy in Nubia, and the timid man who was (according to Redford) an immovable fanatic in religious policy.

Like Redford, Nicholas Reeves distinguished between Nubia, which remained "relatively—if not wholly—stable" and Syria–Palestine: "From the start, however, Amenophis IV Akhenaten had shown that he cared little for affairs beyond the Nile valley, for warfare, or for the ways of international diplomacy. For all the fine universalist talk of the "Great Hymn" to the Aten, the king's interests and concerns revolved wholly around the home country." Reeves then took the argument much further, asserting that by the time Akhenaten understood the gravity of the situation, his troops were needed for other purposes: "propping up an increasingly unpopular regime at home."[7]

The Egyptian empire, fruit of generations of untiring effort and bravery, was thus lost by a coward, an indolent womanizer, or a religious fanatic. There have been other views. As early as 1884, Alfred Wiedemann asserted that the Aten temple at Soleb in Nubia suggested that there was no "retreat" in foreign relations, even if we possessed no depictions of Akhenaten as leader in war.[8]

Norman de Garis Davies, who knew the pictorial record better than anyone, focused on the 'durbar' scenes of foreign tribute in Year 12. He credited Akhenaten with not following the costly and dangerous policy of military invasion and preferring diplomacy. It was "not unlikely," nonetheless, that there had been military demonstrations on the northern and southern frontiers.[9]

James Baikie was one of Akhenaten's staunchest defenders, paying very keen attention to the rival kings against whom the pharaoh was pitted. For him, Suppuliliumas was a man who seemingly never took the straightest road if a crooked one could be found, one of the slipperiest of customers, who delighted in intrigue for the mere pleasure of the thing, almost as much as for the profits which it brought, and had a perfect genius for getting his accomplices to pull the chestnuts out of the fire for him, and then devouring them while they were still nursing their burnt fingers. . . . Altogether a most unlovely man.

Akhenaten thus had to cope with "the tangled web of intrigue which was being woven for the best part of half a century by the Hittite spider from his northern fastnesses in Cappadocia." This was the prelude to the overthrow of the Mitanni and the confrontation with Egypt in Asia. Closer to home, however, "that there is no evidence of revolt within the borders of Egypt itself during the whole reign is surely ample proof that there was no such abandonment of his royal duties on the part of Akhenaten as has been assumed."[10]

Etienne Drioton and Jacques Vandier were of the view that the person responsible for the collapse of any Egyptian empire was, in reality, Amenhotep III, who relied on diplomatic marriages and loyal vassals. They hinted, meanwhile, at the possibility that Horemheb was active as a general in Palestine late in the reign of Akhenaten.[11]

Joyce Tildesley agreed that Amenhotep was to blame:

Amenhotep III had avoided, through accident or design, all military action. He had not led the fight against the vile Ibhat (in Nubia) in person, delegating the command of the army to the viceroy Merimose, and he had never felt the need to embark on a military command or to make a tour of his foreign possessions.[12]

The evidence
The Amarna Letters
As far as we know, the vast majority of the letters were found at Amarna about 1887 by a peasant woman seeking fertilizer, in what has come to be known as the "Records Office," but they did not come to scholarly attention before they passed through various hands. Further searches, especially by Flinders Petrie, added more letters. They now number 382, more than 200 of which are in Berlin, and almost 100 in London.[13]

They are mostly in Akkadian or Babylonian, so they are the letters received by the Egyptian court. There are nine copies of letters sent by pharaoh.[14] The letters are divided into two very different categories: royal correspondence between kings regarding alliances and gifts (*EA* 1–43), and vassal correspondence from Egypt's client rulers in Syria and Palestine. The foreign writer most frequently preserved is Rib-Hadda of Byblos (seventy letters).[15] Four letters were written by women (*EA* 48, 50, 273, and 274).

It seems agreed that the letters range in date from the late reign of Amenhotep III to the accession of Tutankhamun, who abandoned Amarna. The royal correspondence refers to pharaohs by a garbled version of their names: Amenhotep III is Mimmureya or Nibmu(w)areya (= Nebmaatre); Akhenaten is Naphurureya (= Neferkheperure); and Tutankhamun is Nibmurrereya or Niphurrereya (= Nebkheperure). The crucial letter for assuring these identities is *EA* 27. Akhenaten's correspondents are Burnaburiash II of Babylon, Tushratta of Mitanni, Ashuruballit of Assyria, and Suppuliliumas of the Hittites. A major problem has been that only *three* bear a date: *EA* 23: Amenhotep III Year 36; *EA* 27: Akhenaten Year 2; and *EA* 254: either Year 12 (of Akhenaten) or Year 32 (of Amenhotep III).[16]

There are therefore obvious questions about how they were filed. Aldred raised important questions about the 'Records Office' where these letters were found.[17] Amarna was abandoned. What, then, do the surviving letters represent? Are these only out-of-date letters? It must be stressed that, being in foreign languages, in their present form they would have been intelligible only to a few expert translators. This may not, therefore, have been a real archive, but only the left-over originals. The tablets would have been translated into Egyptian and kept on much more manageable papyrus rolls. Aldred considered, nevertheless, that the archive was fairly complete. Frederick Giles, in contrast, stated that no surviving letter can be dated after the death of Akhenaten, although Amarna was not abandoned, he thought, for another four or five years. This would suggest that when the city was abandoned, the most recent correspondence was removed. There is also no copy of any answer to an eastern correspondent, nor is there any report from the many Egyptian officials stationed in Asia.[18] One possible explanation of the infrequency of royal letters is that instructions to the vassals were conveyed in person by Egyptian commissioners and messengers from Egypt.[19]

The letters to and from Babylon (*EA* 1–14) concern, in the main, royal women for the Egyptian harem and gold in return. Letter 14 gives some idea of the staggering array of gifts which were leaving Egypt at this time. It is interesting that the pharaoh is adamant that no Egyptian princess is ever given in exchange (*EA* 4). The Egyptian–Babylonian alliance went back four generations (*EA* 10).

As striking as that is, the Mitannian correspondence (*EA* 17–29) is even more interesting.[20] Two of the most famous Amarna Letters occur here. One is the letter of Tushratta to Queen Tiye (*EA* 26), obviously shortly after Amenhotep III's death, calling her the "mistress of Egypt" and stating that she knew better than anyone else what had been stated in diplomatic correspondence between Amenhotep and Tushratta, and that she had written to the latter seeking continuation of good relations with her son Akhenaten. Tushratta was, however, displeased because, whereas Amenhotep had sent him statues of solid gold, Akhenaten sent only gold-plated wooden ones. The other important Mitannian letter is 29, a history of relations with Egypt. Tushratta calls himself Akhenaten's father-in-law, apparently because the pharaoh had inherited Tushratta's sister from his father's harem. Tushratta reveals that Thutmose IV obtained from his grandfather, Artatama, the last's daughter in marriage. Amenhotep III obtained from Tushratta's father, Suttarana, his daughter Kelu-Kheba in marriage, and from Tushratta his daughter Tadu-Kheba (one might spare a thought for these Mitannian women traded in this way into far-off foreign harems, never to see their families or their land again). This, it must be admitted, is only a prelude to another extraordinarily lengthy complaint about the lack of gold statues and Akhenaten's detaining of Mitannian messengers. Egypt and the Mitanni, it is revealed, had a mutual-defense pact against the Hittites (*EA* 24).

Correspondence with Cyprus (*EA* 33–40) may relate to Akhenaten: certainly a king has recently come to the throne. Egypt's main concern was with gifts of copper and timber, in return for silver.

Four Hittite letters (*EA* 41–44) complete the royal correspondence. Suppiluliumas desires gold and silver statues. Friendly relations had been established for a generation already (*EA* 41). Khuriya was certainly not

Akhenaten and therefore may be Smenkhkare, in which case the founder of this accord would be Akhenaten.

The standard greeting king to king is interesting: "For your household, for your wives, for your sons, for your magnates, for your chariots, for your horses, for your troops, for your country, and for whatever else belongs to you, may all go very, very well." This applies to correspondence with the Babylonians, Mittani, Cypriots, and Hittites. The mention of "sons" was used by Giles to argue for Akhenaten having had multiple male offspring.[21]

These letters are concerned above all with the exchange of "greeting gifts." This was a free exchange (*EA* 6, 9–11, 19), but sometimes a purpose was specified: for a new palace (*EA* 5), a temple (*EA* 9), a royal mausoleum (*EA* 19, 29). Most frequently a bride price was being paid (*EA* 4, 19, 22, 25, 27, 29).

Amenhotep III's reputation for diplomacy is borne out by the letters: he wrote endlessly to the Mitanni about peace (*EA* 29), and made many marriage alliances (*EA* 22, 29, 31).[22]

Of the vassals, Niqm-Adda of Ugarit asked for a physician to be sent from Egypt (*EA* 49). Abdi-Ashirta of Amurru made endless protestations of loyalty (*EA* 60–65), but was finally taken prisoner in what seems the most celebrated military exploit of the time (*EA* 101, 108, 117, 124, 132, 362). Akizzi of Qatna called for aid against the Hittites, who were supported by Qadesh and others; allies of Egypt were Nukhashshe (south of Aleppo), Nii (near Apamea), Zinzar, and Tunanab (*EA* 53). Following the death of Abdi-Ashirta, a major threat was the kingdom of Amurru (between the Orontes and the sea), under his son Aziru (*EA* 53, 55).

The seventy letters of Rib-Hadda (*EA* 68–138, 362) well illustrate the problems of this archive. It is widely accepted that they fall into two groups, an earlier (*EA* 71–101) until the death of Abdi-Ashirta, and a later (*EA* 102–38), in the time of the latter's sons. Can even broad synchronisms be applied? Edward Campbell suggested that the earlier letters belong to the reign of Amenhotep III, the later to Akhenaten, ranging from Year 33 of the former to Year 5 of the latter (so while he was still at Thebes, note).[23] If *EA* 101–38 may, with a fair deal of confidence, be assigned to the reign of Akhenaten, we hear of the advance of Amurru: the fall of Ullassa (*EA* 104), an attack on Sumur (*EA* 105), the loss of

Sidon and Beirut (*EA* 118), Hittite raids (*EA* 126), the death of an Egyptian commissioner Pewuru (*EA* 131), and the loss of Byblos (*EA* 136).

The following letters may be from Akhenaten's reign, or very shortly after. Aziru had killed the kings of Ammiya, Ardata, and Irqata (all near Tripoli), and had broken into Sumur (*EA* 139). Zimredda of Sidon reported that all his cities had been lost to the Habiru (*EA* 144)—but then Abi-Milku warned that Sidon planned to attack him (*EA* 149), and Tyre was blockaded (*EA* 154).

The letters continue with bad news for Egypt. The Hittites and Qadesh set fire to Egyptian cities (*EA* 174), the Hapiru advance (*EA* 185), Damascus resists various allies of the Hittites (*EA* 197), Abdi-Kheba of Jerusalem reports all lands lost (*EA* 286), the Hapiru take the king's cities, various mayors have been slain, yet the king does nothing (*EA* 288), Gazru and its allies threaten Jerusalem (*EA* 189–90), Byblos is threatened, and a commissioner has been killed (*EA* 362).

To illustrate the volatility of the situation, Sumur was captured by the Hapiru (*EA* 76), it defected (*EA* 83), it was in danger (*EA* 103, 104, 106, 114). Rib-Haddi's main message is the threat to Byblos from the Hapiru[24] and their allies the Amurru. He was finally expelled, not by any of his external foes, but by his brother, and took refuge in Beirut (*EA* 136–38). The contemporary situation in Beirut under Ammunira seems quite calm (*EA* 141–43), and in Sidon, Zimredda reported that all was "safe and sound," although all other cities were lost to the Hapiru (*EA* 144–45). It is paradoxical then that Abdi-Milki of Tyre declared that his enemy was Zimredda (*EA* 146–55).

Aziru of the Amurru, like his father, made wild protestations of loyalty (*EA* 157–71). He was somehow induced to come to Egypt to explain himself (*EA* 169). The Hittites won victories under Lupakku and Zitana, capturing Amqu (*EA* 170). Aziru was not the only vassal summoned: Shuwardata (*EA* 283), Abdi-Kheba (*EA* 286), the ruler of Tyre (*EA* 295), and Shubandu (*EA* 306) were also called. As these kings pointed out, it was impossible to come to Egypt: "the war against me is severe" (*EA* 283).

The letters from *EA* 174 on are by a great mixture of rulers. There are only occasionally small collections: Biryawaza of Damascus (*EA* 194–97), Shuwardata of Qiltu (?) (*EA* 278–84), and Abdi-Kheba of Jerusalem (*EA* 285–90). Qadesh was allied to the Hittites (*EA* 174–75, 363).

The Hapiru capture cities (*EA* 185, 186), and in fact, "the entire land" (*EA* 272–74). Lost are all the lands of the king, lost are all the mayors (*EA* 286, 288). One treasures the almost unique "happy" letter (*EA* 209). The "Labayu episode" illustrates the confused exchange of charge and counter-charge (*EA* 244).

One of the most persistent themes of the letters is also one of the most important: that the city-states of Syria and Palestine are involved in constant warfare with each other; for example, Tyre and Sidon (*EA* 146), Qadesh and Damascus (*EA* 189).

The most fundamental requisite for such correspondence is a postal service. The letters show that messages went back and forth in even the most difficult circumstances, mostly quite securely. Byblos is a case in point: this most persistent correspondent kept up a torrent of letters while under constant threat from enemies. There is occasional reference to messengers being detained for long periods (*EA* 7, 28, 29). A caravan was robbed, but the motive for that was obvious (*EA* 7). And Babylonian merchants were killed in Canaan (*EA* 8). There was a system of passports (or laissez-passer), for example from Mitanni to Egypt via Canaan (*EA* 30; also for merchants, *EA* 39, 40). There is unfortunately very little information on travel times, but a journey "post-haste" from Babylon to Thebes and return in one case took three months (*EA* 27)!

Many of the vassals had ancestral relations with Egypt: from the time of Thutmose III (Nukhashshe, *EA* 51; Tunip, *EA* 59), or for three generations (Damascus, *EA* 194; Lab'aya, *EA* 253; Dagantakala, *EA* 317). It is significant that local rulers mention the rearing of their sons in Egypt (Tunip, *EA* 59; Kumidu, *EA* 198; Gazru, *EA* 296).

The letters provide information on needs of the pharaoh which the vassals had to fulfil: copper and box-wood (?) from Byblos (*EA* 77, 109, 126); daughters in marriage (*EA* 99; from Enishasi, *EA* 187); glass from Tyre (*EA* 148), Akka (*EA* 235), Yursa (*EA* 314), and Ashqaluna (*EA* 323); ships, oil, and wood from Amurru (*EA* 161); beautiful female cup bearers, silver, gold, linen, precious stones, and an ebony chair from Lakishu (*EA* 331); and forty beautiful female cup bearers from Gazru (*EA* 369).

The size of the military operations in Syria and Palestine is often specified, and is surprisingly small. Requests were made for the sending of between twenty (*EA* 149) and four hundred men (*EA* 76, 131).[25]

The key to Egypt's 'control' of Syria–Palestine was apparently the office of "commissioner" *(rabisu)*. They led troops (*EA* 60, 84, 106, 117), or sent them (*EA* 285). They provided grain to the vassals (*EA* 83, 85). They settled disputes between vassals (*EA* 113, 117). They were the major sources of Egyptian intelligence (*EA* 127, 131, 132, 151, 230, 264, 283), far more reliable than the fawning letters of the vassals themselves. Not all, however, were reliable: Pakhura was involved in raids (*EA* 122, 123), Pakhamanata was declared a traitor (*EA* 131), and Pewuru was killed (*EA* 129, 362).

Akhenaten and the vassals

Breasted's summation of the relationship between the pharaoh and his vassals was quite negative. To the desperate appeals of the "faithful vassals," either no reply was sent, "or an Egyptian commander with an entirely inadequate force was despatched to make futile and desultory attempts to deal with a situation which demanded the Pharaoh himself and the whole available army of Egypt. At Akhet-Aten, the new and beautiful capital, the splendid temple of Aton resounded with hymns to the new god of Empire, while the Empire itself was no more."[26] Pendlebury described the letters as giving "the whole story" of "the lapse of the Egyptian empire into anarchy."[27] Redford saw them as throwing light on two fundamental areas: Northern Syria, where the Hittite king Suppuliliumas took over from the Mitanni (*EA* 196), and the Upper Orontes, where the Amurru conquered or won over Sumur, Sidon, Qadesh, Ugarit, and Byblos. Although Aziru was finally brought to Egypt to answer for his crimes, he was allowed to return and become an ally of the Hittites.[28] Few entered a protest. One of these was Baikie: these Egyptian vassals with their endless letters were "the most shameless set of royal beggars that the world has ever seen."[29]

There are fundamental problems of understanding in the letters. It has often been remarked that the diplomatic language (Akkadian) was the native tongue of neither the Egyptians nor their allies and vassals. Mario Liverani has demonstrated that the letters provide abundant evidence that there was much misunderstanding.[30] A number of important things, however, are clear in the royal correspondence. There is no evidence that any one of the kings was accepted by any of the others as the leading power. There is, furthermore, no evidence of a concept of, let alone an aspiration to, a balance of power, a concept that began only much later, in Greek times.[31]

The protocol of the vassal letters is another fundamental issue. A short analysis by Horst Klengel contained one of the most basic yet most overlooked rules in understanding the letters: "Neither the protestations of loyalty, nor the incriminations should be taken literally." He went on to emphasize that it was hardly possible for Akhenaten to obtain a correct picture of events from the letters of his Syrian vassals. No notice should be taken of the claims that the king was not paying attention, for the letters were not his main source of information: that was oral or written reports from his own agents.[32] In the last analysis spare a thought for Akhenaten: this was a chaotic and treacherous world.

Franco Pintore took up Klengel's crucial point about the pharaoh's "failure to pay attention." The pharaoh's silences were not carelessness or apathy, but a penalty: the contempt of a divinity offended by the unreliable behavior of a vassal. We must have regard for the Egyptian understanding of hierarchical relations.[33]

Few have helped our understanding of the protocols as much as Liverani, who made a special study of the correspondence of Rib-Hadda of Byblos. This is often used to draw momentous conclusions about Egypt's peril and Akhenaten's failure to respond. We have seventy letters of the ruler of Byblos and only one reply of the pharaoh. Liverani alerts us to many fundamentals: that the Amarna period is seen as one of "radical crisis of the Egyptian domination in Asia"; that "local social disturbances" are seen as anti-Egyptian movements; that Egyptian "non-intervention" is mistaken for a "ruinous misunderstanding of the Asian situation." To the contrary, the Egyptian administration "knew the local situation and could assess it realistically in relation to Egyptian interests." Rib-Hadda, the most insistent of the pharaoh's correspondents, is a perfect example of "a local ruling class that incessantly tried to draw advantages from its relationship with the dominant power for the attainment of local political ends."[34] In another contribution, Liverani warned against the dominant "catastrophe paradigm" in understanding the letters. This relies especially on disregarding the "non-narrative character" of the letters, composed of "wishes and threats, hypotheses, rhetorical questions" and so on and distorting them into events.[35] Most of the letters, in fact, deal with Egypt's seasonal demand for tribute, made up of preparing "spring" letters from Egypt (*EA* 99, 367, 369, 370) and the replies of the vassals. There are also the "late summer letters," where the vassals, on their own initiative, make a list of complaints (for instance *EA* 271). These last, Liverani emphasized, dealt with "permanent and normal facts," such as local conflicts, not a cumulative crisis.

Alan Schulman demonstrated constant patterns here. The letters of all Egypt's loyal allies

> have virtually the same content: protestations of loyalty and faithfulness of the writer, vitriolic accusations in the most slanderous terms of treason on the part of a rival, requests for help in the person of a few Egyptian troops which, if not granted, will result in the loss of the entire land, often an admonition to the scribes of the Foreign Office to bear witness to the writer's virtue, and finally an acknowledgement that justice and truth will indeed triumph.[36]

In other words, there is a pattern here that demonstrates that a literal reading is quite irrational. Other admissions also show the lie of this pattern: orders had been sent to prepare for the arrival of Egyptian troops, and help was indeed sent (see below).[37]

Barry Kemp sharpened this insight. The two crucial characteristics of the vassal letters are "a long introductory protestation of absolute loyalty couched in obsequious language," with "the direct political message . . . reserved for a final brief sentence or two," and "denunciation of a neighboring prince on grounds of disloyalty to the king of Egypt." In these letters "no trace has survived of anything like an objective comment on an international situation," yet Egypt's foreign relations were conducted rationally.[38] A major theme of the letters, indeed, was the gathering of intelligence. This was managed by clear and simple processes.[39]

Ellen Morris was the first to notice that the vassals couched their letters in varying degrees of sycophancy to the pharaoh.[40] She rated the sycophancy, and then thought to plot her findings on a map. The result—in hindsight not unexpected—was that the less obsequious vassals were farthest away from Egyptian control and most subject to influence from powers such as the Hittites.

A most provocative interpretation has recently been proposed by John Darnell and Colleen Manassa. For them, Akhenaten was simply following the policy of his father in encouraging and promoting the growth of Amurru as a buffer state between Egypt and the Hittites, given the imminent fall of the Mitanni.[41]

The Egyptian 'empire'

One of the first attempts to analyze the administration of the Egyptian empire was made by Abdul-Kader Mohammed (1920–85). The empire was never ruled directly by Egypt, but by a 'system' of local rulers supposed to be vassals (*wr* in Egyptian, *aulum* in Akkadian), who ruled a city or even a group of them. Each vassal had to guard his city, protect the governor, report any hostile activity, provide for Egyptian troops, and pay an annual tribute. In major centers, there was an Egyptian governor (*imy-r* in Egyptian, *rabisu* in Akkadian). They were located in towns such as Iarimtu, Kumidu, Tyre, Qatna, and Ashqalino, and some were in southern Palestine. The governor was in charge of the vassals, of garrisons, and of provisions, and was an arbitrator between the vassals. There seems to have been a department in the Egyptian bureaucracy called the "Office for Correspondence of the Pharaoh," first at Thebes, then at Amarna. The head of this office was responsible for all correspondence, advised the king, could dispatch troops (*EA* 82), or might be sent with them (*EA* 77, 117). Akhenaten is rarely mentioned by Mohammed, except at the very end, to state that Egyptian rule fell to pieces because of his apathy.[42]

Morris considered the duties of the vassals more closely. They included "periodically to appear before the pharaoh, to send tribute regularly, to extradite fugitives, to subjugate their own foreign policy to that of the Egyptians, to contribute troops when requested, to send their heirs to Egypt for safekeeping, to protect the cities and representatives of the king, and to allow intercity feuds to be arbitrated by an Egyptian representative."[43]

Kemp deduced that the letters "point to the existence of a division of the whole area under Egyptian hegemony into three provinces": Amurru (northern coast), Upe (inland Syria), and Canaan (Palestine). Each contained a city in which a senior Egyptian representative resided: Simyra, Kumidu, and Gaza. Kemp has also drawn our attention to general points about western Asia. First, from the archaeological evidence, one would never know that an Egyptian empire existed. Second, it is clear that the Egyptian presence did not usher in a golden age of peace and prosperity. This was simply because of Egypt's inability to gain supremacy over the Mitanni or Hittites. One gains a strong impression, however, that the diplomacy of Amenhotep III went far to ushering in peace.[44]

Rolf Hachmann refined Kemp's analysis in a very detailed study of the administrative centers as shown by the letters. There were two administrative centers in Palestine: Gaza and Bethsean. In Syria, there were also two: Sumur and Kumidu. Sumur was the center for the Syrian coast until it was captured by Aziru (*EA* 149). The province of Kumidu stretched from Qadesh to Damascus. Gaza oversaw south Palestine and the coast and, on the fall of Sumur, as far as Byblos. Bethsean controlled middle and northern Palestine and beyond the Jordan.

North of these four 'provinces' lay 'vassals,' such as Ugarit, Nukhash-she, and Tunip, whose links to Egypt went back to the campaigns of Thutmose III. Local rulers were answerable to commissioners, but also protected them. The rulers could correspond directly with the pharaoh. The Egyptian administration did not interfere in local rivalries. Relations with the great powers—the Hittites, Mitanni, Assyria, and Babylon—were restricted to members of the royal personal circle.[45]

Few have equaled the contribution to our understanding of the Egyptian 'empire' made by Liverani. He emphasized that the nature of the relationship between the pharaoh and the 'vassal' was understood completely differently by each side. In a system going back to the earlier second millennium, great and small kings made treaties in which the former promised protection and the latter promised services. For the pharaoh, the relationship was one way, the duty owed him by the vassal, and this was symbolized by the latter's oath of loyalty. Egypt left the local kings to settle their own differences and intervened only when its interests were threatened. Moderns have manufactured a 'crisis' by taking the side of the vassals.[46]

In northern Syria–Palestine, the Hittites took over some Egyptian vassals and, more importantly, eroded the power of the Mitanni. The south remained under Egyptian influence: Horemheb did not have to reconquer it. Akhenaten was following traditional policy. The vassals replied by converting their local troubles into threats to Egypt's power and by depicting themselves not as local kings, but as officials of the pharaoh, protecting his cities (for example, *EA* 148) and obeying his commissioner (*EA* 322): the Asian system had no intermediate hierarchy. In sum, the situation revealed by the letters was not a crisis, but normality: endless local wars, which ultimately left a power vacuum filled by the Hittites.

A further dose of common sense was administered by Michael Several in regard to Palestine. He reads the letters as evidence of various problems here: intercity conflicts; conflict with the Hapiru/SA.GAZ; disruption to trade and communications; disregard of royal orders; and bureaucratic incompetence and corruption. Three of these either pre- or post-dated the Amarnan period. The exception was the disruption of trade, which had not been organized until now. Archaeological evidence shows Palestine as part of a trading system in the eastern Mediterranean and itself enjoying a very rich material culture.

How did Egypt expect to maintain control? First was the threat of military force, but Several cites no example under Akhenaten. Second was the long-established loyalty to Egypt of the local rulers, who had been in power for generations. Reinforcing this was the policy of educating princes in Egypt. Finally, there were Egyptian commissioners (*rabisu*), supported by scribes and messengers. It is highly significant that these messengers could operate even at the worst of times (*EA* 283, 288).

The local princes thus carried out their duties of protecting trade caravans, sending tribute, providing supplies for royal armies, supplying the corvée, keeping the pharaoh informed about the local situation, and defending their cities, all of which indicates a fatal flaw in the customary way the letters are now read: "The pharaoh was still looked upon as the ultimate source of power, and it was believed he could and would exercise that power."[47] If Egyptian power declined in Palestine under Akhenaten, the letters do not document it.

Giles went so far as to argue that conditions were secure: It was possible for Amenhotep III to send only five chariots to escort a Babylonian princess to Egypt (*EA* 11). Even in the north, messengers traveled back and forth between Egypt, the Hittites, the Mitanni, and Assyria. The letters of Burnaburiash of Babylon to Akhenaten make no reference to crisis. To the contrary, they suggest that everything is as usual: "Canaan is your country and its kings are your servants" (*EA* 8). Giles considered the Egyptian policy to be most effective: "The maintenance of a state of unrest in north Syria which left the various princes too hostile towards one another to make a successful combination possible, and only required occasional Egyptian intervention to prevent the complete collapse of one or the other, could only work to the advantage of the Egyptian crown."[48] We, however, have the benefit of hindsight. This all worked splendidly—until the Hittites arrived.

In any assessment, the Amarnan situation needs to be put in context. We need to descend from the 'glories' of Thutmose III to the time of Akhenaten's grandfather and father. Thutmose IV seems to have led an expedition to Naharin/Retenu. Cedar was brought back; booty was dedicated in Karnak; a fortress was established in Syria, so the king asserted[49]—he even went so far as to claim that Naharin and Karoy (Nubia) were subjects of the Aten.[50] Many private tombs mention tribute from Naharin/Retenu.[51]

The letters are not unproblematic when it comes to fitting their retrospectives into what data we have from the pre-Amarna period: Who is Manakhpiya? Thutmose III (Menkheperre), or Thutmose IV (Menkheperure)? Manakhpiya had established princes at Nukhashshe (*EA* 51) and controlled Tunip (*EA* 59). Thutmose IV certainly maintained friendly relations with Babylon (*EA* 1), and finally managed a diplomatic marriage with the Mitanni (*EA* 29). Letter 85 states that "your father" had been in Sidon—but the son in question is not named.[52] Notice should also be taken of letters apparently addressed to Amenhotep III that detailed Hittite advances and Egyptian inactivity (*EA* 75), identifying a major threat to Byblos at the hands of the Hapiru (*EA* 91–92).

It can safely be said that we are a world away from the bold days of the first half of the dynasty, which was intent on the national campaign of liberation and restoration of national pride, and when a king like Thutmose III led expeditions regularly across the Sinai and returned with vast booty, which transformed Egyptian society. For some generations now the kings had been more pacific, relying on a system of international alliances at the highest levels, and a 'network of mayors' and administrators in Syria and Palestine. Two main factors slowly eroded Egyptian influence: the clear aversion of the pharaohs to foreign expeditions, and changes in the balance of eastern power, notably the eclipse of the Mitanni by the Hittites, who were much more aggressive. Over this latter change, the pharaohs obviously could have little influence. Albrecht Goetze acknowledged that by the time of Amenhotep III, Egyptian control of Syria was only nominal.[53]

There is a need to be more insightful about Amenhotep III, who is so often used for unrealistic comparisons with his son. James Weinstein suggested that the former's foreign policy was laissez-faire or worse: "The day-to-day administration of the Asiatic towns was left largely to the native rulers." There was indeed much maritime trade with Syria and Palestine, and almost every site in Palestine possesses an object naming Amenhotep or Tiye. He was dealing with the Levant "from a position of strength unmatched by any pharaoh of the New Kingdom."[54] In blunter terms, "The overriding principle of Egyptian foreign policy in Asia from the reign of Amenhotep III to the death of Horemheb was to gain the greatest economic and political advantage from the smallest commitment of troops."[55]

Schulman offers the context from the other end, the sequel. What of Horemheb? "No real mention is made of his Asiatic wars, mainly because the Egyptian arms were not overly successful, but the fighting, which probably took place in Syria, ended in a Hittite victory and a temporary truce or peace treaty."[56]

There is vital evidence in the letters to which allusion is rarely made by moderns, despite the fact that it is a recurrent theme. The vassals are told again and again to prepare for the arrival of Egyptian troops. Nadav Na'aman has examined this matter. Such orders are referred to by Abdi-Ashtarti of Qiltu (*EA* 65: archers of the king are coming), Ammunira of Beirut (*EA* 141–42: archers), Zimredda of Sidon (*EA* 144), Abi-Milku of Tyre (*EA* 147: "a large army" is arriving; *EA* 153: ships held at the disposition of the king's troops), Arsawuya of Rukhizza (*EA* 191: archers), Twati of Lipana (*EA* 193: archers), Biryawaza of Damascus (?) (*EA* 195: archers), Artamanya of Siribashani (*EA* 201: archers), Amawashe of Bashan (*EA* 202: archers), Abdi-Milki of Shashimi (*EA* 203: troops), the ruler of Qanu (*EA* 204: troops), of Tubu (*EA* 205: troops), of Naziba (*EA* 206: archers), Bawaya in Syria (*EA* 216: archers), unknown writers (*EA* 217–18: troops), Shiptu-risa, town unknown (*EA* 226), the king of Hazor (*EA* 227: Pharaoh himself is expected!), Milkilu of Gazru (*EA* 269: archers), Adda-danu of Gazru (*EA* 292: archers), Yidya of Ashqaluna (*EA* 324–25: troops), Hiziru (*EA* 337: archers), and Endaruta of Ashqaluna

(*EA* 367: archers). The obvious question is whether such repeated orders are to be taken seriously. Na'aman regards them as genuine evidence for an expedition. He does not, however, provide a closer date than "the very last stage of the Amarna archive."[57] Others have been more precise: "toward the end of Akhenaten's reign" (see below).[58]

And what did the vassals have to prepare against the troops' arrival? The longest list is "food, strong drink, oxen, sheep and goats, grain, straw, absolutely everything that the king commanded" (*EA* 325).

That Egyptian troops were expected was one thing. That evidence exists for their actual dispatch is even more telling, and it abounds in the letters. Akizzi of Qatna states that when troops and chariots have come, they have been well provisioned (*EA* 55). Some kings received Egyptian and Nubian troops and archers (*EA* 70). Rib-Hadda did apparently receive reinforcements, but "all the men you gave me have run off" (*EA* 82). Four hundred men and sixty horses were sent to Surata (*EA* 85), and there were Egyptians in Ullassa who escaped to Byblos (*EA* 105). The situation at Sumur became dire "the day the troops of my lord's expeditionary force left" (*EA* 106). Amenhotep III apparently sent archers to Rib-Hadda (*EA* 108), who complains that someone else has a garrison and supplies (*EA* 122), but admits that troops came out and took Sumur and Abdi-Ashirta (*EA* 138). Mention is made of ships sailing into Beirut (*EA* 143). Abi-Milku mentions that "the king gave his attention to his servant and gave soldiers to guard the city of the king" (*EA* 150); he then refers to the departure of the king's troops (*EA* 154). Biridiya of Megiddo mentions the return of archers to Egypt (*EA* 244). Abdi-Kheba states that the king stationed a garrison in Jerusalem, but that it was removed (*EA* 286, 287, 289). And Rib-Hadda of Byblos refers to some people saying that no archers would be sent, but they were (*EA* 362). One reference is extraordinary: Rib-Hadda quotes the king stating that "troops have come out," but Rib-Hadda calls him a liar (*EA* 129). What all these military preparations were for, we will soon see.

Egypt and abroad under Akhenaten

The main danger to Egypt in Asia, as Klengel stressed, was not the local princes, but the Hittites, who were afraid to attack Egyptian allies while Mitanni was her ally. The infamous Aziru remained an Egyptian vassal until the death of Tutankhamun and actually appeared in Egypt to explain himself. Suppuliliumas left Qadesh alone in Akhenaten's time. The Hittite attacks on Amqu began only late in his reign. Akhenaten's diplomacy therefore retained southern Syria under Egyptian control.[59] And if the Hittites made considerable gains at this time, Akhenaten can hardly be singled out for particular blame—the 'Hittite problem' remained for another century, through the reigns of vaunted militarists, from Horemheb to Rameses II.

Thutmose IV, according to Hachmann, was the last king to campaign in Asia (*EA 85*—but see above). Amenhotep III did not campaign (*EA* 116), but relied on diplomacy. What of Akhenaten? He "appears soon after his accession to have lost, for the most part, interest in good relations with the great powers. The impression is that he devoted himself more vigorously and directly to the problem of Egyptian possessions in Asia."[60] For a characteristic letter see *EA 162*.[61]

William Murnane provided an acute analysis of Egypt's position and Akhenaten's policies. Mittani collapsed, and the Hittites withdrew from Syria, but the pharaoh "disregarded the urging of local princes who wanted the vacuum filled by Egypt." Even after the Hittites took over Ugarit and Qadesh, both sides engaged in only a 'cold war.' "What this pattern reveals is not the indecision of a pacifist Akhenaten, but entirely reasonable caution on both sides." War did in fact break out after the death of the Hittite prince who had been sent to marry the Egyptian queen; the conflict lasted sixty years.[62]

Aldred was decisive: "there is nothing to show that under [Akhenaten] Egyptian influence suffered any wholesale collapse."[63] The truth was stated most directly by Alan Gardiner: "It is an often repeated accusation that by his sloth and his hatred of war [Akhenaten] threw away the great Egyptian empire built up in Palestine and Syria by Thutmose III. . . . It may even be doubted whether the much-vaunted Egyptian empire ever existed." Thutmose I defeated the Mitanni. Thutmose III engaged in no fewer than fourteen campaigns "to maintain Egyptian suzerainty." The sea ports may have been strongly held and governors may have been stationed at key points—but that is guesswork, Gardiner stressed. What is not guesswork is that the so-called vassals simply sought support wherever they could find it—and Egypt was not always the most reliable 'superpower.' There was, therefore, no empire to 'hold,' and whatever there was, Akhenaten was not the one who 'lost' it. That was Amenhotep III.[64]

Indeed, as Redford points out, evidence of the possibility or even the likelihood of warfare during Akhenaten's reign was there for everyone to see:

> The army had never been more evident in relief art. Captives abound in heraldic motifs, around the side of the royal dais, and beneath the "window of appearance." At the *ḥb-sd* the "sons of the chiefs of every foreign land" present their tribute, while at every reward ceremony the inevitable parties of Asiatic or Nubian princes raise their hands in adoration. Foreign potentates continue to be intimidated into sending gifts and benevolences: ships from Nubia, Syria and Aegean Greece, whence came the beautiful Mycenaean pottery, crowded the wharves at Akhet-Aten as they formerly did those at Memphis and Thebes.[65]

Julia Samson observed a corroborating detail:

> The Blue Crown, apparently introduced early in the Eighteenth Dynasty as a war crown, perhaps of leather with protective metal discs, was a favourite head-dress with the peace-loving Akhenaten at Amarna, where its construction was probably lighter and easier to wear on informal occasions. He is constantly pictured wearing a high, rather bonnet-like version of it, in contrast to the wider, winged effect of those used earlier in the dynasty. It is as much part of his image as the new tall crown of Nefertiti.[66]

There are further suggestive sources in the letters. One to Aziru (*EA* 162) is understood to be by Akhenaten, or at least by his chancellery. He wrote to Aziru, of all people, rebuking him for his failure to help restore Rib-Hadda to Byblos, and for his friendship with Qadesh, an enemy to Egypt. Threats ensue: "If for any reason whatsoever you prefer to do evil, and if you plot evil, treacherous things, then you, together with your entire family, shall die by the axe of the king!" Where did the modern idea originate that Akhenaten was a pacifist? A list of the enemies of the pharaoh was appended, and Aziru was to hand back the royal messenger Hanni.[67]

Wars?

A Syrian war?

Before turning to wars beyond the frontier, it should be noted that excavations at Tell al-Borg in northern Sinai show that the eastern frontier was guarded during the Amarnan period, and that "Egypt was capable logistically of undertaking and sustaining military operations in the Levant."[68] Aldred saw the evidence: "Forces and supplies were evidently being marshalled for a serious Asiatic campaign at the end of Akhenaten's reign; and indeed such a campaign in the region of Gezer may have been mounted."[69]

The "Restoration Stela" of Tutankhamun states, as an illustration of the unhappiness of Akhenaten's reign, that "if an army was sent to Djahy to broaden the boundaries of Egypt, no success of their cause came to pass";[70] Djahy is Syria–Palestine. Ronald Leprohon took this to be a reference to the lack of discipline in the army, which was also evident in Horemheb's time; he therefore inferred that Horemheb had been the general in question.[71] It is certainly impossible to understand the reference as being to a hypothetical case.

This campaign was treated at greater length by Marc Gabolde. The ports of Tyre, Sidon, and Beirut were all told to prepare for the arrival of a large Egyptian force (*EA* 141, 142, 147, 153, 155). Parallel to this naval attack was a land invasion (*EA* 65, 132, 193–97, 201–206, 227, 292), aimed at Qadesh (*EA* 162). This was before Aziru came to Egypt. It was not a success; the fleet stopped only briefly at Beirut (*EA* 143). Is this the failure Tutankhamun referred to in the "Restoration Stela"? The results were that Qadesh was supported by the Hittites in destabilizing other cities (*EA* 53), and the Hittites raided Amqu (*EA* 170).[72]

A Hittite war?

Schulman pointed to a small number of *talatat* that showed military scenes, which he attributed to a "First Hittite War," dated between Years 1 and 5, on the basis of their presence at Karnak.[73] It has now been demonstrated, however, that these scenes derive from a reuse of these blocks by Tutankhamun, to whom the military reliefs actually belong.[74]

On the basis of some of the letters, Schulman also argued for a war (for him a "Second" one) against the Hittites, the "Amka [Amqu] War." Hittite commanders Lupakku and Zitana are named; Amqu was captured

(*EA* 170); Etakama of Qadesh was a Hittite ally (*EA* 174, 363). Other letters locate the Hittites further inland at Nukhashshe (*EA* 164–65), Byblos was threatened (*EA* 126), and the Mitanni were conquered (*EA* 75).[75]

The historian of the Hittites, Trevor Bryce, accepted that Akhenaten probably did respond to Rib-Hadda's appeals—and reassert control over Abdi-Ashirta—by removing him. He also set out the dilemma facing Akhenaten in dealing with Rib-Hadda's appeals against Abdi-Ashirta's son, Aziru: he had to balance the two against each other, and that against the background of the Hittites' increasing power. "There appeared to be no immediate way of solving this dilemma." By not acting, however, Akhenaten did choose. Rib-Hadda fell. Bryce suggested that Akhenaten deserved credit for understanding the subsequent situation, because he demanded that Aziru appear before him. And Aziru came. Reports of Hittites massing for an attack, however, led to his release. Once again, "Akhenaten's options were very limited. . . . The risks were very great—but there was really no viable alternative." Aziru, not unexpectedly, betrayed whatever promises he had made and allied with the Hittites.[76]

Modern commentators have often suggested that the Hittites were present at the Year 12 'durbar': they point to the five figures with long hair ending in a pigtail and one (the second) certainly bearded.[77] If so, this would date action against the Hittites before Year 12. John Darnell, however, has demonstrated persuasively that they are Keftiu, "from the islands in the midst of the sea."[78]

It is Darnell and Manassa who have suggested that Akhenaten, at the end of his reign, waged war with the Hittites over Qadesh. Aitukama had been installed as ruler and was actively seeking to undermine the loyalty of neighboring vassals (*EA* 53). It was in connection with this campaign that the vassals were told to prepare (*EA* 144, 155). The Egyptians advanced by land and sea. The army marched across Sinai to Gaza. The clash resulted in an Egyptian defeat and a Hittite counter-attack on Amqu just as during Tutankhamun's reign. It was Seti (Dynasty XIX) who recaptured Qadesh.[79]

Nubian unrest

There is only one unequivocal reference to military action under Akhenaten: two inscriptions, almost identical, but varying slightly in date and both missing the regnal year (such are the standard problems of the

Amarna period): either Year 2 or Year 12.[80] They describe the repulse of a raid on the Nile valley by Nubian nomads (Ikayta) from the eastern desert. They were found in the Wadi Allaqi, a gold-mining district, and expelled by the viceroy Thutmose, with the loss of some 360. This was clearly not a serious campaign, but a police operation—or at least so goes the standard version.[81]

Schulman threw an entirely new light on this event. For him the campaign was to be dated definitely to Year 12, according with the presence of Nubian prisoners at the 'durbar.' Two blocks from Pylon II at Karnak show a detachment of soldiers (the first of whom cuts off the hand of a dead Nubian), ships, Egyptian officers, and Nubian captives.[82] The crucial matter, however, is the scale of the operations. Schulman compared the military exploits of Akhenaten's predecessors such as Thutmose III, and concluded that

> the number of captives and slain Nehesi in Ikayta, certainly a barren
> and thinly populated region, was frequently almost the same as
> the body count of the enemy in many of the campaigns against the
> heavily-peopled, or so one assumes, Syro-Palestinian cities. . . . It
> is obvious that both the war of Amunhotpe III in Ibhet and that of
> Akhenaten in Ikayta were, in terms of colonial warfare, for these
> wars were surely colonial, of major proportions.[83]

The subject of Egypt's foreign relations during the Amarna period is extremely complex. Modern analyses have too often been vitiated by relying on assumptions and failing to ask questions or define contexts. What exactly was the Egyptian empire that Akhenaten was supposed to be maintaining? What had his predecessors and successors done with it? How did international relations operate in this part of the world at this time? Finally, and perhaps most fundamentally, how can one rely on a source as fragmentary, contradictory, and undated as the Amarna Letters?

7 Smenkhkare, Neferneferuaten, and the End of Akhenaten's Reign

THE LAST FIVE YEARS of Akhenaten's reign are still shrouded in controversy and uncertainty. While Nefertiti has gained in evidence and importance, Smenkhkare has become a more shadowy figure. In attempting to understand these years and the sequel, a few pieces of evidence are referred to again and again by scholars. Indeed, some have already appeared in our own discussion. It would be most convenient first to set out this jigsaw puzzle of evidence, in order of 'discovery.'[1]

Nine pieces of evidence

1. The scene from the tomb of Meryre ii at Amarna (fig. 91),[2] which shows both Akhenaten and Nefertiti rewarding Meryre and his being rewarded by a king and queen whose cartouches are now obliterated; they must therefore be reconstructed from early copies of the 1840s[3] and a squeeze of the now destroyed inscription first published in 2009: Ankhkheperure, Smenkhkare-djeserkheperu, and the King's Chief Wife "Meryaten," usually read as Merye[t] aten. Her name is, therefore, not fully clear—although it appears in the same abbreviated form alongside the name of Smenkhkare on gold sequins from Tutankhamun's tomb.[4] This tomb also shows the 'durbar' of Year 12.[5]

Fig. 91. Unfinished relief of Smenkhkare and Meryetaten; tomb-chapel of Meryre ii (TA 2).

2a. The so-called Nicholson relief, a block from the Aten temple at Memphis (fig. 92) found by Joseph Hekekyan excavating at Mit Rahina in 1854, but first published by Charles Nicholson in 1870.[6] Much was made of this, especially by Percy Newberry in his 1928 article. It is to be noted that no king's name is anywhere to be seen. It transpires, however, that Nicholson's published drawing is a much elaborated version of Hekekyan's original. Jaromir Malek uncovered the whole story in 1996 and suggested that the now-lost stone showed not a large king followed by a smaller one, but simply a king followed by a fan bearer![7] Amarnan evidence thus appears and then disappears.

2b. Newberry also published at the same time another fragment of stone found by Hekekyan that showed the bottom section of five broken cartouches, two preserving only *kheperu* and a third only the female determinative. He instantly restored them as [Ankh]kheperu[re], [Smenkhkare-djeser]kheperu, and [Meryetaten] (fig. 93).

3. The graffito of Pawah from the tomb of Pairy (TT 139—fig. 94).[8] This was first published by Urbain Bouriant in 1894.[9] It is dated

Fig. 92. The Nicholson relief from Memphis, "improved" for publication to change the figure of a humble fan-bearer into a small king.

Fig. 93. Drawing of a now-lost block from Memphis, found in 1854, including the lower parts of cartouches that can be restored as those of the Aten, Smenkhkare, and Meryetaten.

to Year 3 of Ankhkheperure-mery-A[. . .], Neferneferuaten-mery-A[. . .]. It must be stressed that in both cartouches, the final word is damaged and could read either 'Aten' or 'Amun.' The body of the graffito certainly refers to Amun, but interpretations have been diametrically opposed, as we shall see.

4–5. The German excavations at Amarna (1907–14) produced two vital images: the stela of Pay, showing two royal figures seated beside one another (Berlin ÄM17813: fig. 82), and the unfinished relief of a royal figure pouring liquor for another who is seated (Berlin ÄM20716: fig. 83).[10]

6. A fragment of box from the entrance to Tutankhamun's tomb.[11] On two knobs are the names of Meryetaten and Ankhkheperure-mery-Neferkheperure. Between the knobs is an inscription naming three people: Akhenaten; Ankhkheperure-mery-Neferkheperure, Neferneferuaten-mery-Waenre; and the King's Chief Wife Meryetaten.[12]

The mention of this crucial box fragment from the tomb of Tutankhamun raises the matter of other items that were for many years taken to refer to Smenkhkare. Nicholas Reeves issued a caution: "Contrary to popular belief, there is nothing from this tomb inscribed with the *nomen* of Ankhkheperure Smenkhkare Djoserkheperu."[13] The very next year this statement was refuted.

7. A calcite jar from the tomb of Tutankhamun.[14] This was reexamined by Christian Loeben. It originally bore the double cartouches of two kings, but they are almost completely erased. Howard Carter had hinted at the possibility that the two kings were Amenhotep III and IV, which would make this the only double-dated object attesting the infamous coregency. Loeben reexamined the faint traces in 1991 and showed that, while the first name is certainly Neferkheperure-Waenre Akhenaten, the second is almost certainly Ankhkheperure Smenkhkare-djeserkheperu. There is, therefore, an object with the latter's name (or at least that had once borne his name) in Tutankhamun's tomb, and a further item to add to his scarce documentation.[15]

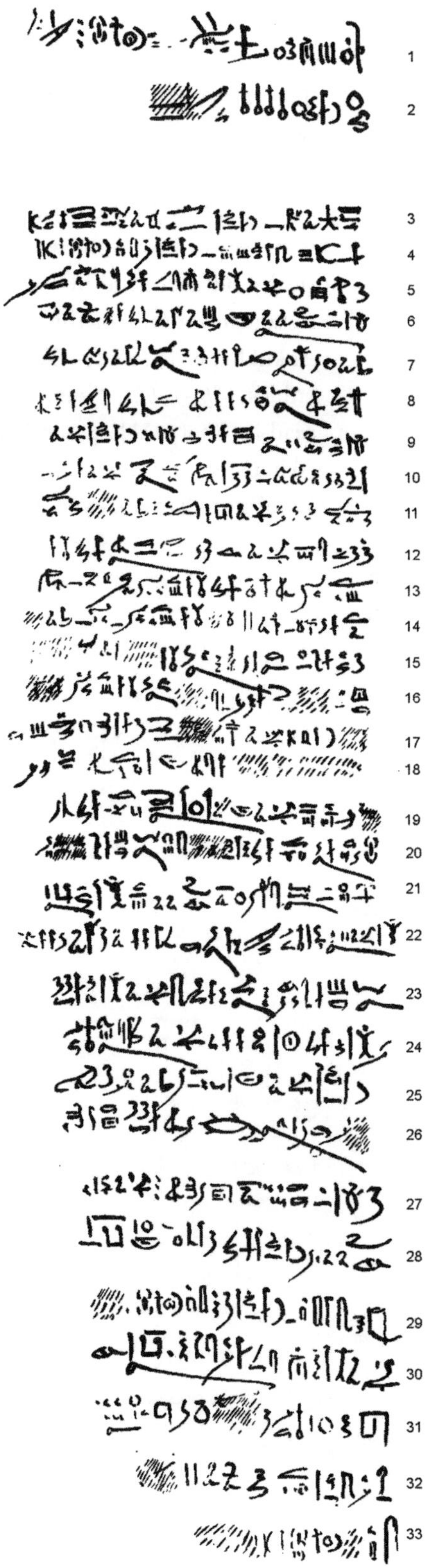

Fig. 94. Facsimile of the Graffito of Pawah in the tomb of Pairy (TT 139), made while it was still intact.

8. The "Coregency Stela" from the "Northern Harem" of the "Central Palace" at Amarna (UCL 410: fig. 95).[16] This was discovered by Flinders Petrie in 1890, but not fully published until sixty years later by Julia Samson. It shows parts of the lower bodies of what must have been two figures, one behind the other, symmetrically on each side of a scene dominated by the Aten, with four cartouches above in the right-hand corner: (1–2) Akhenaten, (3) Ankhkheperure-mery-Waenre, and (4) Neferneferuaten-akhetenhies (*ȝḫt-n-hỉ.s*, "beneficial for her husband"—but long misread as "mery-Akhenaten." They have been variously identified as Akhenaten and Smenkhkare, Akhenaten and Nefertiti, Akhenaten and Tutankhamun, even Akhenaten and Kiya.[17]

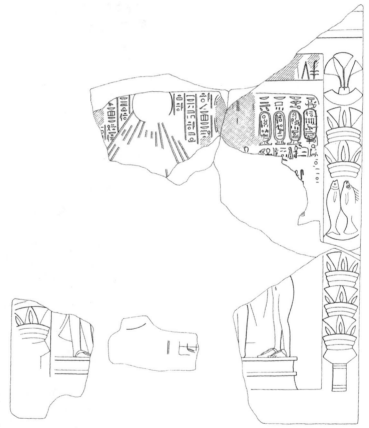

Fig. 95. The "Coregency Stela," from Amarna (Petrie UC410 + Cairo JE 64959).

Fig. 96. The legs of two kings and the much smaller figure of a queen on *talatat* 406-VIIA; from Hermopolis.

9. A block from Hermopolis showing the legs of two kings wearing "sporrans," followed by a female figure on a much smaller scale (fig. 96), none of them named.[18]

These nine pieces of evidence will, for convenience, be referred to by their number in italics in parentheses. Two fundamental questions, often intertwined, must now be kept separate: first, the identification of Smenkhkare and his separation from Neferneferuaten, long believed to be the same person and whom we have seen in the previous chapter to be all but certainly Nefertiti; second, an attempt to reconstruct the last years of Akhenaten.

Identifying Smenkhkare

As early as 1894, Petrie, who was one of the first to read his name correctly, suspected Smenkhkare to have been Akhenaten's coregent because of rings that combined his long-known prenomen "Ankhkheperure" with the epithet "beloved of Neferkheperure"—a crucial mistake that would have major consequences. Thus he might, Petrie thought, have married Meryetaten and have become Akhenaten's successor. Two years later Petrie noted that, from the evidence of wine dockets, Smenkhkare was coregent for a time, even independent by his Year 2.[19]

The most misleading contribution in the whole of Amarnan studies was, in fact, Newberry's attempt in 1928 to gather the documentation on Smenkhkare.[20] He listed the Pairy tomb graffito *(3)*, Tutankhamun's box fragment *(6)*, the scene in the tomb of Meryre ii *(1)*, and the Nicholson relief *(2a)* as all referring to Smenkhkare, whether they bore his name, Neferneferuaten's, or no name at all. The graffito showed, he stated, that by Smenkhkare's reign the cult of Amun was flourishing in Thebes. He "immediately" equated "Neferneferuaten, beloved of Waenre" with Smenkhkare. The Nicholson relief showed Smenkhkare following Akhenaten, but on a much smaller scale. To this Newberry added the other 'Nicholson' block with broken lower halves of three cartouches, which, he claimed, named Smenkhkare and Meryetaten *(2b)*. Newberry's most crucial contribution, however, was his reinterpretation of the stela of Pay *(4)* showing two figures seated side by side. They had, since their discovery, been taken to be Akhenaten and Nefertiti. Now, incited by Carter, Newberry declared them to be Akhenaten and Smenkhkare. To this he added hints of a relationship similar to that between Hadrian and Antinous. The cat was set among the pigeons. These fantasies misled Amarnan studies for almost half a century. In the very same issue of the journal, Newberry suggested that a scene of a king and queen in a garden were Smenkhkare and Meryetaten (fig. 97).[21] Also in the same issue, Alan Gardiner offered a new text with translation and notes of the graffito and elucidated a vital matter mostly overlooked in the sequel: Pawah expresses a wish to see Amun; this is because he is *blind*.[22]

Stephen Glanville attempted an important distinction: he compared the evidence for Smenkhkare from Memphis and from Thebes. In the former, he was called "Smenkhkare" and was still a devotee of Aten and connected with Akhenaten as "beloved of Waenre" or shown in relief with him. At Thebes, on the other hand, he was called "Neferneferuaten," and was associated with Amun.[23] One instantly sees a discrepancy: he is still called by a compound of Aten while supposedly associated with Amun. The problem of his names had to wait another sixty years to be solved.

The publication of the third volume of the British excavations at Amarna in 1951 included a new fragment of the "Coregency Stela" *(8)*. In the light of Newberry's article, this was taken to show Smenkhkare as coregent with Akhenaten. It was noted that Smenkhkare's cartouches showed signs of modification, and Herbert Fairman saw that the second figure was apparently a woman.[24]

Fig. 97. Relief showing a king and queen, often identified as Smenkhkare and Meryetaten (Berlin ÄM 15000).

The first serious study of Smenkhkare remains the long 1958 article of Günther Roeder (1881–1966), in which he attempted a biographical reconstruction, but also, more importantly, to identify his portraits.[25] Regarding his parents, Roeder canvassed two theories: that he was the son of either Amenhotep III or Akhenaten; Roeder *seemed* to favor the latter. Smenkhkare was, he thought, to have been buried in the Royal Tomb at Amarna, and then at Thebes, but his early death prevented adequate preparation, so he was placed in KV 55. Roeder was, in fact, unsure whether this was his original burial or whether he was only moved here some years later. He was sure, however, that the coffin was originally made for him, and that the canopic jars are his.[26]

After eliminating the portraits of Akhenaten and Tutankhamun, Roeder's identification of Smenkhkare's portraits was based on the following criteria: a broad, not hanging chin; a bony jaw; full lips; and a slight depression in the middle of the upper lip as a continuation of the rim of the nose. The mouth is different at different times: when young or idealized (?) it is straight; when older or more natural (?), it is curved, so that the corners of the mouth turn down. To understand these criteria, one must know that Roeder explained Smenkhkare's early death as a result of illness, caused by the genetic weakness of his family. Of Roeder's list of nearly thirty portraits (they have been numbered to facilitate reference), the following are well-known pieces of Amarnan art and will serve as examples:

1 and 2: the two Berlin stelae (figs. 82 and 83);
3. a relief of paired heads;[27]
4. the "kissing king" statue from Amarna P48.2;[28]
11. Smenkhkare and Meryetaten from the tomb of Meryre ii (1);
20. the Berlin limestone relief showing a young king leaning back on a crutch, facing a queen offering him a mandragola, already cited by Newberry (fig. 97);[29]
22. the lower part of a face in yellow jasper,[30] which is usually taken to be a woman.

Apart from the graffito at Thebes (3), Roeder suggested that many items from the tomb of Tutankhamun belonged to Smenkhkare: some gold bands around the mummy, the coffinettes for the viscera, and the second shrine.

Christiane Desroches-Noblecourt naturally paid attention to Smenkhkare as Tutankhamun's putative predecessor. She considered him another son of Amenhotep III and Tiye. She also accepted the portrait of the young king on a crutch (Roeder's no. 20, above) and the stela of Pay (4) as his, as well as a yellow stone statue in the Louvre of a seated king (half of a double statue with his queen) (fig. 22).[31] One might note that if these depict Smenkhkare, the relief shows him with a queen and the stela with a king.

Cyril Aldred, surprisingly, made little mention of Smenkhkare, suggesting only that he was the younger brother of Akhenaten.[32]

Wolfgang Helck thought that Smenkhkare was the son of Akhenaten by a woman of the harem. He accepted that Smenkhkare's mummy was in KV 55 (brought to the Valley of the Kings by Horemheb—already noted above).[33]

In the same year, another German scholar, Peter Munro, reexamined the evidence for Smenkhkare's names.[34] He admitted that his origins are unknown, but if he was buried in KV 55, he was possibly a close relative of Tutankhamun. The things that were certain were the coregency with Akhenaten *(8)* and the marriage with Meryetaten *(1)*. He listed, in fact, most of the nine pieces of evidence above, adding an inscription on a potsherd.[35] These indicate, he suggested, that the king's name was given in two versions:

1. Ankhkheperure-mery-Neferkheperure/Neferneferuaten-mery-Waenre, for example on Tutankhamun's box fragment *(6)*, and

2. Ankhkheperure/Smenkhkare-djeserkheperu, on the tomb of Meryre ii *(1)*.

Smenkhkare does not appear in the 'durbar' in Year 12, Munro noted, but this may simply be in accordance with the common, if paradoxical, custom of emphasizing royal daughters in art.

Smenkhkare, Munro argued, took the expanded form of Nefertiti's name, Neferneferuaten, in Year 13 or 14. It is almost universally understood that Smenkhkare was his original name from birth. It differs, however, from the regular Eighteenth Dynasty names, such as Thutmose or Amenhotep, and is rather a "programmatic" prenomen, assumed on accession (indeed, a Thirteenth Dynasty pharaoh had exactly that prenomen[36]). If that is the case, we do not know his original name. This prenomen signaled his adherence to Re, not Aten: "the one who makes the *ka* of Re alone/excellent/accurate/effective." It suggested the restoration of what has fallen into ruin. A more telling translation would be "the one who reestablishes the value of the *ka* of Re."

His name declared that Re was "the only connecting link between the traditional and the new beliefs." It replaced an earlier Aten name, Neferneferuaten, as shown by some Theban sources *(3, 6)*, but Munro believed the cartouches in the tomb of Meryre ii *(1)* had apparently been reworked with the later name. The earlier name in the tomb of Pairy *(3)* conversely shows that it continued in use until his third year. The early form with the epithet "beloved of Akhenaten" could indeed make sense only during the latter's lifetime; hence it was used in monuments which showed the kings together *(6, 8)*. Munro, like Glanville, had seen the importance of the names, but still had not untangled them.[37]

The great upset occurred in 1973, when John Harris suggested that Smenkhkare was the same person as Nefertiti. The problem with this theory, however, if the former were a woman, was the six occasions in which Neferneferuaten/Smenkhkare is shown with Meryetaten. A basic point which Harris stressed is that Nefertiti disappeared about Year 13, when Smenkhkare appeared. This would, however, more logically mean that they succeeded one another, rather than their being the same people under different names.

Harris followed this the next year by questioning a number of matters concerning Smenkhkare that were almost universally accepted: a coregency of Smenkhkare with Akhenaten, for which he argued that the evidence was slight (see below), and Smenkhkare's marriage to Meryetaten: the scene in the tomb of Meryre ii *(1)*; the block from Memphis *(2b)*; another box from Tutankhamun's tomb; and gold sequins from the same.[38] The only one that contains an illustration, the tomb of Meryre, is, Harris argued, "ambiguous" regarding gender. He further argued that Meryetaten's title of "Great Wife of the King" was "functional" and did not necessarily indicate marriage: Akhenaten's mother, Tiye, alongside him on the gilded shrine from KV 55, bears that title.[39]

The burden of riposte to Harris and Samson was undertaken by Sayed Tawfik.[40] He perversely attempted to reclaim for Smenkhkare visual evidence such as the Berlin reliefs *(4–5)*. As for texts, Smenkhkare's name—as understood by Tawfik—was preserved in two cartouches some sixteen times. Fifteen times it carried the epithet "beloved of Akhenaten." Tawfik saw this as a sign of his respect for the older king (the obviously more natural interpretation was that this was Nefertiti, as we shall see). He also placed great emphasis on the graffito from the tomb of Pairy *(3)*. This, he asserted, was dated to Smenkhkare's Year 3. There has rarely, it must be stated, been a more cavalier use of this last text. Tawfik himself recognized the major problem with his interpretation. The coregent's name in the form Smenkhkare does not appear anywhere that we would expect it, only Neferneferuaten. Tawfik's answer was simply that he had changed his name to this form.

Rolf Krauss devoted a monograph to these problems: *Das Ende der Amarnazeit.*[41] Smenkhkare, in fact, makes only a brief appearance. He was married to Meryetaten, but she died. He then intended to marry her younger sister Ankhesenpaaten, but he died! He did, however, rule for three years. His funerary temple was connected with Amun *(3)*, but he resided at Amarna.[42] Like Tawfik, Krauss had been careless with the graffito.

The "Coregency Stela" *(8)* was a crucial but seriously damaged piece of evidence. William Murnane reexamined it closely and stated that it showed two figures on either side, in a symmetrical scene. He could make out the remains of the cartouches of Ankhesenpaaten and Neferneferu-aten, whom he took to be Smenkhkare. He suggested that originally the stela had shown Akhenaten with three daughters; the cartouches of the younger king were therefore a *recutting.*[43]

Our understanding of this evidence was transformed, however, in 1988 by James Allen. He took up Murnane's insights, but made an even closer examination of the fragments—admittedly based on photographs. The stela came from the 'North Harem' of the 'Central Palace' at Amarna. It shows *two pairs* of figures facing a central Aten. The epithets of the god show the Later form of his name. In the upper right-hand corner, he read two pairs of cartouches: first, "Lord of the Two Lands: Neferkheperure-Waenre; Lord of Crowns: Akhenaten"; second, "Lord who performs the ritual: Neferkheperure, beloved of Waenre; Unique Lord: Neferneferuaten, beloved of Akhenaten" (the last epithet wrongly read, as noted above: a mistake for *3ḫt-n-ḥỉ.s*: "effective for her husband"). Under the third cartouche, Allen thought, were traces of the name Ankhesenpaaten. What Allen descried is that the third and fourth cartouches are replacements for an earlier reading, where there were only three cartouches, that is, Akhenaten and Nefertiti. In fourth place, he reconstructed the name of Meryetaten but with her name also in a cartouche.

The four original figures on the stela were, therefore, Akhenaten and Nefertiti, Meryetaten and Ankhesenpaaten: probably Akhenaten and the eldest daughter on one side, and Nefertiti and their third daughter on the other. In the revised version, Nefertiti and Meryetaten were replaced by two cartouches of king Neferneferuaten. Meryetaten was still a princess, not yet a queen, and she was still a 'King's Daughter' at the end of Akhenaten's reign, for she is shown on Hermopolis *talatat* with Ankhesenpaaten and her daughter.[44] Since Ankhesenpaaten was not shown on the 'Later Proclamation' of Year 6 at Amarna,[45] she could hardly have borne a daughter before the end of her father's reign. Allen thus wished to date the "Coregency Stela" in its original version to year 17. Where now, however, was Smenkhkare? By definition he succeeded Akhenaten, and was married to Meryetaten.[46]

It was in 1991 that Allen made his most important contribution, finally sorting out the tangle of names that had bedeviled all earlier scholarship and assigning them to either Neferneferuaten or Smenkhkare. He concluded that Ankhkheperure Neferneferuaten, with epithets relating to Akhenaten, and Ankhkheperure Smenkhkare, without epithets, "share a common throne name, Ankhkheperure, but nothing else." Smenkhkare ruled *no more than one year* and was buried in KV 55. Tutankhamun was probably his brother, their father was most likely Akhenaten, but their mother uncertain: Nefertiti, Kiya, or someone else.[47]

As already noted, it was Malek who in 1996 conducted a first-rate piece of detective work *by checking the original sources* in a very ingenious way. Since the famous Nicholson 'two kings' relief *(2a)* had since disappeared, everyone had relied on Sir Charles's published drawing. This was made almost certainly by Joseph Bonomi, whom Nicholson mentions, and was in turn derived from a drawing by Joseph Hekekyan, the excavator, whose papers survive in the British Library. On checking this original drawing, Malek discovered that Bonomi had turned the subordinate figure, which seems to have been a fan bearer, into a king wearing the Blue Crown with uraeus! This evidence for two kings was thus shown to be entirely invented.[48]

Marc Gabolde accepted the distinction between Smenkhkare and Neferneferuaten and was responsible also for the final proof that the latter was a woman. Smenkhkare was married to Meryetaten, but Gabolde stated that he was not known at the court of Amenhotep III or Akhenaten. His name is a compound of Re, as were those of the two youngest daughters of Akhenaten. There was, in fact, another

Smenkhkare in the Thirteenth Dynasty,[49] but the name is "abnormal," Gabolde thought, more like a prenomen (as Munro had argued). Only one date was known for him: a wine docket of Year 1. To confirm the length of his reign, Gabolde turned therefore to small objects bearing his name, such as rings. Eighteen are known for Ay, who ruled for about four years, but only six for Smenkhkare: a reign lasting only one year therefore looked correct.

Gabolde's startling theory was, however that Smenkhkare was the Hittite prince Zannanza. He was not killed on his way to Egypt, but reached there, married Meryetaten, and was assassinated a year later. The puzzle of his prenomen that he shares with Neferneferuaten, whom Gabolde took to be Meryetaten, was explained as being "to maintain the efficiency of administrative and religious affairs": husband and wife therefore had the same name.

An important piece of evidence that seems to contradict this, Gabolde admitted, is the calcite vase from the tomb of Tutankhamun (7) showing cartouches of Akhenaten and Smenkhkare. They do not, of course, have to be coregents, but the evidence is so suggestive that Gabolde was forced to argue that the cartouches had been erased because they were "incorrect."[50]

The major problem with this revolutionary thesis is twofold: first, there is not a shred of evidence for the claim that a Hittite prince ruled Egypt about 1330 BC; indeed, the fact that the Hittites had become the main threat to Egyptian foreign interests makes it most unlikely that a daughter of Akhenaten could single-handedly devise and impose this situation on the Egyptian court and army. Second, there was an Egyptian prince, and he did come to the throne.

Allen offered further notes. He suggested that Smenkhkare was a son of Amenhotep III, and therefore brother of Akhenaten, and father of Tutankhamun. He reigned for only one year.[51]

Aidan Dodson, in accepting the identification of the mummy in KV 55 as Smenkhkare, suggested that the most important object which belonged to, and depicted the features of, Smenkhkare could be the second coffin from the tomb of Tutankhamun (fig. 98). Dodson believes that Smenkhkare was the younger brother of Akhenaten.[52]

Summing up: on the origins of Smenkhkare there is no agreement: a son of Amenhotep III and therefore a younger brother of Akhenaten,

Fig. 98. Face of the second coffin of Tutankhamun (Cairo JE 60670).

by Tiye, or by Sitamun—or a son of Akhenaten. The endless portraits assigned to Smenkhkare by the fantasies of Newberry and the broad nets of Roeder and Krauss are now reduced to a minimum. The relief in the tomb of Meryre ii is certain to be of him, but is hardly revealing given its present condition. The second coffin of Tutankhamun may well be the best portrait we have. To this may be added tentatively the Berlin portrait (fig. 99).

Allen's brilliant distinguishing of the royal names of the two rulers called Ankhkheperure has had a vital result: Smenkhkare is hardly attested! He appears in the tomb of Meryre ii and on a wine docket dated to Year 1—unless this is Tutankhamun's first year! This is otherwise the latest year of reign known for him, but

Fig. 99. A plaster face, sometimes identified as a portrait of Smenkhkare (Berlin ÄM 21354).

that datum could be overturned at any time. Some claim that his name was the second one on the coffin in KV 55, but since these secondary names were hacked out in the second intrusion into the tomb, this hardly constitutes stable evidence.

Armed with these sparse findings on the person of Akhenaten's and Nefertiti's eldest son-in-law, we may now turn to an even more daunting task: the reconstruction of the last five years of Akhenaten's reign.

The end of Akhenaten's reign
Petrie was obviously one of the first to try and clarify matters, but he limited himself to listing the reigns at the end of the dynasty: Akhenaten, Smenkhkare (twelve years!), Tutankhamun (nine years), Ay (twelve years!), and finally Horemheb. Amarna was abandoned, he believed, only after the death of Tutankhamun. It was Horemheb who abolished the worship of the Aten and destroyed Amarna: not a stone was left standing.[53] Petrie's source for the lengthy reigns for some of these ephemeral kings was Manetho.

James Breasted stated that Akhenaten was undermined by "a powerful priestly party," while his neglect of the empire in Asia "aroused indignation" in the military class. Sakere [*sic*] was appointed coregent and succeeded Akhenaten: his was "an obscure and ephemeral reign." Tutankhamun then returned to Thebes and restored the worship of Amun.[54]

Walter Wolf believed that Smenkhkare briefly succeeded Akhenaten and restored the worship of Amun, while also maintaining the cult of the Aten. He was also at loggerheads with Nefertiti. It was Tutankhamun who completely restored the old cults and returned to Thebes.[55]

John Pendlebury took sinister factionalism much further, and it was to have a long and misleading history. When Nefertiti was, according to this theory, disgraced and retired to the Northern Palace, Meryetaten and Smenkhkare were sent to Thebes to conciliate the priesthood of Amun. When Nefertiti died in Year 3 of Tutankhamun, he returned to Thebes.[56]

Reginald Engelbach made a famous collection of sources for the history of Akhenaten's reign. There was an estrangement in the royal family about Year 16, with Akhenaten and Smenkhkare in one part of Amarna and Nefertiti and Tutankhamun in another. Nefertiti "had every reason to hate the Aten and Smenkhkare." It is a shame that these reasons were not explored. Smenkhkare was made coregent about Year 17 and went to Thebes to seek reconciliation with the priesthood of Amun, but both he and Akhenaten died around the same time.[57]

Fairman agreed that Akhenaten and Smenkhkare were coregents. The latter ruled three years, but it was uncertain whether he predeceased Akhenaten. That Tutankhamun succeeded Smenkhkare was proven by the fact that he stayed at Amarna for three to four years.[58]

The theory of factionalism was very influential. According to Etienne Drioton and Jacques Vandier, Akhenaten attempted a reconciliation with the priesthood of Amun and became estranged from Nefertiti, who retired to the Northern Palace with Tutankhamun. Smenkhkare was appointed coregent with Akhenaten, but after three years both of them died. Tutankhamun remained at Amarna for about three years before returning to Thebes.[59]

One of the most fantastic reconstructions of this period of history was invented by Keith Seele. According to him, Akhenaten and Nefertiti became estranged, heading different "factions." Smenkhkare returned with Meryetaten to Thebes, but he was "beloved of Waenre" (that is, Akhenaten). His deadly mission was, in fact, a plot masterminded by Nefertiti, and he and his wife were assassinated![60]

John Wilson accepted the idea of a plot, but offered a new cause for the split. In his variation, the army was on Akhenaten's side, but the priesthood and old bureaucracy were disaffected. The empire had been lost, and there was an economic crisis. The turning point came in Year 12 with the visit of Queen Tiye ("an alert little pragmatist"!). Nefertiti was exiled with Tutankhamun and Ankhesenpaaten to "the northern end of town" and her name was given to Akhenaten's younger brother, Smenkhkare. Another variant was that he, not Tutankhamun, returned to Thebes by Year 3.[61] One can only rejoin that the evidence for Tiye's visit (in the tomb of her steward Huya) attests, to the contrary, the most cordial relations between her and her son and daughter-in-law.

Roeder saw the appointment of Smenkhkare as a sign of the loss of power by Nefertiti, who moved to the Maru-Aten (in the south), where later her name was replaced by Meryetaten's. While Akhenaten was still alive, Smenkhkare moved back to Thebes, in an attempt by Akhenaten to effect a reconciliation with the Amun priesthood, but Smenkhkare died soon after (in Year 17?). His true religious feelings, however, are revealed by the objects buried with him (KV 55): jewelry that bears the Earlier form of the Aten name, and the uraeus on the coffin with the Later name.[62]

William Hayes painted a dramatic picture:

In Egypt itself, the king's preoccupation with his personal design for living had not only made him many enemies, but had led him to neglect his administrative responsibilities, so that outside of Amarna itself disorder and corrupt practices by military and civil officials were added to the woes of a population already suffering from widespread distress.

Hayes is obviously drawing on the "Restoration Stela" of Tutankhamun.[63] As for Akhenaten himself, he was "ill and disillusioned." This caused the overtures to Amun and the split with Nefertiti. Smenkhkare returned to Thebes (the graffito: 3). He outlived Akhenaten by a few months.[64]

In Gardiner's classic history of Egypt, Nefertiti was still recorded as falling into disgrace after Year 12, because her name was supposedly replaced in inscriptions by that of her daughter Meryetaten, whose husband took Nefertiti's expanded name. Smenkhkare returned to Thebes and the worship of Amun (the graffito). Akhenaten, Gardiner claimed, was not buried at Amarna, because his canopic box was never used.[65] This deduction was based on Pendlebury's excavation of the Royal Tomb in the 1930s.

Christiane Desroches-Noblecourt thought Smenkhkare was crowned about Year 14, because after three years' reign, he and Akhenaten died at approximately the same time. He replaced Nefertiti in the king's affections, but was conciliatory toward Amun.[66]

Donald Redford, in his early study of chronology, emphasized for the first time that the famous graffito (3) that had been taken to suggest a restoration of the cult of Amun in Year 3 was in fact hidden in an abandoned tomb, and even if a temple had been built, this did not mean that Smenkhkare had returned to Thebes. These were rarely voiced cautions.

In an admittedly subjective reconstruction, Redford suggested that Smenkhkare was appointed coregent about Year 15/16, so that he ruled only one year by himself. He and Nefertiti were enemies, and she had to leave Amarna. On his death she returned, championing Tutankhamun.[67]

In Aldred's biography, Nefertiti disappeared after Years 12 and 13: she had not been disgraced, but had died. He was able at last to state that there was no evidence for earlier theories of disgrace. He also revealed that Fairman had told him that the supposed objects from the Northern Palace naming Nefertiti and Tutankhamun—fundamental to the 'factional' view—did not exist. Akhenaten's younger brother Smenkhkare was appointed coregent (about Year 13) and ruled three to four years. Aldred still accepted Newberry's homosexual interpretations. Smenkhkare's funerary equipment showed him to have been an adherent of *both* the Aten and Amun. His tomb was prepared at Thebes (the graffito: 3). By the time Akhenaten died in Year 17, Smenkhkare too was dead, and Akhenaten was therefore succeeded by Tutankhamun.[68] Munro followed the same conventional line.[69]

Helck's reconstruction led in another direction. Meryetaten appears in the Amarna Letters as a figure of influence in her father's reign (*EA* 10,

11, 155). Helck still believed that her name and portrait replaced those of Nefertiti in the Southern Palace, which proved that the latter was dead. A trio then came to power: Akhenaten, Smenkhkare, and Meryetaten (shown by Tutankhamun's box fragment: 6). It was Smenkhkare, however, and not Meryetaten, who took over the names and position of Nefertiti. Meryetaten is shown with a daughter, Meryetaten the Younger, fathered by Smenkhkare.[70] For Helck the "Coregency Stela" (8) attested a coregency of Akhenaten and Neferneferuaten, that is, Smenkhkare, by still reading the epithet as "beloved of Akenaten" instead of "beneficial for her husband." In sum, Helck posited that Nefertiti died in Year 12 or 13, and that in Year 17, by which time Meryetaten also was dead, Smenkhkare was briefly coregent, before ruling alone for three or four years. At the end of this time the temple of Amun at Thebes was reopened.[71]

For Krauss, the crucial evidence was not contemporary sources, as hitherto, but the third-century priest Manetho, who claimed that Akhenaten was succeeded by his wife and daughter Akencheres. Jurgen von Beckerath had already suggested that an "and" had slipped out: the text should have read Akhenaten's daughter *and* Akencheres, that is, Smenkhkare.[72] Krauss explained this Greek form as "Ankhkheperure," of which a feminine form was known. The queen was Meryetaten, and she was followed by "Rathotes," who was Nebkheperure, that is, Tutankhamun. Krauss then turned to the famous letter from the Egyptian queen recorded in the annals of Suppuliliumas, which also proved, in his view, that Akhenaten was succeeded by a woman. As Murnane responded in a review: "Manetho's historicity and his relationship to his sources are two separate questions: together they form a morass from which there is no easy removal."[73]

Krauss's reconstruction was as follows: after the death of Akhenaten, his daughter and wife Meryetaten ruled for approximately one year (*EA* 10, 11, 155). She then married Smenkhkare, but died before him. Her sister Ankhesenpaaten then became "first lady," shown with Smenkhkare on a block from Hermopolis[74] and the "Coregency Stela" (8). Smenkhkare intended to marry her, but he died. By his Year 3, however, Amun was connected with his funerary temple (the graffito: 3), but his name still contained 'Aten' and he still resided at Amarna. It was Tutankhaton who married Ankhesenpaaten, changed his name to Tutankhamun, and left Amarna in his Year 1, because no later jar seals of his are found there.[75] Krauss also dated his "Restoration Stela" to Year 1.[76]

Helck instantly accepted this theory of the position of Meryetaten. He tried to provide additional evidence by assigning the two famous Berlin reliefs (4–5), recently reassigned to Akhenaten and Nefertiti, to Akhenaten and Meryetaten. He simply asserted that they were "late" Amarnan in date, that Nefertiti had by this time disappeared, and that she never wore the Blue Crown! He was content, however, if a regnant queen could not wear such a crown, to give it to a princess as "designated successor." He attempted to bolster this by a long argument suggesting that Amenhotep III had intended his daughter Sitamun to be his successor.[77] He followed this theory only three years later with another totally novel account.

On the death of Nefertiti in Year 13/14, Kiya was elevated to King's Wife. She produced a daughter in Year 16, who became the chief heiress, thus displacing Meryetaten. When Akhenaten died, Kiya and her daughter were murdered by the supporters of Meryetaten and Ankhesenpaaten.[78] These are 'facts' totally unknown to any other scholar in the field.

Dodson initially interpreted the evidence of the box fragment in Tutankhamun's tomb (6) as a clear indication that Meryetaten was the queen of Neferneferuaten, who was her husband, and thus could not be Nefertiti.[79] He would later change his mind completely. Gay Robins replied that such a queen was not necessarily shown next to her husband. Kings, for example, were shown with their mothers, who would still bear the royal title. There is no evidence on the box fragment, however, that Meryetaten was married to Akhenaten. She may have borne the title in a ceremonial capacity.[80]

In Redford's biography of Akhenaten, Smenkhkare married Akhenaten's eldest daughter Meryetaten, whose importance is attested by *EA* 11, and became coregent in Year 15 (aged 14). It is "beyond dispute" that Smenkhkare began building to Amun at Thebes, and he may himself have returned there if he was buried in KV 55. Redford seemed to date Smenkhkare's death after Akhenaten's, to accord with the age of the mummy in KV 55. He also introduced another major consideration in Akhenaten's last years: a devastating plague that began in the east (*EA* 126). This may have caused the deaths of the three youngest princesses.

Redford must, however, be given credit for his honesty about this period: "We have no clear idea, therefore, whether our chronicle includes the truly important events and conveys a generally accurate record, however brief, of the heretical reign."[81]

Whether recognized at the time or not, at this point (1991) came the solution to one of the most tormenting puzzles, and the undermining of all the assertions thus far that Smenkhkare ruled for three years: Allen's analysis and separation of the two rulers with the same prenomen.

Joyce Tyldesley still believed that by Year 14/15 Nefertiti was either dead or in retirement. Smenkhkare reigned a maximum of three years, mostly as Akhenaten's coregent. He was succeeded by Tutankhamun, who moved back to Thebes in his Year 3/4.[82]

Reeves painted an unparalleled dramatic picture of the reign toward its end. It is a challenging exercise to analyze this account asking for evidence, while trying to steer clear of simple assertions, pejorative language ("complete and utter groveling"), reinforcing adverbs and phrases ("clearly," "there is little doubt," "quite likely") and even the invention of people's private thoughts. There is one category of evidence alluded to, but not documented: troops with batons. Reeves prefers to refer to this evidence generically for a good reason: in the whole six volumes of the Amarnan tombs, there are but three scenes showing Akhenaten with a military escort, and they are all grand ceremonial occasions.[83]

Reeves turned next to the Pawah graffito *(2)* to prove the "despondency" in Egypt at this time. He equated Year 3 of the coregent with Year 14 of Akhenaten. Once again adjectives are on high show: the "heart-rending appeal to Amun." The Amun priesthood was operating in the coregent's mortuary temple. "The Amarna revolution had clearly entered a new phase": the coregent was taking "a softer line." Reeves accepted that Nefertiti was elevated to be coregent and finally pharaoh, but Akhenaten's physical condition declined (again no evidence). Reeves even hints that he went mad, and that his death was "assisted." It was thus Nefertiti who wrote to the Hittite king.[84]

Helck made his last entry into the debate in his posthumously published study of KV 55. He reemphasized Manetho's statement that Akhenaten was succeeded by his *daughter* Akencheres (Ankhkheperure), Meryetaten, whose reign was short. It was she and her husband who were "likely" shown on the two famous Berlin stelae *(4–5)*. The problem is that Meryetaten is linked to both kings with the same prenomen Ankhkheperure. They have, of course, different nomina:

1. Smenkhkare-djeserkheperu (the tomb of Meryre ii: *1*), and
2. Neferneferuaten, with epithets meaning "beloved of Akhenaten" (Tutankhamun's box: *6*).

It had to be admitted that Neferneferuaten was preeminently the expanded name of Nefertiti. Helck confessed, as well he might, that this was "a grotesque situation."

To solve the problem he turned to a neglected criterion: provenance. Smenkhkare is found almost only at Amarna *(1)*, apart from one block at Memphis. Neferneferuaten-mery-Waenre is dominant at Thebes: the tomb of Pairy *(3)*, all the items from Tutankhamun's tomb (boxes, canopic coffins, bracelets), and the block from Hermopolis.[85] The same king thus had two names: Neferneferuaten in Amarna, Smenkhkare in Thebes (this would be unique in Egyptian history, we may note). He was married to Meryetaten, the "interim queen," and was buried in an unprepared tomb, perhaps after a "violent overthrow." A new group headed by Ay (the so-called Akhmim group) took over with Tutankhamun as king. Amarna was abandoned. Tutankhamun also perhaps was overthrown, and replaced by the military.

After this sequence of violence, Helck then admitted that the two young kings might have been victims of a plague raging at the time (*EA* 11, 35, 96). His interpretation of Ay is also contradictory: under him Amarna was abandoned, but as Akhenaten's tutor he played a leading role in the revolution: his accession was "a coup d'état of the chief ideologue." This also "belittled" the military—but Ay himself had been one of the most powerful military generals: the commander of the cavalry.[86]

Dodson, in his 2009 studies, suggested that Smenkhkare, Akhenaten's younger brother, was coregent about Years 13 and 14. His reason for this date was the scene in the tomb of Meryre ii, which also showed the 'durbar' of Year 12. For the first time it was argued that these scenes were chronologically close. This meant that the normal sequence was reversed: Smenkhkare was *followed* by Nefertiti as coregent from Year 14. *She* is the king in the tomb of Pairy *(2)*, and her third year is independent of Akhenaten, whom she survived for seven years. All this was to secure the continuation of the "revolution" and the accession of Tutankhamun, with whom she also coruled, until she died or was deposed.

Dodson realized that there were problems with this interpretation: if Meryetaten was born most likely in Year 3/4, she would be only ten years of age. He nevertheless dated Smenkhkare's coregency to this one year, Akhenaten Year 13/14.[87]

Dimitri Laboury relied mostly on Gabolde's analysis. In his scenario, Nefertiti had died, because the Amarna Letters show Meryetaten as "mistress of the house" (*EA* 11). She was the one who wrote for a husband to the Hittite king (in that case, her *father* is the husband who has died). She was about thirteen at this time. It was all an intrigue, to exclude her brother Tutankhaten from the throne. The Hittite prince arrived and was known in Egypt as Smenkhkare, but ruled for only one year. Meryetaten took over as Ankhkheperure Neferneferuaten: the epithets emphasized her connection with her father, to give her legitimacy. She ruled for three years and was succeeded by Tutankhaten.[88] Here we can employ Occam's Razor. If we have a queen bearing a name used by Nefertiti and emphasizing her connection with Akhenaten, is this more likely to be Nefertiti or her daughter (who, after all, was not very "effective" for her husband)?

Conclusion

The above journey can only be called extraordinary. It must be acknowledged that historians can only work with the evidence before them at any time. And in the problems analyzed above, that evidence has been not only constantly increasing, but also changing. It is the most fundamental betrayal of sound historical method, however, to go beyond the available evidence in pursuit, as we have seen, of fantasy, melodrama, and sensationalism.

The last five years of Akhenaten's reign had long been without datable documents. The last fixed event was Year 12, the celebration of the famous 'durbar,' and the apparently contemporaneous visit to Amarna by Queen Tiye. At the 'durbar' all six daughters are shown, which almost certainly indicates that they were all alive at that time.

Taking Year 12 as a *terminus post quem*, a number of subsequent events were known, although their dates were not: the death of Queen Tiye (there is evidence for her burial in the Royal Tomb); the deaths not only of Meketaten, but also of two of her younger sisters (the evidence of rooms *alpha* and *gamma* in the Royal Tomb has recently been reinterpreted); elevation of Queen Nefertiti to the position of 'king'; and the marriage of Smenkhkare to Meryetaten and his elevation to coregent. It was only in the last few years that just one of these events, the elevation of Nefertiti to full king, has been narrowed down to late in Year 16 or in Year 17 by the Bersha graffito, which makes Year 16, III *3ḥt* 15, a *terminus post quem* for the event.

The important evidence of the two Berlin stelae (figs. 82, 83)—first taken to be Akhenaten and Nefertiti, then, because of Newberry, totally misread as two male kings—has now been reinterpreted as a king and a queen, usually again Akhenaten and Nefertiti, but sometimes Smenkhkare and Meryetaten (by Roeder, for instance).

The misunderstanding of the name replaced by Meryetaten's in the Maru-Aten has been corrected: the name was not Nefertiti's, but Kiya's. With that, there collapsed fantasies that had been bandied about for decades concerning 'factions' and divisions over Atenism within the royal family. The simple proof that this was all fantasy is that the members of the 'factions' were identified in totally contradictory ways, as were their relationships with Atenism!

The graffito of Pawah *(3)* is the most contentious piece of evidence. It is continually discussed, but with incredible clumsiness. It mentions no fewer than *four* people. The tomb belongs to Pairy (TT 139), *waab* priest and overseer of the peasants of Amun; he is the first person. His tomb is dated to the reign of Amenhotep III.[89]

In this tomb is the graffito of Pawah, *waab* priest and scribe of the divine offerings of Amun in the Mansion-of-Ankhkheperure-in-Thebes; Pawah is the second person mentioned in the graffito. He, however, is not its author. That was his brother, Batchan, draftsman in the same "mansion" and the third person mentioned. Why should he have inscribed this text in Pairy's tomb? No one asks, let alone attempts an answer. The graffito is dated to Year 3 of "Ankhkheperure-mery- A[. . .], Neferneferuaten-mery-A[. . .]," who is the fourth person mentioned: the epithets, however, are damaged. There is also a "mansion" of an "Ankhkheperure" in Thebes. Given the lack of any epithets, is this Smenkhkare rather than Neferneferuaten?

The graffito is in two parts: First a hymn to Amun, which is standard; for example, "pleasant is the utterance of your name; it is like the taste of life." The second part is a prayer: "Come back to us, O lord." From where is Amun returning? "You shall come from afar." The key, however, is "as you have caused me to see the darkness which is yours to give, make light for me so that I can see you." Pawah is blind (as Gardiner told us in 1928). This is why his brother makes the inscription for him—but we have no idea why it was placed in this tomb.

The use of this text has been extraordinary. It has been offered endlessly as evidence for Smenkhkare and his length of reign—the one king whose name does not appear—owing to his long-standing confusion with Neferneferuaten. It is also used endlessly to claim that "Smenkhkare" restored the worship of Amun. The graffito states no such thing: it is a prayer by an Amunist for the return of Amun. And what exactly is meant by "return" is unsure: gods traveled about in Egypt for ritual reasons.[90] This fact only heightens the mystery, for Pawah was already in the service of Amun! And the lack of clear epithets in the king's name makes the final identity of even that figure uncertain. The text clearly raises more questions than it answers, but it has been the very linchpin of most reconstructions.

The scene from the tomb of Meryre ii *(1)*, which features the 'durbar' of Year 12, shows parallel scenes of Meryre being rewarded by Akhenaten and Nefertiti and by Smenkhkare and Meryetaten. Attempts to impugn the identity and relationship of the last two seem forced. What chronologically, however, is the relationship between the 'durbar' and this scene?

On the box from Tutankhamun's tomb *(6)*, the two knobs name Meryetaten and Ankhkheperure, "beloved of Neferkheperure" (that is, of Akhenaten). The text in between names Akhenaten, Ankhkheperure/ Neferneferuaten, "beloved of Akhenaten" in both cases, and Meryetaten, "the King's Chief Wife." This is complicated, because of Meryetaten. Of whom was she the chief wife? All we know is that at some point she married Smenkhkare.

The "Coregency Stela" *(8)* shows two kings, because there are four cartouches: Akhenaten and Ankhkheperure Neferneferuaten, "beloved of Akhenaten." As happened so often, the text has been changed. It seems that originally the stela showed Akhenaten and Nefertiti and two daughters. Nefertiti is the candidate for the second king in the reworked version.

So much for the basic texts. Scholars are totally divided about whether Smenkhkare ruled during Akhenaten's lifetime or succeeded him, although there is a strong majority and strong probability for the former. The beginning of his coregency, however, was dated to anywhere between Years 12 and 15, but that is mostly to accommodate the now outdated minimum of the three years' reign that actually belonged to Neferneferuaten.

Views of Smenkhkare's part in Atenism have changed dramatically from the early melodrama based on 'factions' and the overconfident citing of the graffito, which lasted from Pendlebury until Aldred denounced it. This made him the main agent of compromise and reconciliation with the Amunists. Smenkhkare is now seen as more ambivalent, because the evidence is contradictory. And Marianne Eaton-Krauss has assembled a long catalogue of evidence to demonstrate that Tutankhamun was the king who turned against the Aten. He associated himself deliberately with the policies of Amenhotep III: restoring his temple on the west bank, resuming building of his Pylon X, and constructing his own funerary temple—for both of which he used Akhenaten's *talatat*. The first attacks on Akhenaten's memory date from Tutankhamun.[91] The latter's change of name is also compelling evidence.

What of Nefertiti's role after Year 12? In the guise of Neferneferuaten she is now to be assigned the famous graffito *(3)* that used to be taken as Smenkhkare's, which would indicate that she ruled for at least three years as king. As to when this might have begun, the most recent piece of evidence to have come to light turns out to be of vital importance: in the Bersha graffito from Year 16, almost at the end of her husband's reign, Nefertiti was still a simple queen, not yet a female king, so that her full coregency with Akhenaten could have only lasted for a few months at most, perhaps following a significantly longer period with kingly regalia but not yet a king's titulary.

The crucial questions are her relationship with Akhenaten, Smenkhkare, and Tutankhamun. She was certainly a crowned queen, without kingly titles, during Akhenaten's reign, as the stelae show. Given the late date of the Bersha graffito (but the existence of the Tutankhamun box fragment), she will have been her husband's full coregent only during his last months—or even weeks—and thus Nefertiti's power as a fully fledged king will have been exercised mainly after Akhenaten's death. For how long she ruled beyond her Year 3 we do not know. Indeed, were these years spent as Akhenaten's independent successor, or only ever as coregent with the young Tutankhamun? Manetho's garbled note may be useful: Akhenaten was succeeded by a woman, Akencheres.[92] If this conceals Ankhkheperure, then it should be Nefertiti. We are forced to admit, however, if we observe the strict conventions of serious history, that after a century of unrelenting debate, the details of the last five years of Akhenaten—and those that directly followed them—remain almost as much a mystery as they ever were.

This assessment clearly raises more questions. Why should this negative result be so? The nine pieces of constantly quoted evidence contain most of the answers. One (the Nicholson relief, 2) has been removed. The "Coregency Stela" (8) has lost almost all of its image, and only cartouches of three royal persons remain. The Hermopolis block (9) shows merely the lower legs of three presumably royal persons. The box from Tutankhamun's tomb (6) gives five royal names, and the calcite jar from the same tomb (7) gives only the names of Akhenaten and Smenkhkare. What can be made from such pitiful remains?

Other items are admittedly more complete, most usefully the two scenes from the tomb of Meryre (1) and the two reliefs from Amarna (4–5). On calm consideration, out of all the possible royal couples of the Amarna period, Akhenaten and Nefertiti should always have been the obvious identifications. It thus becomes apparent that we have only one text, the graffito of Pawah (3), but this was meant to do anything but assist later historians to reconstruct the end of Akhenaten's reign.

A major problem must never be lost sight of in all these sources: there is not a date in sight. It is no wonder that some have turned to other texts. The Amarna Letters throw a few fitful beams—but only that—and so resort has been had to even the tortured text of the third-century BC Manetho, where his names can be claimed to represent almost anyone known from contemporaneous texts.

To the above archaeological sources (1–9) can, of course, be added other things: the constantly cited mummy from KV 55, and the hardly mentioned statue of the "mature" Nefertiti. It is by now obvious that faced with this dilemma, scholars since Petrie have thrown the most basic cautions of historical method to the winds, and indulged in pure fantasy. It is very disturbing that the motivation often seems to have been prejudice against Nefertiti, to displace her in the affections of Akhenaten. It is incredible to note that assassinations and coups d'état have been claimed to involve every major figure. Often national schools of interpretation, particularly English and German, have restricted, not enlarged, our understanding. In these circumstances, credit must be given to those careful scholars who have been responsible for major steps forward: such as by Allen on the vital distinction of royal names, and reexamination of the "Coregency Stela," and Malek's turn to primary sources for the Nicholson relief.

The parlous situation of our historical knowledge is unlikely to change. And here another fundamental principle of historical method applies: when we do not have evidence, we must admit it.

8 Two Royal Tombs

The royal tomb at Amarna

In the 'Earlier Proclamation' for the founding of the new capital at Akhet-Aten, Akhenaten specified that a tomb was to be built in the eastern mountains for himself, Nefertiti, and Princess Meryetaten. No matter where any of them might die, that was to be their burial place. Had he died while he still ruled at Thebes as Amenhotep IV, he presumably would have been buried in the Valley of the Kings: perhaps in WV 23, ultimately used by Ay, or the unfinished WV 25.[1]

Many stories circulated regarding the first discovery of the Amarna Royal Tomb. William John Loftie, English clergyman and collector, was told in 1883/84 that the locals had discovered the tomb—or the pitiful fragments left in it—and from them he acquired various articles that were soon sold to the Royal Scottish Museum (now absorbed into National Museums Scotland). Three finger rings passed to the collection of Sir Rider Haggard. He missed out, however, on "gold winding sheets" (presumably gold bands holding the shroud in place, as found on the mummy of Tutankhamun), supposedly bearing the names of Tiye and Nefertiti.[2]

The official history of the tomb begins in December 1891, when Alexandre Barsanti (1858–1917), conservator at the Cairo Museum, was sent by Eugene Grébaut (1846–1915), Director General of Antiquities, to

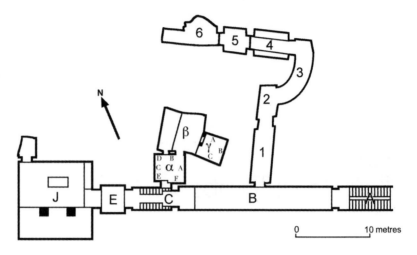

Fig. 100. Plan of the Royal Tomb at Amarna.

find the Royal Tomb, which Barsanti stated was hitherto unknown. After he had walked for five hours along the wadi that leads eastward into the desert behind the city of Amarna, the entrance was found almost blocked by fallen rocks. Barsanti found the burial chamber of Meketaten *(alpha)* in a side chamber, with fragments of a red granite sarcophagus and the relief of the mourning king and queen. The principal burial chamber (E) allegedly contained the fragments of a white limestone sarcophagus. In 1892, Barsanti was sent back by the new Director General, Jacques De Morgan (1857–1924), to clear the tomb (fig. 100).

In room 4 of the corridor that opened from the right wall of the main axis, Barsanti found a slab showing Akhenaten, Nefertiti, and two daughters worshiping (fig. 72). Of the reliefs in the burial chamber of Meketaten, he observed: "What could be more true but unexpected" than the scene of the king in his grief holding the arm of the queen. He commented on the absence of any husband for the dead Meketaten, but stated that no conclusion was to be drawn from the presence of only four princesses, when there were six in Year 12 (see below). He thus dated Meketaten's death between Years 12 and 18.[3]

Intriguing, however, were the stories of human remains. These derive from Archibald Sayce, professor of Assyriology at Oxford, who told in 1923 of the "official discovery" of the tomb in 1891 and Georges Daressy's finding outside of the remains of a mummy "torn to shreds."[4] A decade later, in a letter to the *Egyptian Gazette* of 8 January 1932, he gave further authority for the story: he was with Daressy at the time. Sayce himself was sure that this was the mummy of Akhenaten. There is no reason to disbelieve Sayce's recollections, even so long after the event, although the identity of the mummy is of course wholly uncertain. John Pendlebury in 1931/32 found two fragments of "very thin skull bone" in or near the tomb—whether human or animal is unknown.[5]

The next official visitor was Urbain Bouriant, director of the French Archaeological Mission, in 1896. He identified the burial chamber of Meketaten and read the names of Akhenaten, Nefertiti, and Meryetaten in the main burial chamber: this suggested that the tomb might not have been Akhenaten's after all.[6] Bouriant had observed accurately, but he had drawn the wrong conclusion about Akhenaten's burial. The tomb was copied and photographed under his direction and published alongside a number of private tomb chapels in 1903.[7] These copies have since proved invaluable, as the tomb was vandalized in 1934.

During 1931/32, the Egypt Exploration Society undertook a new clearance and copying campaign at the request and expense of the Egyptian Antiquities Service. Work was conducted both inside the tomb and in the wadi outside, in particular on the dump left behind by Barsanti, and further fragments of sarcophagi and broken shabtis were found there, as well as parts of the king's alabaster canopic chest, a granite bowl of Thutmose III, fragments of a diorite bowl of the Fourth Dynasty king Khaefre (!), and an alabaster vase of Amenhotep III.[8]

Restored in 1939 by Ghazi Effendi Ali, the canopic chest (fig. 101) followed the basic pattern of such chests since the middle of the Eighteenth Dynasty in having a protective divine figure at its corners, but rather than the four tutelary goddesses it had the falcon-headed Re-Horakhty, thus dating it to the very earliest years of Akhenaten's reign (no royal nomen was preserved). The dado of the box was decorated with *djed* and *ankh* signs, which Mahmud Hamza suggested "probably denote the protection of both Isis and Osiris." Hamza assumed that Akhenaten's sarcophagus had the same four Horus protectors at each corner—but he was to be proven wrong. He also stated that the canopic box showed no staining from

Fig. 101. Akhenaten's reconstructed canopic chest (Cairo JE 59454).

unguents. This suggested that it had not been used, and therefore that Akhenaten was never buried in the tomb.[9] As Geoffrey Martin was to declare, however, this deduction is "open to serious question."[10]

In 1934 rumors arose of a new tomb found near the Royal Tomb. The Antiquities Service therefore excavated in the neighborhood. They found no such tomb, but did unearth many fragments of Akhenaten's shabtis, of granite sarcophagi, and of vases.[11] That same year, however, rival gangs of guards at the tomb vandalized rooms *alpha* and *gamma*, destroying significant parts of the decoration, the interpretation of much of which became increasingly contested in subsequent years. Our modern understanding of the Royal Tomb thus relies very much on the records made by the teams of Bouriant and the Egypt Exploration Society, as finally supplemented, collated, and published through the extraordinary labor and scholarship of Geoffrey Martin.[12]

In the burial chamber (E) the decoration had been almost entirely destroyed, but Martin was able to reconstruct three of the scenes. One showed the royal family, including four princesses, offering to the Aten (half the time using the Earlier form of his name, the other half using the Later form). The others were two scenes of mourning, one with the female figure beneath a canopy and Akhenaten and Nefertiti to the right. Martin suggested that the dead person was most probably Queen Tiye.

Akhenaten's sarcophagus could be reconstructed from the numerous fragments of pink, grey, and white granite found in and around the tomb: the Aten was shown on all sides, and, as already noted, at each corner Nefertiti replaced the traditional goddesses (fig. 102). The name of the Aten was in its Later form. More than two hundred shabtis were found (fig. 103): "Every object was systematically smashed into small

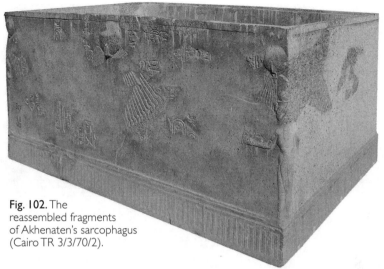

Fig. 102. The reassembled fragments of Akhenaten's sarcophagus (Cairo TR 3/3/70/2).

fragments." "The vengeance taken (on the sarcophagus) by the king's enemies was terrible: with few exceptions none of the fragments is more than a few centimetres wide. . . . This destruction also applies to every object in the tomb, no matter how massive or solid."[13]

The corridor in which Bouriant found the relief of the royal family (rooms 1–6) was unfinished, but can only have been intended, Martin argued, for Nefertiti. In the suite of rooms (rooms *alpha* to *gamma*) that included the burial chamber of Meketaten, who died in or after Year 12, room *alpha* had niches for 'magic bricks' and was therefore at least ultimately intended for a burial. Wall A showed king and queen greeting the rising Aten; the royal figures had been recut "to convert them from the 'exaggerated' style of the early Amarna years in which they were originally rendered to the more conventional and sedate style in vogue during the later part of the reign."[14] Wall B was divided into seven registers that depicted the "sovereignty of the Aten over all Creation,"[15] the upper four the inhabitants of Egypt, the lower three those of Nubia and Asia. Wall D, a continuation of B, showed charioteers, soldiers, and some

Fig. 103. A shabti of Akhenaten (MMA 1982.50).

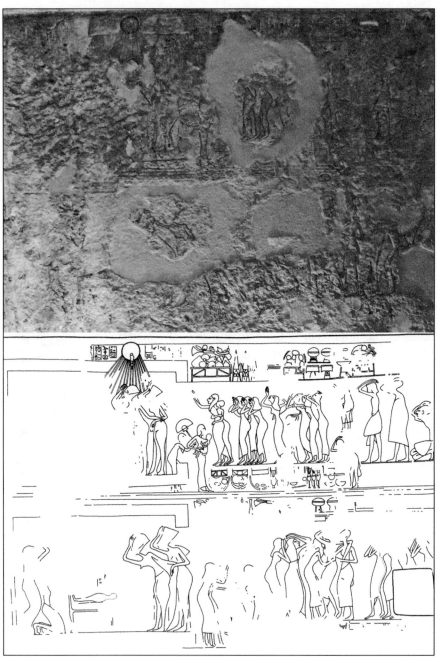

Fig. 104. Akhenaten and Nefertiti mourning at the biers of their daughters (Royal Tomb, room *alpha*, wall F).

foreigners. Wall C was a counterpoint to wall A, showing the adoration of the sun's setting, with Wall E, a continuation of C, also in seven registers and showing foreigners worshiping the Aten.

Wall F, however, was very different, its decoration possibly a late insertion, showing two registers with apparently the same scene, "unparalleled in the royal iconography of ancient Egypt":[16] Akhenaten and Nefertiti are viewing the bier of the deceased (fig. 104). Women mourn, as do some men, including the vizier, while a woman outside the death chamber holds an infant in the upper register; the relevant area of the lower register was already too damaged in the 1890s to be sure of the situation there. No texts survived at all on the wall, apart from some of the epithets of the Aten.

Although room *beta* was undecorated, room *gamma* was adorned in relief. Wall A bore a scene very similar to those on wall F of room *alpha*, including the female mourners, vizier, and nurse with an infant (fig. 105). In this case, however, the deceased is identified as Meketaten, while the nurse and infant are accompanied by a damaged label text that included the name of Nefertiti. Wall B (extending onto C) showed the deceased

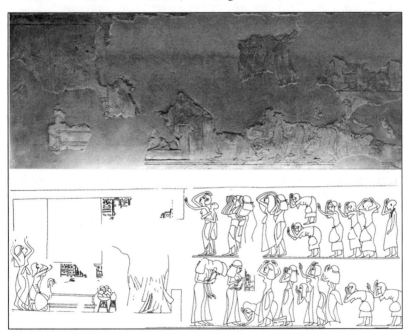

Fig. 105. Akhenaten and Nefertiti mourning at the bier of Maketaten (Royal Tomb, room *gamma*, wall A).

Fig. 106. Akhenaten, Nefertiti, and their surviving daughters mourning at the funerary bower of Maketaten (Royal Tomb, room *gamma*, wall B).

princess in a bower, mourned by her parents and three of her sisters (fig. 106). The Aten above was given the Later form of his name.

Most observers concluded that the child was the newborn of Meketaten, who had therefore died in childbirth. The label text was generally restored along the lines of "[NAME OF BABY born of the King's Daughter of his body, his beloved, Meketaten] born of the King's Chief Wife, his beloved Neferneferua[ten]-Nefertiti, who lives for ever and eternity," but a number argued that there was no space for such a reconstruction. Kurt Sethe, on the other hand, identified the baby as Neferneferuaten-tasherit.[17] Rolf Krauss suggested that it was Tutankhaten,[18] and Marc Gabolde believed that he could read traces of a male determinative in the old photographs and copies (this element of the wall was totally destroyed in 1934), and perhaps even firm signs that the name was that of Tutankhaten, with the label simply identifying him as a son of Nefertiti, who was present as a member of the royal family.[19]

This reading was, however, rejected by others: Lanny Bell, William Murnane, and, in particular, Jacobus van Dijk, concluded that the label named Meketaten herself, shown as a baby after her death, having undergone some process of rebirth or symbolic of new life, presumably as an aspect of the little-known Amarnan funerary beliefs.[20] This resolved an issue that had troubled many as to whether Meketaten had been old enough to have borne a child during her father's reign, given the probability that she was born about Year 5.

The death scenes in room *alpha* were also long interpreted as depicting the aftermath of death in childbirth, and sometimes as simply duplicates of the Meketaten relief. It was only in 1993 that Claude Vandersleyen argued that all scenes could hardly portray the same funeral, because that would entail so much repetition, as well as ignoring vital differences: a nurse and infant are shown in the upper, but not the lower scene—but the lower scene is damaged precisely in the area where the nurse and baby would appear.[21] He further noticed something very particular in the scenes in room *gamma* for Meketaten: together with their parents only *three* princesses are shown. That makes sense if room *alpha* depicts the deaths of two other princesses; he thus suggested that they were Neferneferure and Setepenre, the two youngest daughters.[22]

The very next year, Maarten Raven offered a far-reaching reassessment of the sarcophagus fragments and their lids from the tomb, which Martin had assigned to monuments of Akhenaten and Meketaten.[23] Relying on the type and thickness of the stone, the texts inscribed on it, and other objects such as Tiye's shrine from KV 55, Raven reassigned some sixty or more fragments which Martin had thought constituted the lid of Akhenaten's sarcophagus and the shell[24] of Meketaten's to restore the sarcophagus of Tiye. What Martin had taken to be the lid of Akhenaten's monument was now shown to fit that newly identified sarcophagus.[25] It is interesting that Edwin Brock (1946–2015) came independently to the same conclusions around the same time (fig. 107).[26]

Amid the destruction wreaked on the Royal Tomb and its contents, Julia Samson noted regarding the desecrators: "their aim to destroy the identity of the owners and prevent their names from being spoken in eternity was a complete failure, and as dismal as their actions. We do not know who *they* were. But the world will not forget Akhenaten and Nefertiti."[27]

Tomb 55 in the Valley of the Kings

Fig. 107. Edwin and Lyla Brock's reconstruction of the foot-end of the sarcophagus of Tiye.

In January 1907, the New York businessman Theodore Davis (1837–1915), who had become interested in Egyptology and who had obtained a permit to excavate in the Valley of the Kings and already discovered or cleared a dozen more of its tombs, made one of the most controversial discoveries ever made there.[28] Opposite the place where the tomb of Tutankhamun would be found fifteen years later, his team uncovered a corridor and chamber (fig. 108), the contents of which still puzzle Egyptologists. Davis promptly dubbed this tomb that of Queen Tiye, because her name was on the first item found, a dismantled funerary shrine made for her by Akhenaten, and he perpetuated this identification in his 1910 publication.[29]

The door had been closed with large and small stones, originally cemented or plastered together, but pulled down to a remaining level one meter high. Within the mouth of the tomb, up to a meter or so from the door and to within one or one and one-third meters of the ceiling, the tomb had been filled with stones. On these stones were lying two wooden 'doors' of a shrine.[30]

Beyond the shrine, the corridor continued down into a chamber, at the center of which was a partly collapsed wooden coffin (fig. 109), adorned with gold foil and glass, while to one side lay further sections of the shrine, and in a niche four canopic jars. Within the coffin lay a mummy, badly damaged by damp, with its arms reported as arranged

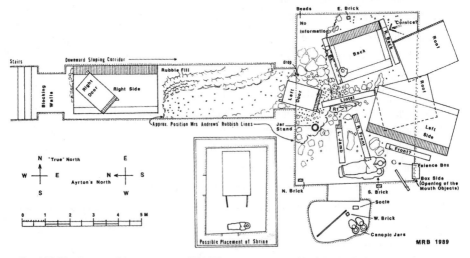

Fig. 108. The layout of the contents of KV 55, as reconstructed by Martha Bell.

Fig. 109. The coffin in KV 55 as originally found.

in the normally female pose of the left arm bent across the breast and the right arm straight at the side, a bent gold-sheet vulture collar at its head recalling a crown (fig. 110), with a gold necklace its only apparent adornment. Apart from Tiye's names, and one of Amenhotep III, on the shrine, all cartouches had been cut out from the shrine and the coffin, the gold face of which had been torn away.[31] Four 'magic bricks' belong-

ing to Akhenaten were present. A large box at the head of the coffin contained glazed ritual objects, while a uraeus with the Aten cartouches was found on the floor. In a corner was another box containing instruments for the opening of the mouth that included Tiye's name.

In Davis's account, the scandalous treatment of the mummy, which was reduced to a skeleton, remains indelibly imprinted on the reader's mind.[32] The archaeologist in charge was Edward Ayrton (1882–1914), who had been trained by Petrie. He gave an account of the clearing of the tomb entirely inadequate in

Fig. 110. The vulture collar found around the head of the mummy in KV 55 (Cairo JE 39630 = CG 52643).

its summary nature, and managing to mistake its orientation (his north is west).[33] In the *Proceedings of the Society for Biblical Archaeology* in the same year, Ayrton provided a slightly fuller account, in which he identified the right side of Tiye's shrine in the corridor as a great square coffin. The two accounts, in fact, barely overlap.

For Davis's publication, Georges Daressy, Deputy Keeper in the Cairo Museum, catalogued the items found and added much. He noted the erasures of Akhenaten's names on the shrine and coffin, that a piece of gold foil found with the mummy bore the Earlier form of the name of the Aten, that the canopic jars bore feminine features and had once borne a uraeus which had been broken off, and that they carried an inscription that had been obliterated. He declared the coffin to be very rich, of the *rishi* (feathered) type. Other objects included a figurine of Thoth and a statuette of Bes.[34]

The mummy was examined by Grafton Elliot Smith (1871–1937), an Australian, Professor of Anatomy at Cairo. In July 1907, he judged that it belonged to a man, aged twenty-five to twenty-six, plus or minus two to three years, perhaps up to twenty-eight. He also stated that the cranium showed unmistakably "the distortion characteristic of a condition of hydrocephalus" (fig. 111).

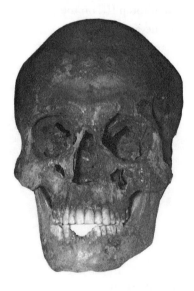

In September 1907, Archibald Sayce, an Assyriologist, note, unwisely entered the fray. The *Times* having announced Smith's analysis of the mummy, Davis thereupon wrote to Sayce, presumably a private communication which Sayce decided to make public. Sayce began by pointing out that the mummy case (meaning the shrine) stated that it was made by Akhenaten for Tiye, and that the coffin bore the (obliterated) name of Akhenaten (or, rather, an excised cartouche: no trace of a name remained). The main burden of the letter was to try to undermine Smith's analysis by stating that the mummy was first seen by Dr. Pollock of Luxor and "a prominent American obstetrician" (who has forever resisted identification)

Fig. 111. The skull from the mummy in KV 55 (Cairo CG 61075).

and on the basis of pelvic angles they had declared the mummy that of a female—and for Davis this was Tiye.[35]

Smith himself replied a month later. With barely concealed contempt, he noted that the pelvic measurements were actually at the opposite end of the scale from those allegedly observed by the Americans and were in fact "ultra-masculine." And how could the bones of a twenty-five-year-old man be those of Tiye, who died in her forties? The main index of age that Smith here emphasized was the fusion of the epiphyses (articular ends of bones). This process of fusion is generally complete by the age of twenty-five. He stated firmly, following the evidence of Antiquities Inspector Arthur Weigall, who had been present at the excavation, that the coffin bore only the name of a king. Smith now for the first time declared that this was "strong presumptive evidence" that the mummy was Akhenaten's own. Some confusion, he admitted, might have occurred during the transfer from Amarna. The only other man in question would be Smenkhkare (as Norman Davies had suggested).

Smith now proceeded to argue further for the mummy being Akhenaten's. For the mummy to be that of a young man in his mid-twenties who had ruled for seventeen years, he must have come to the throne aged about nine. Smith's colleague, Alexander Ferguson, agreed that the body showed hydrocephalus. The cranium was flattened, and thickenings on the inner walls indicated diseases such as epilepsy. This would accord with Lombroso's published criteria for the founder of a new religion[36]—a reference to Cesare Lombroso (1836–1909), the controversial Italian psychiatrist and criminologist.[37]

Smith was to return to the mummy yet again when he published in 1912 a more extensive analysis in the volume on royal mummies for the Cairo Museum's *Catalogue général*.[38] He stressed that the mummy had not been plundered or rewrapped and asserted that Akhenaten's name appeared on both the coffin and "gold bands" on the mummy. The "bands" remain a mystery, having allegedly been found by Smith in the same box that had contained the mummy's bones, but according to a conversation (not made public until 1961) between Smith and Warren Dawson (1888–1968), a historian of mummification, "they were put . . . into a drawer intending to take them next day to Maspero at the Museum, but before he could do so were stolen by one of the laboratory attendants."[39]

In any case, Smith confidently stated that "There can no longer be any doubt that the body found in this tomb was either that of the heretic king or was believed to be his corpse by the embalmers." The only problem, he admitted, was its age. Smith later suggested, in a popular lecture in 1926, that Akhenaten suffered from Fröhlich's Syndrome, a condition that not only distorts the body, but also may mean that a skeleton appears younger than its actual age.[40]

The final summary was provided in the introduction to Davis's 1910 publication, which was written by Gaston Maspero, Director General of Antiquities. According to Maspero, KV 55 was not a tomb, but a "secret burying-place," to save the items it contained, and this deposit must be dated to the reign of either Tutankhamun or Ay. The mummy was that of Akhenaten, but it was now "little more than disconnected bones, with a few shreds of skin and flesh adhering to or hanging from them."[41]

In sum, although this was "not a tomb" and it contained objects belonging to a number of people, Davis and Maspero still called the book *The Tomb of Queen Tîye*. It was an inauspicious beginning, and this book of forty-five pages, alarming in its superficiality, did not appear until three years after the find.[42]

Maspero also examined the canopic jars in a popular essay of uncertain date, comparing their lids with various portraits of Akhenaten, notably the seated statue in the Louvre (fig. 22); he claimed a close correspondence. These lids, he pointed out, had only one uraeus, whereas it was increasingly normal for queens to have two.[43]

There was, of course, another vital figure involved in the work on the tomb: Arthur Weigall, the government Inspector General, who was unmentioned in Davis's 1910 publication (see below). A final participant, universally overlooked, and whose account was not published until 1958, was the artist Davis employed, Joseph Lindon Smith (1866–1950). He, in fact, instantly added another name to those present: Howard Carter. Smith claimed that because of his slimness, he was the first to crawl into the tomb, which must have been difficult because the rubble reached to within about half a meter of the ceiling! Everyone else entered after lunch. It was only then that Maspero called for a photographer. Smith claimed also to have been invited by Maspero to "dismember" the mummy![44] After such chaotic beginnings, the sequel is not surprising.

In 1916, Daressy published an article on the coffin. He was able to report more fully on it now than when he had written about the list of objects from the tomb in 1910, because the coffin lid had now been restored in the Cairo Museum (fig. 112)—the debris of the shell still awaited attention. The wood had virtually rotted away. Daressy noted the similarity in the head-dress on the coffin and that on the canopic jars and stressed the enormous work that went into making the coffin: it was covered with 1,500 incrusted feathers, made of red, blue, and clear glass, "a polychrome mosaic." Daressy then carefully for the first time identified six inscriptions on the coffin: five were on gold bands: A—lid, chest to foot; B and C—around the uppermost rim of the shell, each side; D—inside the lid; E—at the bottom of the shell; F—on the gold foil–covered footboard of the shell.

The titles indicated to Daressy that Akhenaten's name had once been in the cartouches. Daressy was the first to recognize, however, that the pronouns had been changed from feminine to masculine. The coffin had therefore originally belonged to a woman, whom he identified as Queen Tiye. He went on to suggest that she stayed at Thebes and even fell out with her son (despite the last trace of her being her visit to Amarna about Year 12!).

As to the identity of the mummy, he took the view that it might never be known, but the pectoral apparently converted into a crown indicated royal rank. Perhaps it was Tutankhamun. He observed that Akhenaten's so-called hydrocephalus was imposed on the whole family: deformation became a "divine sign." The canopic jars certainly did not show Akhenaten's features: the wig, he thought, was male, so perhaps again they belonged to Tutankhamun.[45]

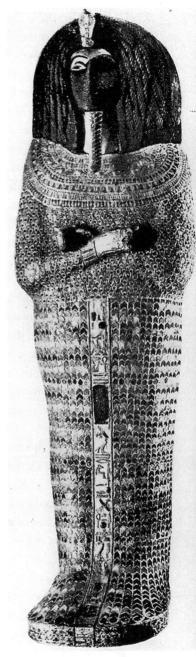

Fig. 112. The restored coffin lid from KV 55 (Cairo JE 39627).

In 1921, Sethe raised very proper cautions about the identity of mummies that had been found in the caches of royal bodies in the later nineteenth century. That in KV 35 (Amenhotep II) supposedly included the body of Akhenaten's grandfather Thutmose IV, whose body had been assessed by Elliot Smith as having died in his mid-twenties. Since Sethe believed that Thutmose had celebrated a *ḥb-sd*, and that this was a celebration of thirty years' reign, this could not be his body.[46] That in KV 55, similarly, could not be Akhenaten, who also celebrated a *ḥb-sd*. In support of this, Sethe cited jewelry on the body that bore the Earlier form of the Aten name. The body was therefore that of someone who died in the first nine years of Akhenaten's reign.[47]

Weigall told his version of the story in 1922, long after the deaths of Maspero, Davis, and Ayrton. As Inspector General supervising work at the tomb in 1907, his most revealing comment was that "the greatest tact had to be used in order to impose proper supervision on his [Davis's] work and check his enthusiastic but quite unrestrained interference in what he quite naturally regarded as his own affair," namely, excavations in the Valley of the Kings. Weigall was most keen to prove that the mummy was Akhenaten's. For this purpose he had to show that the age of thirty at most could fit. Amenhotep III and Thutmose IV were married by the age of twelve or thirteen, and Akhenaten would have been the same, being under the regency of his mother when he came to the throne (*EA* 26). Akhenaten did not, therefore, have to be more than thirty when he died.

Weigall emphasized a vital point. There was no possibility of confusion about the mummy sent to Cairo: he himself had soaked the bones in paraffin wax. The skull showed many similarities to that of Amenhotep III, and "the general structure of the face, especially the jaw, is exactly that portrayed in the statues of Akhenaten." The coffin was Akhenaten's and gold bands around the mummy bore his name.

Weigall's interpretation of the tomb was that it had originally been made for Tiye. When Tutankhamun returned to Thebes, the body of Akhenaten was also reburied there. Priests later removed his mother and defaced his cartouches. The canopic jars must also be Akhenaten's, as they bore a single uraeus; a queen's jars would have had two, and Tiye's would have been removed with her body; attempts were made also to take away her shrine. Weigall thought that the tomb was entered first by the agents of Akhenaten to erase the name of Amun, and later to remove Tiye and erase Akhenaten's name.[48]

The next stage was the work of Reginald Engelbach and Douglas Derry in 1931. Engelbach, Chief Keeper at the Cairo Museum and trained by Petrie, noted that Akhenaten's figure and what seemed to have been his names had been erased from the shrine, coffin, and canopic jars. The head of the mummy wore not a crown but a pectoral, and the wig on the coffin was male, but not royal; he also noted that the uraei had been *added* to the canopic jars. He saw no room for Tiye's name and titles in the inscriptions on the coffin. On a piece of gold that had originally lined the coffin he read "Beloved of Waenre," that is, beloved of Akhenaten. It was therefore a coffin prepared for someone as a private person who later became royal: Smenkhkare. The odd female pronoun was a mistake (thus misunderstanding a vital clue). Engelbach attempted to bolster this interpretation by claiming (following Newberry's 1928 paper) that many works of art showed Akhenaten and Smenkhare displaying close affection, adding the "Kissing King" (Cairo JE 44866) to the two unfinished Berlin stelae (figs. 82, 83).

Engelbach thus restored the inscription on the coffin as originally being for Smenkhkare as "Royal favorite of Akhenaten," which was then emended when he became king, with Akhenaten's cartouches changed to his own. He proposed that the person who made these changes was Tutankhamun, meaning that Smenkhkare died after Akhenaten. And it was Tutankhamun who intended to bury Smenkhkare in the tomb of Tiye at Amarna, but, finding it plundered, brought its remains to the Valley of the Kings (what, then, were the 'magic bricks' of Akhenaten doing there?). The erasures of cartouches on the coffin, canopic jars, and shrine were probably made in the reign of Horemheb; Engelbach noted, however, that the Aten prayers were untouched. This meant that Tiye's equipment was plundered and damaged twice. Engelbach would not make any suggestion about the parentage of Smenkhkare or Tutankhamun, although he admitted that their relationship was close.[49]

An anatomist examined the mummy for the second time in 1931. Douglas Derry (1874–1961), Professor of Anatomy at Cairo, revealed disturbing facts.[50] The skull examined by Smith was "considerably damaged"; "the face was completely broken." Most of the pieces had fortunately been kept in the box with the skeleton, and so most of it could be restored. Derry denied traces of hydrocephalus: the skull was of unusual shape, but a type not uncommon in the royal family; it was rather platycephalic, the very reverse of hydrocephalic. He argued further that, as Egyptians show the union of the epiphyses of the upper limbs earlier than Europeans, this skeleton could have been no more than twenty-three years old. Derry had undertaken the unwrapping and examination of Tutankhamun's mummy. Since the two bodies' heads closely resembled one another, they were, he stated, probably brothers.

The next significant contribution came almost three decades later, by Alan Gardiner, the master philologist. He rightly deplored Davis's publication for its lack of a plan and its inadequate and contradictory explanations. Apart from the coffin and mummy, Davis had referred variously to a "sepulchral canopy," "hearse," "catafalque," and "shrine." This, Gardiner corrected, was actually a shrine made by Akhenaten for his mother, but also mentioning her husband Amenhotep III, and thus meant for the funeral of Tiye.

Gardiner saw the state of the shrine and the seals of a kind found in the tomb of Tutankhamun as evidence that the cache had been found and plundered. If the mummy is Smenkhkare's, there is no mention of his name in what was then believed to be one of his epithets: "Beloved of Waenre" (which actually belonged to Neferneferuaten). Gardiner also suggested that the canopic jars were "secondarily furnished" with "ill-fitting but exceedingly beautiful heads"—in other words the lids were not original.

Gardiner declared the coffin "at once the most interesting and the most enigmatic object" of the tomb: it was entirely covered with gold foil and inlaid with precious stones (in actuality glass). It resembled Tutankhamun's middle coffin and bore a uraeus that has the Later form of the Aten's name (this proved to be an error—there were two uraei found in the tomb, one with the name, one without, and there was from almost the moment of discovery confusion between them). The shell and lid had been lined with gold, which had become detached, so that the lining of the lid fell in on the mummy. Gardiner's great contribution was the demonstration that the traditional placement of speeches of Nephthys at the head of the coffin and Isis at the foot had been adapted for this piece:

now it was Nefertiti addressing the king, a fascinating example of the adaptation of earlier forms by the new cult (just as Nefertiti had replaced the traditional goddesses on the corners of Akhenaten's sarcophagus). For Gardiner, "There [was] no reason to believe that the coffin ever belonged, or was intended to belong, to anyone other than Akhenaten." This was a paradox, since Gardiner also recognized that in the inscription on the foot of the coffin, all feminine first-person suffixes had been changed to masculine in the address to the king. The speaker could then only be, in Gardiner's view, Smenkhkare (Newberry's view of the kings' relationship was still then accepted).

Whose tomb did Gardiner believe KV 55 to be? "The person responsible for the burial" believed it was Akhenaten's, as proved by the four 'magic bricks.' Following Akhenaten's death the Royal Tomb had been ransacked, but the king's followers rescued the coffin, put in it a body they thought to be his, and added the shrine of Tiye from the tomb. The assemblage was taken to KV 55, where it was later desecrated by people who may have destroyed Akhenaten's body and substituted Smenkhkare's, and hacked out cartouches.

Gardiner added something further to the debate: the first plan of the tomb, from the time of its discovery, was by an American, Emma Andrews, Davis's mistress, in her diary in the Metropolitan Museum, to which Gardiner had been alerted by Warren Dawson.[51] This was followed in 1961 by a modern plan of the tomb by Elizabeth Thomas.[52]

Tucked away in a book review in the same journal only two years after the 1957 article, however, was Gardiner's recantation: persuaded by Aldred, he now took the view that the coffin was originally meant for a princess, and later adapted for the king himself, but it "was not up to Pharaonic standard."[53]

Cyril Aldred made his first contribution in the matter in 1957. In an interesting discussion of wigs, he alerted readers to the frequent difficulty of distinguishing gender in Amarna art. A good example was the affectation by both men and women of the "Nubian" wig: both wore it in the multiple-fringed style, but Aldred looked at the back of the heads of the canopic jars in the tomb and emphasized what others had not noticed: that here it is cut upwards to reveal the nape of the neck; clearly then it represented a woman, not a man. Further, influenced by the thought that the mummy might be that of Smenkhkare, he identified that woman as his wife, Meryetaten. He described her features as "rather gaunt, faintly consumptive," in contrast to Ankhesenpaaten's "chubbier face with more rounded contours."[54]

Günther Roeder in 1958 agreed that the mummy was that of Smenkhkare. He was to have been buried in the Royal Tomb at Amarna, but was then transferred to Thebes. His early death prevented proper preparations, so he was put in KV 55. Roeder was unsure whether this was his original burial or a transfer some years later. He was sure, however, that the coffin was originally made for him, as were the canopic jars. The mummy was accepted as that of a man twenty-three to twenty-five years of age, and the skull declared to be of "Armenoid" type, like Yuya's.[55]

No fewer than three articles appeared on the subject in the 1961 issue of the *Journal of Egyptian Archaeology*. Herbert Fairman raised more directly the fundamental problems Engelbach had alluded to regarding the inscriptions: What was the original position of those found detached inside the coffin? What was the original text? What was "patched"? And where did the patches fit? Daressy had noted that the patches were in thinner gold with the hieroglyphs less carefully inscribed. It was very likely that considerable sections of four of the five strip texts that Daressy had identified were missing; the extant sections did not make sense and were not capable of reconstruction. Only Daressy's text A was complete on the lid, running from the arms to the feet.

Fairman was guided by two principles: that the titles preceding the effaced cartouches were once for a nonroyal person, and that the inscription on the foot of the shell was inscribed for a woman. He compared two inscriptions of Akhenaten's lesser wife Kiya and found them "an exact duplicate" of the five strips from the coffin.[56] Her titulary was, however, too long to fit at the beginning of the strips. Fairman considered only one other Amarnan woman a possibility: Meryetaten.

The foot inscription (Daressy's text F) was in two parts: lines 1–9 (lid) and 9–12 (shell). Fairman completely rejected Gardiner's analogy of the traditional Isis speech at the foot of the coffin, arguing that no one would "impersonate" the old gods (it was rather another example of replacing them). For him, it was the dead person addressing the Aten or the king, and he restored the name and titles as those of Meryetaten.

Fairman then turned to the four 'magic bricks.' He reexamined the three in the Cairo Museum and declared that only one was indisputably Akhenaten's. His main problem was that each one bears the name Osiris before the king's name, suggesting that they must belong to the beginning of his reign and have been left behind in Thebes. He concluded that the coffin was reused for Smenkhkare, because Tutankhamun took over much of his funerary equipment (now recognized as that of Neferneferuaten). Ay therefore placed Smenkhkare's mummy in Meryetaten's coffin, equipped "with a small and makeshift collection of miscellaneous objects of various persons that happened to lie conveniently to hand."[57]

Fairman's article was followed in the journal by Aldred's reconsideration of the coffin. He resorted to what seems an obvious—but yet untried—comparison: other coffins of the Eighteenth Dynasty. As it happens, we have only a series at the end of the previous dynasty, and then those of Tutankhamun. These showed, however, that the *rishi*-style (feathered) coffin, of which the one in KV 55 was an example, was common. This coffin had another feature: "a kind of imbricated shawl swathing the upper part of the body over which is placed the elaborate 'Amarna style of collar," a feature of women's coffins. Male coffins always have a vulture rather than the shawl. Aldred recognized the possibility that Akhenaten could have refused to have a vulture (recalling Nekhbet) on his coffin: in that case he could have had a falcon (Re-Horakhty), as on his canopic chest. Also missing was a royal headdress: instead there was a Nubian-style wig, while the uraeus looked as if it were an addition.

The uraei on the canopic jars were also later additions. They were originally not royal, and seem to be for a woman. Aldred suggested a strong resemblance between the face on the coffin and these heads;[58] already in 1957 he had identified the canopic jars with the coffin as having been made for Meryetaten.[59]

Aldred therefore restored the inscription on the foot of the coffin as a prayer by a king's daughter to *her father* (*sc.* Akhenaten), since an appeal could not be made directly to the Aten: Aldred offered six parallels from Amarnan tombs. The spelling of the name of Maat (which changed later in Akhenaten's reign) was used to show that the coffin was made early in Akhenaten's reign. This ruled out Meketaten, as she had died after the 'durbar' of Year 12, and Aldred preferred Meryetaten, whose burial was already being provided for in Year 5 (although he does not explain why Meketaten's coffin could not have been made in advance). Since she married Smenkhkare, and as a queen would have merited new burial furniture, the old coffin was stored as "surplus." Brought out of store, it was adapted for a king by emending the texts, replacing the facemask, and adding a uraeus (with the Later form of the Aten name) and a beard (found nearby detached).[60]

Regarding the mummy, Andrew Sandison, Senior Lecturer in Pathology at the University of Glasgow, who was assisting Aldred, declared that the Karnak portraits showed that Akhenaten suffered from an endocrine disease, which he identified as Fröhlich's Syndrome. For the KV 55 mummy, Sandison, relying on the notes and two photographs of the skull provided by Smith, declared the pelvis gynaecoid, the bones slender, the cranium broad and flat, and the mandible large, with some prognathism. From these he diagnosed secondary hypogonadism, but would not rule out hydrocephalus, and pituitary cranial dysplasia. The deceased, if normal, would be aged in his mid-twenties, but Fröhlich's Syndrome would allow a greater age—appropriate to Akhenaten. It also would make it almost impossible for him to have had children: in that case, Aldred stated, one would have to look for another father! Aldred drew attention to the female pose of the mummy's arms, waxing ironic over possible doubts by the embalmers as to the gender of the body they were handling and the "feminine" coffin in which it was placed.

The magic bricks were clearly Akhenaten's, but lacked their amulets, without which they would be ineffective. Aldred suggested that these must have been removed by the desecrators of the burial, who broke two, but did not scratch out the names on the other two. Judging also by the way in which the tomb had been last entered in antiquity and also because gold had been left, he argued that the reopening was not by robbers but by necropolis officials.

Since it belonged to someone other than Akhenaten, the shrine of Queen Tiye was seen by Aldred as the odd item. The coffin was against the western wall, so could not have been enclosed by the shrine, but may have been erected in the main space. Was it being moved in or out? Its chaotic positioning suggested not that it was being readied for erection, but that it was in the process of being taken away. For Aldred, this suggested that Queen Tiye had once also been buried here: small objects bear her name. Aldred's solution was that Akhenaten and Tiye had once lain in the tomb together, but that the queen had later been transferred elsewhere. His preferred reconstruction was that Tiye would have intended originally to be buried with her husband, but that she joined Akhenaten at Amarna and was perhaps to be buried there in the Royal Tomb (as it is now clear she was).

Aldred claimed that "from the start there was never any intention of burying Akhenaten in the tomb he had made in the Eastern Mountain." The decision had "already been taken" to abandon Amarna for Memphis as soon as Akhenaten had died. So Akhenaten was buried in KV 55, along with the removed body of Tiye. Then, in the early Nineteenth Dynasty, a king decided to move Tiye from the presence of Akhenaten, perhaps to her husband's tomb. After the removal of all her equipment, save the shrine, the cartouches of Akhenaten were everywhere defaced, the pectoral twisted into a false crown, the coffin mask torn off, and the uraei snapped off the canopic jars.[61]

It was only in 1961 that further objects from the tomb came to light. They had been in the possession of Harold Jones, the artist employed by Davis, and were now given to the University of Wales Swansea.[62] They included a clay seal of Tutankhamun and a fragment of glass with the name of Amenhotep II, joining a fragmentary vase found ten years earlier in that king's tomb (KV 35). While some have questioned whether the glass really came from KV 35, and suggested that it may have been accidentally mixed with KV 55 finds, it is interesting that it was in KV 35 that the mummy of the "Elder Lady," possibly that of Tiye, was found.

Aldred and Sandison restated their case at greater length the very next year: either Derry was right and the mummy was that of a man aged about twenty-three, or Smith was right, and it was an older man who suffered from some disorder which delayed skeletal development. In other words, either Smenkhkare or Akhenaten. This conclusion, however, was not based on a reexamination of the mummy itself ("not readily available for study"), but "the published evidence." The "new" article repeated the earlier one virtually word for word, although there is a comprehensive bibliography.[63]

This analysis was rightly dismissed as "scholarly but purely theoretical" by Ronald Harrison, Professor of Anatomy at the University of Liverpool, who now reinvestigated the actual remains in 1963 (their *third* examination, but the first since Derry in 1931). It seemed unlikely that these skeletal remains would ever need reexamination after Harrison's exhaustive analysis (twenty-five pages, with thirty-four plates and figures). The skull was declared brachycephalic, large, but "within the normal range of European skulls." Hydrocephalus was ruled out. There was no evidence for pituitary abnormality, hypogonadism was minimal, and Marfan's Syndrome was excluded. The teeth, of great value in assessing age, indicated the lower end of a range from eighteen to twenty-two years. There was no evidence of caries, and very slight wear. There was no sign of prognathism. The pelvis was inconsistent with wide hips. In sum, the skeleton was that of a man younger than twenty-five years of age (Harrison was prepared to say twenty.) A facial reconstruction showed a "striking resemblance" to Tutankhamun (although the face used as direct comparison was that on Tutankhamun's second coffin—which seems *not* to have been that of Tutankhamun.[64] Since the mummy is male, there is only one possible candidate: Smenkhkare.[65]

Aldred, of course, returned to the matter in his biography of Akhenaten, accepting Harrison's conclusions and agreeing that on the basis of age the body could only be that of Smenkhkare. His revised reconstruction was that when Smenkhkare died (before Akhenaten), a coffin from store originally made for Meryetaten was adapted for her husband's use, enclosing his body most strangely mummified in a female pose. Akhenaten then died, but was never buried at Amarna. KV 55 was therefore used for Akhenaten, Smenkhkare, and Tiye (the latter two brought from Amarna), until Akhenaten and Tiye's bodies were removed during Ramesid times (Akhenaten's probably for destruction), leaving Smenkhkare's behind, deprived of his identity.[66]

A very extensive discussion was next offered by Yuri Perepelkin in his 1968 book, translated into English ten years later as *The Secret of the Golden Coffin*. He began with the inscriptions on the shell, noting the remaining feminine pronouns in texts D and F. He judged that the prayer on the foot (F) was in its final form to Re *for* the king, but was originally *to* the king. The remains of the original titles followed the pattern of those of Kiya, as seen at the Maru-Aten: she was therefore the coffin's original owner. To judge from the use of the old Osirian epithet "true of voice," and the sun's address as Re-Horakhty, it would have been made relatively early in Akhenaten's reign.

As for the mummy, Perepelkin accepted an age of twenty, so it could not be Akhenaten's, although those who placed the body in the coffin were sure that it was his. He rightly drew attention to the paradox that, among the various names in the tomb, Smenkhkare's was nowhere found, but the mummy could only be his. Perepelkin also emphasized that the 'magic bricks' belonged to Akhenaten, but contained references to Osiris, and that the wigs on the canopic jars could be either male or female, but were, in any case, the same as on the coffin.

Perepelkin concluded that the equipment in KV 55 was for a second burial of the king: fanatics had destroyed his original burial. Although the canopic chest in the Royal Tomb at Amarna seemed unused, shabti figures were present. In KV 55, Perepelkin believed that the shrine of Tiye had originally stood around the coffin, but the reburial had been interfered with under Horemheb: Akhenaten's body was removed and his name erased. Would the mummy of Akhenaten not, however, have been destroyed by the fanatical desecrators, and where had the mummy of Smenkhkare, which replaced it, been in the interval?[67]

Nicholas Reeves attempted another examination of the deposit, suggesting that the construction of the tomb had been abandoned because of faults in the rock in the ceiling. Davis had found materials from two burials, those of Tiye and Akhenaten. Reeves proposed that the material had been deposited on two separate occasions and partially cleared on a third. Tiye was originally buried with her husband, as shown by her objects in his tomb (he relied on Carter's unpublished excavation notes), while Akhenaten was buried first in his Royal Tomb at Amarna. Was Tiye reburied here first, and then removed before the end of the Twentieth Dynasty? Defacement of the other coffin occurred at this time. Reeves raised a terrible possibility: that the bones now identified as coming from the tomb had somehow become jumbled with others. Could the body originally found there have been female (as the first examination suggested)? Worse than confusion: hoax (at that time a suggestion had been made that Elliot Smith might have been the Piltdown hoaxer[68]). In short, the body found originally was possibly Meketaten's. Reeves was oblivious of Weigall's evidence about the paraffin wax.[69]

Martin next made a close examination of the canopic jar in the Metropolitan Museum. Contrary to previous investigators, he argued that the uraeus was not a later addition. The inscription had been very thoroughly obliterated, but he thought that he could make out on the bottom left three signs from the name of Akhenaten. He concluded that both the coffin and canopic jars had all been made for Akhenaten, and the obliteration of the texts on the jars was done, not by the iconoclasts, but so that someone else could use them.[70]

The definitive study of the canopic jars was undertaken soon afterward by Krauss in 1986. In a stunning work of reconstruction, he examined all four jars (fig. 76) for any remaining traces of hieroglyphs from the erased texts, which were, of course, the same on each. He next made a composite of the traces from each, and they were found to correspond almost exactly with the inscription on the calcite vase of Kiya. Examination of the lids showed that the uraeus was indeed secondary (it had been set into the altered hairstyle). Krauss also noted that the erasure of the inscription had been in two phases: the right-hand third had been removed by abrasion, the left-hand two-thirds by chiseling. The vases had thus been converted for a new owner, but then the text had been savagely obliterated. He accepted that the KV 55 burial was of Smenkhkare: the coffin and canopic jars of Kiya had been reworked for him, although his name survived on neither.[71]

Aldred revised his position in 1988, accepting Kiya's original ownership of the coffin. Otherwise, his reconstruction of the origin and fate of the deposit was little changed.[72]

In view of the apparently exhaustive analysis of the mummy in 1966, it was astounding that in 1988 a paper was presented to the Fifth International Congress of Egyptologists stating that "Estimation of the age was done from the wear of the teeth and periodontal recession (Harris) and from the bones (Hussein). The dentition, using the Nubian standards, indicate[s] the middle 30s. Utilizing anthropological standards and x-ray of the bones, it was also concluded that the skeleton was more than 35 years." The paper was never published, only presented to the world as an abstract.[73] This was enough for those who think the latest contribution must always be right to claim that Harrison's findings had been overturned.

In the same 1988 paper that began the separation of Smenkhkare from Neferneferuaten, James Allen discussed the inscriptions on the KV 55 coffin and the four magic bricks. Of the latter, two were incised with hieroglyphs and two inscribed in hieratic: one of the former allows the name to be read: Neferkheperure-Waenre. Allen was cautious over the question of whether the bricks belonged to the same burial as the coffin and canopic jars. The last two did, he believed, belong together, being made for Queen Kiya, but then they were altered, apparently for a pharaoh. He concluded that the inscription on the foot of the coffin had originally been a prayer addressed to Akhenaten by Kiya, which had then been changed to show a man speaking, with cartouches at beginning and end (later destroyed, of course). Allen suggested that the new owner was a successor of Akhenaten, who was addressing him as "father Re-Horakhty Akhenaten." The space available in the effaced cartouches was assessed as fitting Smenkhkare, rather than Neferneferuaten.[74]

A key essay appeared in 1990: "An Armchair Excavation of KV 55" by Martha Bell. This attempted to provide a more complete list with extensive notes of the objects from the tomb now in Cairo and New York, and reconstructed plans (including our fig. 108), both of which are invaluable. Major attention was given to the largest item in the tomb, the shrine: the Aten names were all in their Later form; Maat was spelled phonetically; and the shrine seemed to have been made at Amarna, given the reference to the "House of the Aten in Akhet-Aten."

Bell turned next to the mummy, providing one of the most memorable phrases in the history of Egyptology: "a mummified penis seems fairly indestructible." In other words, there was none (but with a number of king's mummies the penis was flattened against the leg[75]). She began to suggest, indeed, that the body was that of a woman: witness the position of the arms, the bracelets, and that the earlier owner of the coffin was a woman. All this is undercut two pages later: "I do not insist that the mummy is Akhenaten"—but she believed that it was.

She rightly stressed the range of material in the tomb beginning with Amenhotep III (vases and so on) and Tiye (the shrine) and going down to Tutankhamun. Much was non-Atenist: a Thoth plaquette, Bes figures, the Nekhbet pectoral, and the Osirian 'magic bricks' (she compared the pectoral reused as a "crown" with Tutankhamun's Nekhbet skullcap). Bell stressed, however, that two of the three cartouches found with the mummy had the Earlier form of the Aten name; the uraeus and shrine, however, had the Later form.

Bell's reconstruction of events was that the burial was for two people. The first seems to have been Tiye, given the vases, opening-of-the-mouth equipment, shrine, fragments of other furniture, perhaps a Thoth plaquette, and fragments of a pall. The second seems to have been Akhenaten: the coffin, canopic jars, and bricks. The seals indicated that they were buried here under Tutankhamun. The tomb was then sealed with the (inner) ashlar wall. The tomb was later reopened, and all of Tiye's burial removed except the shrine, her mummy being taken perhaps to KV 35 (Amenhotep II). At the same time traces of Akhenaten's name were removed. This second opening was possibly to be dated (with Reeves) to the reign of Rameses IX, during the excavation of KV 6. The tomb was then resealed with the outer rubble fill.[76]

Aidan Dodson in 1992 tried to account for some puzzles. The coffin and canopic jars were made for Kiya, who fell from grace, so the material was stored (which raises intriguing questions about her burial). On the other hand, he noted, Tutankhamun's burial includes equipment prepared for Smenkhkare (in fact, Neferneferuaten): the four canopic coffinettes, and perhaps even the second coffin, because the face did not match the other two. Dodson's solution was that Smenkhkare was "by no means a devoted Atenist" and died before Akhenaten, who arranged for his burial, keeping back "traditional" equipment Smenkhkare had made (the coffin, for example), and adapting older equipment. He was, in this case, presumably buried originally at Amarna (in TA 27, 28, or 29).[77]

A *fourth* examination of the skeleton was undertaken in 2000 by Joyce Filer, specialist in human and animal remains in the Department of Egyptian Antiquities in the British Museum, working in collaboration with Nasry Iskander. She began with the disconcerting assertion by Reeves and Harris and Hussein that the skeleton was "incomplete." To the contrary, it was "almost complete and overall is in quite good condition," "virtually intact." Contrary to the oft-run theory that the body is not the one from KV 55, many of the bones had opaque flakes adhering to them: the very paraffin wax in which Weigall stated that he had soaked them.

There was no question that the remains were male. The age, twenty to twenty-five, is shown by dental development and the fusion of the epiphyses (Smith was wrong to claim that they are all fused). The skull bore a striking resemblance to that of Tutankhamun, and was "somewhat brachycephalic." And Filer finally stated "quite bluntly" that there was no evidence of pathology.[78]

Wolfgang Helck's study of the tomb was published posthumously in 2001. He raised the problem of the reason for the dismantling of the shrine. It could have been to allow the removal of the coffin—but it had been left. For him there was no plan to take the shrine away: it was used in the corridor to make a floor (a purpose for which it was entirely unsuited). The main object was to remove the stone sarcophagus that contained the coffin. Helck believed that the tomb was broken into twice: first to remove the sarcophagus, perhaps under Horemheb; and then by robbers when the tomb of Rameses IX was being built.

The identification of the mummy by anatomy, he declared, was not possible: only the inscriptions on the coffin could solve this. The obliteration of cartouches suggested to him that the last occupant was Akhenaten, although the coffin had originally been for a female who was not royal (the uraeus being secondary): this was Kiya. The second occupant was not, however, Akhenaten, but the "beloved of Waenre," that is, Smenkhkare—as he had not yet been untangled from the regular user of that epithet, Neferneferuaten! Akhenaten's cartouches were destroyed when the sarcophagus was removed. The portraits on the canopic jars, according to Helck, were originally male and had been reworked. The inscriptions were first changed from Kiya to Smenkhkare, and then erased by the anti-Atenists.[79]

Yet another examination of the coffin and its inscriptions was undertaken in connection with a Munich exhibition in 2001 that was sparked by the astonishing emergence on the antiquities market of the shell of the KV 55 coffin. Badly decayed, its debris, primarily gold foil and glass inlay, had been recorded in 1915 as awaiting restoration, but it had apparently been stolen shortly afterward; the fragments had then surfaced in the hands of a dealer in the 1970s.[80] By the 1990s, the foil and inlays had been fitted to a plexiglass form, and by the end of the decade they were in the Staatliche Sammlung Ägyptischer Kunst in Munich.

After the exhibition, the restored shell was returned to Cairo.

In the catalogue of the exhibition, Alfred Grimm challenged orthodoxy on many counts. For him, there was nothing feminine about the lid: the shawl, wig, and necklaces. In materials and technique, moreover, the coffin compared favorably with the second (wooden) coffin of Tutankhamun. The owner was easily determined. "The good ruler" instead of "good god" which begins each inscription, "Great in his lifetime" (inscriptions B and C), and "the beautiful child of the living Aten who shall live forever continually" were usages exclusive to Akhenaten. The woman speaking in the inscription at the foot of the coffin was (with Gardiner) Nefertiti replacing the traditional Isis. At some later date, the seated woman signs were all changed to a seated god, except for line seven. This was very carefully done, in contrast to a later revision, when all the royal cartouches were removed. Grimm thus contradicted what had become the recent agreed view, that the coffin was prepared for Kiya: Grimm's view was that it was prepared for Akhenaten, but became unusable after what Grimm called the "great Aten-Reform" (Years 9–14). Maat was spelled both with her original hieroglyph and phonetically, while the 'magic bricks' were similarly outdated, referring to Akhenaten as Osiris. Grimm accepted the canopic jars as originally belonging to Kiya. All this equipment from the Amarnan 'funerary depot' was then used for Smenkhkare: the mummy found in the tomb was his.

Grimm's most original contribution is his analysis of the style of the coffin. Many have commented on its rank, with very contradictory judgments. Fundamental, however, is its place in the *rishi* class, a type that began in the Seventeenth Dynasty and continued into the Nineteenth.

> In type and motif th[is] anthropoid or anthropomorphic *rishi* coffin thus combined the central themes about death in ancient Egyptian beliefs: the post-mortem ascent to heaven of the *ba* and the cyclical rebirth in the other world in the body of the goddess of heaven, Nut. Their iconographic conversion resulted in the shape of an anthropoid or anthropomorphic mixture of a feathered human body with bird's wings. The *rishi* motif at the same time represented the iconographic representation of the blending of the *ba* with the corpse and thereby the unity of the sun god Re *(ba)* with the god of

the dead and ruler of the afterlife, Osiris (the corpse). The clothing of feathers of the *rishi* coffin is also the 'ikon' for the unity of the king and the falcon (Horus).[81]

In short, this coffin could not be more traditional.

Grimm's reassessment of the origins of the coffin found little favor with the wider community of Amarna specialists. Marc Gabolde reasserted that the original owner of the coffin and canopic jars was indeed Kiya, and that the last owner of the coffin was Akhenaten, because of the epithets "great in his lifetime," although band D read "beloved of Waenre," when it should therefore have read simply "Waenre." He sought a parallel: Thutmose I was reburied by Hatshepsut in her own sarcophagus—but a coffin is not a sarcophagus, and the sarcophagus was a woman's because the reburier was a woman!

Gabolde then turned to a reexamination of the mummy, which he accepted as Akhenaten's. He drew attention here to a persistent problem with modern anatomy. Modern medical estimates of the age of Egyptian mummies, he claimed, consistently *underestimate* the age of the person at death: historical evidence contradicts the autopsy. Then came a remarkable contradiction: Gabolde *accepted* the medical estimates of the age of the mummy in KV 55: "18–25 is the most probable case." This is simply because he believed that Akhenaten came to the throne at the age of ten.

His further assertion (similar to Grimm's) that the coffin was "not Atenist at all" is an exaggeration. All band inscriptions refer to the Aten, it being only the foot inscription (F) that refers to Re-Horakhty, not in use, according to Gabolde, after Year 14. The same feature was revealed in the bricks, which refer to "the Osiris king Neferkheperure true of voice," showing orthodox Osirian beliefs.[82]

In the last sensational medical analysis in 2010 by Zahi Hawass and a large team, the body in KV 55 was identified as Akhenaten, genetically the father of Tutankhamun, whose mother was not Nefertiti or Kiya, but a sibling of Akhenaten: the "Younger Lady" in KV 35, they asserted. In the mummy accepted as Akhenaten's, there were, it was declared, no signs of pathological abnormality.[83]

There have been many criticisms made of this investigation, both in method (the lack of adequate control groups) and in presentation (the allegation that the results were published giving only the preferred interpretations of the raw data). We have already noted that the genetic option that Tutankhamun's parents could have been third-generation first cousins is just as valid as that they were siblings (with less historical effect), while also missing from Hawass's presentation was the fact that Tutankhamun's father and any paternal uncles would have shared a DNA profile. Since an option favored by a number of scholars has been that Smenkhkare was a younger brother of Akhenaten,[84] the KV 55 mummy could still be Smenkhkare, especially in light of the majority view of the age of the bones, consistently assigned to a man at the oldest in his early twenties. One of Hawass's team, in contrast, has stated that the body was that of a man in his forties—without any published explanation of how or why this should vary so greatly from the vast majority of examination of the remains.[85]

In estimating the age of ancient human remains, crucial comparative material is provided by the analysis of the eighteenth/nineteenth century Spitalfields cemetery in London.[86] Human remains of which the age at death was known with certainty from their coffin plates were here examined by physical anthropologists, with the worrying result that "there was a systematic error which depended on the age of the individual, those under 40 being over-aged, those over 70 being under-aged. . . . Less than 30% of the sample were correctly aged— i.e. to within five years of the real age; but 50% were assessed to within ten years, and three-quarters to within fifteen years of the correct age."[87] Among cases of under-aging, individuals who were known certainly to have died in their late eighties or their nineties appeared according to the anatomical criteria to be in their sixties, or in one case late fifties! All this chimes with the concerns about the ages assigned to royal mummies that seem not to match what is known historically about the length of their reigns.

Until the late 2000s it was generally assumed that whoever the occupant(s) of KV 55 were, the final desecration had been carried out under Horemheb, the earlier Ramesids, or even Rameses IX. In 2008, however, Stephen Cross published his first results of a study into the hydrology of the Valley of the Kings, which suggested that the area of the valley occupied by KV 55, plus the tomb of Tutankhamun and the embalmers' cache, KV 63, found in 2006, had been sealed by a flash flood not long after the final closure of Tutankhamun's tomb.[88] He would now place the flood no later than the end of Ay's reign (as huts for the building of the tomb of Horemheb were built above the flood layer), preferring a date within a year of Tutankhamun's death.[89]

If correct, this means that the final disposition of the KV 55 deposit will have been made shortly after the death of Tutankhamun. Dodson, who takes the view that the deposit was established on the abandonment of Amarna as the capital in Tutankhamun's Year 3 and contained the bodies of Akhenaten (on the basis of the magic bricks), Tiye (the shrine), and Smenkhkare (the age of the remaining mummy), suggested that as soon as Tutankhamun was dead, KV 55 was reentered, Akhenaten's mummy removed for destruction, Tiye relocated, and Smenkhkare stripped of his name, before all was lost soon afterward in the flood, under which the tomb lay undisturbed for three thousand years.[90]

By way of a conclusion

The fundamental problem with KV 55 has been the way in which it was excavated. As Aldred declared of the excavators, "these men, two of them at least with specialized training and experience, somehow managed to conduct one of the worst pieces of excavation on record in the Valley."[91] Or as Harry James put it: "a notably mismanaged operation from the start . . . the inadequacy of the work compounded by a very indifferent publication. . . . It is not surprising that material from the tomb passed into the hands of the Luxor dealers."[92] To think how many problems would not now exist had George Reisner, for example, made the discovery.

The magic bricks are generally taken to belong to Akhenaten, but it has been observed by Aldred that they are not a set, two being thinner and made of different mud, with two in hieroglyphs and two in hieratic.[93] Fairman claimed that only the northern one certainly belonged to Akhenaten, but the presence of even one would seem to imply that Akhenaten was at least intended at some point to lie in the tomb.[94]

The canopic jars have been assigned to every possible candidate: Tiye (Davis), Tutankhamun (Daressy), Akhenaten (Weigall), Smenkhkare (Engelbach), Kiya (Perepelkin, Krauss, Gabolde, Grimm), and Kiya then Smenkhkare (Allen, Helck, Dodson, Grimm). Most modern analysis, therefore, favors Kiya as the original owner, although the lids have been considered by some not to fit, and therefore coming perhaps from a different set of jars, albeit of the same period.

The coffin has been understood as *originally* for Tiye (Daressy, Martin); for Akhenaten (Weigall, Carter, and Gardiner [1957—and they suggested it remained his], Grimm); for Smenkhkare before he became king (Engelbach, Roeder); for a princess (Gardiner [1959]); for Meryet-aten (Fairman, Aldred); and again for Kiya (Perepelkin, Krauss, Allen, Helck, Dodson, Gabolde). It was then *adapted* for use by Smenkhkare (Engelbach [after he became king], Fairman, Dodson, Krauss, Allen, Helck, Grimm); or Akhenaten (Gardiner, Aldred, Perepelkin, Gabolde). Modern scholars therefore increasingly class the coffin along with the canopic jars as originally Kiya's. It was then adapted for a man, most commonly taken to be Smenkhkare (perhaps influenced by the proposed identity of the mummy as his, but also doubt that the long-reigning Akhenaten would end up in a second-hand coffin). Fairman identified the main problem: the total mishandling of the delicate gold bands on the coffin, with their overlaid emendations.

It is the *corpus delicti* which is the most perplexing. One would think that the most basic questions could be answered about a mummy when subjected to anatomical examination. This is, in fact, the most examined mummy in Egyptian history, investigation presumably made easier by its reduction to a bare skeleton. After preliminary statements that it was a woman, it has thenceforth been regarded as male, even though the pose is female! The age is usually given as in the twenties, with preference toward the lower end. That would seem to rule out Akhenaten, and therefore the majority of scholars have accepted it as the mummy of Smenkhkare, although recent DNA work and associated anatomical examinations have attempted to revive the claims for Akhenaten. Doubts have sometimes been raised over whether the mummy now in Cairo said to be from KV 55 is in fact the right one, but that doubt should be allayed by the evidence of paraffin wax on the bones, with which Weigall explicitly states they were treated.

Beyond these few agreements over contents, the history of the tomb is still a puzzle. For whom was it originally cut (most have called it a private tomb)? How many people were originally buried here? When were they buried: together or singly? When was the tomb last opened and closed in ancient times (although this seems now to have been given a *terminus ante quem*)? What was the purpose of these reopenings? On much of this, we seem no closer to solutions. The main responsibility for that lies with the original 'excavators' of the tomb.

Afterword

There are few things which one can state with a degree of confidence or even with some degree of probability about Akhenaten and his associates (subject to new data becoming available). Akhenaten himself died after seventeen years of rule and was buried in the Royal Tomb at Amarna. Nefertiti, who had risen to great heights of power, even kingship, alongside him, lived into middle age, probably witnessing the reigns of two of her sons-in-law, the fleeting Smenkhkare and the short-lived Tutankhamun, who abandoned Amarna and made (or was made to make) his peace with Amun and died aged only about eighteen. The last member of the Amarnan circle to become pharaoh was the old general Ay, perhaps Nefertiti's father and Akhenaten's uncle.

The Amarnan family effectively marked the end of the Eighteenth Dynasty. Power was then seized by another military figure, Horemheb, who set about effacing every trace of Akhenaten and his family, demolishing all their buildings at Karnak and burying the remains in the heart of the great pylons he erected to the glory of Amun. The restoration of Amun was complete, as evidenced by the striking portraits of the dutiful pharaoh standing before him. The destruction at Amarna was carried out by the Ramesids, who followed Horemheb's lead and buried most of its stone buildings across the river at Hermopolis in the foundations of their constructions. The final stroke was to obliterate Akhenaten and his family from the royal record, as evidenced by the Abydos king-list, which paraded Horemheb as successor to Amenhotep III. Akhenaten and his family, Amarna, and all his constructions were never meant to be seen again.

The historian knows that it is rarely possible to carry out such obliteration. The French expedition in 1798 hurried past Amarna, but plotted the few remains to be seen above ground, which included the tombs of the courtiers in the eastern cliffs. Nineteenth-century travelers barely gave the site a glance, but the diplomatic archive in cuneiform of the major Near Eastern powers of the time was by chance uncovered, and it opened new vistas of the world of the Levant of the fourteenth century BC. Petrie then began his excavations in 1891, and the city, its ruler, his family, and its people reentered the pages of history. The later work of the German Oriental Society, the Egypt Exploration Society, and the Amarna Trust has widened and deepened our knowledge of a site whose importance contines to grow. Davies painstakingly published the tombs of Akhenaten's courtiers, while in 1922 the most spectacular Egyptological find ever paradoxically brought one of the minor players to the attention of the world. From the 1920s the pylons at Karnak began to give up their secrets, and from 1939 the remains of Amarna began to be uncovered at Hermopolis. Since the beginning of the twentieth century Amarna has been the most discussed site in all of Egypt. And despite the most desperate efforts of his enemies to bury him forever, Akhenaten (along with his son Tutankhamun) has become the most famous of all the pharaohs, and Nefertiti not only the best known of queens but also the possessor of one of the most instantly recognizable images in the world.

Notes

Notes to Chapter One

1   Maspero 1921: 248.

2   Traunecker 1986: 17.

3   Cook, introduction to Baikie 1926: xiii. One example may be cited of the incredible nonsense which the Amarnan period has inspired: Philipp Vandenberg's *Nefertiti: An Archaeological Biography* (1975), English translation, New York 1978. There is virtually no archaeology in it. Dates which are contested by Egyptologists within the span of a decade or more are given here not only by year, but even by day and month. Both Tiye and Nefertiti are Mitannian. Nefertiti is Tadukhepa, first married to Amenhotep III. She was an adulteress, whose last three daughters were not by Akhenaten—and the same may be true even for Ankhesenpaaten. The Amarna Letters were written on stone. The heart was one of the organs placed in the canopic jars. Akhenaten had an incestuous relationship with his mother: their child was Baketaten (when Tiye was fifty-six). Akhenaten came to the throne aged twelve, when Nefertiti was seventeen. Akhenaten's "whole life was an unremitting attempt to free himself from dependence on his father" who "possessed the one human being to whom the entire libido of the young Akhenaten was directed—his mother." "One fact cannot be disputed—he was a pacifist." The age of the mummy in KV 55 is twenty. The durbar was held on 21 November 1352. Akhenaten was a homosexual (the reproduction of the Pasi stela is a travesty). The missing left eye of the Nefertiti bust in Berlin was the revenge of the sculptor Thutmose, the queen's rejected lover. Nefertiti wrote the letter seeking a Hittite husband (the Hittites, by the way, are Babylonian). Tutankhamun was murdered. Vandenberg also wrote a book on the "Pharaoh's Curse," in which he declared Flinders Petrie's death at the age of 89 to be "mysterious."

4   Lepsius 1851: 40–46.

5   Petrie 1894: 41.

6   Petrie 1896: II, 214.

7   Moret 1912: 68.

8   Breasted 1912: 339. One recalls Breasted relinquishing his plans to be a minister of religion, when the "present and visible evidences" were found wanting.

9   Davies 1923a: 152. Davies was a Unitarian minister.

10   Borchardt 1917: 31.

11   Schäfer 1918a: 37.

12   Hall 1921: 45.

13   Baikie 1926: 233, 234, 269, 260. Baikie was a minister in the Scottish Free Church.

14   Budge 1923: 107–108.

15   Baikie 1926: 260.

16   Drioton and Vandier 1952: 343.

17   Černý 1952: 64, 65.

18   Gardiner 1961: 214, 220.

19   Aldred 1968: 260.

20   Murnane 1995: [89.11].

21   Murnane 1995: [5].

22   Perepelkin 1978: 55.

23   Giles 1970: 92.

24   Hornung 1982: 244, 249.

25   Murnane 1995: [108].

26   Redford 1984: 58, 232–35.

27   Leprohon 1985: 100–102.

28   Murnane 1995: [88].

29   Schlögl 1986: 99, 107–109.

30   Assmann 1995: 223, 226.

31   Tyldesley 1998: 89.

32   Gabolde 1998: 23.

33   Reeves 2001: 193.

34   Davies 1903–1908: IV, pl. 12, but see IV, 16, where Davies describes no such thing.

35   Helck 2001: 4, cf. 65.

36   G. Johnson 1992: 59.

37   At this point, one should register admiration for Barry Kemp for one of the most recent books on Amarna, his splendid *City of Akhenaten and Nefertiti* (2012), beautifully written and full of insights about every aspect of life in the city (one example: the "reach of the city," p. 199). It is, more importantly, a beacon of wisdom and common sense in a field littered with extremism and sensationalism. I would especially like to draw attention to his discussion of archaeological problems and method (pp. 197–99), which might well have been placed at the very beginning of the book. It is curious, however, that Kemp is rather out-of-date regarding the political history of the period, especially over the Smenkhkare/Neferneferuaten question.

38   White 1948: 108.

39   Montserrat 2000: 41.

40   Murnane 1995: 12.

41   Desroches-Noblecourt 1963: 169.

42 Laboury 2010: 220–21.
43 Murnane 1995: [19-A].
44 Murnane 1995: [19-D].
45 Murnane 1995: [35-A].
46 Murnane 1995: [22].
47 Murnane 1995: [37.1].
48 Murnane 1995: [38.1].
49 Murnane 1995: [38.5].
50 Murnane 1995: [38.6].
51 Murnane 1995: [66.6].
52 Murnane 1995: [55].
53 Murnane 1995: [47-C].
54 Trigger 1981: 181.
55 A caution, however: contrary to the assumptions of most scholars, the situation
    with Eighteenth Dynasty mummies is precarious. To state the matter most directly,
    we have absolute certainty about the identity of only three of them: Yuya and Tjuiu
    (parents of Tiye), and Tutankhamun. Almost all the others come from the two
    'caches' where they were found as having been rewrapped in antiquity (cf. ch. 2
    n.1).
56 Gabolde 2009: n.44.
57 Martin 1974–89: 1:104.
58 'Heresy' comes from the Greek word *hairesia*, meaning 'choice,' then a school
    of philosophy (Polybios 5.93.8 in the second century BC), or a religious sect: for
    example, the Essenes (Josephos *BJ* 2.8.1) or the Christians (*Acts of the Apostles* 24.5).
59 Not that he himself was immune—far from it.
60 Kozloff and Bryan 1992: 60; for a recent summary see Dodson 2014a: 74–76.
61 Wilson 1973: 235.
62 As an example of rigorous (and therefore rare) method, one may single out Samson
    1982b, who demonstrates with devastating clarity how commonly evidence is
    manipulated. She is rarely cited.

Notes to Chapter Two

1   Amenhotep III was originally buried in WV 22. A mummy is preserved in the
    Egyptian Museum in Cairo, found in KV 35 in 1898 and labeled Amenhotep III,
    that is, identified as such by priests in the Twenty-first Dynasty, who restored the
    plundered mummies. The DNA and use of wet natron as a mummifying agent suit
    the late Eighteenth Dynasty, but padding under the skin is reminiscent of,
    but not in any way identical to, Twenty-first Dynasty practice (Dodson 2014a:
    83–84). The mummy of the 'Elder Lady' in KV 35 was identified as that of
    Queen Tiye in 2010 (see p. 214).
2   See the fascinating statistics produced by Redford (2013: 12). This article is a
    brilliant survey of the reign, utilizing texts from the *talatat*.
3   L'Hôte 1840: 53–76.
4   Lepsius 1851: 40–46.
5   Mariette 1882: 133.

6   Brugsch 1879: I, 491.

7   Stuart 1879: 81.

8   Dodson 1990; Wildung 1998 (with only a nod to Dodson); Cabrol (2000: 163–68) suggests that Thutmose died late in his father's reign; Dodson 2009c; Dodson (2014a: 44–45) later suggests that he died in Year 30 of Amenhotep III's reign.

9   Cairo JE 61995 (Carter and Mace 1923–33: III, 97).

10 See Cabrol (2000: 139–62) and Laboury (2010: 54–57) for a recent overview on Akhenaten's sisters.

11 Van de Walle 1968.

12 Hayes 1948.

13 Epigraphic Survey 1980: pl. 57.

14 Davies 1903–1908: III, pl. 4, 6, 18.

15 As suggested by Cabrol (2000: 150–53), and borne by Kiya, Tiye having become her foster mother after Kiya's disappearance.

16 Eaton-Krauss 1983.

17 Cf. the relief from the tomb of Heqaerneheh (TT 64), showing his father, Heqareshu, tutor to Thutmose IV, with the child-size king on his lap, facing Heqaerneheh, also a royal tutor with a young man (the later Amenhotep III) in front of him and six other princes, including a Prince Amenemhat behind him.

18 Davies 1923b: 42–43.

19 Davies 1933: 39, pl. 35.

20 Dodson 1990: 94 n.68.

21 Laboury 2010: 81.

22 Murnane 1995: [78.2].

23 Hayes 1959: 159.

24 W.S. Smith 1958: 160–72 (an excellent account: the excavations have not been published); excavations have now been resumed by the Metropolitan Museum of Art.

25 Hayes 1951: 35.

26 Schäfer 1919: 29.

27 Aldred 1968: 211–13; Cabrol agreed regarding Memphis (2000: 169).

28 Hari 1985: 5.

29 Laboury 2010: 85.

30 Weigall 1922a: 42.

31 Redford 1984: 233.

32 For a recent review of the whole concept of coregency in Egypt, arguing that it was actually a very rare institution, see Dodson 2014b.

33 Petrie 1896: 210, 219–20.

34 For example, Carter and Mace 1923–33: III, 3–4; Borchardt 1933; Pendlebury 1935: 10–14; Giles 2001: 25–137.

35 In Pendlebury 1951: 152–57.

36 For principal references down to the mid-1970s, see Murnane 1977: 123–69, 231–33; subsequent contributions have been Gabolde 1998: 62–98; Dorman 2009; Laboury 2010: 87–92; Dodson 2014b.

37 W.R. Johnson 1996 (cf. 2014); the view also has a vocal current advocate in Francesco Martin Valentin, who relies on the presence of cartouches of both Amenhotep III and IV on (separate) columns in the tomb of the former's vizier,

Amenhotep-Huy (Asasif FK-28), to suggest a coregency between them, lasting from the father's jubilee in Year 30 (Valentin and Bedman 2014).

38 Murnane 1977: 237.
39 Laboury 2010: 87.
40 Murnane and van Siclen 1993: 154–55.
41 Murnane 1995: [38.5].
42 Murnane 1995: [38.6].
43 Hornung et al. 2006: 492.
44 Wenig 1975: 211.
45 Aldred 1968: 213.
46 Schäfer 1918a: 28; 1919: 480.
47 Gabolde (2009: 27), forced on him owing to his acceptance of both the identity of the mummy from KV 55 as Akhenaten's and the lower estimates (eighteen to twenty-five) of its age at death, with supporting evidence claimed for early representations of the king (for example, the tomb of Ramose, TT 55) as showing "a fat young boy."
48 Baikie stated that he was under the control of his mother for two or three years, and married to Nefertiti when she was eight or nine (1926: 240, 243).
49 Petrie 1894: 38; Laboury 2010: 62; "no later than his father's 25th year" (Redford 2013: 13).
50 Gabolde (1998: 11), because his religious revolution was the work of "a rebellious adolescent"! This is hard to believe as the comment of a historian.
51 Aldred 1988: 260; Luban 1999: 18–22.
52 Desroches-Noblecourt 1972: 240.
53 Harris and Wente 1980: 255. This is, however, based on the bizarre calculation that Akhenaten had a daughter *prior to the move to Amarna* by his own daughter Meryetaten, who must therefore have been at least twelve, and her father *must* have been at least fourteen years older than her.
54 Sethe 1921: 130; Kitchen 1962: 5–39; early 20s: Schäfer 1931: 12.
55 Epigraphic Survey 1980: pl. 9, cf. pl. 13, facing his parents, offering libation and incense, from the northern wall of the entrance, and pl. 12, adjoining, a hecatomb to Re-Horakhty.
56 Laboury 2010: 98.
57 The best illustration we now have is Lepsius 1897–1913: IV, pl. 97; for a recent photograph, see Dodson 2014a: 97, fig. 81; a Swedish expedition has now rerecorded the stela.
58 Schiff-Giorgini 1965–98: V, pl. 4–11; Laboury 2010: 97.
59 Petrie 1894: 38; Baikie 1926: 240.
60 Desroches-Noblecourt 1974: 21.
61 Thomas 1966: 81–82; Reeves 2001: 127.
62 Laboury 2010: 108.
63 Vergnieux and Gondran 1997: 37–41; Kemp 2012b: 60.
64 Redford 2013: 18.
65 L'Hôte 1840: 93; Lepsius 1849–59: III, pl. 52, 110; Prisse d'Avennes 1843: pl. 10–11. They were also mentioned by Brugsch 1862: II, 69, pl. 57 and Wiedemann 1884: II, 399.

66 Pillet 1922: 248–51; 1923: 129–34; 1924: 81–82.

67 Pillet 1923: 109–11; 1925: 5–8. These notes are of the briefest. On the work of Legrain, see Traunecker and Golvin 1984: 153–77; of Pillet, Traunecker and Golvin 1984: 179–82.

68 Chevrier 1926: 129; 1927: 149–50; 1928: 123; 1929: 144–45; 1930: 168–69; 1932: 112; 1936: 141–43; 1937: 193; 1938: 141–43.

69 Chevrier 1949a: 7–8; 1949b: 242–49; 1950: 430–33; 1952: 230–36; 1955: 22–36; Adam and el-Shaboury 1959: 35–52. On Chevrier, see Traunecker and Golvin 1984: 182–200; Redford stated that he was "a notoriously bad recorder and published virtually nothing by way of reports."

70 Sauneron and Sa'ad 1969.

71 Sauneron and Sa'ad 1969.

72 Sa'ad 1967.

73 Smith and Redford 1976: 68–75.

74 Redford 1973.

75 Redford 1973: 80–81.

76 Redford 1975.

77 Smith in Smith and Redford 1976: 19–63.

78 Tawfik in Smith and Redford 1976: 58–63.

79 Redford in Smith and Redford 1976: 76–94.

80 Redford 1984: 228; 1983: 212, 214; Reeves (2001: 91) suggested that the demolitions began under Tutankhamun. Aldred posed, however, a crucial question: how can the buried statues bear the king's original name, Amenhotep? Had they been in existence after his change of name, they would have been altered. Aldred's answer, logically, was that Akhenaten himself buried them (1968: 196).

81 Redford 1977.

82 Redford 1981b.

83 Redford 1983.

84 See Smith and Redford 1976, endpapers.

85 Redford 1984: ch. 7.

86 Redford 1991.

87 Redford 1999: 56.

88 Laboury 2010: 157–65.

89 For a complete catalogue see Manniche 2010: 23–84, an invaluable historiographical analysis.

90 Kozloff 2010; 2012.

91 W.R. Johnson 2012–13.

92 Wolf 1957: 454; Pillet 1961; Westendorf 1963; Wildung 1989: 179–80; more especially Akhenaten in this role: Aldred 1961a: 73–74; Lange and Hirmer 1968: 457; Spieser 2004.

93 Desroches-Noblecourt 1974; Robins 1997.

94 Hari 1985.

95 Desroches-Noblecourt 1972: 248–49.

96 Freed 1999: 113.

97 W.R. Johnson 2014: 417.

98 Westendorf 1963.

99 Murnane 1995: [37.4], [70.8].
100 Davies 1903–1908: IV, pl. 31.
101 Murnane 1995: [70.8].
102 Murnane 1995: [89.11].
103 "By the end of his reign Amenhotep is shown, rejuvenated, as Hapy, a youthful, plump, and potent god bringing wealth to his people" (Fletcher 2000: 92).
104 Leblanc 1980.
105 Russmann 1989: 115; Vandersleyen 1995: 420; Hornung 1999: 44.
106 Angenot 2008.
107 Chevrier 1930: 169.
108 Manniche 2010: 48–60.
109 J.R. Harris 1977b; accepted as Nefertiti: Vandersleyen 1984; Reeves 2001: 166.
110 Schäfer 1918a: 8–14.
111 Vandersleyen 1984.
112 W.R. Johnson 2014: 416.
113 Spieser and Sprumont 2004: 171–72.
114 Westendorf 1963: 269–77.
115 Robins 1993; cf. J.R. Harris 1977b and Vandersleyen 1984.
116 W.R. Johnson 2014: 416.
117 Samson 1972: 23.
118 Barta 1975; for the story, see Pritchard 1969: 23–25.
119 Redford 1977: 25.
120 Manniche 2010: 93–96.
121 Traunecker 1984.
122 Epigraphic Survey 1980: pl. 32, 34, 36, 38, 40.
123 Traunecker 1986.
124 Cf. Davies 1903–1908: VI, pl. 4.
125 Vergnieux and Gondran 1997.
126 Redford 2013: 22.
127 Chappaz 1983.
128 Traunecker 1986.
129 Murnane 1995: [5].
130 Murnane 1995: [6].
131 Murnane 1995: [10D].
132 Murnane 1995: [10F]; Laboury 2010: 174–78 stressed the enormous resources devoted to the cult, celebrated throughout Egypt (Murnane 1995: [9, 33.5]).
133 Murnane 1995: [10G].
134 Doresse 1955.
135 Redford 1984: 71; Reeves 2001: 94–95.
136 Gohary 1992: 219 n.83.
137 Dodson 2014a: 97–98 suggests that the *bnbn* may actually have been Thutmose IV's obelisk.
138 Redford 1984: 82. For a modern reconstruction of *Tni-mnw*, see Vergnieux and Gondran 1997: 124–33; for a summary, Laboury 2010: 165–72.
139 Redford in Smith and Redford 1976: 95–101.
140 Tawfik 1988. For reassembled *talatat* showing the ritual, see Vergnieux and

Gondran 1997: 142–53.

141 Griffith 1918; Murnane 1995: [11].

142 Schäfer 1919.

143 Aldred 1959: 24[1]; Davies 1941: pl. 23; nos. 2–3: Ranke 1951: 50, 51[4]; Aldred 1973: [5]; Asselberghs 1923: 36.

144 Murnane 1995: [37.4].

145 Assmann 1972a. Laboury agreed that the festival signaled the birth of Atenism as the state religion (2010: 181); on the Sed festival in general, see Redford 1984: 122–36.

146 Redford 2013: 19.

147 Eight hundred fifty out of 35,000 *talatat* relate to the festival. For the relevant *talatat*, see Vergnieux and Gondran 1997: 174–77; Murnane 1995: [10.I.6–7].

148 Redford 1999: 56–57.

149 But cf. Gohary 1992: 40, 42, 43, pls. 1–2, 72–73.

150 Gohary 1992: especially 29–39, 167–69; for an earlier paper, see Gohary in Smith and Redford 1976: 64–67.

151 Redford 1984: 63, cf. 138; Uphill 1963.

152 Darnell and Manassa 2007: 26–27.

153 Murnane 1995: [37.4].

154 Davies 1903–1908: VI, pl. 6.

155 Aldred 1968: 168.

156 Uphill 1963.

157 Aldred 1988: 266–67, 271.

158 Redford 1984: 148, cf. 186.

159 Reeves 2001: 97.

160 Laboury 2010: 178.

161 Helck and Otto 1972–92: V, 109.

162 Murnane 1995: [22].

163 Murnane 1995: [37.1].

164 Laboury interpreted the two dates as a year apart, and dated the change between early Year 5 and early Year 6 (2010: 138–41).

165 Murnane 1995: [37.1].

166 Breasted 1912: 322; Gardiner 1961: 222; Aldred 1968: 185.

167 Englund 1978; Friedman 1986.

168 Fecht 1960: 83–91, relying on Edel 1948; Albright 1946: 7–25.

169 Govan, MacFarlane, and Callander 1991: 826.

170 Aldred 1968: 137.

171 Burridge 1993.

172 Aldred 1973: fig. 42.

173 Hornung (1971) therefore dismissed medical explanations: the representation of the king was "ideological." Lauffray noted that many of Akhenaten's "abnormalities" were often found among Nubians (1979: 160–61). One of the best discussions is Risse 1971. For the fantasies of the analysts of Akhenaten's *mental* condition, sample Abraham 1935: antipathy to his father; Strachey 1939: a "negative Oedipus complex"; Giles 1970: he was "mentally deranged."

Notes to Chapter Three

1   Murnane and van Siclen 1993; Fenwick 2006; there is a neat summary in Aldred 1988: 44–51 and Dodson 2014a: 107, 111.

2   Murnane 1995: [37.1, 38.1, 5, 6].

3   Davies 1903–1908, V.19–34.

4   Fenwick 2006.

5   Modern antagonists of Akhenaten have made much of these assertions. Redford 1984: 165: "The emotional overtones of his vow to disregard the advice of others also signals clearly his qualms about his own weakness of resolve, and a fear of the powers of persuasion of the queen and his coterie"; Reeves 2001: 103: the move was "characteristically impulsive and peremptory."

6   Fairman 1935.

7   Recognizing that the words might well mean that he would keep the city within the set limits, Pendlebury nevertheless could not resist a sneer: "Here then Akhenaten lived in his little Utopia for the remaining eleven years of his life" (1935: 18).

8   On this tomb for the Mnervis bull, see Montserrat 2000: 37.

9   Baikie 1926: 272; Erman 1952: 144; Doresse 1941/42: 191; Gabolde 1998: 30.

10   Aldred 1968: 193–94.

11   Helck 1958: 300; Redford 1984: 164.

12   Helck 1958: 300–301; Aldred 1988: 50, 270.

13   Hoffmeier 2014: 162.

14   Helck 2001: 4; Reeves 2001: 111. "Events in Thebes which brought about the removal of the capital to Amarna" (W.S. Smith 1958: 186) or the Amun priests saying more evil things about Akhenaten than they had said about his father or grandfather (Hart 1986: 41) hardly illuminate; the text is quite mishandled by Tyldesley (1998: 74).

15   Cabrol 2000: 282.

16   Aldred 1976: 184.

17   Hoffmeier 2014: 141–57.

18   Wells 1987; Murnane 1987a. Two years later, Wells reworked this alignment from the altar in the "Mansion of the Aten" (*Ḥwt-'Itn*).

19   Van de Walle 1976; Murnane 1987a.

20   Jomard 1809–18: II, 13–15, and IV, pl. 63.

21   Wilkinson 1847: 306–307.

22   Champollion 1909: 141; Rosellini 1994: 86–87.

23   L'Hôte 1840: 60–68, 76.

24   On Lepsius, see Mode 1984.

25   Lepsius 1853: 114, 322.

26   Lepsius 1849–59: VI, pls. 92–111; 1904: II, 123–49. Lepsius could never compile the text and gave his journal to Eduard Naville; the work was edited by Kurt Sethe, assisted by Ludwig Borchardt.

27   Petrie 1894: 1, 2, 4, 18.

28   Petrie 1894: 2.

29   Petrie 1894: 7.

30   Petrie 1894: 8.

31   Petrie 1894: 11, 12.

32 Some further fragments showing servants have recently been identified in London: Weatherhead 1995.

33 This was the largest building after the temple and palace, which Petrie thought belonged to a very high official. Pendlebury called it the "King's House" (1951: 86).

34 Petrie 1894: 32.

35 Petrie 1894: 38–44.

36 For a description, see Chubb 1954: 44–47 and Owen 2009.

37 See Davies 1903–1908: I, pl. 32, top left: well with steps and *shaduf*; this was previously thought to be simply a garden pool.

38 Berlin ÄM 20496, 20716 (the relief), 21364, 21835; Cairo JE 43520.

39 An extensive search failed to reveal the first names of these three.

40 Cairo JE 44865 (Aldred 1973: fig. 2); on the genuineness of this piece, see Krauss 2009.

41 For a recent overview of the workshop, see Seyfried 2012: 170–86.

42 Borchardt 1913: 28–50.

43 Pendlebury 1935: 168.

44 Janssen 1983: 274.

45 Kemp and Garfi 1993: 71.

46 Peet and Woolley 1923.

47 Peet and Woolley 1923: 5–9, 15–17, 19–20, respectively.

48 Badawy 1956.

49 Newton 1924; Griffith 1924, 1926; Whittemore 1926.

50 Kemp and Garfi 1993: 44.

51 Kemp 2012a: 146–51.

52 Frankfort and Pendlebury 1933.

53 Frankfort and Pendlebury 1933: 44.

54 Pendlebury 1951: 5–32.

55 Pendlebury 1951: 22–25, pl. 8.

56 Pendlebury 1951: 26–27, pl. 11.

57 Pendlebury 1951: 33–85. It is now that a major problem makes itself felt: the very complicated descriptions are not keyed in to the excellent plates, making them very hard to follow.

58 Pendlebury 1951: 80.

59 Pendlebury 1951: 86–105, pl. 16.

60 Weatherhead 1995.

61 Kemp 2012b: 133–35.

62 Most recently Kemp 2012b: 86.

63 Pendlebury 1951: 113–30, pl. 19.

64 The vast teams that have worked here with Kemp over the last thirty-five years are unfortunately too numerous to list, unlike the modest équipes of earlier expeditions.

65 Kemp 2012b: 60–63.

66 Kemp and Garfi 1993: 50–57; Kemp 2012b: 87–95.

67 Kemp 2014: 1–17.

68 Mallinson 1989.

69 Kemp 2012b: 137–46.

70 Kemp 2012b: 140.

71 Kemp 2012b: 151–53.

72   Ricke 1932: 58–63; Whittemore 1926: 4.

73   Hölscher 1941: I, 37–59.

74   Kemp 1976.

75   Pendlebury 1951: 121–22.

76   Kemp 1979.

77   Kemp 1987: 33.

78   W.S. Smith 1958: 192.

79   Kirby and Tooley 1989.

80   Kemp 2005: 22.

81   Kemp 2005: 22.

82   Kemp 2006: 44.

83   Kemp 2006: 27–37.

84   Kemp 2006: 23–27; 2007: 1–11; 2008: 1–13; 2009: 1–11.

85   Davies 1903–1908: I, 19. It is noteworthy that in one scene in Meryre ii (TA 2) the cartouches of Smenkhkare and Meryetaten stand in the places normally occupied by Akhenaten and Nefertiti (Davies 1903–1908: II, pl. 41).

86   Davies 1903–1908: II, 7.

87   Davies 1903–1908: IV, 8.

88   Davies 1903–1908: IV, 4.

89   Laboury 2010: 261, 282.

90   Davies 1903–1908: II, 1–8.

91   Davies 1903–1908: III, pl. 4 (banquet); pls. 13, 15 ('durbar'); pl. 18 (family); II, pl. 37 (Meryre ii); IV, 15 (Mahu).

92   Davies 1903–1908: II, pl. 5, cf. 10, 13, 15.

93   Capart 1957: 211.

94   Davies 1903–1908: I, pls. 22–27, 33; II, pls. 5, 12, 20; VI, pls. 1, 3, 7, 8; VI, pls. 16; IV, pl. 15; IV, pl. 31; V, pl. 3; VI, pl. 26.

95   Davies 1903–1908: III, pl. 8, 12; III, pl. 30, 32; I, pl. 10, 20; IV, pl. 5, 7; II, pl. 13–17.

96   Kemp 2012b: 153.

97   Laboury 2010: 255–59.

98   Laboury 2010: 292.

99   Erman 1952: 157.

100 Davies 1903–1908: III, pl. 4, 6, 7; II, pl. 32; III, pl. 3; IV, pl. 10.

101 Davies 1903–1908: III, pl. 13–15; II, pl. 37–40.

102 Maspero 1907a: 77; Aldred 1957c: 114; Redford 1959: 37; Bille-de-Mot 1966: 132; Schulman 1982; Darnell and Manassa 2007: 125–27; Fletcher 2004: 314; Dodson 2009a: 13.

103 Allen 2009. Laboury (2010: 294–97) raises the interesting question why this scene was shown in only two tombs, and with a precise date. Were Huya and Meryre present in an official capacity?

104 Davies 1903–1908: III, pls. 33–36 (Meryre ii); I, pl. 30 (Meryre i); IV, pls. 8–9 (Pentju); II, pls. 10–11 (Panehsy); VI, pls. 4, 7 (Parennefer); VI, pls. 17–18 (Tutu); IV, pls. 17–19 (Mahu); VI, pls. 28–31 (Ay).

105 Redford 1984: 60.

106 Davies 1903–1908: I, pls. 6–9; III, pls. 16–17; VI, pls. 19–21.

107 Davies 1903–1908: III, pls. 18, 22–24; IV, pls. 20–22, 24–26.

108   Murnane 1995: [58.B8], [68.1], [84B], [86].

109   Reeves 2001: 133.

110   Kemp 1981: 96, cf. Kemp 2012b: 17: "20,000 or maybe twice that number"; Reeves 2001: 119; Tyldesley 1998: 110, 113; Laboury 2010: 266; Janssen 1983.

111   Tietze 1985.

112   Laboury 2010: 280.

113   Kemp 2012b: 110, 116.

114   Engelbach 1940: 145.

115   Tyldesley 1998: 119, cf. 118.

116   Reeves 2001: 163—giving no reference to the extensive iconography.

117   Bouriant, Legrain, and Jéquier 1903.

118   Janssen 1983; Kemp and Garfi 1993: 77; Kemp 2012b: 125, 155.

119   Aldred 1973: 181.

120   Pendlebury 1935: 41.

121   Kemp 1977/78: 126.

122   Kemp 1981: 88.

123   Kemp 2012b: 47.

124   Janssen 1983. "There was no overall plan," yet it had "a sound economic basis." The "primitive" sanitation, on the other hand, is a focus of interest: Tyldesley 1998: 118.

125   Borchardt 1911: 12.

126   Laboury 2010: 275.

127   Kemp 2012b: 166–68, 190.

128   Baikie 1926: 265.

129   Pendlebury 1935: 17.

130   Gardiner 1961: 220; Redford 1984: 14.

131   Reeves 2001: 116; Tyldesley 1998: 116.

132   Tietze 1985: 58.

133   Laboury 2010: 266.

134   Erman 1952: 150. For something toward a list of these men, see Laboury 2010: 270–72.

135   Gardiner 1961: 223.

136   Murnane 1995: [70.1], [80.9].

137   Redford, in Smith and Redford 1976: 122–25.

138   Redford 1984: 165.

139   Van de Walle 1979: 359.

140   Murnane 1995: [68.2], [70B1].

141   Murnane 1995: [99]; pointed out by Leprohon 1985: 98.

142   Aldred 1968: 59.

143   Aldred 1968: 259; 1988: 164–65; and so Kemp 2012b: 41.

144   Murnane 1995: [67.2B].

145   Redford 1984: 180; Lichtheim 1973–80: I, 60–80, 125–29; II, 135–40.

146   Assmann 1972a: 109.

147   Stressed by Laboury 2010: 313.

148   Kemp 1977/78: 126.

149   Hornung 1990: 28.

150   Sheppard 2018.

151 Sheppard 2018: 206, 30 December 1929.
152 Sheppard 2018: 219, 9 October 1930.
153 Sheppard 2018: 221.

Notes to Chapter Four

1   As translated by Murnane 1995: [58.B4]; there are other translations in Gardiner
    1961: 225–27; Wilson in Pritchard 1969: 369–70; Aldred suggests that Ay, "as the
    king's private secretary [sic—there is no evidence for such a role for Ay], is most likely
    to have given the full authorised version" (1968: 187–89); Lichtheim 1976: 96–100.
2   Petrie 1896: 214; Davies 1903–1908: I, 47; Schäfer 1918a: 37; Gardiner 1961: 225;
    Redford 1980: 24; Assmann 1992: 145; Hoffmeier 2014: 212.
3   Breasted 1912: 335.
4   Hayes 1959: 281.
5   Redford 1980: 24.
6   Allen 1989; he began by counting four themes, but added a "final theme."
7   Assmann 2003: 214–28.
8   Hoffmeier 2014: 222–25.
9   Murnane 1995: [60.A1], [61.B1], [69.6], [70.8], [89.7].
10 Davies 1903–1908: IV, 27–29; Murnane 1995: [70.8]; Laboury wrote of a
    "centralized codification" (2010: 191).
11 Murnane 1995: [70.8].
12 Erik Hornung is one of the few to have noticed this: "there is no word of god"
    (1992: 48).
13 Statue Florence 1722 (Murnane 1995: [21]).
14 Murnane 1995: [33.3].
15 Murnane 1995: [68.1].
16 Murnane 1995: [70.7].
17 Davies 1903–1908: IV, 26.
18 Murnane 1995: [37.4].
19 Murnane 1995: [38.1].
20 Murnane 1995: [66.7, 66.10].
21 Murnane 1995: [89].
22 Cairo TR 30/10/26/12 (Aldred 1973: fig. 33).
23 For example, Desroches-Noblecourt 1963: 129, with fig. 69; Vandersleyen 1984;
    Davies 1923a: 139.
24 Davies 1903–1908: I, pl. 22; II, pl. 5; IV, pl. 31; V, pl. 33; VI, pl. 16.
25 Davies 1903–1908: I, pls. 11, 26, 27, 33.
26 Davies 1903–1908: III, pl. 30.
27 Davies 1903–1908: IV, pl. 60.
28 Davies 1903–1908: II, pls. 10, 32; III, pls. 16, 17; VI, pls. 4 (holding a uraeus to
    the king), 19, 29; there is a slightly whimsical touch in Davies 1903–1908: I, pl. 6,
    where the Aten rests a hand on the roof in very human style.
29 Davies 1903–1908: I, pl. 30; II, pl. 41; IV, pl. 7; VI, pls. 17, 20, 30.
30 Davies 1903–1908: I, pls. 10, 17; IV, pls. 20, 22.
31 Davies 1903–1908: II, pl. 13; III, pl. 32A.

32   Davies 1903–1908: III, pl. 4—but not on pl. 6.
33   Cairo JE 44862; Berlin ÄM 14145 (Aldred 1973: 11, fig. 2, [16]).
34   Davies 1903–1908: I, pls. 10, 22; II, pl. 10; IV, pl. 31.
35   Davies 1903–1908: I, pl. 27; III, pl. 8, 16.
36   Gardiner 1961: 227.
37   Hornung 1992: 48.
38   Gunn 1923, responding to Sethe 1921: 101–21.
39   For the range of potential translations, see Bennett 1965: 208.
40   For a stress on the flux in the Early form: Hoffmeier 2014: 72–76; on Re-Horakhty
     and Shu: 82–87.
41   Murnane 1995: [66.6], [71.1].
42   See Dodson 2014a: 91, fig. 75.
43   Laboury 2010: 127.
44   Gunn 1923.
45   Davies 1903–1908: II, pls. 7–8, vs. pls. 10, 12.
46   Sethe 1921.
47   Pendlebury 1951: 152.
48   Aldred 1968: 238.
49   Redford 1984: 186.
50   Gabolde 1998: 105–18.
51   Laboury 2010: 206, 314–21.
52   Bennett 1965.
53   This led to the tomb's open court, at the rear of which was the actual chapel, dating
     to the latter years of Amenhotep III; at the time Davies wrote, it was not known
     that the two elements belonged to the same monument.
54   Davies 1923a.
55   Murnane 1995: [25].
56   Laboury 2010: 193; that the solar god has become also the god of the monarchy is not,
     however, an innovation; Horus the sky god was the god of kingship in the Old Kingdom.
57   Aldred 1959; it should be noted that Gunn, in his 1923 discussion of the names of
     the Aten, had gone on to list the features of the god, including cartouches, uraeus,
     royal epithets, celebration of jubilees, and even taking the place of Akhenaten for
     dating (Stela S; Davies 1903–1908: III, pl. 13).
58   Sa'ad and Manniche 1971.
59   Redford 1976: 55–56.
60   Petrie 1894: 13.
61   Davies 1903–1908: I, pl. 22; II. pls. 5, 12, 18; IV, pl. 15; V, pl. 3; VI, pls. 16, 26;
     Cooney 1965: pls. 9, 10.
62   Davies 1903–1908: I. pl. 14, III, pl. 30.
63   Kemp 2012b: 96–105.
64   Murnane 1995: [5].
65   Aldred 1968: 185–86, 190.
66   Aldred 1968: 186.
67   Davies 1903–1908: II, 15; on the triad, see also Tyldesley 1998: 47–50, who
     accepted both the Aten–Akhenaten–Nefertiti triad and "effectively" a secondary
     triad of Akhenaten–Nefertiti–daughter; also Spieser 2001: 28.

68   Allen 1996: 5.
69   Hornung 1980: 88.
70   Badawy 1973: 68.
71   Zabkar 1954.
72   Hornung 1980: 86.
73   Murnane 1995: [58.B7.D].
74   Assmann 1980: 21, 28.
75   Breasted 1912: 348; Baikie 1926: 330.
76   Posener 1975.
77   Assmann 1980.
78   Murnane 1995: [58.B7.J].
79   Murnane 1995: [68.1].
80   Černý 1952: 65.
81   Gardiner 1961: 230.
82   Baikie 1926: 248–50, 211, 323. Pendlebury made the same points (1935: 155).
83   Wilson 1956: 211.
84   Stewart 1960.
85   Pritchard 1969: 373 (modified: author has removed archaisms).
86   Hornung 1992: 49.
87   Breasted 1909: 361, also 377; 1912: 331; see also Moret 1912: 63.
88   Erman 1952: 142.
89   Foster 1999: 102.
90   Hoffmeier 2014: 223.
91   Weigall 1922a: 152.
92   Giles 1970: 135.
93   Assmann 2003: 219.
94   Murnane 1995: [37.3], [82], [90D], [70.8], [70.8], [77.B.12], [70.11].
95   Martin 1974–89: II, 33, fig. 4, pl. 43.
96   Brunner 1962: 152–53.
97   Aldred 1968: 246.
98   Redford 1984: 142, 175.
99   Bille-de-Mot 1966: 54.
100   Reeves 2001: 154.
101   Breasted 1909: 363; Wilson 1956: 221.
102   Davies 1923a: 139.
103   Epigraphic Survey 1980: pl. 13.
104   Tyldesley 1998: 74.
105   Murnane 2000b: 19.
106   Breasted 1909: 362; Wilson 1956: 222.
107   Hari 1984: 1041; 1985: 15.
108   Baikie 1926: 274.
109   Murnane 1995: [79].
110   Murnane 1995: [68.1].
111   Murnane 1995: [58.B8].
112   Tawfik 1976.
113   Murnane 1995: [70.9], [71.3].

114   Louvre C 286 (Lichtheim 1973–80: II, 81–86).

115   Moret 1912: 61.

116   Borchardt 1914: 27.

117   Eaton-Krauss 2003.

118   Dodson 2014a: 129.

119   Gabolde 1998: 29–34.

120   Tawfik 1973b: 84.

121   Redford 1984: 141, 175.

122   Gabolde 1998: 29.

123   Murnane 1995: [35A].

124   Laboury 2010: 108, 198.

125   Laboury 2010: 108; Reeves 2001: 154.

126   Aldred 1968: 195–96; 1988: 289.

127   Dodson 2009a: 46; 2014a: 127.

128   Murnane 1995: [22].

129   Murnane 1995: [47 D], [21], [29], [55].

130   Borchardt 1914: 16.

131   Hari 1984: 1039–41.

132   Tyldesley 1998: 74.

133   Murnane 1995: [99].

134   Redford 2013: 18.

135   Hoffmeier 2014: 195–96.

136   Murnane 1995: [33.5]: Theban tomb of Parennefer, TT 188; see also Leprohon 1985: 97.

137   Kemp 2012b: 27.

138   Murnane 1995: [94].

139   Murnane 1995: [55].

140   Davies 1943.

141   Winlock 1923: 32.

142   Winlock 1929: 36 and note, figs. 48–49, 51–52.

143   Caminos and James 1963.

144   Davies 1941: 32.

145   Murnane 1995: [29].

146   Drioton 1943.

147   Murnane 1995: [81].

148   Tomb of Pahery at el-Kab: Lichtheim 1976: II, 15–20.

149   Murnane 1995: [28].

150   Murnane 1995: [23].

151   Murnane 1995: [54].

152   Murnane 1995: [58 B 8].

153   Murnane 1995: [70.4], [80.3], [89.2].

154   Murnane 1995: [66.1].

155   Murnane 1995: [66.14]

156   Hari 1984: 1050.

157   Van de Walle 1979: 359.

158   Gabolde 1998: 108.

159   Cairo JE 31378 (Murnane 1995: [34 D]).

160   DM 1352; Porter and Moss 1960–64: 688.

161   Hari 1984: 1050–55.

162   Hornung 1992: 48.

163   Brunner 1961: 162.

164   Davies 1923a: 150.

165   Wilson 1956: 224–26; Pendlebury's judgment was gross: the Amarna age was "an ephemeral butterfly age with that total lack of moral standards usually associated with happy morons" (1935: 160).

166   Williams 1971: 285–87.

167   Hoffmeier 2014: 247–56.

168   Hayes 1959: 280.

169   Gardiner 1961: 229.

170   Assmann 2003: 221.

171   Baikie 1926: 329.

172   Breasted 1912: 336.

173   Weigall 1922a: 105.

174   van de Walle: 1979, already pointed to by Zabkar 1954: 94–96. The texts can be found in Murnane 1995: [58.B.8], [68.1], [89.1], [89.7], [89.10], [58.B.8], [89.7].

175   Wolf 1924: 111.

176   pBulaq 17 (Pritchard 1969: 365–67).

177   BM EA 826 and Cairo CG 34051 (Pritchard 1969: 367–68).

178   Wilson in Pritchard 1969: 36.

179   Gardiner 1961: 227.

180   Fecht 1967.

181   In the tombs of that king (KV 34), of Hatshepsut (KV 20), and of Vizier User (TT 61).

182   Piankoff 1964.

183   Breasted 1906: I, 747.

184   Redford 1976: 48–52.

185   The best collection of these sources is Giles 1970: 111–27.

186   BM EA 65800 (Shorter 1931: 23–25).

187   Bryan 1991: 354.

188   Shorter 1931: 24.

189   Murnane 1995: [1], [2A], [2B], [2D], [2E], [2E], [2F], [2G], [23], [24], [31].

190   Schäfer was already resolutely refuting Borchardt's view that a formal cult of Aten went back to Amenhotep III; that a barge was called "the Aten Gleams" did not prove a formal cult (1918a: 24–25). Borchardt had also misidentified Berlin ÄM 2072 (fig. 20) as a usurped Amenhotep III piece, and on that mistaken basis suggested that it was evidence for a falcon-headed Aten under Amenhotep III (see Dodson 2014a: 186 n.95). Wolf queried whether there was a cult of Aten under Amenhotep III and declared that all the evidence cited turned out to be from Akhenaten's reign (1924: 11).

191   Breasted 1906: II, 882, 887, 888, 905.

192   BM EA 38272 (Glanville 1929b: 5).

193   Wilson 1956: 210; Tawfik 1973a: 79.

194   Murnane 1995: [100F].

195   Redford railed against what he called this "canard which has bedevilled Amarna studies," attempts to identify Amarnan and earlier solar theology (2013: 11).

196 Assmann 1972a.
197 Breasted 1906: II, 187–242, 246–95.
198 Lichtheim 1973–80: II, 146–63.
199 Assmann 1989.
200 Assmann 2003: 223.
201 Assman 1995. This book is anomalous in Amarnan scholarship: it discusses the solar journey, then Amunist theology in the early Eighteenth Dynasty, and Amun-Re theology in the Ramesside period.
202 Hornung 1982: 244–50.
203 Brunner 1962: 158, 161.
204 Redford 1976: 47.
205 Petrie 1894: 417.
206 Davies 1923a: 150; Tyldesley 1998: 90 (although Tyldesley later suggests that it was "an idiosyncratic brand of monotheism" (1998: 179)). Dodson seemed to prefer henotheism (2014a: 129).
207 Laboury 2010: 202–207.
208 Wilson 1956: 209.
209 Morenz 1973: 142.
210 Wiedemann 1884: II, 396.
211 Breasted 1909: 363.
212 Gardiner 1961: 227.
213 Redford 1984: 158.
214 Hari 1985: 3.
215 Assmann 1992: 143; 2003: 213.
216 Foster 1999: 101.
217 Hoffmeier 2014: 227.
218 Zabkar 1954: 93.
219 Hayes 1959: 280.
220 Aldred 1968: 190, 246; 1988: 244.
221 Redford 1980: 21–23; 1984: 176.
222 Hornung 1980: 84; 1982: 246.
223 Murnane 1995: [7].
224 Mentioned by Redford 1984: 172.
225 Moret 1912: 41.
226 Drioton and Vandier 1952: 343–44.
227 Wilson 1956: 216.
228 Hayes 1959: 280.
229 Redford 1984: 158–62.
230 Reeves 2001: 32–48.
231 Breasted 1906: II, 187–88, 655.
232 Breasted 1906: II, 810–11.
233 Hari 1985: 6.
234 Assmann 2003: 214.
235 Aldred 1968: 191.
236 Murnane 1995: [99].
237 Redford 1984: 178.

238 Redford 1995: 175–76, 180.
239 Redford 1976: 26.
240 For a most convenient survey of these various temples, Hoffmeier 2014: 165–92.
241 Murnane 1995: [51B].
242 Habachi 1965: 79–84.
243 Maspero 1881: 116; Wilbour 1936: 82–83; Murnane 1995: [49]; a similar block is Washington 1421.
244 Cairo CG 34175 (Lacau 1909: 214, pl. 65; Murnane 1995: [48]).
245 Löhr 1974.
246 Frankfort and Pendlebury 1933: pl. 57A; III, 182, fig. 123; Murnane 1995: [47E].
247 Murnane 1995: [68.2].
248 Pendlebury 1951: pl. 81 [5, 12].
249 Murnane 1995: [79].
250 Bakry 1972.
251 Löhr 1975.
252 Petrie in Engelbach 1915: pl. 54[6, 10].
253 Sa'd and Manniche 1971; Helck 1973b.
254 Murnane 1995: [22], [26B], [24], [29]. Meryneith/Meryre later served as Memphite High Priest of the Aten under Tutankhamun, changing his name back to Meryneith; for his tomb, see Raven and van Walsem 2014.
255 Malek 1997.
256 Gabra 1931; Murnane 1995: [52]; Hoffmeier 2014: 171–72.
257 el-Masry 2002.
258 Hoffmeier 2014: 170.
259 Naville 1901: 62.
260 Breasted 1902/3.
261 Macadam 1949: xii.
262 Trigger 1976: 129.
263 Blackman 1937.
264 Spence et al. 2011: 36; Hoffmeier 2014: 144–46.
265 Bonnet 2001; Valbelle 2006; W.R. Johnson 2012: 93.
266 Kendall 2009; W.R. Johnson 2012: 93.
267 Hari 1984: 1041–43.
268 Assmann 1972a: 109.
269 Hoffmeier 2014: 178–92.
270 Trigger 1981: 179–80.
271 Breasted 1909: 390.
272 Gardiner 1961: 229.
273 Schäfer 1918a: 37.
274 Wolf 1924: 117.
275 Erman 1952: 139, 152.
276 Daressy 1901.
277 Hari 1985: 14.
278 The god Bes also had a feminine form (Beset), shown holding her tail; she was apparently an Amarnan invention, an apotropaic deity especially associated with the sun god (Bosse-Griffiths 1977).

279   Hari 1984: 1043–46.
280   Kemp 2012b: 236–45.
281   Wente 1990: 94–96.
282   Foster 1999: 109.
283   Davies 1920: 25.
284   Baikie 1926: 143–45.
285   Tyldesley 1998: 78, 83–84.
286   Reeves 2001: 139, 181.
287   Allen's translation.
288   Martin 1986: 109–129.
289   Ikram 1989.
290   Giles 1970: 139.

Notes to Chapter Five

1   W.S. Smith 1958: pl. 44B.
2   W.S. Smith 1958: pl. 61.
3   Tyldesley 1994: 197, 199–200.
4   Bouriant 1885.
5   Seele 1955: 170.
6   Maspero 1895–99: II, 316–17.
7   Baikie 1926: 243; Pendlebury 1935: 9.
8   Petrie 1896: 207–10; Drioton and Vandier 1952: 384.
9   Worms 1916.
10   Gardiner 1961: 214.
11   Bille-de-Mot 1966: 40.
12   Bouriant, Legrain, and Jéquier 1903.
13   Wilson 1973: 239.
14   For example, Senwosret A (father of Amenemhat I), Mentuhotep A (father of Sobekhotep III), and Haankhef A (father of Neferhotep I, Sihathor, and Sobekhotep IV).
15   Borchardt 1905.
16   On the history and refutation of this theory, see Robins 1983a.
17   Davies 1903–1908: VI, 23–24.
18   Seele 1955: 169, 178.
19   Worms 1916.
20   He suggested that the marriage was shown in Ay's tomb (Davies 1903–1908: VI, pl. 29).
21   Accepted by many later writers, including Aldred 1968: 90–91; Reeves 2001: 88; Dodson 2009a: 96–97; Laboury 2010: 224–30.
22   Dodson 2009a: 99; his position was subsequently modified in light of the DNA evidence (see 2014a: 87–88).
23   Senenmut with Hatshepsut's daughter Neferure; Ahmose under Amenhotep II (TT 224); Sennefer (TT 99—also "Father of the King's Son Siamun"); Imhotep ("Father of the Children of the King Thutmose I"); Heqareshu, tutor to Thutmose IV (TT 64).

24 Brunner 1961; Schaden 1992; also accepted by Redford in Smith and Redford 1976: 79–80.
25 As Borchardt himself stressed, *the eye had never been inserted*. For a clear photograph, see Seyfried 2012: 182.
26 Borchardt 1913: 43, fig. 19; for a recent description of the discovery based on Borchardt's notebooks, see Seyfried 2012: 180–85, with further extracts 336, 429, 442, 446.
27 This is not entirely true; some pieces are in Cairo.
28 Borchardt 1923: 38.
29 Borchardt 1913: 41; 1923: 31.
30 Borchardt 1923.
31 Anthes 1968: 19; cf. 5.
32 Krauss 1978.
33 On this visit and the photographs, Petersen 2012.
34 Borchardt, quoted by Matthes 2012: 429.
35 Wilson 1964: 156.
36 Krauss 1989b: 102–11.
37 Krauss 1989b: 106.
38 Borchardt's judgment is borne out, in fact, because in Terrace and Fischer 1970: 127–28, the relief is indeed one of the forty-three "treasures."
39 Borchardt 1913: 28–50, 43 for Nefertiti.
40 MFA 11.1738.
41 Borchardt 1923.
42 Krauss 1989b: 109–10.
43 Krauss 1989b: 102.
44 Samson 1973a.
45 Smith and Redford 1976: pls. 23.2, 32.7.
46 Davies 1903–1908: V, pl. 42.
47 Davies 1903–1908: V, pl. 40.
48 Samson 1973a: 50.
49 Ertman 1992b.
50 Kozloff and Bryan 1992: 473–74.
51 Redford 1975: 11; van de Walle 1980; Laboury 2010: 226–31, who stressed her connection with Hathor and the imitation of Amenhotep III, the solar god, and Tiye as Hathor.
52 Aldred 1973: [29], fig. 34.
53 Aldred 1973: 31.
54 Davies 1903–1908: I, pls. 22, 30; Brooklyn 16.48 (Aldred 1973: [121]); the only three-dimensional representation appears to be Berlin ÄM 21263—see Ertman 1976.
55 Arnold 1996c: 79.
56 Davies 1903–1908: II, pl. 8; VI, pl. 26(?).
57 Also called the "pointed wig" (*Zipfelperücke*—Hanke), "winged wig" (*Flügelperücke*—Mainz catalogue), or "pointed Nubian wig" (Werner).
58 Daressy in Davis 1910: 27.
59 Aldred 1957a.

60 Schulman 1964: 52; J.R. Harris, 1973b: 9.

61 Smith and Redford 1976, passim; Davies 1941: pl. 33; Aldred 1973: fig. 17.

62 Davies 1903–1908: III, pl. 4; VI, pl. 3; Aldred 1973: [48].

63 Cairo JE 62028 (Desroches-Noblecourt 1963: pl. 6); cf. Bosse-Griffiths 1980: 79.

64 Eaton-Krauss 1977: esp. 30.

65 Rammant-Peeters 1985.

66 Weigall 1922a: 116.

67 Blackman 1922: 522.

68 The stela of Pay has no provenance and no date of discovery. It was first published by Schäfer (1912–13: 136–37, fig. 68). Its accession number (17813) falls after 15000 (acquired in 1899) but before the Borchardt finds in 1912, which are numbered from 21000; Pay is not known to Hari (1976c).

69 Newberry 1928a.

70 Schäfer 1931: pl. 30. Giles completely misread the scene, giving the Aten two cartouches, Akhenaten three, and "Smenkhkare" two (1970: 89).

71 Wolf 1930: 100.

72 Cf. the material discussed by Montserrat 2000: 168–82.

73 So Schäfer 1931: pl. 31; Aldred 1968: pl. 82.

74 J.R. Harris 1973b. Perepelkin (originally published in Russian in 1968) had noted that there were only three cartouches for two "kings" (1978: 92–93). Roeder had seen this fact, but been unable to discern what it meant, not to mention the physique, the secondary figure's left arm, and the gesture of the main king (1958: 47). Tawfik misread Harris to say that Nefertiti was *not* wearing the blue crown here (Tawfik 1975: 159; J. R. Harris 1973b: 11). Tawfik then contradicted himself by stating that Schäfer's rule on the shape of the royal necks was undermined by the *talatat*, which mostly show both Akhenaten's and Nefertiti's necks as straight. Tawfik took this argument to overthrow totally Harris's identifications of Nefertiti where Smenkhkare had been posited. Helck reasserted the identification of Akhenaten and Nefertiti (as with Berlin ÄM 20716) (1984a: 164).

75 Davies 1903–1908: II, pl. 32. Ankhesenamun is also shown thus on Tutankhamun's golden shrine (Edwards 1977: 56).

76 J.R. Harris 1973b: 12; Werner 1979 raised the question of the identity of the king and queen on the *talatat* reliefs from the temple at Karnak. He used two criteria, the pointed Nubian wig and the double uraeus, to identify the queen and to reassign images to Nefertiti (Aldred 1973: [23], [27]; Settgast 1976: [18], [19], [20]).

77 Tawfik 1973b: 83–84.

78 Tawfik 1973b: 82–86.

79 Tyldesley 1998: 58.

80 Wilson 1973: 197.

81 This reversal of the Aten's name had been noted by Davies in 1903 (1903–1908: I, 9); Tawfik responded by stressing that it was the god's name that was changed to face the queen's (1973b: 82). He later refined this observation: the 'Neferneferuaten' name referring to Nefertiti as queen always has the Aten name written backwards to face the queen; when used for a king, all hieroglyphs in the cartouche were made to face the same way (1981: 470).

82 Smith and Redford 1976: pl. 77.

83   Davies 1903–1908: II, pls. 18, 37, 38; III, pl. 13.
84   Vandersleyen observed something else: a Berlin relief (ÄM 13135) of the king and queen with three daughters shows Akhenaten sitting on a plain stool, while Nefertiti's is decorated with the Union of the Two Lands (1984: 9).
85   Wilson 1973.
86   Tawfik 1975: 163, fig. 1 and pl. 52a; Tyldesley (1998: 144) rejected all this: there is "absolutely no proof that she was ever an official, or even an unofficial, queen regnant." Her evidence for this was that Nefertiti's size in relation to her husband varied; the most remarkable evidence, Nefertiti as queen smiting the enemy, she sidelined. The stela of Pay, on the other hand, she admitted, showed a "regally crowned" Nefertiti; this was written, of course, before the final proof of the femininity of Neferneferuaten.
87   Tawfik 1973a: pl. 29a.
88   Tawfik 1973b.
89   Wilson 1973: 239.
90   Samson 1976.
91   Murnane noted that she is referred to by both names in this particular text (1995: [37.2]). Laboury dated the new name to between Stela K and Stela X, so later than the change to her husband's (2010: 336).
92   Cairo JE 60688–91 (Porter and Moss 1960–64: 574; Beinlich and Saleh 1989: 106–117[266g]).
93   Cairo JE 60673 (Beinlich and Saleh 1989: 83, 85–88[256a–b]).
94   Cairo JE 61517, 61902a (Porter and Moss 1960–64: 581; McLeod 1970: 10–12, pls. 17, 20; Beinlich and Saleh 1989: 22[h]).
95   Cairo JE 62416 (Porter and Moss 1960–64: 583; Beinlich and Saleh 1989: 222[620(41–42)]).
96   Cairo JE 61944 (Beinlich and Saleh 1989: 96[261p(1)]; Gabolde 1998: 17–19).
97   Cairo JE 61495 (Porter and Moss 1960–64: 579; Beinlich and Saleh 1989: 31–32 [79]).
98   Samson 1982c.
99   J.R. Harris 1973a; in this he continues to be followed by Reeves 1999: 88–91.
100 Krauss 1978: 36–47.
101 Allen 1991, adumbrated in Allen 1988.
102 Gabolde 1998: 147–66.
103 Cairo JE 60714 (Edwards 1977: 191).
104 On plaster from the North Riverside Palace at Amarna, and the canopic coffinettes and a pectoral reused by Tutankhamun.
105 Allen 2010: 27–41.
106 Gabolde 1998: 157.
107 See Moran's translation, 1992: 23 n, where he accepted the identification, but admitted that "the line of thought (is) curious."
108 Allen 2009.
109 Dodson 2009b.
110 W. R. Johnson 2015b. The head is Hanover 1970.49.
111 Davies 1903–1908: III, 1–8.
112 Davies 1903–1908: V, 19–34.

113 Redford 1975: 10.
114 Redford 1984: 79.
115 Redford in Smith and Redford 1976: 83–92.
116 Redford 1984: 149.
117 Dodson 2009a: 23–24.
118 Laboury 2010: 314–22.
119 Murnane and van Siclen 1993: 175–78.
120 Petrie (1894: 38) and Laboury (2010: 62, 224) dated the marriage to Year 4; the latter noted that there was no mention of Nefertiti in *EA* 26, 27.
121 Roeder 1969: pl. 19[234/VI].
122 Brunner 1938; Aldred accepted Akhenaten's marriages with three of his daughters (1968: 242).
123 Wilson 1973: 237.
124 Redford 1975: 11–12.
125 Roeder 1969: pl. 106 [451/VIIC].
126 Redford 1975: pl. 7.
127 Meyer 1984.
128 Wente in Harris and Wente 1980: 137–40.
129 Redford 1975: pl. 3.
130 Wente in Harris and Wente 1980: 139, 255.
131 Allen 2009: 15–18.
132 Murnane and van Siclen 1993: 177.
133 Petrie 1896: II, 232; Breasted 1909: 379.
134 Inter alia, Carter and Mace (1923), Hall (1923), Bille-de-Mot (1966), Aldred (1968), Roeder (1969), Giles (1970), Ray (1975), Samson (1985), Kozloff and Bryan (1992), Tyldesley (1998), Reeves (2001), Fletcher (2004), Dodson (2009a, 2014a), Hawass et al. (2010), and Laboury (2010).
135 Roeder 1969: pl. 105 [56–VIII A], 106 [831–VIII C].
136 Dodson 2009a: 15–17; 2014a: 130; Laboury 2010: 317.
137 Cf. Dodson and Hilton 2004.
138 Peet and Woolley 1923: 123–24.
139 Peet and Woolley 1923: 155.
140 Peet and Woolley 1923: 123, 151, 154.
141 Glanville 1929a: 131–32.
142 Engelbach 1931: 105–106; Carter and Mace 1923–1933: III, 17–18; Gardiner 1961: 233.
143 Pendlebury 1935: 28; Seele 1955.
144 Baikie 1926: 281.
145 Perepelkin 1978: 58–59.
146 Perepelkin 1978: pl. opp. p. 74; cf. Peet and Woolley 1923: pl. 32.
147 Aldred 1968: 242–43; 1988: 228–29; so Wilson 1973: 241.
148 Helck 1969a, reinforced fifteen years later in Helck 1984a.
149 Tyldesley 1998: 166, 174, 176.
150 Gabolde 1998: 170–74; Laboury 2010: 323, relying on the Amarna Letters.
151 Berlin AM 17555.
152 Brunner-Traut 1982: 519.

153 Pendlebury 1935: 28.
154 Redford 1967: 170–82, and Smith and Redford 1976: 94.
155 Perepelkin 1978: 125.
156 Redford 1975: 11–12; in his 1994 discussion of Smenkhkare, Allen accepted
     Nefertiti as Akhenaten's coregent Neferneferuaten; either she died about the same
     time as her husband, or was deposed by Smenkhkare and lived into the reign of
     Tutankhamun; Allen later changed his view.
157 Harris 1973a; 1973b; Samson 1973b.
158 Samson 1977: 97.
159 Krauss 1997.
160 Peet and Woolley 1923: 166.
161 Helck 1969a: 202.
162 Krauss 1979: 841.
163 Dodson 2009a: 38–42, 45, 52, noting the various items of Neferneferuaten's
     funerary equipment in Tutankhamun's tomb: coffinettes for the viscera, mummy
     trappings, a bow, a box fragment, bracelets, and a pectoral.
164 Aldred 1968: 242.
165 Luban 1999.
166 Gabolde argued that this was a woman in her thirties. His evidence: Honoré de
     Balzac thought that a woman of that age already had her life behind her (Gabolde
     1998: 11)! Amarnan scholarship is full of the fantasy of historical fiction: Helck
     thought that Nefertiti returned [sic] to Asia with her three daughters after Year 13
     (2001: 44–45). For Fletcher, she succeeded Akhenaten, returned to Thebes, and
     compromised with the Amunists, but then sought a Hittite husband, and was then
     buried perhaps in KV 56 (2004: 327, 330, 334–46).
167 Van der Perre 2014.
168 Murnane 1995: [37.4].
169 Brooklyn 33.51 (Aldred 1968: pl. 108).
170 Loeben 1986.
171 Murnane 1995: [46.E3].
172 Aldred 1988: 229.
173 Krauss 1997.
174 Eaton-Krauss 1990: 551.
175 Numbered Cairo CG 61071 (Smith 1912: 39–40), although never taken to the
     museum.
176 Cairo CG 61070 and 61072 (Smith 1912: 38–39, 40–42).
177 Harris and Wente 1978; Harris et al. 1979.
178 Germer 1984.
179 Robins 1983b.
180 Hawass et al. 2010: 644.
181 James 2001.
182 Luban 1999.
183 Fletcher 2004: 340–57.
184 James 2003.
185 G.E. Smith 1912: 40–41.
186 Hawass et al. 2010.

187 Gabolde 2013.

188 See for example Aldred 1968: 88–90, but going back further.

189 Dodson 2014a: 167.

190 Cf. Marchant 2011; 2013: 196–211; Dodson 2014a: 163–67.

191 Hayes 1959: II, 294.

192 BM EA 65901 (Fairman 1961: 29–30, pl. 6; Murnane 1995: [45A]).

193 Perepelkin 1978: 85–129, whose discussion is vitiated by his failure to identify the pieces of archaeological evidence in the standard ways (for example, Berlin ÄM 17813), or to key them into the text. He writes, for example, simply of "the Hermopolis stones"! He also begins referring to "the estate" (for example, p. 102), which is finally revealed (p. 112) as the Maru-Aten.

194 To which are devoted two pages.

195 Perepelkin 1978: 116.

196 Perepelkin 1978: 110.

197 Perepelkin 1978: 120, 121.

198 Perepelkin 1978: 120, 121.

199 Perepelkin 1978: 129.

200 Accepted by Harris, Hanke, Helck, and Krauss. The definitive examination of the canopic jars was by Krauss, who showed that they were originally made for Kiya (1986). They had been variously ascribed to Tiye (Davis 1910: 24), Nefertiti (Schäfer 1918b), Meryetaten (Aldred 1957a: 141–47), Smenkhkare (Roeder 1958: 65), Kiya (J.R. Harris 1974a: 30), and Akhenaten (Manniche 1975).

201 Murnane 1995: [45A–F].

202 J.R. Harris 1974a.

203 Reeves 1988.

204 Harris cites Roeder 1969: pls. 12, 14, 21, 126, 172, 186(?), 198, 200, 215.

205 For instance, Cooney 1965: pl. 18b.

206 Hanke 1975.

207 Eaton-Krauss 1981: 257; Roeder 1969: pls. 21–22 (statues in relief), MMA 21.114.1; Cairo JE 44866 (Aldred 1973: [105]; fig. 54) (three-dimensional).

208 Krauss 1986.

209 Although some have argued that the lids did not originally belong to the jars.

210 Cooney 1965: pl. 13b.

211 Berlin ÄM 21245 (Aldred 1973: [103]).

212 W.R. Johnson 2015a; the preserved fraction of the scenes is, however, very small and, in truth, the evidence for the identity of the king in question is less solid than it might seem.

213 Reeves 1988.

214 Roeder 1969: pl. 111[438/VIIA].

215 Van Dijk 2009: 83–88.

216 Helck 1984a; 2001.

217 Tyldesley 1998: 162, using as evidence the Royal Tomb, room *alpha*, wall F.

218 Fletcher 2004: 325.

219 Van Dijk 1997; Gabolde 1998: 166–70, 180, 184 (repetition makes certain); Laboury 2010: 322.

220 J.R. Harris 1974a; Samson 1985: 70, 92; Kozloff and Bryan 1992: 44; Tyldesley

221 Helck 1984a; Krauss 1986; Tyldesley 1998: 129; Laboury 2010: 323.
222 Cf. Edel 1948.
223 This text was first published by Forrer 1926.
224 Federn 1960.
225 Suppuliliumas frag. 28, trans. Goetze in Pritchard 1969: 319.
226 Redford 1967: 158–62. Reeves agreed (2001: 176–77).
227 Kitchen 1968: 318–20.
228 Stempel 2007.
229 Dodson 2014a: 200–201, n.14.
230 Helck 1981: 207.
231 Helck 2001: 45.
232 Krauss 1979, a paper given at the first International Congress of Egyptologists (1976); the same case was already better argued in Krauss 1978: 37–47. Schlögl (1986: 117–20) agreed with Krauss (Hachmann 1982: 21–22).
233 Schlögl 1986: 117–20.
234 Hachmann 1982: 21–22.
235 Gabolde 1998: 187–212.
236 Laboury 2010: 333–34.
237 So Winlock 1923: 12; Sturm 1933; Edel 1948: 14; Gurney 1952: 31, 217; Guterbock 1956: 94; Gardiner 1961: 241; Campbell 1964: 59; Hornung 1966: 101; Kitchen 1968: 318; Helck 1968: 197; von Beckerath 1975; Bryce 1990 and 1998: 193; Murnane 1999: 182.
238 Carter and Mace 1923–33: II, 196.
239 Van Dijk 1993: 54–57.
240 Bryce 1990.
241 Dodson 2009a: 89–94.

Notes to Chapter Six

1 Breasted 1909: 355.
2 Hall 1921: 42–43, 44, 45.
3 Pendlebury 1935: 14, 20, 21, 25, 27, 28.
4 Wilson 1956: 2, 30f.
5 Aldred 1968: 240–41.
6 Redford 1984: 194–95, 202–203.
7 Reeves 2001: 152–53.
8 Wiedemann 1884: II, 400.
9 Davies 1903–1908: II, 42.
10 Baikie 1926: 95, 269.
11 Drioton and Vandier 1952: 411–14.
12 Tyldesley 1998: 33. Giles completely misunderstood the royal correspondence and the "greeting gifts" to claim that Amenhotep III was paying large sums of gold each year to Babylon (*EA* 7) and to the Mitanni (*EA* 16). He posited a treaty between Egypt and Mitanni, whereby the latter policed their frontiers and Egypt paid large sums toward the expense (1970: 159–60).

13 For the now-standard English edition, see Moran 1992, a splendid translation and commentary; an attempt has been made from this point to standardize spelling of proper names, following Moran's usage, but there are bound to remain inconsistencies.

14 By Amenhotep III (*EA* 1, 5, 31) and an unnamed king (99, 162, 163, 367, 369, 370).

15 Aldred 1968: 205.

16 Moran 1992: xxxiv–xxxv suggested a span of some thirty years, from Amenhotep III's Year 30 to Tutankhamun, with the Mitannian letters dating from Amenhotep III's Year 30 to Akhenaten's Years 4 and 5; the Babylonian letters from Amenhotep III to late Akhenaten; and the Assyrian letters are late Akhenaten.

17 Aldred 1968: 204–205; 1988: 189.

18 Giles 1970: 148–57.

19 Na'aman 2000: 135.

20 See especially Artzi 2000.

21 Giles 1970: 53.

22 There is, however, a major problem here, involving two important letters: reference is made to a visit to Sidon by "your father" (*EA* 85). Campbell takes the earlier king to be Thutmose IV (1964: 86); Goetze and Kitchen take it to be Amenhotep III (Goetze 1975: 11; Kitchen 1962: 20). In *EA* 116, in the later Rib-Adda letters, Moran translates "did not your father come out and visit his lands and his mayors?" (Moran 1992: 191–92) but Campbell takes it to be a statement: "your father did not . . . ." (1964: 87).

23 Campbell 1964: 87. Helck is uncertain under which king the Rib-Hadda letters belong (1975). Cohen and Westbrook incredibly offer nothing (2000: 90–96).

24 Not the ancestors of the Hebrews, as long thought, but plundering nomads; see Albright 1975: 110–14.

25 Other requests were for fifty (*EA* 238, 289, 295), forty (twenty Egyptians and twenty Nubians), eighty (*EA* 152), 100–200 and fifty chariots (*EA* 132), two hundred (*EA* 196), two hundred men and thirty chariots (*EA* 127), three hundred (*EA* 93).

26 Breasted 1909: 389.

27 Pendlebury 1935: 21–22.

28 Redford 1984: 198–202.

29 Baikie 1926: 104.

30 Liverani 1983b.

31 Ragionieri 2000: 49, 51.

32 Klengel 1965.

33 Pintore 1983: 332.

34 Liverani 1971. Giles diagnosed Rib-Hadda as suffering from neurosis: he had quarreled with almost every major Egyptian official. He was right, however, to detect the essential truth: "He was always tottering on the brink of disaster, constantly crying for help, and yet, after almost fifteen years of these pleas being ignored, the peril of his position never changed, until his own city got rid of him" (1970: 169–71).

35 Liverani 1990.

36 Schulman 1964: 61.

37 These letters were analyzed by Pintore (1972) and Na'aman (1990).

38   Kemp 1978: 17. Albright noted the "extraordinary extent" of the recriminations, unparalleled in any comparable archive. This he attributed to the demoralization of two centuries of Egyptian rule (1975: 104).

39   Cohen 2000.

40   Morris 2006.

41   Darnell and Manassa 2007: 156–72.

42   Mohammad 1959.

43   Morris 2006: 195.

44   Kemp amazingly makes hardly any reference to Akhenaten (1978).

45   Hachmann 1982.

46   Liverani 1967.

47   Several 1972.

48   Giles 1970: 158, 174.

49   Cumming 1982–95: III, 1552, 1554, 1556.

50   If the "Aten scarab" is genuine.

51   For example, TT 95 (Cumming 1982–95: III, 1570).

52   Giveon 1969. He is usually taken to be Thutmose III, but Giveon favors Thutmose IV, and the appeal to memory is more likely to the more recent king. Aldred thought it was Amenhotep III (1968: 240).

53   Goetze 1975: 2.

54   Weinstein 1998.

55   Darnell and Manassa 2007: 142.

56   Schulman 1964: 69.

57   Na'aman 1990.

58   Cohen and Westbrook 2000: 232.

59   Klengel 1965: 133.

60   Hachmann 1982: 49.

61   Hachmann 1982.

62   Murnane 2000a.

63   Aldred 1968: 259.

64   Gardiner 1961: 230; he thought that it was Amenhotep III who ignored appeals for help against the advancing Hittites (*EA* 53–55, 59), but these were actually addressed to Akhenaten.

65   Redford 1984: 193–94.

66   Samson 1973a: 50.

67   This letter has been analyzed by Pintore (1983) to provide the most basic insights into the pharaoh's understanding of hierarchical relations. Unlike the usual formulaic demand for supplies or services, it responds to a particular situation. Pintore understands line 14 not (as Moran 1992: 248) as referring to the men whom Aziru handed over to Rib-Hadda ("Were you ignorant of the treacherousness of these men?"), but as a general judgment on mankind: "Were you ignorant of the treacherousness of men?"

68   Hoffmeier and van Dijk 2010: 205.

69   Aldred 1968: 241.

70   Murnane 1995: [99].

71   Leprohon 1985: 97–98.

72 Gabolde 1998: 195–205. It must be noted that Gabolde dates these movements to shortly before and after Akhenaten's death because he believed the Egyptian queen who wrote to Suppuliliumas to be Nefertiti. The one chronological indicator we have is the *terminus ante quem* of the stela.

73 Schulman in Redford 1988: 53–79.

74 W.R. Johnson 2009.

75 Schulman 1978.

76 Bryce 1998: 185–86, 189.

77 Davies, 1903–1908: II, 42; Drenkhahn 1967; Giles 1970: 196; Redford 1984: 186; Aldred 1988: 279.

78 Darnell 1991: 123–24.

79 Darnell and Manassa 2007: 172–78.

80 Murnane 1995: [55–56].

81 Helck 1980.

82 Legrain 1929: fig. 87; Chevrier 1955: pl. 1.

83 Schulman 1982; see also Darnell and Manassa 2007: 118–19.

Notes to Chapter Seven

1   Fundamental is Samson 1982b.

2   Davies 1903–1908: II, pl. 41; Murnane 1995: [95A].

3   Lepsius 1849–59: VI, pls. 98–99; copies also survive made by Hay, L'Hôte, and Prisse d'Avennes.

4   Cairo JE 62654 (Beinlich and Saleh 1989: 20 [46gg]).

5   The squeeze was obscurely published in Moseley 2009: 144, fig. 7.8, and a drawing based on it inserted into Davies's copy of the scene in Dodson 2009a: 27–29.

6   Nicholson 1870.

7   Malek 1996.

8   Murnane 1995: [94].

9   Bouriant 1893: 70–71; Gardiner 1928.

10 Borchardt 1912: 28.

11 Cairo JE 61500 (Beinlich and Saleh 1989: 4 [1k]; Murnane 1995: [92]).

12 This is, remarkable to say, mentioned by many but pictured by few; it is illustrated by Reeves 1990: 193 and Dodson 2009b: 34.

13 Reeves 1990: 169.

14 Cairo JE 62172 (Beinlich and Saleh 1989: 185 [405]).

15 Loeben 1991.

16 Pendlebury 1951: III, pl. 107; Murnane 1995: [93A].

17 Samson 1972: 103–106; Dodson 2009b: 43.

18 Roeder 1959: pl. 16 [406/VIIA].

19 Petrie 1894: 42–43; 1896: 219.

20 Newberry 1928a.

21 Newberry 1928b; Schäfer 1931: pl. 33; Aldred 1973: no. 120.

22 Gardiner 1928.

23 Glanville 1929a.

24 Fairman quoted in Pendlebury 1951: 232–33.

25 Roeder 1958. This essay is marred by chaotic organization and mistakes in references, while the details in the chronological table do not correspond with the text. As Redford pointed out, Roeder's methods in identifying portraits are far from convincing (Redford 1967: 172).
26 For the whole controversy over KV 55, see chapter 8.
27 Cairo JE 59294; Aldred 1973: fig. 49.
28 Cairo JE 44866; Aldred 1973: fig. 54.
29 Berlin ÄM 15000; Aldred 1973: [120].
30 MMA 26.7.1396; Aldred 1973: [21].
31 Desroches-Noblecourt 1963: 109, 120, 165–68.
32 Aldred 1968: 243, 246.
33 Helck 1969a: 203–13. More fantastic musings about this time may be consigned to this note: Giles at one time dated Smenkhkare's coregency to Year 12, at another to Year 14/15. There was "more than tentative evidence" of a homosexual relationship with Akhenaten. And there is, he suggested, a possibility that Smenkhkare was murdered (Giles 1970: 88–90, 95–106).
34 Munro 1969.
35 Pendlebury 1951: pl. 86 [35].
36 Gardiner 1961: 440; Manetho 6.21.
37 Munro 1969.
38 For the box, Cairo JE 61495, see Beinlich and Saleh 1989: 31–32 [79/574]; for the sequins, see ch. 7, n. 4, above.
39 Samson essentially repeated these arguments (1973b, 1976).
40 Tawfik 1975; 1981: 471.
41 Krauss 1978.
42 Krauss 1978: 48–53.
43 Murnane 1982.
44 Not in Roeder 1969: 56–57[III.N.3].
45 Murnane 1995: [38].
46 Allen 1988.
47 Allen 1991, restated three years later 1994. Laboury attributes this breakthrough, of course, to Gabolde (2010: 334).
48 Malek 1996.
49 Gardiner 1961: 440; Manetho 6.21.
50 Gabolde 1998: 162–66, 213–26.
51 Allen 2009.
52 Dodson 2009b: 29–36; 2014a: 143–46.
53 Petrie 1894: 42–44.
54 Breasted 1909: 391–93.
55 Wolf 1930: 100–102.
56 Pendlebury 1935: 28.
57 Engelbach 1940: 135–43.
58 Fairman, in Pendlebury 1951: 157.
59 Drioton and Vandier 1952: 346–47.
60 Seele 1955: 173–74.
61 Wilson 1956: 231.

62   Roeder 1958.

63   Murnane 1995: [99].

64   Hayes 1959: 296–97.

65   Gardiner 1961: 232–33.

66   Desroches-Noblecourt 1963: 109, 120, 165–68.

67   Redford 1967: 170–82.

68   Aldred 1968: 242–46.

69   Munro 1969.

70   Roeder 1959: pl. 17 [500/VIIIC].

71   Helck 1969a: 203–13.

72   Beckerath 1967: 11—but the next entry relates back to the daughter. Hari thought that Akencheres was Mutnedjmet, who he argued ruled between Ay and Horemheb (1965: 227).

73   Murnane 1983: 282.

74   Roeder 1959: pl. 10 [826/VIIIA].

75   Murnane 1995: [98B].

76   Krauss 1978: 203–13; see Murnane for the "Restoration Stela" (1995: [99]). Murnane rejects Krauss's date.

77   Helck 1981: 207.

78   Helck 1984a.

79   Dodson 1981.

80   Robins 1981.

81   Redford 1984: 185–92.

82   Tyldesley 1998: 160–75.

83   Davies 1903–1908: I, pl. 10; II, pl. 13; III, pl. 31.

84   Reeves 2001: 162–77.

85   Roeder 1959: pl. 10 (826/VIIIA).

86   Helck 2001: 58.

87   Dodson 2009a: 38–52. Five years later, he assigned Smenkhkare to "soon after" Year 12, and Nefertiti's elevation as coregent to Year 17, based on the then-new Bersha graffito, with Neferneferuaten's reign spanning the transition Akhenaten–Tutankhamun (2014a: 144).

88   Laboury 2010: 329–45.

89   Manniche 1987: 136.

90   I thank most sincerely the series editors for this very important suggestion.

91   Eaton-Krauss 2003: 195.

92   How is one to rely on Manetho, whose account of the Eighteenth Dynasty is a nightmare? He begins with Thutmose I, omits Hatshepsut (instead apparently listing Amenhotep I's mother Ahmes-Nefertiry), conceals Thutmose III under "Misphragmuthosis" (which is supposedly Menkheperure Thutmose), conceals Tutankhamun under "Rathotes," and concludes with some *three* kings (one a woman) all called "Akencheres," and all reigning twelve years.

Notes to Chapter Eight

1   Thomas 1966: 81–82; Schaden 1979; Reeves 1990: 40–42.
2   Blackman 1917: 45.
3   Barsanti 1894.
4   Sayce 1923: 282; Pendlebury 1935: 31–32.
5   Martin 1974–89: I, 37.
6   Bouriant 1896.
7   Bouriant, Legrain, and Jéquier 1903: 5–23.
8   Pendlebury 1931b.
9   Hamza 1940.
10   Martin 1974–89: I, 105.
11   Kamal 1935.
12   Martin 1974–89. Translations of texts are provided conveniently in Murnane 1995: [46]. Martin worked at the tomb from 18 January to 21 March 1980: what such study entailed is revealed by his note that this required a brisk walk two hours each way each day. It was, however, "one of the happiest experiences of many years' work in Egypt" (1974–89: II, ix).
13   Martin 1974–89: I, 104.
14   Martin 1974–89: II, 30.
15   Martin 1974–89: II, 32.
16   Martin 1974–89: II, 38.
17   Sethe 1921: 115–16.
18   Krauss, in *Tutanchamun in Köln* (1980): 51–52.
19   Gabolde 1998: 118–24. He later read the name of Nefertiti in front of the nurse in room *gamma*, and restored the rest of the inscription to include the name of Tutankhamun, as the son of Nefertiti and Akhenaten (2002: 42). As Vandersleyen declared, "to draw such an important conclusion from such vanished traces is unacceptable" (1993: 193).
20   Bell 1985; Murnane 2001: 15; van Dijk 2009; Dodson 2009a: 23.
21   I thank most sincerely Professor Salima Ikram for pointing this out.
22   Vandersleyen 1993.
23   Martin 1974–89: I, 16–30.
24   To distinguish the lower and major part of the coffin which holds the body from its lid, I have used the term used by Carter and Mace 1923–33: II, 73.
25   Raven 1994.
26   Brock 1996.
27   Samson 1985: 93.
28   We now have a fully rounded portrait of Davis by Adams, and eagerly await the transcription of the diary of his mistress Emma Andrews, who accompanied him in Egypt (Adams 2013).
29   Davis 1910: 1–41. This publication offered the first of what Alfred Grimm could in 2001 count as thirty-one theories concerning the tomb (Grimm 2001a).
30   Davis 1910: 1. They were, in fact, the right door and the right side of the shrine.
31   Davis 1910: 2–3.
32   Davis 1910: 2–3.
33   Davis 1910: 7–10.

34 Davis 1910: 13–40. For a checklist of all items known from the tomb, see Martin 1985: 117–20.
35 Sayce 1907.
36 G.E. Smith 1907.
37 Lombroso 1891: 336–52.
38 G.E. Smith 1912: 51–56.
39 Aldred 1961b: 57 n.5.
40 G.E. Smith 1926.
41 Davis 1910: xiii–xxii.
42 Maspero added an account of his own in the *Journal des débats*. He implied that Davis was the first to enter the tomb; he confused Tiye's shrine with the sledge on which the coffin was carried; the mummy was described as "rolled in twenty flexible gold plates" (1907b).
43 Republished in Maspero 1913: 113.
44 J.L. Smith 1958: 45–75.
45 Daressy 1916.
46 Most scholars today accept that Thutmose's alleged jubilee was simply a prospective wish and that he died after only a decade of reign.
47 Sethe 1921: 122–30.
48 Weigall 1922a: xxvii; Weigall 1922b; Hankey 2001: 90.
49 Engelbach 1931: 98–114.
50 Derry 1931.
51 Gardiner 1957.
52 Thomas 1961.
53 Gardiner 1959.
54 Aldred 1957a.
55 Roeder 1958.
56 Murnane 1995: [45A].
57 Fairman 1961.
58 Aldred 1961b.
59 Aldred 1957a.
60 Aldred 1961b.
61 Aldred 1961b.
62 Bosse-Griffiths 1961.
63 Aldred 1962.
64 Harrison 1966; Aldred rightly stated that this was a "minute and fully documented investigation which set entirely new standards in the medical examination of the royal mummies" (1988: 201).
65 This comparison was later used by Dodson to attribute the original ownership of that coffin to Smenkhkare (2009a: 41–42; cf. p. 306).
66 Aldred 1968: 151–54; résuméd in 1988, ch. 18, where Perepelkin's evidence was accepted: the coffin originally for Kiya, and the mummy of Smenkhkare. The tomb was a "family vault"!
67 Perepelkin 1978: 26–35, 131–67.
68 Millar 1972.
69 Reeves 1981.

70   Martin 1985.
71   Krauss 1986.
72   Aldred 1988: 195–218.
73   Hussein and Harris 1988.
74   Allen 1988.
75   G.E. Smith 1912: 27, 31, 34.
76   Bell 1990.
77   Dodson 1992.
78   Filer 2000.
79   Helck 2001.
80   Cf. Reeves 1990: 57 n.147, pl. 3.
81   Grimm 2001b and c.
82   Gabolde reasserted that the mummy was Akhenaten's. While upholding the
     reliability of the ancient rewrappers of the royal mummies, he tried to undermine
     modern anatomical analysis (2009; 2013).
83   Hawass et al. 2010.
84   Rationalized most recently by Dodson 2009a: 38–39.
85   Hawass et al. 2010.
86   Reeve and Adams 1993.
87   Molleson and Cox 1993: 169.
88   Cross 2008.
89   Cross 2009; 2014: 146–48.
90   Dodson 2009a: 76; 2014a: 159–60.
91   Aldred 1988: 195.
92   T.G.H. 1992: 134.
93   Aldred 1961b: 53.
94   Fairman 1961: 37.

Bibliography

Abbreviations for periodicals used in bibliography

AncEg   *Ancient Egypt Magazine* (Manchester: Ancient Egypt Magazine)

AO   *Acta Orientalia* (Copenhagen: Munksgaard)

ASAE   *Annales du service des antiquités de l'Égypte* (Cairo: Institut français d'archéologie orientale/Supreme Council of Antiquities Press)

BASOR   *Bulletin of the American Schools of Oriental Research*

BIFAO   *Bulletin de l'Institut français d'archéologie orientale du Caire* (Cairo: Institut français d'archéologie orientale)

BHM   *Bulletin de la Société française d'histoire de la médecine*

BiOr   *Bibliotheca Orientalis* (Leiden: Nederlands Instituut voor het Nabije Oosten)

BMMA   *Bulletin of the Metropolitan Museum of Art* (New York: Metropolitan Museum of Art)

BSEG   *Bulletin de la Société d'égyptologie de Genève* (Geneva: Societé d'égyptologie de Genève)

BSFE   *Bulletin de la Societé français d'égyptologie* (Paris: Societé français d'égyptologie)

CdE	*Chronique d'Egypte* (Brussels: Fondation égyptologique Reine Elisabeth)
EgArch	*Egyptian Archaeology: The Bulletin of the Egypt Exploration Society* (London: Egypt Exploration Society)
GM	*Göttinger Miszellen* (Göttingen: Universität Göttingen, Ägyptologisches Seminar)
JA	*Journal Asiatique* (Paris: Société asiatique)
JAMA	*Journal of the American Medical Association* (Chicago: American Medical Association)
JAOS	*Journal of the American Oriental Society* (New Haven, &c: American Oriental Society)
JARCE	*Journal of the American Research Center in Egypt* (New York, &c: Eisenbraun)
JCS	*Journal of Cuneiform Studies* (Cambridge MA: American Schools of Oriental Research)
JEA	*Journal of Egyptian Archaeology* (London: Egypt Exploration Fund/Society)
JEH	*Journal of Ecclesiastical History*
JMAA	*Journal of Mediterranean Anthropology and Archaeology* (Xanthi: Anthropological Museum of the International Demokritos Foundation)
JNES	*Journal of Near Eastern Studies* (Chicago: Chicago University Press)
JSSEA	*Journal of the Society for the Study of Egyptian Antiquities* (Toronto: Society for the Study of Egyptian Antiquities)
Kmt	*Kmt: A Modern Journal of Ancient Egypt* (San Francisco, &c: Kmt Communications)
MDAIK	*Mitteilungen des Deutschen Archäologischen Instituts, Kairo* (Mainz: Philipp von Zabern)
MDOG	*Mitteilungen der Deutschen Orient-Gesellschaft zu Berlin* (Berlin: Deutschen Orient-Gesellschaft)
OLZ	*Orientalistische Literaturzeitung* (Leipzig: Hinrichs'/Berlin: Akademie Verlag)
OMRO	*Oudheidkundige Mededelingen uit het Rijksmuseum van Oudheden te Leiden* (Leiden: Rijksmuseum van Oudheden)
PEQ	*Palestine Exploration Quarterly*

PSBA	*Proceedings of the Society for Biblical Archaeology* (London: Society for Biblical Archaeology)
RAL	*Rendiconti dell'Accademia Nzaionale dei Lincei*
RdE	*Revue d'égyptologie* (Leuven: Peeters)
REA	*Revue des études anciennes*
RecTrav	*Recueil de travaux relatifs à la philologie et à l'archéologie égyptiennes et assyriennes* (Paris: Librairie Edouard Champion)
SAK	*Studien zur altägyptschen Kultur* (Hamburg: H. Buske Verlag)
S&N	*Sudan and Nubia: The Sudan Archaeological Society Bulletin* (London: The Sudan Archaeological Research Society)
SPAW	*Sitzungsberichte der Preussischen Akademie der Wissenschaften, Berlin*
TRSL	*Transactions of the Royal Society of Literature* (London: Royal Society of Literature)
ZÄS	*Zeitschrift für Ägyptische Sprache und Altertumskunde* (Leipzig: J.C. Hinrichs'sche Buchhandlung/Berlin: Akademie Verlag)

Bibliography

Abraham, K. 1935. "Amenhotep IV: A Psycho-analytical Contribution to the Understanding of His Personality and the Monotheistic Cult of Aton." *Psychoanalytic Quarterly* 3: 537–69.

Adam, H., and F. El-Shaboury. 1959. "Report on the Work of Karnak during the Seasons 1954–5 and 1955–6." *ASAE* 56: 35–52.

Adams, J. 2013. *The Millionaire and the Mummies: Theodore Davis's Gilded Age in the Valley of the Kings.* New York: St. Martin's Press.

Albright, W. 1946. "Cuneiform Material for Egyptian Prosopography." *JNES* 5: 7–25.

———. 1975. "The Amarna Letters from Palestine." In *Cambridge Ancient History* II/2: *History of the Middle East and the Aegean region, c.1380–1000 B.C.*, edited by I.E.S. Edwards, 98–116. Cambridge: Cambridge University Press.

Aldred, C. 1957a. "Hair Styles and History." *BMMA* NS 15: 141–47.

———. 1957b. "The End of the El-'Amārna period." *JEA* 43: 30–41.

———. 1957c. "Year 12 at El-'Amārna." *JEA* 43: 114–17.

———. 1959. "The Beginning of the El-'Amārna period." *JEA* 45: 19–33.

———. 1961a. *New Kingdom Art in Ancient Egypt during the Eighteenth Dynasty.* London: Tiranti.

———. 1961b. "The Tomb of Akhenaten at Thebes," *JEA* 41: 41–60.

———. 1962. "The Pharaoh Akhenaten: A Problem in Egyptology and Pathology." *Bulletin of the History of Medicine* 36: 293–316.

———. 1968. *Akhenaten, Pharaoh of Egypt: A New Study*. London: Thames and Hudson.

———. 1973. *Akhenaten and Nefertiti*. New York: Brooklyn Museum.

———. 1976. "The Horizon of the Aten." *JEA* 62: 184.

———. 1988. *Akhenaten, King of Egypt*. London: Thames and Hudson.

Allen, J.P. 1988. "Two Altered Inscriptions of the Late Amarna Period." *JARCE* 25: 117–26.

———. 1989. "The Natural Philosophy of Akhenaten." In *Religion and Philosophy in Ancient Egypt*, edited by W.K. Simpson, 89–101. New Haven: Yale University Press.

———. 1991. "Akhenaten's Mystery Co-regent and Successor." *Amarna Letters* 1: 74–85.

———. 1994. "Nefertiti and Smenkh-ka-re." *GM* 141: 7–17.

———. 1996. "Religion in Amarna." In *The Royal Women of Amarna*, edited by D. Arnold, 3–5. New York: Metropolitan Museum of Art.

———. 2009. "The Amarna Succession." In *Causing His Name to Live: Studies in Egyptian Epigraphy and History in Memory of William J. Murnane*, edited by P.J. Brand and L. Cooper, 9–20. Leiden: Brill.

———. 2010. "The Original Owner of Tutankhamun's Canopic Coffins." In *Millions of Jubilees: Studies in Honor of David P. Silverman* 1, edited by Z. Hawass and J. Houser Wegner, 27–41. Cairo: Conseil suprême des antiquités.

Ameline, M., and P. Querey. 1920. "Le pharaon Amenophis IV, sa mentalité: Fut-il atteint de lipodystrophie progressive?" *Revue neurologique* 36: 448–62.

Andreu, G. 1987. "Le policier S'sha: A propos de quelques talatat du IXe pylône de Karnak." *BIFAO* 87: 1–20.

Angenot, V. 2008. "Le role de parallaxe dans l'iconographie d'Akhenaton." *BSFE* 171: 28–50.

Anthes, R. 1952. *Die Maat des Echnaton und Amarna*. Baltimore: American Oriental Society.

———. 1968. *The Head of Queen Nofretete*. Berlin: Mann.

Anus, P. 1971. "Un domaine thébain d'époque amarnienne." *BIFAO* 69: 69–88.

Arnold, D., ed. 1996a. *Royal Women of Amarna*. New York: Metropolitan Museum of Art.

———. 1996b. "An Artistic Revolution: The Early Years of King Amenhotep IV/Akhenaten." In *Royal Women of Amarna*, edited by D. Arnold, 17–39. New York: Metropolitan Museum of Art.

———. 1996c. "The Workshop of the Sculptor Thutmose." In *Royal Women of Amarna*, edited by D. Arnold, 41–83. New York: Metropolitan Museum of Art.

———. 1996d. "Aspects of the Royal Female Image During the Amarna Period." In *Royal Women of Amarna*, edited by D. Arnold, 85–119. New York: Metropolitan Museum of Art.

Arramon, J., and E. Crubezy. 1994. "Le pharaon Akhenaten avait-il une maladie auto-motive?" *Synoviale* 28: 30–33.

Artzi, P. 2000. "The Diplomatic Service in Action: The Mitanni File." In *Amarna Diplomacy*, edited by R. Cohen and R. Westbrook, 205–11. Baltimore: Johns Hopkins University Press.

Asselberghs, H. 1923. "Ein merkwürdiges Relief Amenophis IV." *ZÄS* 58: 36–38.

Assmann, J. 1972a. "Die Häresie des Echnaton: Aspekte der Amarna-religion." *Saeculum* 23: 109–26.

———. 1972b. "Palast oder Tempel? Überlegungen zur Architektur u. Topographie von Amarna." *JNES* 31: 143–55.

———. 1980. "Die loyalistische Lehre Echnatons." *SAK* 8: 1–32.

———. 1989. "State and Religion in the New Kingdom." In *Religion and Philosophy in Ancient Egypt*, edited by W. Simpson, 55–88. New Haven: Yale University Press.

———. 1992. "Akhanyati's Theology of Light and Time." *Proceedings of the Israel Academy of Sciences and Humanities* 7/4: 143–76.

———. 1995. *Egyptian Solar Religion in the New Kingdom: Re, Amun and the Crisis of Polytheism*. Translated by A. Alcock. London: Kegan Paul.

———. 2003. *The Mind of Egypt: History and Meaning in the Time of the Pharaohs*. Translated by Andrew Jenkins. Cambridge MA: Harvard University Press.

———. 2004. "Theological Responses to Amarna." In *Egypt, Israel and the Ancient Mediterranean World*, edited by G. Knoppers and A. Hirsch, 179–91. Leiden: Brill.

Ayrton, E. 1907. "The Tomb of Thyi." *PSBA* 29: 85–86, 277–81.

Badawy, A. 1956. "Maru-Aten: Pleasure Resort of Temple?" *JEA* 42: 58–64.

———. 1961. "The Symbolism of the Temples at Amarna." *ZÄS* 87: 79–95.

———. 1968. *A History of Egyptian Architecture*, 3. Berkeley: University of California Press.

———. 1973. "Aberrations about Akhenaten." *ZÄS* 99: 65–72.

Baikie, J. 1926. *The Amarna Age*. London: A.C. Black.

Bakry, H. 1972. "Akhenaten at Heliopolis." *CdE* 47: 55–67.

Balcz, H., and K. Bittel 1932. "Grabungsbericht Hermopolis 1932." *MDAIK* 3: 9–45.

———. 1934. "Grabungsbericht Hermopolis 1933." *MDAIK* 5: 11–44.

Barsanti, A. 1894. "Sulla scoperta della tomba del faraone Amenofi IV." *RAL* 5/3: 245–48.

Barta, W. 1975. "Zur Darstellungsweise der Kolossalstatuen Amenophis IV aus Karnak." *ZÄS* 102: 91–94.

Beckerath, J. von. 1967. "Methode und Ergebnisse aegyptischer Chronologie. *OLZ* 62: 5–14.

———. 1975. "Eje." In *Lexikon der Ägyptologie*, 1, edited by W. Helck and E. Otto, 1211. Wiesbaden: Harassowitz.

———. 1997. *Chronologie des pharaonischen Ägypten*. Mainz: von Zabern.

Beinlich, H., and M. Saleh. 1989. *Corpus der Hieroglyphischen Inschriften aus dem Grab des Tutanchamun*. Oxford: Griffith Institute.

Bell, L. 1985. "A Possible Motif of Rebirth and Resurrection in New Kingdom Popular Art." In *Abstracts of Papers: Fourth International Congress of Egyptologists*, 9. Munich: International Association of Egyptologists.

Bell, M. 1990. "An Armchair Excavation of KV 55." *JARCE* 27: 97–137.

Bennett, J. 1965. "Notes on the Aten." *JEA* 51: 207–209.

Bentley, J. 1980. "Amenhotep III and Akhenaten: Co-regency Proved?" *JEA* 66: 164–65.

Beresford, J. 2010. "Tutankhamun's DNA." *Minerva*, May–June 2010: 8–10.

Bille-de-Mot, E. 1966. *The Age of Akhenaten*. London: Evelyn, Adams, and Mackay.

Blackman, A. 1917. "The Nugent and Haggard Collections." *JEA* 4: 43–46.

———. 1922. "A Study of the Liturgy Celebrated in the Temple of the Aten at el-Amarna." In *Recueil d'études égyptologiques dédiées à la memoire de Jean François Champollion*, 505–27. Paris: Ecole des Hautes-Etudes.

———. 1937. "Preliminary Report on the Excavations at Sesebi." *JEA* 23: 145–51.

Blankenbergh van Delden, C. 1969. *The Large Commemorative Scarabs of Amenhotep III*. Leiden: Brill.

Bogoslovskij, E. 1983. Review of Perepelkin 1967. *GM* 61: 53–63.

Bonnet, C. 2001. "Kerma, rapport préliminaire." *Kerma-Soudan* 49: 199–219.

Booth, C. 2009. *Horemheb: The Forgotten Pharaoh*. Stroud: Amberley.

Borchardt, L. 1905. "Der ägyptische Titel 'Vater des Gottes' als Bezeichnung für 'Vater oder Schwiegervater des Königs'." *Berichte über die Verhandlungen der Königlich-Sächsischen Gesellschaft der Wissenschaften, philosophische-historiche Klasse* 57: 254–70.

———. 1907. "Voruntersuchung von Tell el-Amarna im Januar 1907." *MDOG* 34: 14–31.

———. 1911. "Ausgrabungen in Tell el-Amarna 1911." *MDOG* 46: 1–32.

———. 1912. "Ausgrabungen in Tell el Amarna 1911/12." *MDOG* 50: 1–40.

———. 1913. "Ausgrabungen in Tell el Amarna 1912/1913." *MDOG* 52: 1–55.

———. 1914. "Ausgrabungen in Tell el Amarna 1913/1914." *MDOG* 55: 3–39.

———. 1915. "Excavations at Tell el-Amarna Egypt in 1913–1914." *Smithsonian Institution Annual Report* 1915: 445–57.

———. 1916. "Das ägyptischen Wohnhaus im 14 Jh.v.Ch." *Zeitschrift für Bauwesen* 66: 510–58.

———. 1917. "Aus der Arbeit an den Funden von Tell el-Amarna." *MDOG* 57: 1–32.

———. 1923. *Porträts der Konigen Nofretete aus den Grabungen 1912/1913 in Tell el-Amarna*. Leipzig: Deutsche Orient-Gesellschaft.

———. 1933. "Amenophis IV. Mitkönig in den letzten Jahren Amenophis III?" In *Allerhand Kleinigkeiten*, 23–29. Leipzig: Privatdruck.

Borchardt, L., and H. Ricke. 1980. *Die Wohnhäuser in Tell el-Amarna*. Berlin: Mann.

Bosse-Griffiths, K. 1961. "Finds from the Tomb of Queen Tiye in the Swansea Museum." *JEA* 47: 66–70.

———. 1977. "A Beset Amulet from the Amarna Period." *JEA* 63: 98–106.

———. 1980. "Two Lute-players of the Amarna Age." *JEA* 66: 70–82.

Bouriant, U. 1884. "Deux jours de fouilles à Tell el Amarna." In *Mémoires publiés par les membres de la mission archéologique français au Caire* 1: 1–22.

————. 1885. "A Thebes, II: A propos des débris du temple d'Aten à Karnak." *RecTrav* 6: 51–55.

————. 1893. "Notes de voyage." *RecTrav* 14: 67–74.

————. 1896. "Notes de voyage: 21: Tombeau royal." *RecTrav* 18: 144–50.

Bouriant, U., G. Legrain, and G. Jéquier. 1903. *Monuments pour servir à l'étude du culte d'Atonou en Egypte, tome premier: Les tombes de Khouitatonou.* Cairo: Institut français d'archéologie orientale.

Breasted, J.H. 1902/3. "A City of Ikhnaton in Nubia." *ZÄS* 40: 106–13.

————. 1906. *Ancient Records of Egypt.* 5 vols. Chicago: University of Chicago Press.

————. 1909. *History of Egypt.* 2nd ed. New York. Charles Scribner's Sons.

————. 1912. *The Development of Religion and Thought in Ancient Egypt.* London: Hodder and Stoughton.

Brock, E. 1996. "The Sarcophagus of Queen Tiy." *JSSEA* 26: 8–21.

Brugsch, H. 1862. *Recueil des monuments égyptiens dessinés sur lieux.* Leipzig: Hinrichs.

————. 1879. *History of Egypt under the Pharaohs.* Translated by P. Smith. 2 vols. London: Murray.

Brunner, H. 1938. "Eine neue Amarna Prinzessin." *ZÄS* 74: 104–108.

————. 1961. "Der 'Gottesvater' als Erzieher des Kronprinzen." *ZÄS* 86: 90–100.

————. 1962. "Echnaton und sein Versuch einer religiösen Reform." *Universitas* 17: 149–62.

Brunner-Traut, E. 1982. "Nofretete." In *Lexikon der Aegyptologie* 4, edited by W. Helck and E. Otto, 519–21. Wiesbaden: Harrassowitz.

Bryan, B. 1991. *The Reign of Thutmose IV.* Baltimore: Johns Hopkins University Press.

Bryce, T. 1990. "The Death of Niphururiya and Its Aftermath." *JEA* 76: 97–105.

————. 1998. *The Kingdom of the Hittites.* Oxford: Oxford University Press.

Budge, E.W. 1923. *Tutankhamen: Amenism, Atenism, and Egyptian Monotheism.* London: Martin Hopkinson.

Bunsen, C. 1848–67. *Egypt's Place in Universal History.* 5 vols. London: Longman.

Burridge, A. 1993. "Akhenaten: A New Perspective. Evidence of a Genetic Disorder in the Royal Family of 18th Dynasty Egypt." *JSSEA* 23: 63–73.

Cabrol, A. 2000: *Amenhotep III le magnifique.* Paris: Pygmalion.

Caminos, R., and T.G.H. James. 1963. *Gebel el Silsilah.* London: Egypt Exploration Society.

Campbell, E. 1964. *The Chronology of the Amarna Letters.* Baltimore: Johns Hopkins University Press.

Capart, J. 1957. "Dans le studio d'un artist." *CdE* 32: 199–217.

Carter, H., and A.C. Mace. 1923–33. *The Tomb of Tut.ankh.amen.* 3 vols. London: Cassel.

Cattaino, J., and L. Vicario. 1999. "Myotonic Dystrophy in Ancient Egypt." *European Neurology* 41: 59–63.

Cavaignac, E. 1930. "Les annales de Subbiluliumas." *REA* 32: 229–44.

Černý, J. 1952. *Ancient Egyptian Religion*. London: Hutchinson.

Champollion, J.-F. 1827. *Notice descriptive des monuments égyptiens au musée Charles X*. Paris: Crapelet.

———. 1835–45. *Monuments d'Egypte et de la Nubie*. Paris: Firmin Didot.

———. 1909. *Lettres et journaux écrits pendant le voyage d'Egypte*, ed. Hermine Hartleben. Paris: Leroux.

Chappaz, J-L. 1983. "Le premier édifice d'Amenophis IV à Karnak." *BSEG* 8: 13–42.

Chevrier, H. 1926. "Rapport sur les travaux de Karnak (mars–mai 1926)." *ASAE* 26: 119–30.

———. 1927. "Rapport (nov. 1926–mai 1927)." *ASAE* 27: 134–53.

———. 1928. "Rapport (1927–1928)." *ASAE* 28: 114–28.

———. 1929. "Rapport." *ASAE* 29: 133–49.

———. 1930. "Rapport (1929–1930)." *ASAE* 30: 159–73.

———. 1931. "Rapport (1930–1931)." *ASAE* 31: 81–97.

———. 1932. "Rapport (1931–1932)." *ASAE* 32: 97–114.

———. 1933. "Rapport (1932–1933)." *ASAE* 33: 167–86.

———. 1936. "Rapport (1935–1936)." *ASAE* 36: 131–57.

———. 1937. "Rapport (1936–1937)." *ASAE* 37: 173–200.

———. 1938. "Rapport (1937–1938)." *ASAE* 38: 567–608.

———. 1947. "Rapport." *ASAE* 46: 147–93.

———. 1949a. "Rapport (1947–1948)." *ASAE* 49: 1–35.

———. 1949b. "Rapport (1948–1949)." *ASAE* 49: 241–300.

———. 1950. "Rapport (1949–1950)." *ASAE* 50: 527–467.

———. 1952. "Rapport (1951–1952)." *ASAE* 52: 229–50.

———. 1955. "Rapport (1952–1953)." *ASAE* 53: 7–42.

———. 1956. "Chronologie des constructions de la salle hypostyle." *ASAE* 54: 35–38.

Chubb, M. 1954. *Nefertiti Lived Here*. London: Geoffrey Bles.

Clayton, P. 1994. *Chronicle of the Pharaohs*. London: Thames and Hudson.

Cohen, R. 2000. "Intelligence in the Amarna Letters." In *Amarna Diplomacy*, edited by R. Cohen and R. Westbrook, 85–98. Baltimore: Johns Hopkins University Press.

Cohen, R., and R. Westbrook, eds. 2000. *Amarna Diplomacy*. Baltimore: Johns Hopkins University Press.

Connolly, R.C., R. Harrison, and S. Ahmed. 1976. "Serological Evidence for the Parentage of Tut'ankhamūn and Smenkhkarē'." *JEA* 62: 184–86.

Cooney, J. 1965. *Amarna Reliefs from Hermopolis in American Collections*. Brooklyn: Brooklyn Museum.

Costa, P. 1978. "The Frontal Sinuses of the Remains Purported to be Akhenaten's." *JEA* 64: 76–79.

Crocker, P. 1985. "Status Symbols in the Architecture of el-Amarna." *JEA* 71: 52–65.

Cross, S.W. 2008. "The Hydrology of the Valley of the Kings." *JEA* 94: 303–12.

———. 2009. "The Re-Sealing of KV62." *AncEg* 10/2: 16–22.

————. 2014. "The Workmen's Huts and Stratigraphy in the Valley of the Kings." *JEA* 100: 133–50.

Cumming, B. 1982–95. *Egyptian Historical Records of the Later Eighteenth Dynasty*. 3 vols. Warminster: Aris & Phillips.

Daressy, G. 1893. "Tombeaux et stèles-limites de Hagi Qandil." *RecTrav* 15: 36–64.

————. 1901. "Rapport sur la trouvaille de Hatiay." *ASAE* 2: 1–13.

————. 1916. "Le cercueil de Khu-n-Aten." *BIFAO* 12: 145–59.

Darnell, J. 1991. "Supposed Depictions of Hittites in the Amarna Period." *SAK* 18: 113–40.

Darnell, J., and C. Manassa. 2007. *Tutankhamun's Armies: Battle and Conquest during Ancient Egypt's Late Eighteenth Dynasty*. Hoboken: Wiley.

Davies, N. de G. 1903–1908. *The Rock Tombs of El Amarna*. 6 vols. London: Egypt Exploration Fund.

————. 1920. "The Work of the Tytus Memorial Fund." *BMMA* 15 Supplement: 24–32.

————. 1921. "Mural Paintings in the City of Akhetaten." *JEA* 7: 1–7.

————. 1923a. "Akhenaten at Thebes." *JEA* 9: 132–52.

————. 1923b. "The Graphic Work of the Expedition." *BMMA* 18 Part II: 40–53.

————. 1933. *The Tomb of Menkheperrasonb*. London: Egypt Exploration Society.

————. 1941. *The Tomb of the Vizier Ramose*. London: Egypt Exploration Society.

————. 1943. *The Tomb of Rekh-mi-Re at Thebes*. London: Egypt Exploration Society.

Davis, T.M. 1907. *The Tomb of Iouiya and Touiyou*. London: Constable.

————. 1910. *The Tomb of Queen Tiyi*. London: Constable.

Dawson, W. 1924. "Note on Some Ostraka Found at el-'Amārnah." *JEA* 10: 133.

Derry, D. 1931. "Note on the Skeleton Hitherto Believed to be that of King Akhenaten." *ASAE* 31: 115–19.

Desroches-Noblecourt, C. 1963. *Tutankhamen*. London: Michael Joseph.

————. 1972. "Un buste monumental d'Amenophis IV." *Revue du Louvre* 4/5: 239–50.

————. 1974. "La statue colossale fragmentaire d'Amenophis IV." *Fondation Piot. Monuments et mémoires* 59: 1–44.

————. 1984/85. "Les vestiges du règne d'Amenophis IV découverts dans le domaine de Monthou à Tod." *ASAE* 70: 253–76.

Dodson, A. 1981. "Nefertiti's Regality: A Comment." *JEA* 67: 179.

————. 1990. "Crown Prince Djhutmose and the Royal Sons of the Eighteenth Dynasty." *JEA* 76: 87–96.

————. 1992. "KV 55 and the End of the Reign of Akhenaten." In *VI Congresso Internazionale di Egittologia* I, 135–39. Torino: Sesto congresso internazionale d'Egittologia.

————. 2002. "The Canopic Coffinettes of Tutankhamun and the Identity of

Ankhkheperure." In *Egyptian Museum Collections around the World: Studies for the Centennial of the Egyptian Museum, Cairo*, edited by M. Eldamaty and M. Trad, I, 275–85. Cairo: Supreme Council of Antiquities.

———. 2009a. *Amarna Sunset: Nefertiti, Tutankhamun, Ay, Horemheb, and the Egyptian Counter-Reformation*. Cairo: American University in Cairo Press.

———. 2009b. "Amarna Sunset: The Late-Amarna Succession Revisited." In *Beyond the Horizon: Studies in Egyptian Art, Archaeology and History in Honour of Barry J. Kemp*, edited by S. Ikram and A. Dodson, 29–43. Cairo: Supreme Council of Antiquities Press.

———. 2009c. "On the Alleged 'Amenhotep III/IV Coregency' Graffito at Meidum." *GM* 222: 25–28.

———. 2014a. *Amarna Sunrise: From Golden Age to Age of Heresy*. Cairo: American University in Cairo Press.

———. 2014b. "The Coregency Conundrum." *Kmt* 25/2: 28–35.

Dodson, A., and D. Hilton. 2004. *The Complete Royal Families of Ancient Egypt*. London: Thames and Hudson.

Doresse, M. 1955. "Les temples atoniens de la région thébaine." *Orientalia* 24: 113–35.

Doresse, M., and J. Doresse. 1941/42. "Le culte d'Aton sous la XVIII dynastie." *JA* 233: 181–99.

Dorman, P.F. 2009. "The Long Coregency Revisited: Architectural and Iconographic Conundra in the Tomb of Kheruef." In *Causing His Name to Live: Studies in Egyptian Epigraphy and History in Memory of William J. Murnane*, edited by P.J. Brand and L. Cooper, 65–82. Leiden: Brill.

Drenkhahn, R. 1967. "Ausländer (Hethither und Marijannu?) in Amarna." *MDAIK* 22: 60–63.

Drioton, E. 1943. "Trois documents d'époque amarnienne." *ASAE* 43: 15–43.

Drioton, E., and J. Vandier. 1952. *L'Egypte*. 3rd ed. Paris: Presses universitaires de France.

Eaton-Krauss, M. 1977. "The *khat* Headdress to the End of the Amarna Period." *SAK* 5: 21–39.

———. 1981. "Miscellanea Amarniensia." *CdE* 56: 245–64.

———. 1983. "Eine rundplastische Darstellung Achenatens als Kinde." *ZÄS* 110: 127–32.

———. 1984. "Ramses II." In *Lexikon der Aegyptologie* 5, edited by W. Helck and E. Otto, 108–14. Wiesbaden: Harrassowitz.

———. 1988. "Tutankhamun at Karnak." *MDAIK* 44: 1–11.

———. 1990. "Akhenaten versus Akhenaten." *Orientalia* 47: 541–59.

———. 2003. "Restorations and Erasures in the Post-Amarna Period." In *Egyptology at the Dawn of the Twenty-first Century: Proceedings of the Eighth International Congress of Egyptologists*, edited by Z. Hawass and L. Pinch Brock, 194–201. Cairo: American University in Cairo Press.

Edel, E. 1948. "Neue keilinschriftliche Unterschreibung." *JNES* 7: 11–24.

Edwards, E. 1977. *Tutankhamun: The Tomb and Its Treasures*. New York: Metropolitan Museum of Art.

Engelbach, R. 1915. *Riqqah and Memphis VI*. London: Egyptian Research Account.

————. 1931. "The So-called Coffin of Akhenaten." *ASAE* 31: 98–114.

————. 1940. "Material for a Revision of the Heresy Period." *ASAE* 40: 133–84.

Englund, G. 1978. Akh: *Une notion religieuse dans l'Egypte pharaonique.* Uppsala: Almqvist & Wiksell.

Epigraphic Survey. 1980. *The Tomb of Kheruef.* Chicago: Oriental Institute.

Erman, A. 1952. *La religion des Egyptiens.* 3rd ed. Translated by H. Wild. Paris: Payot.

Ertman, E. 1976. "The Cap Crown of Nefertiti." *JARCE* 13: 63–67.

————. 1992a. "Is There Visual Evidence for a King Nefertiti?" *Amarna Letters* 2: 51–55.

————. 1992b. "The Search for the Significance and Origin of Nefertiti's Tall Blue Crown." In *VI Congresso internazionale di Egittologia* 1, 189–93. Turin: Sesto congresso internazionale d'Egittologia.

Evelyn-White, H. 1915. "The Egyptian Expedition 1914–1915." *BMMA* 10: 253–56.

Fairman, H.W. 1935. "Topographical Notes on the Central City, Tell el-'Amarnah." *JEA* 21: 136–39.

————. 1960. "A Block of Amenophis IV from Athribis." *JEA* 46: 80–82.

————. 1961. "Once Again the So-called Coffin of Akhenaten." *JEA* 47: 25–40.

Fakhry, A. 1935. "Blocs décorés provenant du temple de Louxor." *ASAE* 35: 35–51.

Fecht, G. 1960. "Amarna Probleme." *ZÄS* 85: 83–118.

————. 1967. "Zur Frühform der Amarna Theologie." *ZÄS* 94: 25–50.

Federn, W. 1960. "Dahamunzu." *JCS* 14: 33.

Fenwick, H. 2006. "The Amarna Survey." *JEA* 92: 52–54.

Filer, J. 1995. *Disease.* London: British Museum Publications.

————. 2000. "The KV55 Body: The Facts." *EgArch* 17: 13–14.

Fischer, H. 1976. "An Early Example of Atenist Iconoclasm." *JARCE* 13: 131–32.

Fletcher, J. 2000: *Chronicle of a Pharaoh: The Intimate Life of Amenhotep III.* Oxford: Oxford University Press.

————. 2003. "Looking for Nefertiti." *Weekend Australian Magazine* 19–20 July: 20–27.

————. 2004. *The Search for Nefertiti.* London: Hodder and Stoughton.

Forbes, D. 1992. "Who Stands in Pharaoh's Shadow on Karnak's Third Pylon?" *Amarna Letters* 2: 9–17.

————. 1998. *Tombs, Treasures and Mummies.* Sebastapol: KMT Communications.

Forrer, E.E. 1922–26. *Die Boghazkoi Texte in Umschrift.* 2 vols. Leipzig: Hinrich.

Foster, J. 1999. "The New Religion." In *Pharaohs of the Sun,* edited by R. Freed, Y. Markowitz, and S. D'Auria, 97–109. Boston: Museum of Fine Arts.

Frankfort, H., ed. 1929. *The Mural Painting of el-'Amarnah.* London: Egypt Exploration Fund.

Frankfort, H., and J.D.S. Pendlebury. 1933. *The City of Akhenaten,* 2: *The North Suburb and the Desert Altars.* London: Egypt Exploration Society.

Freed, R. 1999. "Art in the Service of Religion and the State." In *Pharaohs of the Sun*, edited by R. Freed, Y. Markowitz and S. D'Auria, 110–30. Boston: Museum of Fine Arts.

Friedman, F. 1986. "*Akh* in the Amarna Period." *JARCE* 23: 99–106.

Friedrich, J. 1925. *Aus dem hetitischen Schrifttum*. Leipzig: Hinrich.

Fritz, W. 1991. "Bemerkungen zum Datierungsvermark auf der Amarnatafel Kn 27." *SAK* 18: 207–14.

Gabolde, M. 1998. *D'Akhenaton à Tutankhamoun*. Lyon: Université Lumière-Lyon 2.

———. 2002. "La parenté de Toutankhamon." *BSFE* 155: 32–48.

———. 2009. "Under a Deep Blue Starry Sky." In *Causing His Name to Live: Studies in Egyptian Epigraphy and History in Memory of William J. Murnane*, edited by P.J. Brand and L. Cooper, 109–20. Leiden: Brill.

———. 2013. "L'ADN de la famille royalle amarnienne et les sources égyptiennes." *Egypte nilotique et méditerranéenne* 6: 177–203.

Gabra, S. 1931. "Un temple d'Amenophis IV à Assiut." *CdE* 6: 237–43.

Gardiner, A. 1928. "The Graffito from the Tomb of Pere." *JEA* 14: 10–11.

———. 1945. "Regnal Years and Civil Calendar in Pharaonic Egypt." *JEA* 31: 11–28.

———. 1953. "The Coronation of King Horemheb." *JEA* 39: 13–31.

———. 1957. "The So-called Tomb of Queen Tiye." *JEA* 43: 10–25.

———. 1959. Review of J. Smith, *Tombs, Temples and Ancient Art. JEA* 45: 107–108.

———. 1961. *Egypt of the Pharaohs*. Oxford: Oxford University Press.

Germer, R. 1984. "Die angebliche Mumie der Teje. Probleme interdisciplinärer Arbeiten." *SAK* 2: 85–90.

———. 2001. "Die Mumie aus dem Sarg in KV55." In *Das Geheimnis der goldenen Sarges*, edited by A. Grimm and S. Schoske, 58–63. Munich: Staatliches Museum.

Ghaliounghui, P. 1947. "A Medical Study of Akhenaten." *ASAE* 47: 29–46.

Gilbert, P. 1964. "Les corégences d'Amenophis IV et l'art thébain durant la période amarnienne." *CdE* 39: 15–24.

———. 1962. "La filiation de Toutankhamon." *CdE* 37: 19–22.

Gilderdale, P. 1984. "The Early Amarnan Canon." *GM* 81: 7–20.

Giles, F. 1970. *Ikhnaton: Legend and History*. London: Hutchison.

———. 1997. *The Amarna Age: Western Asia*. Warminster: Aris and Phillips.

———. 2001. *The Amarna Age: Egypt*. Warminster: Aris and Phillips.

Girling, R., and P. Bennett. 2003a. "Looking for Nefertiti." *The Weekend Australian Magazine* (19–20 July): 20–27.

———. 2003b. "Nefertiti." *The Weekend Australian Magazine* (26–27 July): 21–27.

Giveon, R. 1969. "Tuthmosis IV and Asia." *JNES* 28: 54–59.

Glanville, S. 1929a. "Amenophis IV and His Successors in the Eighteenth Dynasty." In *Great Ones of Ancient Egypt*, edited by W. Brunton, 105–39. London: Hodder and Stoughton.

———. 1929b. "Notes on Material for the Reign of Amenophis III." *JEA* 15: 3–8.

Goetze, A. 1951. Review of E. Cavaignac, *Les Hittites*. *JAOS* 71: 79.

———. 1975. "The Struggle for the Domination of Syria 1400–1300 BC." In

Cambridge Ancient History II/2: *History of the Middle East and the Aegean Region, c.1380–1000 B.C.*, edited by I.E.S. Edwards, 1–20. Cambridge: Cambridge University Press.

Gohary, J. 1992. *Akhenaten's Sed-festival at Karnak.* London: Kegan Paul International.

Gordon, C. 1947. "The New Amarna Tablets." *Orientalia* 16: 1–21.

Govan, A., P. MacFarlane, and R. Callander. 1991. *Pathology Illustrated.* 3rd ed. Churchill: Livingstone.

Green, L. 1966. "The Royal Women of Amarna." In *The Royal Women of Amarna*, edited by D. Arnold, 7–15. New York: Metropolitan Museum of Art.

———. 1992. "Queen as Goddess: The Religious Role of Royal Women in the Late Eighteenth Dynasty." *Amarna Letters* 2: 28–40.

———. 2000. "Crowned Heads: Royal Regalia of the Amarna and Pre- and Post-Amarnan Periods." *Amarna Letters* 4: 61–75.

———. 2004. "Some Thoughts on Ritual Banquets at the Court of Akhenaten." In *Egypt, Israel and the Ancient Mediterranean World*, edited by G. Knoppers and A. Hirsch, 203–22. Leiden: Brill.

Griffith, F.Ll. 1910. "Egypt: History." In *Encyclopedia Britannica*. 11th ed. IX: 80–88.

———. 1918. "The Jubilee of Akhenaten." *JEA* 5: 61–63.

———. 1924. "Excavations at Tell el-'Amarnah 1923–1924." *JEA* 10: 299–305.

———. 1926. "A Stela in Honour of Amenophis III and Teya from Tell el'Amarnah." *JEA* 12: 1–2.

———. 1931. "Excavations at Tell el-'Amarnah. Statuary." *JEA* 17: 179–84.

Griffith, N. 1923. "Akhenaten and the Hittites." *JEA* 9: 78–79.

Grimm, A. 2001a. "Ägyptologisches Kaleidoskop." In *Das Geheimnis des goldenen Sarges*, edited by A. Grimm and S. Schoske, 121–36. Munich: Staatliches Museum Ägyptischer Kunst.

———. 2001b. "Das Geheimnis des anonymen Sarge." In *Das Geheimnis des goldenen Sarges*, edited by A. Grimm and S. Schoske, 115–20. Munich: Staatliches Museum Ägyptischer Kunst.

———. 2001c. "Goldsarg ohne Geheimnis." In *Das Geheimnis des goldenen Sarges*, edited by A. Grimm and S. Schoske, 101–14. Munich: Staatliches Museum Ägyptischer Kunst.

———. 2001d. "Von Amarna im Tal der Könige." In *Das Geheimnis des goldenen Sarges*, edited by A. Grimm and S. Schoske, 51–57. Munich: Staatliches Museum Ägyptischer Kunst.

Gunn, B. 1923. "Notes on the Aten and His Names." *JEA* 9: 168–76.

Gurney, O. 1952. *The Hittites.* London: Penguin.

Guterbock, H. 1956. "The Deeds of Suppuliliuma." *JCS* 10: 41–130.

Habachi, L. 1958. "The Clearance of the Tomb of Kheruef at Thebes." *ASAE* 55: 325–50.

———. 1965. "Varia from the Reign of Akhenaten." *MDAIK* 10: 70–92.

———. 1971. "Akhenaten in Heliopolis." *Beiträge zur ägyptischen Bauforschung und Altertumskunde* 12: 35–45.

Hachmann, R. 1982. "Die äg. Verwaltung in Syrien während der Amarnerzeit." *Zeitschrift des Deutschen Palästina-Verein* 98: 17–49.

Hall, H.R. 1921. "Egypt and the External World c.1350." *JEA* 7: 39–53.

Hamza, M. 1940. "The Alabaster Canopic Box of Akhenaten and the Royal Alabaster Canopic Boxes of the Eighteenth Dynasty." *ASAE* 40: 537–43.

Hanke, R. 1975. "Änderungen von Bildern und Inschriften während der Amarna Zeit." *SAK* 2: 79–94.

———. 1978. *Amarna Reliefs aus Hermopolis*. Hildesheim: Gerstenberg.

Hankey, J. 2001. *A Passion for Archaeology: Arthur Weigall*. London: Tauris.

Hankey, V. 1981. "The Aegean Interest in El-Amarna." *JMAA* 1: 38–49.

Hari, R. 1965. *Horemheb et la reine Moutnedjemet*. Geneva: La Sirène.

———. 1976a. "Un nouvel élément de la corégence Amenophis III-Akhenaton." *CdE* 51: 252–60.

———. 1976b. "La reine d'Horemheb était-elle la soeur de Nefertiti?" *CdE* 51: 39–46.

———. 1976c. *Répertoire onomastique amarnienne*. Geneva: Editions de Belles-Lettres.

———. 1984. "La religion amarnienne et la tradition polythéiste." In *Studien zu Sprache und Religion Ägyptens zu Ehren von Wolfhart Westendorf*, 2: 1039–55. Gottingen: Junge.

———. 1985. *The Great Hymn to the Aten*. Leiden: Brill.

Harris, J.E., and E. Wente. 1978. "The Mummy of the 'Elder Lady' in the Tomb of Amenhotep II." *Science* 200: 1149–51.

Harris, J.E., and E. Wente, eds. 1980. *X-ray Atlas of the Royal Mummies*. Chicago: University of Chicago Press.

Harris, J.E., E.F. Wente, C.F. Cox, I. El Nawaway, C.J. Kowalski, A.T. Storey, W.R. Russell, P.V. Ponitz, and G.F. Walker. 1979. "The Identification of the 'Elder Lady' in the Tomb of Amenhotep II as Queen Tiye." *Delaware Medical Journal* 51/2: 89–93.

Harris, J.R. 1968. "How Long Was the Reign of Horemheb?" *JEA* 54: 95–99.

———. 1973a. "Neferneferuaten." *GM* 4: 15–17.

———. 1973b. "Nefertiti rediviva." *AO* 35: 5–13.

———. 1974a. "Kiya." *CdE* 49: 25–30.

———. 1974b. "Neferneferuaten regnans." *AO* 36: 11–21.

———. 1975. "Contributions to the History of the Eighteenth Dynasty." *SAK* 2: 95–101.

———. 1977a. "A Fine Piece of Egyptian Faience." *Burlington Magazine* 119: 340–43.

———. 1977b. "Akhenaten or Nefertiti?" *AO* 38: 5–10.

Harrison, R. 1966. "An Anatomical Examination of the Pharaonic Remains Purported to Be Akhenaten." *JEA* 52: 95–119.

Harrison, R., and A.B. Abdallah. 1972. "The Remains of Tutankhamun." *Antiquity* 46: 8–18.

Harrison, R., R. Connolly, and A. Abdallah 1969. "The Kinship of Smenkhkare and Tutankhamun Demonstrated Serologically." *Nature* 224: 325–26.

Hart, G. 1986. *Dictionary of Egyptian Gods and Goddesses*. London: Routledge and Kegan Paul.

Hassan, S. 1938. "A Representation of the Solar Disk with Human Hands and Arms." *ASAE* 38: 53–61.

Hauza, M. 1940. "The Alabaster Canopic Box of Akhenaten." *ASAE* 40: 537–43.

Hawass, Z., Y.Z. Gad, S. Ismail, R. Khairat, D. Fathalla, N. Hasan, A. Ahmed, H. Elleithy, M. Ball, F. Gaballah, S. Wasef, M. Fateen, H. Amer, P. Gostner, A. Selim, A. Zink, and C.M. Pusch. 2010. "Ancestry and Pathology in King Tutankhamun's Family." *JAMA* 303/7: 638–47.

Hayes, W. 1948. "Minor Art and Family History in the Reign of Amenhotep III." *BMMA* 6: 272–79.

———. 1951. "Inscriptions from the Palace of Amenhotep III." *JNES* 10: 35–56, 82–112, 156–83, 231–42.

———. 1959. *The Scepter of Egypt*, 2. New York: Metropolitan Museum of Art.

Helck, W. 1954. "Die Sinai Inschrift des Amenmose." *Mitteilungen des Instituts für Orientforschung* 2: 189–207.

———. 1958. *Zur Verwaltung des Mittleren und Neuen Reiches*. Leiden: Brill.

———. 1968. *Geschichte des alten Aegyptens*. Leiden: Brill.

———. 1969a. "Amarna Probleme." *CdE* 44: 200–31.

———. 1969b. "Die Tochterheirat äg. Könige." *CdE* 44: 22–25.

———. 1973a. "Probleme der Zeit Horemhebs." *CdE* 48: 251–65.

———. 1973b. "Zur Opferliste Amenophis IV." *JEA* 59: 95–99.

———. 1975. "Abdi-Aširta." In *Lexikon der Ägyptologie*, I, edited by W. Helck and E. Otto, 2. Wiesbaden: Harassowitz.

———. 1980. "Ein Feldzug unter Amenophis IV gegen Nubiens." *SAK* 8: 117–26.

———. 1981. "Probleme der Königsfolge in Darübergangszeit von 18 zu 19 Dynastie." *MDAIK* 37: 207–15.

———. 1984a. "Kiye." *MDAIK* 40: 159–67.

———. 1984b. "Semenchkare." In *Lexikon der Ägyptologie*, V, edited by W. Helck and E. Otto, 837–41. Wiesbaden: Harassowitz.

———. 2001. *Das Grab nr 55 im Königsgräbertal*. Mainz: von Zabern.

Helck, W., and E. Otto. 1972–92. *Lexikon der Ägyptologie*. 7 vols. Wiesbaden: Harassowitz.

Hoeppli, R. 1973. "Morphological Changes in Human Schistosomiasis and Certain Analogies in Ancient Egyptian Sculpture." *Acta Topica* 30: 1–11.

Hoffmeier, J. 2014. *Akhenaten and the Origins of Monotheism*. New York: Oxford University Press.

Hoffmeier, J., and J. van Dijk. 2010. "New Light on the Amarna Period from N. Sinai." *JEA* 96: 191–205.

Hölscher, U. 1941. *The Mortuary Temple of Ramesses III*. Chicago: Oriental Institute.

Hornung, E. 1966. "Aja als Kronprinz." *ZÄS* 92: 99–102.

———. 1971. "Gedanken zur Kunst der Amarnazeit." *ZÄS* 97: 74–78.

———. 1980. "Monotheismus im pharaonischen Agypten." In *Monotheismus im alten Israel und seiner Umwelt*, edited by O. Keel, 84–97. Fribourg: Verlag Schweizerisches Katholisches Bibelwerk.

———. 1982. *Conceptions of God in Ancient Egypt*. Translated by J. Baines. Ithaca: Cornell University Press.

————. 1990. *The Valley of the Kings*. New York: Timken.

————. 1992. "The Rediscovery of Akhenaten and His Place in Religion." *JARCE* 29: 43–49.

————. 1999. *Akhenaten and the Religion of Light*. Ithaca: Cornell University Press.

Hornung, E., and A. Piankoff. 1962. "Das Grab Amenophis III." *MDAIK* 17: 111–27.

Hornung, E., R. Krauss, and D.A. Warburton, eds. 2006. *Ancient Egyptian Chronology*. Leiden: Brill.

Hussein, F., and J. Harris. 1988. "The Skeletal Remains from Tomb no. 55." In *Fifth International Congress of Egyptology*, 140–41. Cairo.

Ikram, S. 1989. "Domestic Shrines in the Cult of the Royal Family at el-Amarna." *JEA* 75: 89–101.

James, S. 2001. "Who is the Mummy Elder Lady?" *Kmt* 12/2: 42–50.

————. 2003. "Duelling Nefertitis." *Kmt* 14/3: 22–30.

James, T.G.H. 1982. *Excavating in Egypt: The Egypt Exploration Society 1882–1982*. London: British Museum Publications.

————. 1992. *Howard Carter*. London: Kegan Paul.

Janssen, J. 1983. "El-Amarna as a Residential City." *BiOr* 40: 273–88.

Johnson, G. 1992. "Norman de Garis Davies and the Rock Tombs of el Amarna." *Amarna Letters* 2: 56–69.

————. 2000. "The Royal Tomb of Horemheb in the Valley of the Kings." *Amarna Letters* 4: 121–59.

Johnson, M. 2000. "The Royal Heiress Sitamun." *Amarna Letters* 4: 20–29.

Johnson, W.R. 1996. "Amenhotep III and Amarna: Some New Considerations." *JEA* 82: 65–82.

————. 1998. "Monuments and Monumental Art under Amenhotep III." In *Amenhotep III: Perspectives on His Reign*, edited by D. O'Connor and E. Cline, 80–85. Ann Arbor: University of Michigan Press.

————. 2009. "Tutankhamen-Period Battle Narratives at Luxor." *Kmt* 20/4: 20–33.

————. 2012. "Akhenaten in Nubia." In *Ancient Nubia: African Kingdoms on the Nile*, edited by M.M. Fisher, P. Lacovara, S. Ikram, and S. D'Auria, 92–93. Cairo: American University in Cairo Press.

————. 2012–13. "Same Statues, Different King." *Kmt* 23/4: 49–53.

————. 2014. "Sexual Duality and Goddess Iconography on the Amenhotep IV Sandstone Colossi at Karnak." *BES* 19: 415–19.

————. 2015a. "The Duck-throttling Scene from Amarna." In *Joyful in Thebes: Egyptological Studies in Honor of Betsy M. Bryan*, 293–99. Atlanta: Lockwood.

————. 2015b. "An Amarna Royal Head at Hanover's Museum August Kestner: Evidence for King Ankhkheperure Neferneferuaten." *Kmt* 26/3: 22–29.

————. 2015/16. "A Royal Fishing and Fowling Talatat Scene from Amarna." *Kmt* 26/4: 40–50.

Jomard, E.F. 1809–18. *Description de l'Egypte*. 20 vols. Paris: Imprimerie impériale.

Jørgensen, M. 2005. *Egyptian Art from the Amarna Period*. Copenhagen: Ny Carlsberg Glypotek.

Junge, F. 1991. "Ein Bruckstück vom Kopf einer Achenaten-Statue aus Elephantine." *MDAIK* 47: 191–94.

Kamal, M. 1935. "Fouilles de service des antiquités à Tell el-Amarna en 1934." *ASAE* 35: 193–96.

Kees, H. 1961. *Ancient Egypt: A Cultural Topography*. London: Faber & Faber.

Kemp, B. 1976. "The Window of Appearances at el-Amarna and the Basic Structure of the City." *JEA* 62: 81–99.

———. 1977/78. "The City of el-Amarna as a Source for the Study of Urban Society in Ancient Egypt." *World Archaeology* 9: 123–39.

———. 1978. "Imperialism and Empire in New Kingdom Egypt." In *Imperialism in the Ancient World*, edited by P. Garnsey and C. Whittaker, 7–57. Cambridge: Cambridge University Press.

———. 1979. "Wall Paintings from the Workmen's Village at el-Amarna." *JEA* 65: 47–53.

———. 1981. "The Character of the Southern Suburb at Tell el-Amarna." *MDOG* 113: 81–97.

———. 1987. "The Amarna Workmen's Village in Retrospect." *JEA* 73: 21–50.

———. 1995. "Amarna Expedition, 1994–5." *JEA* 81: 9–10.

———. 1996. "Tell el Amarna, 1996." *JEA* 82: 12–14.

———. 1997. "Tell el Amarna, 1996–7." *JEA* 83: 8–13.

———. 1998."Tell el Amarna, 1997–8." *JEA* 84: 12–16.

———. 1999. "Tell el Amarna, 1998–9." *JEA* 85: 13–18.

———. 2000. "Tell el Amarna, 2000." *JEA* 86: 12–18.

———. 2001. "Tell el Amarna, 2000–01." *JEA* 87: 16–21.

———. 2002. "Tell el Amarna, 2001–02." *JEA* 88: 12–21.

———. 2003. "Tell el Amarna, 2003." *JEA* 89: 10–21.

———. 2004. "Tell el Amarna, 2004." *JEA* 90: 14–28.

———. 2005. "Tell el Amarna, 2005." *JEA* 91: 15–30.

———. 2006. "Tell el Amarna, 2006." *JEA* 92: 21–56.

———. 2007. "Tell el Amarna, 2007." *JEA* 93: 1–64.

———. 2008. "Tell el Amarna, 2008." *JEA* 94: 1–68.

———. 2009. "Tell el Amarna, 2009." *JEA* 95: 1–34.

———. 2010. "Tell el Amarna, 2010." *JEA* 96: 1–29.

———. 2011. "Tell el Amarna, 2011." *JEA* 97: 1–10.

———. 2012a. "Tell el Amarna, 2012." *JEA* 98: 1–26.

———. 2012b. *The City of Akhenaten and Nefertiti: Amarna and Its People*. London: Thames and Hudson.

———. 2013. "Tell el Amarna 2012–2013." *JEA* 99: 1–34.

———. 2014. "Tell el Amarna, 2014." *JEA* 100: 1–35.

Kemp, B., and S. Garfi. 1993. *A Survey of the Ancient City of el-'Amarna*. London: Egypt Exploration Society.

Kemp, B., A. Stevens, G.R. Dabbs, M. Zabecki, and J.C. Rose. 2013. "Life, Death and Beyond in Akhenaten's Egypt: Excavating the South Tombs Cemetery at Amarna." *Antiquity* 87/335: 64–78.

Kendall, T. 2009. "*Talatat* Architecture at Jebel Barkal: Report of the NCAM Mission 2008–2009." *S&N* 13: 2–16.

Kirby, C., and A. Tooley. 1989. "Report on the 1987 Excavations: The Excavation of Q48.4." In *Amarna Reports* 5, 15–63. London: Egypt Exploration Society.

Kitchen, K. 1962. *Suppiluliuma and the Amarna Pharaohs*. Liverpool: Liverpool University Press.

———. 1968. "Further Notes on New Kingdom Chronology and History." *CdE* 43: 313–24.

Klengel, H. 1965. "Einige Bemerkungen zur Syrienpolitik des Amenophis IV/ Echnaton." *Das Altertum* 2: 131–37.

Kozloff, A.P. 2010. "Chips Off the Old Block: Amenhotep IV's Sandstone Colossi, Re-cut from Statues of Amenhotep III." In *Millions of Jubilees: Studies in Honor of David P. Silverman*, edited by Z. Hawass and J. Houser Wegner, I: 279–94. Cairo: Conseil suprême des antiquités.

———. 2012. "Chips off Old Statues: Carving the Amenhotep IV Colossi at Karnak." *Kmt* 23/3: 18–32.

Kozloff, A.P., and B. Bryan. 1992. *Egypt's Dazzling Sun: Amenhotep III and His World*. Cleveland: Cleveland Museum of Art.

Krauss, R. 1978. *Das Ende der Amarnazeit*. Hildesheim: Gerstenberg.

———. 1979. "Meritaten as Ruling Queen of Egypt and Successor of Her Father Nepkhururia-Akhenaten." In *Acts of the First International Congress of Egyptologists*, 403–406. Berlin: Akademie Verlag.

———. 1986. "Kiya—ursprüngliche Besitzerin der Kanopen aus KV 55." *MDAIK* 42: 67–80.

———. 1989a. "Neues zu den Stelenfragmenten UC London 410 und Kairo JE 64959." *BSEG* 13: 83–87.

———. 1989b. "1913–1988: 75 Jahre der Nofretete/Nefret-iti in Berlin." *Jahrbuch des Preußischer Kulturbesitz* 24: 87–124.

———. 1990. "Einige Kleinfunde mit Namen von Amarnaherrschen." *CdE* 65: 206–18.

———. 1997. "Nefertitis Ende." *MDAIK* 53: 209–19.

———. 2009. "Nefertiti's Final Secret." *Kmt* 20/2: 18–28.

Laboury, D. 2010. *Akhenaten*. Paris: Pygmalion.

Lacau, P. 1909. *Les stèles du Nouvel Empire*. Cairo: Institut français d'archéologie orientale.

Lacovara, P. 1999. "The City of Amarna." In *Pharaohs of the Sun*, edited by R.E. Freed, Y. Markowitz, and S.H. D'Auria, 61–71. Boston: Museum of Fine Arts.

Lange, K. 1951. *König Echnaton und die Amarna-Zeit*. Munich: Gesellschaft für Wissenschaftlichen Lichtbild.

Lange, K., and M. Hirmer. 1968. *Egypt*. 4th ed. London: Phaidon.

Larson, J. 1992. "Other Amarna Letters: A Scholarly Honeymoon on the Nile: The Breasteds at el Amarna Jan. 10–17, 1895." *Amarna Letters* 2: 116–25.

Lauffray, J. 1979. *Karnak d'Egypte*. Paris: CNRS.

Leblanc, C. 1980. "Piliers et colosses de types 'osiriaque' dans le context des temples de culte royale." *BIFAO* 80: 69–89.

Lefébure, E. 1891. "Sur différents mots et noms égyptiens, V." *PSBA* 13: 470–83.

Lefebvre, G. 1929. *Histoire des grands prêtres d'Amon à Karnak*. Paris: Geuthner.

Legrain, G. 1902. "Les stèles d'Amenophis IV à Zernik et à Gebel Silsileh." *ASAE* 3: 259–66.

———. 1903. "Fragments de canopes." *ASAE* 4: 138–49.

———. 1929. *Les temples de Karnak*. Brussels: Vromant.

Leibovitch. J. 1953. "Gods of Agriculture and Welfare in Ancient Egypt." *JNES* 12: 73–113.

Leprohon, R. 1958. "Cultic Activities in the Temples at Amarna." Smith and Redford 1976: II: 47–51.

———. 1985. "The Reign of Akhenaten Seen through the Later Royal Decrees." In *Mélanges Gamal Eddin Mokhtar*, edited by P. Posener-Kriéger, 2: 93–103. Cairo: Institut français d'archéologie orientale.

Lepsius, C.R. 1849–1859. *Denkmaeler aus Aegypten und Aethiopien*. 12 vols. Berlin: Nicolai.

———. 1851. *Uber den ersten ägyptischen Götterkreis und seine geschichtlich-mythologische Entstehung*. Berlin: Hertz.

———. 1853. *Letters from Egypt, Ethiopia and the Peninsula of Sinai*. Translated by J. and L. Horner. London: Bohn.

———. 1897–1913. *Denkmaeler. Text*. 5 vols. Leipzig: Hinrichs.

L'Hôte, N. 1840. *Lettres écrites d'Egypte en 1838 et 1839*. Paris: Firmin Didot.

Lichtheim, M. 1973–80. *Ancient Egyptian Literature*. 2 vols. Berkeley: California University Press.

Liverani, M. 1965. "Implicazioni sociali nella politica di Abdi-Aserta di Amurru." *Riv. degli studi orientali* 40: 267–77.

———. 1967. "Contrasti e congruenze di concezioni politiche nell'età d'el-Amarna." *Revue d'Assyriologie* 61: 1–18.

———. 1971. "La lettera del Faraone a Rib-Adda." *Oriens Antiquus* 10: 253–68.

———. 1972. "Elementi 'irrazionali' nel commercio amarniano." *Oriens Antiquus* 11: 297–317.

———. 1979. *Three Amarna Essays*. Malibu: Undena.

———. 1983a. "Aziru, servitor di due padroni." In *Studi orientalistici in ricordo di Franco Pintore*, edited by O. Cannuba, M. Liverani, and C. Zaccagnini, 93–121. Pavia: GJES.

———. 1983b. "The Political Lexicon and Political Ideologies in the Amarna Letters." *Berytus* 31: 41–56.

———. 1990. "A Seasonal Pattern for the Amarna Letters." In *Lingering Over Words*, edited by T. Abusch, 337–48. Atlanta: Scholars' Press.

Lloyd, S. 1933. "Model of a Tell el-'Amarnah house." *JEA* 19: 1–7.

Loeben, C. 1986. "Eine Besttattung der grossen königlichen Gemahlin Nofretete in Amarna?" *MDAIK* 41: 97–107.

———. 1991. "'No Evidence of Co-regency': Zwei getilgte Inschriften aus dem Grab von Tutanchamun." *BSEG* 15: 81–90.

———. 1994. "'No Evidence of Coregency': Two Erased Inscriptions from Tutankhamun's Tomb." *Amarna Letters* 3: 105–109.

Löhr, B. 1974. "Akhanjati in Heliopolis." *GM* 11: 33–38.

———. 1975. "Akhanjati in Memphis." *SAK* 2: 169–87.

Lombroso, C. 1891. *The Man of Genius*. London: Walter Scott.

Luban, M. 1999. "Do We Have the Mummy of Nefertiti?" http://www.oocities. org/scribelist/do_we_have_.htm.

Lucas, A. 1931. "The Canopic Vases from the Tomb of Queen Tiyi." *ASAE* 31: 120–22.

Lucas, P. 1705. *Voyage au Levant*. 2 vols. The Hague: Uytwerf.

Macadam, M.F.L. 1949. *The Temples of Kawa*. 2 vols. Oxford: Oxford University Press.

———. 1957. *Corpus of Inscribed Funerary Cones*. Oxford: Griffith Institute.

Malaise, M. 1981. "Aton, le sceptre ouas et la fête sed." *GM* 50: 47–60.

Malek, J. 1996. "The 'Coregency Relief' of Akhenaten and Smenkhkare from Memphis." In *Studies in Honor of William Kelly Simpson*, edited by P. Der Manuelian, II: 553–59. Boston: Museum of Fine Arts.

———. 1997. "The Temples at Memphis." In *The Temple in Ancient Egypt*, edited by S. Quirke, 90–101. London: British Museum Press.

Mallinson, M. 1989. "Report on the 1987 Excavations: Investigation of the Small Aten Temple." *Amarna Reports* 5: 115–42.

Manniche, L. 1975. "The Wife of Bata." *GM* 118: 33–35.

———. 1978. "Symbolic Blindness." *CdE* 53: 13–21.

———. 1987. *The City of the Dead: Thebes in Egypt*. London: British Museum.

———. 1991. *Music and Musicians in Ancient Egypt*. London: British Museum Publications.

———. 2010. *The Akhenaten Colossi of Karnak*. Cairo: American University in Cairo Press.

Marchant, J. 2011. "Curse of the Pharoah's DNA." *Nature* 472: 404–406.

———. 2013. *The Shadow King: The Bizarre Afterlife of King Tut's Mummy*. Boston: Da Capo Press.

Mariette, A. 1855. "Renseignements sur les soixante-quatre Apis." *Bulletin archéologique de l'Athenaeum français* 1: 45–50, 53–58, 66–68, 85–90, 93–100, reprinted in *Sérapéum* 1882, 114–202.

———. 1882. *Le Sérapéum de Memphis*. Paris: Gide.

———. 1890. *The Monuments of Upper Egypt*. Boston: Mansfield and Dearborn.

Martin, G. 1974–89. *The Royal Tomb at El-'Amarna*. 2 vols. London: Egypt Exploration Society.

———. 1985. "Notes on a Canopic Jar from Kings' Valley Tomb 55." In *Mélanges Gamal Eddin Mokhtar*, edited by P. Posener-Kriéger, II: 111–24. Cairo: Institut français d'archéologie orientale.

———. 1986. "Shabtis of Private Persons in the Amarna Age." *MDAIK* 42: 109–29.

———. 1991a. *A Bibliography of the Amarna Period and Its Aftermath*. London: Kegan Paul International.

———. 1991b. *The Hidden Tombs of Memphis*. London: Thames and Hudson.

Maspero, G. 1881. "Notes sur quelques points de grammaire et d'histoire." *ZÄS* 19: 116–31.

————. 1895a. "Une capital oubliée de l'Egypte pharaonique." *Journal des débats* 27 Sept.

————. 1895–99. *Histoire ancienne des peuples de l'Orient*. 3 vols. Paris: Hachette.

————. 1896. *The Struggle of the Nations*. Translated by M. McLure. London: Society for the Promotion of Christian Knowledge.

————. 1907a. *Causeries d'Egypte*. Paris: Guilmot.

————. 1907b. "Le tombeau de la reine Tiye." *Journal des débats*, 20 March.

————. 1913. *Egyptian Art*. Translated by E. Lee. London: Fisher Unwin.

————. 1921. *Histoire ancienne des peuples d'Orient*. Paris: Hachette.

El-Masry, Y. 2002. "New Evidence for Building Activity of Akhenaten in Akhmim." *MDAIK* 58: 391–98.

Matthes, O. 2012. "Ludwig Borchardt, James Simon and the Colourful Nefertiti Bust in the First Year after Her Discovery." In *In the Light of Amarna*, edited by F. Seyfried, 427–37. Berlin: Ägyptisches Museum und Papyrussammlung.

McLeod, W. 1970. *Composite Bows*. Oxford: Griffith Institute.

Meyer, C. 1984. "Zum Titel ḥmt nswt bei den Töchtern Amenophis III und IV und Ramses II." *SAK* 11: 253–63.

Millar, R.W. 1972. *The Piltdown Men: A Case of Archaeological Fraud*. London: Gollancz.

Mode, M. 1984. "Die Entdeckung von Tell el Amarna. Der Beitrag von Lepsius zur Erforschung der Amarna Zeit." *Das Altertum* 30: 93–102.

Mohammad, A.-K. 1959. "The Administration of Syro-Palestine during the New Kingdom." *ASAE* 56: 105–37.

Molleson, T., and M. Cox. 1993. *The Spitalfields Project: II: The Anthropology, the Middling Sort*. York: Council for British Archeology.

Montserrat, D. 2000. *Akhenaten: History, Fantasy and Ancient Egypt*. London: Routledge.

Moran, W. 1992. *The Amarna Letters*. Baltimore: Johns Hopkins University Press.

Morenz, S. 1973. *Egyptian Religion*. Ithaca: Cornell University Press.

Moret, A. 1912. *Kings and Gods of Egypt*. New York: Putnam.

Morris, E. 2006. "Bowing and Scraping in the Ancient Near East: An Investigation into the Obsequiousness in the Amarna Letters." *JNES* 65: 179–95.

Moseley, S. 2009. *Amarna: The Missing Evidence*. Calshot: Peach Pixel.

Mueller, M. 1976. "L'art et la fin de la XVIIIe dynastie." *SAK* 4: 237–53.

Munro, I. 1987. Review of Perepelkin 1984. *BiOr* 44: 137–43.

Munro, P. 1969. "Die Namen Semenech-ka-Ra's." *ZÄS* 95: 109–16.

————. 1981. "Frühform oder Deckname des Jati in Heliopolis." *MDAIK* 37: 359–67.

————. 1991. "Anmerkungen zu zwei Königsplastiken der Amarna Zeit." *MDAIK* 47: 255–62.

Murnane, W. 1977. *Ancient Egyptian Coregencies*. Chicago: Oriental Institute.

————. 1982. Review of Samson 1968. *JNES* 41: 141–44.

————. 1983. Review of Krauss, *Das Ende der Amarnazeit*. *Orientalia* 52: 274–84.

———. 1987a. "The First Occasion of the Discovery of Akhet-Aten." *SAK* 14: 239–46.

———. 1987b. Review of Krauss, *Das Ende der Amarna Zeit*. *Orientalia* 52: 274–84.

———. 1995. *Texts from the Amarna Period in Egypt*. Atlanta: Scholars Press.

———. 1999. "The Return to Orthodoxy." In *Pharaohs of the Sun*, edited by R. Freed, Y.J. Markowitz, and S.H. D'Auria, 177–85. Boston: Museum of Fine Arts.

———. 2000a. "Imperial Egypt and the Limits of Power." In *Amarna Diplomacy*, edited by R. Cohen and R. Westbrook, 101–11. Baltimore: Johns Hopkins University Press.

———. 2000b. "Soleb Renaissance: Reconstructing the Nebmaatre Temple in Nubia." *Amarna Letters* 4: 6–19.

———. 2001. "The End of the Amarna Period Once Again." *OLZ* 96: 11–21.

Murnane, W., and C. van Siclen. 1993. *The Boundary Stelae of Akhet-Aten*. London: Kegan Paul International.

Na'aman, N. 1990. "Praises to the Pharaoh in Response to His Plans for a Campaign in Canaan." In *Lingering Over Words: Studies in Ancient Near Eastern Literature in Honor of William L. Moran*, edited by T. Abusch, 397–405. Atlanta: Scholars Press.

———. 2000. "The Egyptian-Canaanite Correspondence." In *Amarna Diplomacy*, edited by R. Cohen and R. Westbrook, 125–40. Baltimore: Johns Hopkins University Press.

Naville, E. 1894–1908. *The Temple of Deir el Bahri*. 6 vols. London: Egypt Exploration Fund.

Newberry, P. 1928a. "Akhenaten's Eldest Son-in-law 'Ankhkheprurē'." *JEA* 14: 3–9.

———. 1928b. "Notes on a Sculptured Slab no 15000 in the Berlin Museum." *JEA* 14: 117.

Newton, F. 1924. "Excavations at el-'Amārnah, 1923–24." *JEA* 10: 289–98.

Nicholson, Sir C. 1870. "On Some Remains of the Disk Worshippers Discovered at Memphis." *TRSL* 9: 197–214.

Nicholson, P.T. 2007. *Brilliant Things for Akhenaten: The Production of Glass, Vitreous Materials and Pottery at Amarna Site O45.1*. London: Egypt Exploration Society.

Nims, C. 1973. "The Transition from the Traditional to the New Style of Wall Relief under Amenhotep IV." *JNES* 32: 181–87.

Norden, F. 1757. *Travels in Egypt and Nubia*. Translated by P. Templeman. 2 vols. London: Davis and Reymers.

O'Connor, D., 1989. "City and Palace in New Kingdom Egypt." *Cahiers de recherches de l'Institut de papyrologie de Lille* 11: 73–87.

O'Connor, D. and E. Cline, eds. 1998. *Amenhotep III: Perspectives on His Reign*. Ann Arbor: University of Michigan Press.

Owen, G. 2009. "*Bayt* Doctor Barry: Progress and Ritual." In *Beyond the Horizon: Studies in Egyptian Art, Archaeology and History in Honour of Barry J. Kemp*, edited by S. Ikram and A. Dodson, 339–46. Cairo: Supreme Council of Antiquities.

Pansaers, C. 1921. "Khouen-Aton, le pharaon de la Paix Eternelle." *Revue mondiale* ser. 7, 145: 29–45.

Paulshoch, B. 1980. "Tutankamun and His Brothers." *JAMA* 244: 160–64.

Peet, T.E., and C.L. Woolley. 1923. *The City of Akhenaten*, I: *Excavations of 1921 and 1922 at El-'Amarneh*. London: Egypt Exploration Society.

Pendlebury, J. 1931a. "Preliminary Report of the Excavations at Tell el-'Amarnah (1930–1931)." *JEA* 17: 233–44. See also Frankfort and Pendlebury.

———. 1931b. "Report on the Clearance of the Royal Tomb at el-'Amarna." *ASAE* 31: 123–25.

———. 1932. "Preliminary Report of the Excavations at Tell el-'Amarnah (1931–1932)." *JEA* 18: 143–49.

———. 1935. *Tell el Amarna*. London: Lovat Dickson.

———. 1951. *The City of Akhenaten*, 3: *The Central City and the Official Quarters*. London: Egypt Exploration Society.

Perepelkin, Y.Y. 1967, 1984. *Perevorot Amen-xotpa IV*. 2 vols. Moscow: Academy of Sciences of the USSR.

———. 1978. *The Secret of the Gold Coffin*. Moscow: Nauka Publishing House.

Perring, J. 1843. "On Some Fragments from the Ruins of a Temple at el Tell." *TRSL* 2/1: 140–48.

Petersen, L. 2012. "Nefertiti in Focus." In *In the Light of Amarna*, edited by F. Seyfried, 445–51. Berlin: Aegyptisches Museum und Papyrussammlung.

Petrie, W.M.F. 1890. *Kahun, Gurob and Hawara*. London: Kegan Paul, Trench, Trübner.

———. 1894. *Tell el Amarna*. London: Methuen.

———. 1896. *A History of Egypt*, 2. London: Methuen.

Pflüger, K. 1936. *Haremhab und die Amarnazeit*. Zwickau: Ullmann.

———. 1946. "The Edict of King Horemheb." *JNES* 5: 260–68.

Phillips, J. 1991. "Sculpture Ateliers of Akhet-Aten." *Amarna Letters* 1: 31–45.

Piankoff, A. 1964. "Les grandes compositions religieuses du Nouvel Empire." *BIFAO* 62: 207–18.

Piankoff, A. and E. Hornung. 1961. "Das Grab Amenophis III im Westtal der Könige." *MDAIK* 17: 111–27.

Pillet, M. 1922. "Rapport sur les travaux de Karnak (1921–1922)." *ASAE* 22: 235–60.

———. 1923. "Rapport sur les travaux de Karnak (1922–1923)." *ASAE* 23: 99–138.

———. 1924. "Rapport sur les travaux de Karnak (1923–1924)." *ASAE* 24: 53–88.

———. 1925. "Rapport sur les travaux de Karnak (1924–1925)." *ASAE* 25: 1–24.

———. 1950. "A propos d'Akhenaton." *RdE* cahier complémentaire: 63–82.

———. 1961. "L'art d'Akhenaten." In *Mélanges Mariette*, 81–95. Cairo: Institut français d'archéologie orientale.

Pinch, G. 1983. "Childbirth and Female Figurines at Deir el-Medina and el-Amarna." *Orientalia* 52: 405–14.

Pinch-Brock, L. 2000. "An Unpublished Photograph of the KV55 Burial Chamber." *GM* 175: 65–71.

Pintore, F. 1972. "Transiti di truppe e schemi epistolari nella Siria egiziana." *Oriens antiquus* 11: 101–31.

———. 1983. "Il carattere dell'autorità faraonica in base ad alcuni passi epistolari amarniani." In *Studi orientalistici in ricordo di Franco Pittore*, ed. O. Cannuba, M. Liverani, and C. Zaccagnini, 323–33. Pavia: GJES.

Porter, B., and R.L.B. Moss. 1934. *Topographical Bibliography of Ancient Egyptian Hieroglyphic Texts, Reliefs and Paintings*, IV: *Lower and Middle Egypt*. Oxford: Clarendon Press.

———. 1960–64. *Topographical Bibliography of Ancient Egyptian Hieroglyphic Texts, Reliefs and Paintings*, I: *The Theban Necropolis*. 2nd ed. Oxford: Clarendon Press/Griffith Institute.

Posener, G. 1975. "La pieté personelle avant l'age amarnienne." *RdE* 27: 185–210.

Prisse d'Avennes, E. 1843. "Remarks on the Ancient Materials of Some of the Propyla at Karnak." *TRSL* 2/1: 76–92.

———. 1878. *Histoire de l'art égyptien*. Paris: Bertrand.

Pritchard, J.B., ed. 1969. *Ancient Near Eastern Texts Relating to the Old Testament*. 3rd ed. Princeton: Princeton University Press.

Proskauer, F. 1932. "Zur Pathologie der Amarnazeit." *ZÄS* 68: 114–19.

Ragionieri, R. 2000. "The Amarna Age, an International Society in the Making." In *Amarna Diplomacy*, edited by R. Cohen and R. Westbrook, 42–53. Baltimore: Johns Hopkins University Press.

Rammant-Peeters, A. 1985. "Les couronnes de Nefertiti à el-Amarna." *Orientalia Lovanensia Periodica* 16: 21–48.

Ranke, H. 1951. *Masterpieces of Egyptian Art*. London: Alan and Unwin.

Raven, M. 1994. "A Sarcophagus for Queen Tiy and Other Fragments from the Royal Tomb at el-Amarna." *OMRO* 74: 7–20.

Raven, M., and R. van Walsem. 2014. *The Tomb of Meryneith at Saqqara*. Turnhout: Brepols.

Ray, J. 1975. "The Parentage of Tutankhamun." *Antiquity* 49: 45–47.

Redford, D. 1959. "Some Observations on Amarna Chronology." *JEA* 45: 34–37.

———. 1967. *The History and Chronology of the Eighteenth Dynasty*. Toronto: University of Toronto Press.

———. 1973. "Studies on Akhenaten at Thebes I: Report on the Work of the Akhenaten Temple Project of the University Museum, University of Pennsylvania." *JARCE* 10: 77–94.

———. 1975. "Studies on Akhenaten at Thebes II: Report on the Work of the Akhenaten Temple Project of the University Museum, University of Pennsylvania for the Year 1973–1974." *JARCE* 12: 9–14.

———. 1976. "The Sun Disk in Akhenaten's Program: Its Worship and Antecedents, I." *JARCE* 13: 47–61.

———. 1977. "Preliminary Report of the First Season of Excavation in East Karnak 1975–1976." *JARCE* 14: 9–32.

————. 1978. "The Razed Temple of Akhenaten." *Scientific American* December: 100–10.

————. 1979. "The Akhenaten Temple Project and Karnak Excavations." *Expedition* 21/2: 54–59.

————. 1980. "The Sun Disk in Akhenaten's Program: Its Worship and Antecedents, II." *JARCE* 17: 21–37.

————. 1981a. "Interim Report on the Excavations at East Karnak, 1977–78." *JARCE* 18: 11–29.

————. 1981b. "Interim Report on the Excavations at East Karnak (1979 and 1980 Seasons)." *JSSEA* 11: 243–83.

————. 1981c. "A Royal Speech from the Blocks of the Tenth Pylon." *BES* 3: 87–98.

————. 1983. "Interim Report on the Excavations at East Karnak (1981–1982 Seasons)." *JSSEA* 13: 203–23.

————. 1984. *Akhenaten: The Heretic Pharaoh*. Princeton: Princeton University Press.

————. 1987. "The Monotheism of the Heretic Pharaoh." *Biblical Archaeology Review* 13/3: 16–32.

————. 1988. *The Akhenaten Temple Project, 2: Rwd-mnw, Foreigners and Inscriptions*. Toronto: Akhenaten Temple Project.

————. 1991. "East Karnak Excavations 1987–1989." *JARCE* 28: 75–106.

————. 1994a. *The Akhenaten Temple Project, 3: East Karnak Excavations*. Toronto: Akhenaten Temple Project.

————. 1994b. "East Karnak and the Sed Festival of Akhenaten." In *Hommages à Jean Leclant*, II, 485–92. Paris: Institut français d'archéologie orientale.

————. 1995. "The Concept of Kingship during the Eighteenth Dynasty." In *Ancient Egyptian Kingship*, edited by D. O'Connor and D. Silverman, 157–84. Leiden: Brill.

————. 1997. "The Excavations of the Cairo Museum Akhenaten Temple Project at Karnak." *Expedition* 19/4: 33–38.

————. 1999. "The Beginning of the Heresy." In *Pharaohs of the Sun*, edited by R. Freed, Y. J. Markowitz, and S. D'Auria, 50–59. Boston: Museum of Fine Arts.

————. 2013. "Akhenaten: New Theories and Old Facts." *BASOR* 369: 9–34.

Reeve, J., and M. Adams. 1993. *The Spitalfields Project*. London: Council for British Archaeology.

Reeves, C.N. 1981. "A Reappraisal of Tomb 55 in the Valley of the Kings." *JEA* 67: 48–55.

————. 1988. "New Light on Kiya from Texts in the British Museum." *JEA* 74: 91–101.

————. 1990. *The Complete Tutankhamun*. London: Thames and Hudson.

————. 1999. "The Royal Family." In *Pharaohs of the Sun*, edited by R. Freed, Y.J. Markowitz, and S. D'Auria, 81–95. Boston: Museum of Fine Arts.

————. 2001. *Akhenaten: Egypt's False Prophet*. London: Thames and Hudson.

Ricke, H. 1932. *Der Grundriss des Amarna-Wohnhauses*. Leipzig: Deutschen Orient-Gesellschaft.

Risse, G. 1971. "Pharaoh Akhenaten of Ancient Egypt: Controversies among Egyptologists and Physicians Regarding His Postulated Illness." *Journal of the History of Medicine* 26: 3–17.

Robins, G. 1981. "*Ḥmt nsw wrt* Meritaton." *GM* 52: 75–81.

———. 1983a. "A Critical Examination of the Theory that the Right to the Throne of Ancient Egypt Passed through the Female Line in the 18th Dynasty." *GM* 62: 67–77.

———. 1983b. "The Value of the Estimated Ages of the Royal Mummies at Death as Historical Evidence." *GM* 45: 63–68.

———. 1993. "The Representation of Sexual Characteristics in Amarna Art." *JSSEA* 23: 29–41.

———. 1997. "The 'Feminization' of the Male Figure in New Kingdom Two-Dimensional Art." In *Chief of Seers: Egyptian Studies in Memory of Cyril Aldred*, edited by E. Goring, C.N. Reeves, and J. Ruffle, 251–65. London: Kegan Paul International.

Roeder, G. 1958. "Thronfolger und König Smench-ka-Re." *ZÄS* 83: 43–74.

———. 1959. *Hermopolis 1929–1939*. Hildesheim: Gerstenberg.

———. 1969. *Amarna Reliefs aus Hermopolis*. Hildesheim: Gerstenberg.

Romer, J. 1981. *The Valley of the Kings*. London: Joseph and Reinbird.

Rosellini, R. 1994. *Giornale della spedizione letteraria Toscana in Egitto negli anni 1828–1829*. Pisa: ETS.

Russmann, E. 1989. *Egyptian Sculpture*. Austin: University of Texas Press.

Sa'ad, R. 1967. "New Light on Akhenaten's Temple at Thebes." *MDAIK* 22: 64–67.

———. 1970. "Les travaux d'Amenophis IV au IIIe pylône du temple d'Amon-Re à Karnak." *Kemi* 20: 187–93.

Saad, R., and L. Manniche. 1971. "A Unique Offering List of Amenophis IV Recently Found at Karnak." *JEA* 57: 70–73.

Sabbahy, L. 2000. "The Mnervis Bull at 'Horizon of the Disk.'" *Amarna Letters* 4: 37–43.

Samson, J. 1972. *Amarna: City of Akhenaten and Nefertiti*. Warminster: Aris and Phillips.

———. 1973a. "Amarna Crowns and Wigs." *JEA* 59: 47–59.

———. 1973b. "Royal Inscriptions from Amarna." *CdE* 48: 243–50.

———. 1976. "Royal Names in Amarna History." *CdE* 51: 30–38.

———. 1977. "Nefertiti's Regality." *JEA* 63: 88–97.

———. 1978. *Amarna: City of Akhenaten and Nefertiti*. 2nd ed., *Nefertiti as Pharaoh*. Warminster: Aris & Phillips.

———. 1979. "Akhenaten's Successor." *GM* 32: 53–58.

———. 1982a. "Akhenaten's Coregent Ankheperure-Neferneferuaten." *GM* 53: 51–54.

———. 1982b. "The History of the Mystery of Akhenaten's Successor." In *L'égyptologie en 1979*, II, 91–297. Paris: Centre national de la recherche scientifique.

———. 1982c. "Neferneferuaten-Nefertiti." *GM* 57: 61–67.

———. 1985. *Nefertiti and Cleopatra*. London: Rubicon Press.

Sauneron, S. 1951. "La tradition officielle relative à la XVIIIe dynastie d'après un ostracon de la Vallée des Rois." *CdE* 26: 46–49.

Sauneron, S., and R. Sa'ad. 1969. "Le démontage et l'étude du IXe pylône à Karnak." *Kemi* 19: 137–78.

Sayce, A. 1907. Letter to the *Times*, 17 September 1907.

———. 1923. *Reminiscences*. London: Macmillan.

Schaden, O. 1979. "Preliminary Report on the Re-clearance of Tomb 25 in the Western Valley of the Kings (WV-25)." *ASAE* 63: 161–68.

———. 1992. "The God's Father Ay." *Amarna Letters* 2: 92–115.

———. 2000. "Paintings in the Tomb of King Ay (WV 23)." *Amarna Letters* 4: 89–110.

Schäfer, H. 1912–13. "Kunstwerke aus der Zeit Amenophis' IV. (um 1375 v. Chr.)." *Amtliche Berichte aus den Königliche Kunstsammlungen Berlin* 34: 127–46.

———. 1918a. "Altes und neues zur Kunst und Religion von Tell el-Amarna." *ZÄS* 55: 1–43.

———. 1918b. "Die angeblichen Kanopenbildnisse König Amenophis IV." *ZÄS* 55: 43–49.

———. 1919. "Die Anfänge der Reformation Amenophis des IV." *SPAW*: 477–84.

———. 1923. *Kunstwerke aus el-Amarna*. 2 vols. Berlin: Bard.

———. 1931. *Amarna in Religion und Kunst*. Berlin: Deutschen Orient-Gesellschaft.

———. 1934. "Die Simonsche Holzfigur eines Königs der Amarnazeit." *ZÄS* 70: 1–25.

Schiff-Giorgini, M. 1965–98. *Soleb*. 5 vols. Florence: Sansoni/Cairo: Institut français d'archéologie orientale.

Schlögl, H. 1986. *Amenophis IV. Echnaton*. Hamburg: Rowohlt.

Schnabel, D. 1976. "Die Rätsel des Grabes no 55 im Tal der Könige." *Das Altertum* 22: 226–33.

———. 1980. "Wer waren Tut-ench-Amens Eltern ?" *Das Altertum* 26: 89–95.

Schubert, S. 2004. "Double Entendre in the Stela of Suty and Hor." In *Egypt, Israel and the Ancient Mediterranean World*, edited by G. Knoppers and A. Hirsch, 143–65. Leiden: Brill.

Schulman, A. 1964. "Some Observations on the Military Background of the Amarna Period." *JARCE* 3: 51–69.

———. 1978. "Ankhesenamun, Nofretity and the Amka Affair." *JARCE* 15: 43–48.

———. 1982. "The Nubian War of Akhenaton." In *L'égyptologie en 1979*, II, 299–316. Paris. Centre national de la recherche scientifique.

Seele, K. 1955. "King Ay and the Close of the Amarna Age." *JNES* 14: 168–80.

Seidlmayer, S. 1983. "Zu einigen Architekturinschriften aus Tell el-Amarna." *MDAIK* 39: 183–206.

Sethe, K. 1921. "Beiträge zur Geschichte Amenophis IV." *Nachrichten von der Gesellschaft der Wissenschaften zu Göttingen: philolosophische-historisches Klasse* 1921: 101–30.

Settgast, J. 1976. *Nofretete-Echnaton*. Munich: Haus der Kunst.

Several, M. 1972. "Reconsidering the Egyptian Empire in Palestine." *PEQ* 104: 123–33.

Seyfried, F. 2012. "The Workshop Complex of Thutmosis." In *In the Light of Amarna*, 170–86. Berlin: Aegyptisches Museum und Papyrussammlung.

Sharpe, S. 1846. *The History of Egypt*. 2 vols. London: Edward Moxon.

Shaw, I. 1994. "Balustrades, Stairs and Altars in the Cult of the Aten at el-Amarna." *JEA* 80: 109–27.

Shaw, I., and P. Nicholson, eds. 1995. *British Museum Dictionary of Ancient Egypt*. London: British Museum Press.

Sheppard, K.L. 2018. *"My Dear Miss Ransom . . .": Letters between Caroline Ransom Williams and James Henry Breasted, 1898–1935*. Oxford: Archaeopress.

Shorter, A. 1931. "Historical Scarabs of Tuthmosis IV and Amenophis III." *JEA* 17: 23–25.

Smith, G.E. 1907. Letter to the *Times*, 15 October 1907.

———. 1912. *The Royal Mummies*. Cairo: Institut français d'archéologie orientale.

———. 1926. "The Diversions of an Anatomist in Egypt." *Cambridge University Medical Society Magazine* 4: 34–39.

Smith, J.L. 1958. *Tombs, Temples and Ancient Art*. Norman: Oklahoma University Press.

Smith, W.S. 1958. *Art and Architecture of Ancient Egypt*. Harmonsworth: Pelican.

Smith, W.R., and D. Redford. 1976. *The Akhenaten Temple Project*, 1: *Initial Discoveries*. Warminster: Aris and Phillips.

Snorasson, E. 1946. "Cranial Deformation in the Reign of Akhenaten." *BHM* 20: 601–10.

Sobhy, G. 1930. "Miscellanea: The Persistence of Ancient Facial Types amongst Modern Egyptians." *JEA* 16: 3.

Spence, K. 2004. "The Three-Dimensional Form of the Amarna House." *JEA* 90: 123–52.

Spence, K., P.J. Rose, R. Bradshaw, P. Collet, A. Hassan, J. MacGinnis, A. Masson, and P. van Pelt 2011. "Sesebi 2011." *S&N* 15: 34–38.

Spieser, C. 2001. "Amarna et la négation du cycle solaire." *CdE* 76: 20–29.

———. 2004. "Iconographie composite et pouvoir royal durant la 18e dynastie." *CdE* 79: 5–21.

Spieser, C., and P. Sprumont. 2004. "La construction de l'image du corps de l'élite égyptienne à l'époque amarnienne." *Bulletins et mémoires de la Société d'anthropologie de Paris* 16: 167–85.

Stempel, R. 2007. "Identification of Nibhururiya and the Synchronism in the Egyptian and Hittite Chronology in Light of Newly Reconstructed Hittite Text." *GM* 213: 97–100.

Stevens, A. 2006. *Private Religion at Amarna: The Material Evidence*. Oxford: Archaeopress.

Stewart, H.M. 1960. "Some Pre-Amarnah Sun Hymns." *JEA* 46: 83–90.

———. 1976. *Egyptian Stelae, Reliefs and Paintings from the Petrie Collection*, I: *The New Kingdom*. Warminster: Aris and Phillips.

Strachey, J. 1939. "Preliminary Notes upon the Problem of Akhenaten." *International Journal of Psychoanalysis* 20: 33–42.

Stuart, H.W.V. 1879. *Nile Gleanings Concerning the Ethnology, History and Art of Ancient Egypt, as Revealed by Egyptian Paintings and Bas-reliefs: With Descriptions of Nubia and Its Great Rock Temples to the Second Cataract.* London: J. Murray.

Sturm, J. 1933. "Wer ist Pepkhururias?" *Rev. hittite et asiatique* 2: 161–76.

Tankard, E. 1932. "The Art of the 'Amarnah Period." *JEA* 18: 49.

Tawfik, S. 1973a. "Aton Studies, 1: Aton before the Reign of Akhenaten." *MDAIK* 29: 77–82.

———. 1973b. "Aton Studies, 2: The Reverse Aton in the Long Name of Nefertiti." *MDAIK* 29: 82–86.

———. 1975. "Aton Studies, 3: Back Again to Nefer-neferu-Aton." *MDAIK* 31: 159–68.

———. 1976. "Aton Studies, 4: Was Aton Only a Manifestation of the God Re?" *MDAIK* 32: 217–26.

———. 1979. "Aton Studies, 5: Cult Objects on Blocks from the Aton Temple(s) at Thebes." *MDAIK* 35: 335–44.

———. 1981. "Aton Studies, 6: Was Neferneferuaten the Immediate Successor of Akhenaten?" *MDAIK* 37: 469–73.

———. 1988. "Aton Studies, 7: Did Any Daily Cult Ritual Exist in Aton Temples at Thebes?" *MDAIK* 44: 275–81.

Terrace, E., and H. Fischer 1970. *Treasures of the Cairo Museum: From Predynastic to Roman Times.* London: Thames and Hudson.

Thomas, E. 1961. "The Plan of Tomb 55 in the Valley of the Kings." *JEA* 47: 24.

———. 1966. *The Royal Necropoleis of Thebes, I: The Major Cemeteries.* Princeton: Privately Printed.

Thomas, V. 1964. "From What Disease Did the Pharaoh Akhenaten Suffer?" *Aktuelle Probleme aus der Geschichte der Medizin: Verhandlungen des XIX. Internationalen Kongresses für Geschichte der Medizin, Basel, 7–11. September 1964*, edited by R. Blaser and H. Buess, 177–84. Basel: Karger.

Thompson, K. 2006. "A Shattered Granodiorite Dyad of Akhenaten and Nefertiti from Tell el-Amarna." *JEA* 92: 141–51.

Tietze, C. 1985. "Amarna: Analyse der Wohnhäuser und soziale Struktur der Stadtbewöhner." *ZÄS* 112: 48–84.

Traunecker, C. 1984. "Données nouvelles sur le début du règne d'Amenophis IV et son oeuvre à Karnak." *JSSEA* 14: 60–69.

———. 1986. "Amenophis IV et Nefertiti: Le couple royal d'après les talatates au IXe pylône de Karnak." *BSFE* 107: 17–44.

Traunecker, C., and J.-C. Golvin. 1984. *Karnak: Resurrection d'un site.* Fribourg: Office du Louvre.

Trigger, B. 1976. *Nubia under the Pharaohs.* London: Thames and Hudson.

———. 1981. "Akhenaten and Durkheim." *BIFAO* 81: 165–84.

Tutanchamun in Köln. 1980. Mainz: von Zabern. [no editors given—a 'collective']. See Annual Egyptological Bibliography 1980, item 591.

Tyldesley, J. 1994. *Daughters of Isis: Women of Ancient Egypt.* London: Viking.

———. 1998. *Nefertiti*. London: Viking.
Uphill, E.P. 1963. "The Sed-festivals of Akhenaton." *JNES* 22: 123–27.
———. 1970. "The Per Aten at Amarna." *JNES* 29: 151–66.
———. 1998. "The Boundaries and Orientation of Akhetaten." In *Proceedings of the Seventh International Congress of Egyptologists, Cambridge, 3–9 September 1995*, edited by C.J. Eyre, 1191–95. Leuven: Peeters.
Valbelle, D. 2006. "Les temples du Nouvel Empire à Doukki Gel: Témoignages épigraphiques (1998–2002)." In *Acta Nubica: Proceedings of the X International Conference of Nubian Studies, Rome, 9–14 September 2002*, edited by I. Caneva and A. Roccati, 431–33. Roma: Istituto Poligrafico e Zecca dello Stato.
———. 2008. "Les temples thoutmosides de Pnoubs (Doukki Gel): L'apport de l'épigraphie et de l'iconographie." In *Between the Cataracts: Proceedings of the 11th Conference for Nubian Studies, Warsaw University, 27 August–2 September 2006*, I: *Main Papers*, edited by W. Godlewski and A. Łajtar, 85–93. Warsaw: Warsaw University Press.
Valentin, F., and T. Bedman. 2014. "Proof of a 'Long Coregency' between Amenhotep III & Amenhotep IV Found in the Chapel of Vizier Amenhotep-Huy (Asasif Tomb 28) West Luxor." *Kmt* 25/2: 17–27.
Van der Perre, A. 2014. "The Year 16 Graffito of Akhenaten in Dayr Abū Ḥinnis: A Contribution to the Study of the Later Years of Nefertiti." *JEH* 7: 67–108.
Vandersleyen, C. 1984. "Amarnismes: Le 'disque' d'Aton, le roi asexué." *CdE* 59: 5–13.
———. 1988. "Les deux jeunesses d'Amenhotep III." *BSFE* 111: 9–30.
———. 1993. "Les scènes de lamentation des chambres *alpha* et *gamma* dans la tombe d'Akhenaton." *RdE* 44: 192–94.
———. 1995. *L'Égypte et la vallée du Nil*. Volume 2. Paris: Presses Universitaires de France.
Vandier, J. 1967. "Toutankhamon, sa famille, son règne." *Journal des savants* 1967: 65–91.
Van Dijk, J. 1993. *The New Kingdom Necropolis of Memphis*. Groningen: Rijksuniversiteit.
———. 1997. "The Noble Lady of Mitanni and Other Royal Favourites of the Eighteenth Dynasty." In *Essays on Ancient Egypt in Honour of Herman te Velde*, edited by J. van Dijk, 33–46. Groningen: Styx.
———. 2009. "The Death of Meketaten." In *Causing His Name to Live: Studies in Egyptian Epigraphy and History in Memory of William J. Murnane*, edited by P.J. Brand and L. Cooper, 83–88. Leiden: Brill.
Varille, A. 1940. "Tutankhamon est-il le fils d'Amenophis III et de Satamon?" *ASAE* 40: 651–57.
Vercoutter, J., and C. Vandersleyen. 1995. *L'Egypte et la vallée du Nil*. Paris: Presses universitaires de France.
Vergnieux, R., and M. Gondran. 1997. *Amenophis IV et les pierres du soleil*. Paris: Arthaud.
Walle, B. van de. 1968. "La princesse Isis, fille et épouse d'Amenophis III." *CdE* 43: 36–53.

———. 1976. "La découverte d'Amarna et d'Akhenaton." *RdE* 28: 7–24.

———. 1979. "Les textes d'Amarne se refèrent-ils à une doctrine morale?" In *Studien zu altaegyptischen Lebenslehren*, edited by E. Hornung and O. Keel, 354–62. Fribourg: Universitätsverlag.

———. 1980. "Survivances mythologiques dans les coiffures royales de l'époque atonienne." *CdE* 55: 23–36.

Weatherhead, F. 1995. "Wall Paintings from the King's House at Amarna." *JEA* 81: 95–114.

Weigall, A. 1907. "Akhenaten: Pharaoh of Egypt." *Blackwood's Edinburgh Magazine*, October 1907: 470–82.

———. 1922a. *The Life and Times of Akhenaten*. 4th ed. London: Thornton Butterworth.

———. 1922b. "The Mummy of Akhenaten." *JEA* 8: 193–200.

Weinstein, J. 1998. "Egypt and the Levant." In *Amenhotep III: Perspectives on His Reign*, edited by D. O'Connor and E. Cline, 223–36. Ann Arbor: University of Michigan Press.

Wells, R. 1987. "The Amarna M, X, K Stelae Date: A Modern Calendar Equivalent." *SAK* 14: 313–33.

———. 1989. "The Amarna M, X, K Boundary Stelae Date: *Ḥwt ỉtn* Ceremonial Altar, Initial Results of a New Survey." *SAK* 16: 289–327.

Wenig, S. 1975. "Amenophis IV." In *Lexikon der Aegyptologie*, edited by W. Helck and E. Otto, I: 210–19. Wiesbaden: Harrasowitz.

Wente, E. 1990. *Letters from Ancient Egypt*. Atlanta: Scholars' Press.

Werner, E. 1979. "Identification of Nefertiti in *talatat* Reliefs Previously Published as Akhenaten." *Orientalia* 48: 324–31.

Westendorf, W. 1963. "Amenophis IV in Urgottgestalt." *Pantheon* 21: 269–77.

White, L. 1948. "Ikhnaton: The Great Man vs. the Culture Process." *JAOS* 68: 91–114.

Whittemore, T. 1926. "The Excavations at el-'Amarnah, Season 1924–1925." *JEA* 12: 3–12.

Wiedemann, K. 1884. *Geschichte Aegyptens*. Gotha: Perthes.

Wilbour, C.E. 1936. *Travels in Egypt*. Brooklyn: Brooklyn Museum.

Wildung, D. 1989. *Das Kunst des alten Aegypten*. Freiburg: Hirmer.

———. 1998. "Le frère ainé d'Akhnaton." *BSFE* 143: 10–18.

Wilkinson, J. G. 1837–41. *Manners and Customs of the Ancient Egyptians*. 5 vols. London: Murray.

———. 1843. *Modern Egypt and Thebes*. 2 vols. London: Murray.

———. 1847. *Handbook for Travellers in Egypt*. London: Murray.

Williams, R. 1971. "Egypt and Israel." In *The Legacy of Egypt*, edited by J.R. Harris, 257–90. Oxford: Oxford University Press.

Wilson, J. 1956. *The Culture of Ancient Egypt*. Chicago: University of Chicago Press.

———. 1964. *Signs and Wonders upon Pharaoh*. Chicago: University of Chicago Press.

———. 1973. "Akhenaton and Nefertiti." *JNES* 32: 235–41.

Winlock, H. 1912. "The Work of the Egyptian Expedition." *BMMA* 7: 184–90.

———. 1923. "Harmhab: Commander-in-chief of the Armies of Tutenkhamon." *BMMA* 18, part 2.

———. 1929. "The Egyptian Expedition 1928–1929." *BMMA* 24, Part II.

Wit, C. de. 1960. "Une tête d'oushebti d'Amenophis IV au musée du Cinquantenaire." *CdE* 40: 20–27.

Wolf, W. 1924. "Vorläufer der Reformation Echnatons." *ZÄS* 59: 109–19.

———. 1930. "Zwei Beiträge zur Geschichte der 18. Dynastie." *ZÄS* 65: 98–102.

———. 1957. *Die Kunst Aegyptens*. Stuttgart: Kohlhammer.

Worms, M. 1916. "Nefertiti." *JA* 7: 469–91.

Zabkar, L. 1954. "Theocracy of Amarna and the Doctrine of the *ba*." *JNES* 13: 87–101.

Ziskind, B., and B. Haliqua. 2006. "Pathographie d'Akhenaton." in *1er Colloque internationale de Pathographie*, 159–63. Paris.

Zivie, A.P. 2004. "Hatiay: Scribe du temple d'Aton à Memphis." In *Egypt, Israel and the Ancient Mediterranean World*, edited by G. Knoppers and A. Hirsch, 223–31. Leiden: Brill.

———. 1979. "Une tombe d'époque amarnienne à Saqqarah." *BSFE* 84: 21–32.

Sources of Images

Maps

Figures

17.　Redford 1984: fig 6.

18.　Chevrier 1931: p. 4.

19.　Aidan Dodson.

20.　Aidan Dodson.

21.　Griffith 1918: pl. 8.

22.　Aidan Dodson.

23.　Davies 1903–1908: V, pl. 42.

24.　Davies 1903–1908: V, pl. 40.

25.　Aidan Dodson.

26.　Courtesy Egypt Exploration Society.

27.　Aidan Dodson.

28.　Swiss Institute, Cairo.

29.　Borchardt 1911: pl. 3.

30.　Borchardt 1913: pl. 11.

31.　Aidan Dodson.

32.　Philips 1991: 37.

33.　Aidan Dodson.

34.　Courtesy Egypt Exploration Society.

35.　Courtesy Egypt Exploration Society.

36.　Peet and Woolley 1923: pl. 3.

37.　Peet and Woolley 1923: pl. 16.

38.　Peet and Woolley 1923: pl. 26.

39.　Badawy 1956: 59.

40.　Courtesy Trustees of the British Museum.

41.　Dyan Hilton.

42.　Whittemore 1926: pl. 2.

43.　Courtesy Egypt Exploration Society.

44.　Courtesy Egypt Exploration Society.

45.　Adapted by Aidan Dodson after Pendlebury 1951: pl. 1.

46.　Pendlebury 1951: pl. 2.

47.　Pendlebury 1951: pl. 9[2].

48.　Pendlebury 1951: pl. 4.

49.　Davies 1903–1908: II, pl. 20.

50.　Pendlebury 1951: pl. 10[2].

51.　Pendlebury 1951: pl. 13b.

52.　Pendlebury 1951: pl. 16.

53. Pendlebury 1951: pl. 19.
54. Aidan Dodson.
55. Aidan Dodson.
56. Courtesy Egypt Exploration Society.
57. Davies 1903–1908: III, pl. 38.
58. Davies 1903–1908: VI, pl. 16.
59. Aidan Dodson/Davies 1903–1908: I, pl. 10–10a.
60. Davies 1903–1908: I, pl. 10.
61. Davies 1903–1908: III, pl. 4.
62. Davies 1903–1908: III, pl. 13–15, 38.
63. Davies 1903–1908: VI, pl. 28–30.
64. Davies 1903–1908: VI, pl. 29.
65. Davies 1903–1908: III, pl. 18.
66. Davies 1903–1908: III, pl. 22.
67. Courtesy Brooklyn Museum.
68. Courtesy Brooklyn Museum.
69. Courtesy Metropolitan Museum of Art.
70. Courtesy Egypt Exploration Society.
71. Frankfort and Pendlebury 1933: pl. 21.
72. Courtesy Egyptian Museum, Cairo.
73. Davies 1903–1908: IV, pl. 31.
74. Epigraphic Survey 1980: pl. 11.
75. Aidan Dodson.
76. Aidan Dodson.
77. Martin 1974–89: II, pl. 43.
78. Aidan Dodson.
79. Peet and Woolley 1923: pl. 12[2].
80. Aidan Dodson.
81. Davies 1903–1908: VI, pl. 4.
82. Aidan Dodson.
83. Aidan Dodson.
84. Aidan Dodson.
85. Aidan Dodson.
86. Aidan Dodson.
87. Girling and Bennett 2003a: 21.
88. Girling and Bennett 2003b: 20.

89. Aidan Dodson.
90. Aidan Dodson.
91. Dodson 2009a: fig. 21, adapted from Davies and Lepsius.
92. Nicholson 1870: pl. 1[5].
93. Adapted by Aidan Dodson from Nicholson 1870: pl. 1[4].
94. Aidan Dodson/Gardiner 1928: pl. 5–6.
95. Dodson 2009a: fig. 33, adapted from Stewart 1976: pl. 12 & Allen 1988: fig. 1.
96. Roeder 1969: pl. 15.
97. Aidan Dodson.
98. Frederick Kennett.
99. Roeder 1958: pl. 5.
100. Aidan Dodson.
101. Aidan Dodson.
102. Aidan Dodson.
103. Courtesy Metropolitan Museum of Art.
104. Aidan Dodson/Martin 1974–89: II, pl. 58.
105. Aidan Dodson/Martin 1974–89: II, pl. 63.
106. Martin 1974–89: II, pl. 63.
107. Brock 1996: fig. 4.
108. M. Bell 1990: fig. 5.
109. Davis 1910: pl. 30.
110. Davis 1910: pl. 20.
111. Martin Davies.
112. Engelbach 1931: pl. 1.

Index

Neferkhepru-her-sekheper (mayor) 122
Neferneferuaten the younger 138, 199,
    201, 204, 286
Neferneferure 200, 201, 287
Nefertiti: Amarnan art 105–10,
    112, 135–36, 192–93, 196, 211,
    249–50, 284–87; Ankheperure-
    Neferneferuaten 262; Aten cult
    38–41, 44, 46–49, 53 (at Thebes),
    136–37, 145, 191, 194–95 (in
    Amarna); Berlin stelae 13, 75, 192–
    94, 252, 270–71, 295; burial and
    mummy 212–16; bust 75, 186–89,
    208; crowns 189–90, 194; 'disgrace'
    13, 82, 191, 268; end of Akhenaten's
    reign 249, 252, 254–56, 260–67;
    fate 205–12, 276–78, 341n166;
    foreign policy 226; foundation of
    Amarna 64–66; goddess 197; 'Great
    Hymn' 128; Great Palace 96; 'Hall
    of Foreign Tribute' 91; Hittite
    letter 221–22; jubilee 55; king
    276–77; KV 55 297, 308; marriage
    29; names 197–200; parents 183–85;
    position and importance 111,
    191–97; Royal Tomb 280–87; tomb
    of Ramose 29; unknowns 9; wigs
    190–91
Nefrusy 176
Newberry, Percy 13, 62, 191–94, 206,
    217, 250, 255–56
Newton, Francis 84
Nicholson relief 250, 256, 262, 277–78
Niqm-Adda 232
Nubia 66, 111, 127, 174, 227, 241,
    247–48; see also Kawa; Soleb
Nut 162–63

Osiris 44–45, 47, 71, 112, 140, 151–52,
    155, 159, 170, 174, 179–80, 299,
    303, 308–309

Pa-aten-em-heb 122
Pakhura 235
Panehsy (chief priest) 91, 96, 102–103,
    138, 155, 176, 181
Parennefer 22, 43, 56, 133, 140–41
Pawah (graffito) 74, 151, 172, 211, 250,
    255–56, 260, 268, 271, 274–75, 277
Pay (stela of) 192–94, 200, 217, 252, 256
Peet, Eric 79–84, 191, 193, 205

Pendlebury, Hilda 86
Pendlebury, John 78, 86–95, 120–21,
    206, 209, 226, 235, 266, 281,
    333n165
Pentju (chief physician) 122, 156
Perepelkin, Yuri 4–5, 13, 203–204, 207–
    209, 217–18, 302–303, 342n193
Petrie, Flinders 2, 13, 25, 62, 68–73, 88,
    94, 144, 168, 229, 254–55, 265, 289,
    295, 316
Pewuru (commissioner) 233, 235
Piankoff, Alexandre 163
Pillet, Maurice 33
Pintore, Franco 236, 345n67
Pollock, Dr. 290
Posener, Georges 146
Prisse d'Avennes, Émile 33
Ptah 152, 162, 170, 173, 176
Ptahmay 153, 155, 173
Ptahmose 170
Punt 111
Py 155

Rameses II 173, 202
Ramose (general) 78, 153
Ramose (perfumer) 177
Ramose (vizier) 28–29, 54, 59, 140, 154
Ranke, Hermann 75
Raven, Martin 287
Re 25, 28, 31, 44, 45, 49–50, 52, 54,
    125, 138–41, 146, 151, 155, 160,
    161–65, 170, 175, 262, 299, 303,
    305, 309
Redford, Donald 5, 25, 39, 41–43,
    47–49, 52, 54–56, 66, 111–12, 121–
    23, 129, 139, 141–42, 150, 152–53,
    167–68, 170–71, 201–203, 209, 221,
    227, 235, 245, 268, 270–71, 325n5
Reeves, Nicholas 6, 56, 113–15, 121,
    150, 152, 170, 179, 218, 228, 252,
    271, 303–304, 306
Reisner, George 311
Rekhmire (vizier) 154
Retenutet 176
Rib-Hadda (of Byblos) 226, 230–32,
    236, 243, 245, 247, 344n23
Ricke, Herbert 79, 114
Robins, Gay 47, 270
Roeder, Günther 257–58, 267, 298
Russmann, Edna 45